John Tulloch

English Puritanism and it's Leaders

Cromwell, Milton, Baxter, Bunyan

John Tulloch

English Puritanism and it's Leaders
Cromwell, Milton, Baxter, Bunyan

ISBN/EAN: 9783741186530

Manufactured in Europe, USA, Canada, Australia, Japa

Cover: Foto ©ninafisch / pixelio.de

Manufactured and distributed by brebook publishing software
(www.brebook.com)

John Tulloch

English Puritanism and it's Leaders

ENGLISH PURITANISM AND ITS LEADERS

CROMWELL MILTON BAXTER
BUNYAN

BY

JOHN TULLOCH, D.D.

PRINCIPAL AND PROFESSOR OF THEOLOGY, ST MARY'S COLLEGE, IN THE UNIVERSITY
OF ST ANDREWS, AND ONE OF HER MAJESTY'S CHAPLAINS
IN ORDINARY IN SCOTLAND

Author of " Leaders of the Reformation," &c.

WILLIAM BLACKWOOD AND SONS
EDINBURGH AND LONDON
MDCCCLXI

PREFATORY NOTE.

THE history of English Puritanism still remains to be written. Separate aspects of the subject have been treated in detail by different writers. M. Guizot, Mr Carlyle, Mr Foster, and, from an ecclesiastical point of view, Mr Marsden, have all contributed by their labours to a right understanding of the great constitutional and religious struggle of the seventeenth century. But it cannot be said that the subject, as a whole, in its strange complexity of political, military, religious, moral, and social relations, has received as yet adequate treatment. Who, for example, has pictured to us the living features of those diverse sects, whose presence meets us everywhere in surveying the period, but whose real character and influence it is so difficult to estimate?

The present volume has no pretensions to be a history of Puritanism: it professes merely to give some side-glimpses into that history—openings into a wide field. If it has any peculiar merit, this will probably be found in the analysis which it presents of the moral meaning and characteristics of Puritanism as exhibited in the great lives which it tries to depict. There is nothing in the subject that retains more interest; and this feeling has been present to the writer throughout, and served to give, in his own mind, some degree of unity to the successive sketches of the volume.

St Mary's College, St Andrews,
  5th February 1861.

CONTENTS.

INTRODUCTION.

CROMWELL.

MILTON.

BAXTER.

ENGLISH PURITANISM AND ITS LEADERS

INTRODUCTION

THE history of English Puritanism is the history both of a theological movement and of a great national struggle. The spirit of which Puritanism is the symbol has entered deeply into the national life, and strongly coloured many of its manifestations. It has given depth and passion not only to the religion, but to the literature and patriotism of the country; it has largely contributed alike to its intellectual lustre and heroic fame. No one, therefore, can understand the sources of our mixed civilisation without studying the great Puritanical movement of the seventeenth century. It is necessary to penetrate to the *heart* of this movement, and find some sympathetic point of connection with it, before we can appreciate some of the most powerful influences which have moulded the English people and made them what they are. Otherwise, as with some of our historians, the face of the facts may be observed and delineated, but their genuine meaning will be missed, and the moral forces out of which they grew and consolidated into history will remain unintelligible.

A

Britain was the national soil in which the seeds of the Reformation were destined to take the deepest and most enduring root. Germany did far more to originate and strengthen the movement in its beginnings; France, in many of its highest minds, showed a more ready receptivity and welcome to the new religious ideas; England could boast neither a Luther nor a Calvin: but the spiritual impulses out of which the movement grew, and which constituted its real life and strength, found in the Anglo-Saxon character their most congenial seat, their highest affinities, their most solid nutriment. Slowly, and under many hindrances, they spread, unaided by the powerful influence of any great teacher, but sinking always more into the depths of this character, and gaining a firmer hold of it. While dying out in Germany, and hardly able to maintain themselves in France against the fierce odds with which they had to contend, they continued to propagate and gather force in England amidst all obstacles, and only attained, after the lapse of a century, and under many modifications of struggle and conquest, to their full development.

The English Reformation had a double origin. It sprang at once from the people and the court. It was the effect of a renewed spiritual excitement in the Church and in society; it was also the creature of statecraft and royal policy. Erasmus's Greek Testament, and Tyndall's Bible, were the great agents on the one side; Henry VIII.'s matrimonial necessities, and the traditional anti-Romish policy of the Crown, were the moving springs on the other. In its earlier stages, and for long, the latter element assumed and exercised the predominance. The Reform movement in England became characteristically an official movement: the sovereign was its guide and head; the State aimed to direct and regulate the course of innovation, and to mould the new Protestantism into conformity with the historical constitution and venerated usages of the old Catholicism. But, under all this official guidance, there had lived from the first a religious earnestness and active zeal for reform, impatient of control. The spiritual individualism which the Reformation everywhere called forth was in England held in check, but not extinguished, by the jealous watchfulness of the State. Even the firmness of the Tudor policy was not able to destroy, however it restrained, this moral force. Whether, if this policy had been persevered in, it might have proved successful, and the spiritual element of the Reformation coalesced more completely with the temporal, it is hard to say. The close of Elizabeth's life was not without some signs of such an issue. But, as it was, the spirit of religious reform gathered fresh impulse from the very circumstances which were meant to crush it; and, after years of insult and oppression, it first matched and then mastered the royal policy with which it had been so long in conflict.

It was characteristic of the aggressive spirit of the English Reformation, that it should ally itself with that branch of continental Protestantism which was most thorough and logical in its expression and results. As it was the aim of the state-party, while breaking with the Pope, to preserve unbroken the continuity of Catholicism, so it was the aim of the more radical Reformers to depart as far as possible from Popery. The one side desired to preserve the historical traditions, the medieval forms of worship, and the hierarchical framework of the Church of England; the other side desired, in the spirit of the Swiss and French Protestants, to base the reformation, both of doctrine and discipline, anew and directly upon Scripture. This was a natural consequence of the profound evangelical consciousness quickened by Scripture, and appearing to be everywhere reflected in its pages, out of which the deeper movement sprang. It was the consequence, also, in a great degree, of the peculiar tendencies of the time, and the special character of the Calvinistic Reformation.

Unlike Lutheranism, Calvinism maintained a vigorous and progressive influence long after its first reforming excitement was spent. Less broad and magnanimous in its beginnings, it was far more concentrated and impulsive in its aims. Eliciting in a far less degree the welcoming humours of a free and sympathetic humanity, it found in its very narrowness and inward intensity, rather than genial fulness, its chief strength. It attained to more clear and systematic aims; it knew its own resources and husbanded them; while its dogmatic consistency and intellectual masterliness exercised a powerful charm over many minds at a distance, and gave to its principles a systematic and well-directed efficiency. The result was, that while Lutheranism, after little more than a quarter of a century's living action, was wasting itself in controversy equally violent and feeble, and rapidly passing into a barren dogmatism, Calvinism was still making vigorous conquests, and drawing to itself fresh accessions of force. It came to represent the cause of Protestantism abroad more prominently and boldly than the older movement ; and the Protestant spirit of England, amidst its conflicts, instinctively turned to Geneva, as its great model and guide. Calvinism became, if not the progenitor, yet the nursing-mother of Puritanism.

This movement in England towards the Genevan Reformation was greatly accelerated and strengthened by special circumstances. On the accession of Mary, and the triumph of the medieval party, multitudes of the most active Reformers fled to the Continent. Geneva, and other Swiss and Rhine towns, were the refuges of these Protestant emigrés; and in this manner they came into immediate contact with Calvinism, learned its religious and ecclesiastical spirit of independence, became accustomed to the imposing outline of its doctrine and the simple severity of its ritual, and, in many cases, adopted firmly its constitutional principles. In these years the influence of Calvin's personal character and mental power was at its height; no single man exercised such a sway within the sphere of Protestantism; and all who were brought near it carried away ineffaceable traces of the spirit which it represented and embodied.

In tracing this connection between Puritanism and Calvinism, it is necessary to notice, that it was an ecclesiastical, still more peculiarly than a doctrinal sympathy, that united them. So far as doctrine was concerned, there was no division as yet in the Church of England. It might be too much to say that the English Church was in the sixteenth century universally Calvinistic in its theology. Such an assertion would not allow for those Catholic peculiarities of thought which have always distinguished the highest divines of this Church, and given a certain breadth and freedom to their dogmatic views, even when these were most closely allied to the technical modes of Calvinistic opinion. Jewell and Hooker, for example,

while coinciding with this opinion in their doctrinal
conclusions, are yet far more than Calvinists in a
certain comprehensiveness and genial width of view.
But if not exclusively or rigidly Genevan in doctrine,
even under the primacy of Whitgift, the Church of
England was yet so far from finding any cause of
quarrel in this doctrine, that it embodied it substantially in its thirty-nine articles; while Whitgift's well-
known Lambeth articles * remain to testify how far
more closely he and others were prepared to bring the
creed of the Church of England into conformity with
the Genevan theology in its most extreme forms.

The cause of quarrel, therefore, was not in this source,
but in an entirely different one.   It was the disciplinal
and not the doctrinal element of the Genevan Reform
which, carried back to England, planted the seed of
widening discord in English Protestantism.   Nay, it
was something far narrower in its beginning than even
any general question of church discipline.   Never has
a great movement in a civilised country sprung from
a more trivial cause.   It is like tracing some gigantic
river, renowned for the great cities along which it has
swept, the hurrying interests which it has borne on its
bosom, and the scenes of struggle and associations of
interest which mark its course, to its source in some
streamlet, noisy but insignificant.   In its outset, Puritanism brings us face to face with no vital interest,

---

* Hooker's criticisms on these articles mark very well the difference
indicated in the text between the characteristic theology of the Church
of England and Calvinism.   The comprehensive mind of Hooker, with
its broader and more genial survey of theological literature, at once detected the narrowness of the proposed articles, and nothing can show
better than his remarks the fine balance of his spiritual judgment.
Whitgift's mind was acute and powerful, but narrow and polemical in
comparison with Hooker s.

with no grand circumstance of dogmatic or spiritual earnestness; it seems a mere petty though violent contention between rival bishops; yet it grew into a great creed, a significant principle, a systematic and triumphant policy. It did so because it masked, from the very first, principles of the broadest distinction. The "vestiary" controversy was the mere shaft into the mine in which slumbered elements of the most powerful opposition ready to burst into flame.

It will conduce to the clearness and interest of our succeeding pages to mark briefly the progress of the controversy to the point at which our sketches begin. Up to this point, Puritanism had run through two distinct stages of its career. In the first stage, which may be said to close with the reign of Elizabeth, it continued very much such a contest as it began—a contest in the main regarding church order and ceremony—in which we can trace sufficiently the opening of a deeper issue of principles, but during which it still seemed possible that these principles might find some peaceful solution. In the second stage, which lasted during the reign of James, and that of his son, to the eve of the memorable parliament so associated with the triumphs of Puritanism, the controversy, while still largely retaining its ecclesiastical character, took at the same time a higher and wider range. Starting from the defined basis of the Millenary petition, it became mingled in the course of these reigns with new and exciting interests, both theological and political, and gradually passed into a great party conflict—a wide schism of thought and feeling, of manners and policy. In the ninety years that fill up the interval, a quarrel as to the dress of bishops had grown into an incurable oppo-

sition of faith and an antagonism of constitutional
principle which could only settle itself by the sword.
A case of casuistry, in which prelate had encountered
prelate in the antechamber of Edward VI., had waxed
into a national crisis, and was fast assuming the pro-
portions of a civil struggle.

The appointment of Hooper to the see of Gloucester
in 1550, marks the well-known rise of the Puritan controversy. After his nomination, he refused to be in-
ducted in the customary robes of the Romish priesthood, which had never been abolished. Hooper had
lived abroad, and was the friend of Bullinger. His
natural sensitiveness regarding the idolatrous character of the rites of the Church of Rome, had been quickened and exaggerated by his residence in Switzerland.
He was an able and earnest man, a powerful and untiring preacher,* but possessed of a scrupulous and
somewhat vehement temper. He not only refused to
wear the robes, but he considered himself bound to
preach vehemently against them. Cranmer and Ridley,
especially the latter, interposed in behalf of Episcopal
order ; and the dispute became so hot and intolerable,
that Hooper was confined by order of the Privy Council, first to his house, and then to the Fleet. The
young king, who at first sought to mediate in the controversy, it is said, at length " grew very angry with
Mr Hooper for his unreasonable stiffness."

Two eminent foreign divines, Peter Martyr and
Bucer, filled at this time the respective professorships
of divinity at Oxford and Cambridge. Their counsel
was sought in the case, and both strongly advised

* " He preaches four, or at least three times every day."—*Letter of
his wife to Bullinger,* 1551. BURNET, iii.

Hooper to abandon his scruples; not that they approved of the vestments—Martyr, in fact, expressed a wish that they should be abandoned—but because they did not consider their use in any way sinful or entitled to interfere with admission into his office in the usual manner. Hooper was not immediately moved, but at last he consented to a compromise. He submitted to wear the robes at his consecration, and to appear and preach in them at least once.* Afterwards, he was to be at liberty to do as he liked.

Hooper's episcopate thus contentiously began, terminated ere long in martyrdom. In the sight of the cathedral to which he had been consecrated four years before, he and Ridley, his old opponent, suffered together. Their differences had all vanished in the glory of the testimony which they then rejoiced to render to their common faith. They had been "two in white," in the quaint and touching language of the message that passed between them at the awful moment of their fate; but they were now "one in red."

The excitement of the "vestiary" controversy was not extinguished in the flames of Hooper's martyrdom. For a while, it necessarily sank out of sight during the more serious dangers that menaced Protestantism in the reign of Mary. But the spirit out of which it sprang continued to live on and to gather strength. The national return to Romanism, and the ease in many respects with which the transition was made, only proved to many minds an incentive to de-

---

* These robes, besides the surplice, consisted in the chimere, a long scarlet robe, worn loose down to the foot, and the rochet, a white linen vestment covering the shoulders. These garments, adapted from those of the Jewish priesthood, were held by the Church of Rome to be emblematical of the sacrificial efficacy of the Christian priesthood; and hence their peculiar obnoxiousness to the Puritan.

part further from all its usages, and to identify Protestantism with a form of worship as far as possible removed from all its rites. On the other hand, there were some like Dr Cox, the well-known tutor of King Edward, who gathered from their sufferings only a deeper love for the ritual, such as it had been set forth in the preceding reign, and whose Protestantism, while it remained loyal to the policy of Cranmer, shrank from all further encroachment with extreme jealousy and distaste. With the one class, contact with the Reformed polity abroad elicited sympathy and admiration—in not a few cases led to new convictions and desires; with the other class, it only evoked a more ardent devotion to their home form of worship and all its associations. What have been called the "Frankfort Troubles," were the most significant and notable expression of this disunion during the period of the Marian Exile. These troubles were petty and discreditable to the cause of English Protestantism; and they left behind them a bitterness which served to inflame the discords which soon again broke out in the restored Church of England.

On the accession of Elizabeth the country presented a peculiar aspect. The Catholics, although they had lost their chief support in the Crown, remained a great and powerful party—the most compact and decided party beyond doubt in the country. The Protestants returned from their four and a half years' exile with their hatred of Popery inflamed, and the most illustrious and able among them considerably more advanced in their views of reform. There were, indeed, men like Cox, who had little advanced; but Jewell and Grindal, Sandys, Horn, and Parkhurst, had all learned to dislike the "ceremonies" as savouring of Popery ; while others, such as old Miles Coverdale, and Fox the martyrologist, and Whitehead (whom Elizabeth wished to make primate, but whose conscience scrupled both at the dignity and its accompaniments), not only cherished a deep aversion to the ceremonies, but had strongly imbibed the Calvinistic principle, that nothing should be "ordered" in the Church which was not warranted and required in the word of God.

The Queen herself was genuinely Protestant in conviction. She inherited not only the proud national spirit of her father against Rome, but she understood far more than he did the grounds of theological difference between the Churches, and had given her intelligent assent to the side of Protestantism. At the same time she possessed all her father's love of display and authority. She was no less strong in her admiration of the old ritual, and her determination to uphold the prerogatives of the Crown in the government of the Church, than she was strong in her opposition to Rome and her disbelief of its grosser superstitions. She preserved a crucifix in her own chapel to the last, and she had no idea of any church order that did not emanate from her own royal will and pleasure.

Elizabeth acted as might have been supposed from her circumstances and character. She strengthened her Crown against the Catholics by the *Act of Supremacy*, but she reserved all power of Church reform in her own hands by the *Act of Uniformity*. This act not only prescribed and enforced the *Book of Common Prayer* and the administration of the sacraments, as set forth 5 and 6 Edward VI., and the use of such ecclesiastical ornaments as were customary in the second year of this reign, but empowered the Queen with her commissioners to ordain and publish such further ceremonies and rites as might be "necessary for the advancement of God's glory and the edifying of His Church." It was grievous enough to some of the extreme Protestants to return to the church order of the second year of Edward, with all its superstitious usages as they deemed them ; but this power reserved to the Queen, of adding indefinitely to ecclesiastical ceremonies, was peculiarly obnoxious to them, as it proved peculiarly galling in its exercise.

Upon this "fatal rock of Uniformity," says Neale, "was the peace of the Church of England split." The most eminent of the clergy were in favour of leaving off the usages which had been the subject of so much contention. Grindal and Jewell were strongly committed against the vestments. The latter had spoken of them as the "relics of the Amorites." Even Parker himself was at first liberal, and indisposed to any violent measures. He was glad to have the assistance of old Miles Coverdale (who had been in Edward's reign Bishop of Exeter) in his consecration, although Coverdale refused to appear in anything but his black Geneva gown. He concurred with Grindal in providing a sphere of labour—the church and parish of St Magnus, at the corner of Fish Street—for the stern old man, when no arguments would induce him to resume his episcopal duties. There was even a party at Court secretly inclined to favour the extreme Protestants. Dudley, Earl of Leicester, in the midst of his other intrigues, held close relations with some of them. He courted and patronised them, under the idea that they might be unconsciously serviceable to his criminal ambition.

It is not wonderful if, in such circumstances, many

of the clergy exercised their freedom in the matter of the contested ceremonies. Nay, as might be expected, the spirit of aggression gained ground, and not merely the vestments, but many collateral points —such as holy days, the cross at baptism, kneeling at communion, and the use of organs—were largely canvassed, and their abolition strongly urged by a vigorous and increasing party. Nothing, perhaps, can more strongly show the extent to which this aggressive spirit had spread, than the debate which took place in the Convocation which met after Elizabeth's second Parliament in 1562, when the proposals of the Puritan party for reform, in such matters as have been mentioned, under the leadership of Dean Nowel, the prolocutor, were only lost by a majority of one. The numbers stood 58, 59. Of those present, in fact, a majority voted in favour of the proposals,* but the scale was turned by proxies. So nearly were the parties divided within the Church.

Such a state of things, it may be augured, was far

* The proposals, which were a modification of those originally brought in, less minute, and upon the whole less radical in their spirit, stood as follows :—

"1. That all Sundays in the year, and principal feasts of Christ, be kept holy days ; and that all other holy days be abrogated.

"2. That in all parish churches, the minister in common-prayer turn his face towards the people, and then read distinctly the service appointed, that the people may hear and be edified.

"3. That in baptism the cross be omitted, as tending to superstition.

"4. Forasmuch as divers communicants are not able to kneel for age and sickness at the sacrament, and others kneel and think superstitiously, that therefore the order of kneeling may be left to the discretion of the ordinary.

"5. That it be sufficient for the minister, in time of saying divine service, and ministering of the sacraments (once), to wear a surplice; and that no minister say service or minister the sacraments, but in a comely garment or habit.

" 6. That the use of organs be removed."—NEALE, vol. i. 143.

from pleasing to Elizabeth. In the prevailing disaffection among the clergy, she saw not only her own
supposed rights invaded—a right which no Tudor, and
she least of all, could behold with complacency; but she
and some of her counsellors, moreover, believed that
they saw in it serious danger to her state and crown.
The great idea of the Church of England, being one
and the same (*semper eadem* was her favourite ecclesiastical motto) under all the vicissitudes which it had
undergone, seemed likely to fade away before the growing spirit of innovation. The Catholics, many of whom,
by the preservation of the ceremonies and the framework
of the Church, might be supposed gradually drawn to
submission and loyalty, were likely to be altogether
alienated by further changes. This apprehension as
to the Catholics was real and urgent, and was acknowledged to be such as well by the anxieties of the Puritans as by the fears of the Court. It was the constant
argument of the former, that the retention of the Popish
habits inclined the nation to Popery. " If we compel
the godly to conform themselves to the Papists," wrote
Whittingham, "I fear greatly *lest we fall to Papism.*"
"While Popish superstitions have the broad seal, and
while Popish pomp doth allure and awe the people,
wherewithal," argued Miles Coverdale, "shall they be
restrained from backsliding to Rome ?"—a view which
was encouraged by reported sayings of Bonner and
others, who professed to see, in the retained usages, an
evident symptom that the nation would soon again
relapse into Popery. "An they sup of our broth they
will soon eat of our beef," was the somewhat coarse
joke attributed to Bonner. Accordingly, the Puritans
earnestly identified the triumph of Protestantism with
the abolition of all Popish ceremonies. The offences

done to the Catholics by such an abolition, was to them one of the principal recommendations of the step. It was a blow to Antichrist which would help its downfall ; and the necessities of the State were to them a secondary and unimportant thought. But *this* was necessarily to Elizabeth herself, and men like Cecil —the primary consideration, to which all others must yield. The Catholics could not be outraged and driven to rebellion without peril to the Crown, and ruin to all the best interests of the nation. It is impossible to doubt that this was a real exigency. It is perhaps too much to say that it was a defence of Elizabeth's conduct in the repressive measures which, in conjunction with Parker, she now resolved to adopt against the aggressive or Puritan party in the Church.

In the beginning of 1564-5 the Queen addressed a letter to the archbishop on the subject of " ceremonial diversities " and " novelties of rites " in the Church, which, " through the negligence of her bishops, had crept in and were on the increase." These, she said emphatically, " must needs provoke the displeasure of Almighty God, and *bring danger of ruin to the people and the country;* " and she accordingly charged him to investigate into the disorders, and to take means that " uniformity of order may be kept in every church." The result of this investigation was, that a book of articles was drawn up for enforcing uniformity, which did not, owing to the secret opposition of Dudley and others, receive the sanction of the Privy Council, but which became practically the rule of Episcopal action. The most important of its provisions was, subscription on the part of the clergy to certain promises, which placed them entirely as to preaching under the control of their bishop, and bound them to the use of the apparel and other institutions as already established in the Church.

Fox the martyrologist, Coverdale, and Whitehead, were among the most conspicuous victims of the system of repression upon which Parker now zealously entered. He had not been very forward to move, but, having once " stirred in the affair," he, and some more of the bishops, acted with a determination and vigour which outran the more cautious policy of Cecil. He professed at last to see that not only were " the rites of apparel now in danger, but *all other rites universally*." * Fox refused to subscribe to the promises of the Book of Articles or Advertisements, as it came to be called, and was dismissed in disgrace to his quiet Salisbury prebend. Such respect was entertained for his " age, parts, and pains," that the Bishops did not venture to take any further steps against him. Whitehead was suspended ; but the somewhat singular favour that he enjoyed with Elizabeth as " a man of parts, but more as a clergyman *unmarried*," formed also a shield of protection to him. Upon " poor old Miles " the persecution fell more heavily. He was driven from his humble benefice of St Magnus, and died in a few years in great poverty. Sampson, Dean of Christ Church, and Humphrey, President of Magdalene College, Oxford, were also summoned before the ecclesiastical commissioners, and the former deprived of his deanery. The harshness of this measure was aggravated by the fact that Sampson, along with his companions Humphrey, Lever, and others, were so far from being extreme in their views, that many of the ultra-Puritans looked upon them with dislike, and altogether disowned their preaching.

* STRYPE'S *Parker*, 161 ; *Annals*, ii. 129.

It would be impossible for us to trace minutely the course of the controversy, and the persecutions to which it gave rise in the time of Elizabeth. The subject is a history in itself. We can only briefly glance at the two main phases into which the controversy ran during this period. These phases mark a certain definite advance in the principles which guided both sides.

The first is represented by the dispute between Cartwright and Whitgift. This dispute had its origin in various causes. Personal bitterness between the combatants helped to inflame public animosity. They had been rival disputants at the university of Cambridge. Cartwright, as professor of divinity, had identified himself with the movement party, and ventured freely to discuss the new ecclesiastical policy in his lectures. Whitgift, as vice-chancellor of the university, keenly took the opposite side, and, by his influence, silenced and expelled from his office the professor of divinity. Cartwright was driven abroad, but his spirit survived at home, and circumstances soon occurred to draw him again into the field.

In many of the younger clergy the Protestant schism was fast spreading, and assuming a more definite and irreconcilable form. A small band of more zealous spirits even went the length of establishing themselves into a separate congregation on the basis of the Genevan plan of government. Plumber's Hall, in Anchor's Lane, became the scene of the first meeting of Dissenters from the Church of England, in the month of June 1567. The appearance of the sheriffs dispersed the infant congregation, thirty-one of whom, men and women, were seized and hurried to prison. The fact of such an attempt at ecclesiastical separation was regarded with dismay. Even many among the bishops, who had hitherto befriended those opposed to the ceremonies, and especially the vestments, were shocked at such an open expression of variance from the Church, and joined with their brethren in adopting means to arrest it. Grindal, in so far, was united with Parker, although, with the mildness characteristic of him, he prevailed with Cecil and the Lords of Council to dismiss the present offenders after a brief imprisonment, but, at the same time, with a solemn warning of greater severity should they persist in their factious conduct.

The Parliament of 1571 met amidst continued excitement, and no fewer than seven bills for the "Reformation of Ceremonies in matters of Religion and Church Government" were introduced. The Commons showed a strong sympathy for further reformation. Mr Strickland, a "grave and ancient man, of great zeal," spoke boldly. "There be abuses in the Church of England, there be also abuses of churchmen—all these it were high time were corrected." He received a summons to attend the Privy Council for his plain speaking, and was temporarily detained from the House. Peter Wentworth spoke with no less freedom, and formed one of a committee of six who waited upon the archbishop touching a "model of reformation." Nothing, however, followed these expressions of discontent, except a more determined zeal on the part of the Crown and the Bench to enforce the laws for uniformity. Only three of the seven bills were passed to the House of Lords, and all of them finally fell to the ground.

A new Parliament opened in May 1572, with a speech from the Lord Keeper, in which he complained of the neglect of the "laudable rites and ceremonies of the Church, the *very ornaments of our religion ;*" and recommended that systematic means should be adopted by the bishops for correcting this neglect, "that thus the civil sword might support the sword ecclesiastic."* While this was the temper of the Court, that of many of the clergy was increasing in boldness. Two of their number, of the names of Field and Wilcox, presented, after careful preparation, a document to this Parliament, entitled "An Admonition for Reformation of Church Discipline." It keenly exposed the corruptions of the hierarchy and the proceedings of the bishops; and, after setting forth a new platform of Church government, craved that the Church of England might be remodelled according to it, in greater conformity to the Word of God and the foreign Reformed Churches. Both the authors were apprehended and committed to Newgate; but their boldness only served to call into the field an abler and more vigorous champion, who had already whetted his pen in the controversy.

Thomas Cartwright had lately returned from exile, with all his Puritan convictions deepened and strengthened. He was an attentive observer of the proceedings in Parliament, and when the writers of the original "Admonition" were violently withdrawn from the scene of conflict, he prepared and published a "Second Admonition," more importunate, and to the same effect, which came out, according to Heylin, "with such a flash of lightning, and such claps of thunder, as if heaven and earth were presently to have met together." Whitgift, in the mean time, had joined in the fray ; and, with the direct concurrence of Parker

* D'EWES, 195.

and Cooper, the Bishop of Lincoln published a reply
to the first "Admonition." The sight of his old adversary roused Cartwright's blood, and the controversy
between them became a prolonged and vehement one.
Cartwright replied to his answer; Whitgift rejoined
at great length, both to Cartwright's "Admonition,"
and his attack upon himself; and Cartwright again
returned to the charge. The "untempered speeches,"
"hard words," "bitter reproaches" ("as it were sticks
and coals"), which the Puritan hurled at the churchman, were sufficiently met by the "flouts," "oppro-
bries," "slanders and disdainful phrases," which the
latter imputed to the Puritan.* On both sides rudeness and vituperation too frequently outweigh sense
and reason; and the main drift of the argument loses
itself in the muddy and wearying channel of personal abuse.   Each, however, contended with marked
ability, and, beyond doubt, represented the most vigorous intellect of his party; Cartwright displaying, perhaps, more vigorous eloquence and rough sense in
details, a more pungent and superior polemical learning; Whitgift more elevation, comprehension, and
thoughtful force in general reasoning.

Cartwright, under all his vehemence and bitterness,
gives us the idea of a very manly and honest nature;
a man of fiery impulses, but of a free and courageous
spirit.   There is something, also, pathetic in the hardships and sadness of his fate, in comparison with that
of his prosperous adversary.   Fellow-students and rival
theologians, they had preached from the same university pulpit; the same career seemed before them.

---

* Whitgift does not even disdain to reproach his adversary with
the poverty which his own harshness had inflicted.—*Works* PARKER
SOCIETY, vol. i. pp. 45-6, 84.

But Whitgift then, as afterwards, had chosen the winning side. He was first made Dean of Lincoln, then Bishop of Worcester, and finally raised to the see of Canterbury. Cartwright was twice driven abroad, "little better than a wandering beggar." On his second return he was seized and imprisoned by order of Aylmer, Bishop of London, whose character, amidst the oppressions of the time, stands out as peculiarly contemptible, in the vindictive severities with which it is associated. After his liberation he was jealously watched, forbidden to write, and again, after the death of Leicester, who had patronised him, imprisoned along with a number of other Puritan divines, till he was finally released in 1592, and allowed to die in obscurity. The way of the Puritan was certainly not a way of pleasantness. Only one pleasing gleam lights up the harsh relations between him and Whitgift. After the latter was made primate, he is said to have sought an interview with his old adversary, and to have offered him kindness. A softening impression was left on the minds of both. Whitgift was sufficiently severe; but, unlike Aylmer, there was magnanimity in his severity—he harboured no petty malignity; and after all that had passed between him and Cartwright, he showed the latter such friendliness as to draw from his friend and patron, the Earl of Leicester, a letter of thanks for his "favourable and courteous usage."

The principles maintained in their controversy show the deeper vein into which Puritanism was running. It was no longer merely the accessories of worship that were in dispute, but the subjects of Church government and authority in themselves. Cartwright contended that Scripture was the standard of Church government and discipline as well as of doctrine—nay, that it was the only standard of rule as of truth in the Church, and that the English hierarchy must be reduced to the Presbyterian pattern of Scriptural simplicity. The opposition was no longer merely to the Popish ceremonies, but to the whole structure of the Anglican polity, as at variance with Scripture. Whitgift maintained, on the other side, that Scripture was not designed as a standard of ecclesiastical polity ; that this polity, on the contrary, was a fair subject for arrangement on the part of the State and the superiors of the Church. The Churchman occupied the ground of expediency, destined, ere long, to a far higher elaboration and defence ; the Nonconformist urged the argument of divine right. The latter had already taken up his full dogmatic position ; the former not yet.

During some years the controversy continued with great keenness and with various alternations of feeling towards the Puritans. After Whitgift and Cartwright had laid aside their pens, a swarm of minor writers took up the quarrel, and the famous Martin Marprelate's* pamphlets on the Puritan side, and others not a whit behind them in scurrility on the Church side, † attest the vehemence of excitement which actuated and convulsed the nation.

The death of Parker in 1575, and the appointment of Grindal to the primacy, were favourable to the movement. Grindal's well-known predilections, his natural

---

* "A vizored knight, behind whose shield a host of sturdy Puritans were supposed to fight."—HALLAM, vol. i. p. 220.

† Such as " A Fig for my Godson ; or, Crack me this Nut,"—that is, "A sound Box of the Ear for the Idiot Martin to hold his Peace ;" and "An Almond for a Parrot," by Cuthbert Curry-knave—the pseudonyme of Tom Nash, who was, says Walton, "a man of sharp wit, and the master of a scoffing, satirical, merry pen. "The Cobbler's Book," and " Ha' ye any work for the Cooper?" are specimens of the titles on the Puritan or "Martin Marprelate" side.

mildness and apostolical simplicity of character, con-
duced to mitigate the rule of uniformity, and to open
up the way for a temporary freedom. The "prophesyings," as they were called, had been begun in the preceding primacy. They were designed to meet the
great lack of intelligent and godly preaching throughout the land. The clergy and others in a district met
together, and engaged in the exposition of Scripture,
and in other exercises of religious edification. Such
meetings were the expression of a prevailing spirit of
religious earnestness, but also to some extent of the
growing spirit of ecclesiastical freedom. They were
not likely to be acceptable, therefore, in high quarters.
Elizabeth frowned, and Parker put them down. But
Grindal was no sooner established in his office than he
took the prophesyings under his protection. The result
was, that he came into collision with the Queen, fell
into disgrace, and was banished the Court. He himself
cared little for the royal disfavour in such a cause ; but
the party who looked to him for protection experienced
in many ways the effects of his exclusion from the
national counsels. Aylmer's bigoted and persecuting
activity was allowed to run riot.

The reins of archiepiscopal authority soon passed
into firmer hands. Grindal died in 1583, and Whitgift was promoted to the primacy. "There was no
danger," remarks Strype,* " of *his* Grindalising by
winking at the plots and practices of the Puritan faction." His character was too well established, and his
ecclesiastical position taken up too definitely. Yet the
Queen was not content to leave him merely to his own
impulses. She "straitly" instructed " to be vigilant
and careful for the reducing of all ministers to the

* STRYPE'S *Whitgift*, 114.

settled order and government;" "to restore the discipline of the Church and the uniformity in the service of God established by Parliament, which, through
the connivance of the prelates, the obstinacy of the
Puritans, and the power of some noblemen, was run
out of square."* Whitgift was not slow to justify the
expectations, and to avail himself of the ample powers,
reposed in him. He devised three articles for the
further enforcement of uniformity, and issued orders
for their subscription throughout his province. Many
clergy refused, and in consequence were suspended,
and finally deprived if they continued obstinate. The
primate never for a moment relaxed his watchful jealousy; the Queen was strongly assenting, even when
the law was somewhat stretched to reach offenders;
repression, systematic, and far-seeing, became the order
of ecclesiastical and civil policy. To "root out Puritanism and the favourers thereof," was the undisguised
aim of her Majesty and the primate.

The powers of a great intellect working in the rec-
tory of Boscum, in the diocese of Sarum, were of more
weight in the struggle than all the vigilance of Whitgift, backed by the authority of the High Court of
Commission. Here Hooker was quietly preparing
his great work, which deserves to mark the next and
final stage of the controversy in the reign of Elizabeth. He had retired to Boscum in 1591, after the
contentions of his ministry in the Temple. The seclusion was welcome to one whose nature was essentially tranquil in its loftiness and contemplative
simplicity. He had shown, indeed, that he did not
shrink from the active annoyances of a struggle, the
principles of which he had so deeply pondered. His

* CAMDEN, 288.

ministry in the Temple, if not a popular success, proved him of a resolute and courageous spirit, capable of maintaining his own convictions in the face of opposition and amidst the heats of discussion. Travers had been conjoined with him here, and to this conjunction and its consequences may be traced the bent of Hooker's thoughts to the subject in connection with which his name has become immortalised.

Travers, after Cartwright, must be reckoned the most distinguished leader of the Elizabethan Puritans. "Allowing Mr Cartwright for the head," says Fuller, " Mr Walter Travers might be termed the neck of the Presbyterian party, the second in honour and esteem." * He had been identified since 1574 with a "Plan of Presbyterian Government," concocted at Geneva, and especially adapted to the meridian of London. This plan, revised by Mr Cartwright and other learned ministers, had passed into popularity, and become a sort of programme of the Presbyterian policy. Travers himself stood in high esteem with Lord Treasurer Burleigh, whose domestic chaplain he was. He had resided abroad, like most of the active Puritans. He was a man of earnest and fixed convictions, who cherished his Presbyterianism as the Gospel itself, and was ready to submit to any sacrifice in its defence. Like Cartwright, he was vehement, restless, and impulsive, animated by lofty but narrow principle, and with that tincture of harsh and rude dogmatism which distinguishes the religious spirit of the age (save in such eminent exceptions as Jewell and Hooker). Cartwright appears to us, upon the whole, the manlier and higher character, as he was the more powerful and systematic reasoner: a stronger, more living, and less

* Book ix. p. 136.

captious earnestness marks him as a controversialist. But Travers was evidently more polished and attractive in the pulpit. He appears, in fact, to have been one of the most popular preachers of his day.

It was as a preacher that he came in contact with Hooker. He had been sometime a lecturer in the Temple, when Hooker was appointed to the mastership. He was a great favourite with the congregation, many of whom were deeply imbued with the Puritanical spirit. In the afternoon, when he preached, crowds came to hear him, while Hooker's sermon in the forenoon was but thinly attended. "The pulpit spoke," old Fuller says, "pure Canterbury in the morning, and Geneva in the afternoon;" while the congregation "ebbed" in the former case, and "flowed" in the latter.* The special dispute between them related to some changes in the dispensation of the Lord's Supper that Travers had introduced; but the two men impersonated the opposing religious principles of their day, not in one particular only, but in the whole style and tendency of their thought. The theology of the one is intensely Calvinistic, with that narrowing polemical tone which the mere disciples of a great system are apt to adopt; that of the other embraces but rises above

---

* Fuller's portraits of the rival preachers are graphic, if somewhat one-sided. "Mr Hooker: his voice was low, stature little, gesture none at all; standing stone-still in the pulpit, as if the posture of his body were the emblem of his mind, unmovable in his opinions. Where his eye was left fixed at the beginning, it was found fixed at the end of the sermon: in a word, the doctrine he delivered had nothing but itself to garnish it. His style was long and pithy, driving on a whole flock of several clauses before he came to the close of a sentence; so that when the copiousness of his style met not with proportionable capacity in his auditors, it was unjustly censured for being perplexed, tedious, and obscure. . . . Mr Travers: his utterance was graceful, gesture plausible, manner profitable, method plain, and his style carried in it *indolem pietatis*, a genius of grace flowing from his sanctified heart."

Calvinism. The one is wedded to the Genevan polity, the other has analysed and estimated the foundations of all polity in the intimations of the divine mind revealing itself in nature, reason, and Scripture. Travers no doubt seemed by far the more clever and successful pulpiteer ; but he was only a controversialist—Hooker was a philosopher.

The first four books of the ecclesiastical polity appeared in 1594 ; the fifth some years later, after the author had removed to Bishopsborne, near Canterbury, where he died in the last year of the sixteenth century. It is difficult to estimate the exact effects of these books upon the course of controversy. But there is reason to think that they were considerable, and that, after fifty years' conflict, the agitation somewhat recoiled under the shock of the lofty and far-reaching argument which they developed. Of this there can be no doubt, that they carried the Puritans into a region of discussion where they had difficulty in following the author, and where they certainly could not meet him. The Puritan's strong point, as we have seen, was the supposed warrant of Scripture for his views. Scripture, he urged, had especially laid down rules for the ordering and worship of the Church. "Those things only are to be placed in the Church which the Lord himself in His Word commandeth," was the fundamental principle laid down in the "Admonition." Whitgift had so far met this by saying, that the "substance and matter of government must indeed be taken out of the Word of God;" yet that "the offices in the Church whereby this government is wrought, are not namely and particularly expressed in the Scriptures, but in some points left to the discretion and liberty of the Church, to be disposed according to the state of times, places, and persons." He

met the assertion of the Puritans by a simple negative—
to wit, that the Scriptures are not the only and absolute
source of ecclesiastical polity, but that there is a certain discretion and liberty left in the hands of the gov-
ernors of the Church for the time. He did not, however, see the necessity of any higher principle to meet
and absorb their special doctrine, which, in its defin-
iteness, had a strong affinity for the current theological
temper. He had no spirit of philosophy carrying him
beyond the immediate necessities of the argument to
a larger sphere of moral and political contemplation, in
which the Puritan doctrine should receive at once due
recognition and limitation.

It remained for Hooker to do this in the whole conception of his work   Divine rules must be our guide,.
was the postulate. Granted, was Hooker's argument,
divine rules must be our guide ; but it does not follow
that there are no divine rules except those revealed in
Scripture. All true laws, on the contrary, are equally
with the rules of Scripture divine, as springing out of
and resting on the same source as those of Scripture—
the eternal divine reason. The supreme mind is the
fountain of all law, whether its revelation be in Scripture or in nature and life ; and the excellent and binding character of the law does not depend upon the
special medium of revelation, but on the fact that it is
really a revelation or expression of the highest Order.
The particular rules in dispute, therefore, whether or
not they were expressly contained in Scripture, might
have a clear divine sanction. They might have a
valid authority, both in their substance and direct
origin, in their conformity to reason, and the national
will and position. For divine law might as truly
approve itself in such a conformity as in any mere

verbal imitation of the letter of Scripture. The question accordingly came to be not merely what is laid down in Scripture, but what in all respects is fair and conformable, "behovefull and beautiful" in itself, in harmony with the consecrated usages of history, and the exercise and development of the Christian consciousness in the Church. The ground on which it must be decided, in short, is not any mere dogmatic and self-constituted Scriptural interpretation, but the fitness and excellence of the thing in all its relations of time and circumstance—the eternally good ground of *Christian expediency* against *theoretical ecclesiasticism* of any kind.

Of all the theologians of his age, Hooker was the most unpuritan ; he not only opposed a special church theory which then sought to dominate in Protestantism, but he showed how every such theory must break against the great laws of historical induction and national liberty. He was catholic in judgment and feeling, but he wrote not merely on the interests of Catholicism: it was the rights of reason and of free and orderly national development in the face of all preconception, of whatever kind, that he really vindicated. While others merely argued, he reasoned and philosophised.

The dispute was not destined to rest where Hooker wished to rest it. The age was not ripe for such views as he had expounded, even if his party had seen the right application of them. Their publication tended in some degree to divert the course of controversy, and to help the pause in it which marks the close of Elizabeth's reign. But the controversy had then also begun to slacken of itself. As a mere theological polemic, it was wellnigh exhausted, and men were wearied with its endless iterations on either side. It might have died out if it had not been that there were deeper principles at stake than any mere points of ecclesiastical policy. From the beginning, the ecclesiastical difficulty had masked the far greater difficulty of the liberty of the subject; and it was only Elizabeth's vigorous and enlightened sense of her position, and the consistent pride with which she sought the national glory in its highest sense, and, notwithstanding her apparent deference to the ecclesiastical prejudices of the Catholics, yet maintained herself at the head of Protestantism in Europe, that enabled her to evade this latter difficulty. With all the restlessness of the extreme Protestants during her reign, they yet beheld in her government their only defence against the reactionary plots that were everywhere threatening the very existence of their faith. She might thwart and oppress them, but she remained true upon the whole to the great cause which they prized, and which, but for her, might have been utterly overthrown in England and in Scotland, as it was in France. The political difficulty, therefore, did not emerge in Elizabeth's reign. The Puritans felt that, although oppressed in conscience, they were not sacrificed to any game of political intrigue. Elizabeth, in fact, was as Protestant as she could be; and although they did not recognise this, and their whole conduct indeed protested against it, yet the fact vaguely impressed itself on the national conscience, and kept it steady and loyal amidst all its agitations.

With the accession of the Stuarts a wholly different turn was given to the political aspects of the controversy; while its theological spirit also, after a brief repose, awakened to fresh bitterness, and, on the Anglican or Church side, took a new and intensely dogmatic direction.

It was natural for the Puritans to make advances to James on his first accession to the throne. A monarch who, in Scotland, had seemed for a while warmly to identify himself with Presbytery, and who, in his zeal, had pronounced the Anglican service " an ill-said mass in English," might well excite hopes in their breasts. They would have been untrue to their convictions if they had not besought his countenance; and they met him accordingly on his way to assume his new dignity with their famous Millenary petition. The heads of this petition claim our notice, as showing what were the definite objects of the Puritans after fifty years' struggle. It was their manifesto at the opening of the second great stage of the controversy. It consisted of four heads.

1. Concerning Church Service.—It prayed that the cross in baptism, the interrogatories to infants, baptism by women, and confirmation, should be done away; that the cap and surplice should not be enforced; that examination should precede communion; that the ring in marriage should be dispensed with; that the Lord's-day should be strictly observed; that church music should be moderated and the service abridged; that there should be no bowing at the name of Jesus; and that none but canonical Scriptures should be read.

2. Concerning Ministers.—It prayed that none but able men who can preach be appointed; that non-residence be forbidden, and the lawfulness of the marriage of the clergy fully recognised.

3. Concerning Church Livings.—It required that

bishops abandon all preferment except their bishoprics; that they be not allowed to hold additional livings in *commendam*; that impropriations annexed to
bishoprics and colleges be converted into regular rec-
torial livings; and that lay impropriations—that is to
say, livings in the possession of laymen to whom they
had been given at the Reformation—should be charged
with a sixth or seventh part for the support of a
preacher.

4. Concerning Church Discipline.—It required that
excommunication should not be in the name of lay
chancellors, nor for *twelve-penny* matters, without the
consent of pastors.

With the exception of the first of these heads, which
contains the main points which had been so long controverted, it will be observed how very practical is the
spirit of reform displayed by the Puritans. They had
profited, in some degree, from their hard experience;
they could not lay aside the old subjects of contention—the cross in baptism, the ring in marriage, holy
days and church music; but these are no longer the
sole, or even the chief abuses urged by them. The
lack of preaching, the abuses of Church patronage and
of discipline, occupy a prominent place: and in fix-
ing their attention on such practical and notorious
abuses, while they evaded all allusion to an entire
change of ecclesiastical policy, and shut out of sight
the question of Presbyterianism, they no doubt mor-
ally strengthened their position, and appealed far more
strongly to the common sense and intelligence of the
nation. At no period, in fact, do they, as a party
within the Church, stand higher. It seemed as if, in
the ebb of the polemical bitterness which had so long
raged, they had risen to a truer sense of their position,

and the really urgent necessities of the Church and country. All this was owing, in a great degree, to the wisdom, moderation, and thoughtfulness of their present leader, Dr Reynolds. Distinguished by profound learning and elevated character—serious without gloom, and zealous without harshness—deeply convinced, without pedantry, or ambition, or any personal interest—he stands out as one of the best ecclesiastical characters of his time; and, in a crisis which was most solemn and memorable for the Church of England, he bears a lofty contrast to most of the dignitaries which assembled around James. He was extreme in his Calvinism, and he certainly mistook the character of the men with whom he had to deal; but his calmness and sense never forsook him amidst all the indignities of the Hampton Court Conference; and to one of his suggestions we owe the only valuable result to which that Conference led—to wit, the authorised version of the Scriptures.

It was obvious, from the very first day that the divines assembled together at Hampton, what part James was resolved to take. While the archbishop and bishops went into "the presence-chamber" to consult with the King, the four representatives of the Puritans—Dr Reynolds, Dr Sparks, Mr Knewstubs, and Mr Chaderton—were left "sitting on a form outside." A conference thus begun terminated as might have been expected. James's only interest seemed to be to exhibit his knowledge of divinity, and to browbeat the remonstrants as soon as they ventured to make any suggestions of reform. Even in Barlow's* fawning account of the Conference, this is obvious; and it

---

* Barlow, Dean of Chester, who was one of the seven deans present, published the *Sum and Substance of the Conference.*

C

is difficult to say whether the insolence of the King
or the servility of the prelates is the more contemptible. As to the power of the Church in things indifferent, his Majesty said "he would not argue, but
answer as kings in Parliament, *Le Roy s'arisera.*" "I
will have one doctrine," he added, "one discipline,
one religion, in substance and ceremony." And when
Reynolds at last suggested, in default of any more
extended plan of reform, that the prophesyings, such
as they had been approved of by Archbishop Grindal
and others, should be revived, and the clergy be allowed to meet in provincial constitutions and synods
with the bishops, he kindled into a passion, fancying
they were aiming at a Scotch Presbytery, which, he
said, "agreeth as well with monarchy as God and the
devil. Then Jack and Tom, and Will and Dick,
shall meet, and, at their pleasure, censure me and my
Council, and all our proceedings. Then Will shall
stand up and say, It must be thus: then Dick shall
reply, and say, Nay, marry, but we will have it thus:
here I must once reiterate my former speech, *Le Roy
s'avisera,*" &c.*

It is clear that there was not much to be made of
such a conference. If *le Roy s'avisera* was to settle
everything, the scruples of the Puritans would go for
little; and accordingly it was soon found that the
royal will was to govern the Church as despotically
as ever, and far more insolently. The Hampton Court

* There is a coarse and telling humour in James's taunts about Presbytery, which, if they were not so utterly unbecoming, might make us
smile. He added, in the same vein, "Pray stay one seven years before
you demand that of me, and if then you find me pursy and fat, and my
windpipe stuffed, I will perhaps hearken to you—for let that government be up, and I am sure I shall be kept in breath." There is a tragic
irony in the fearful reply which the Presbyterian Long Parliament
made to this sarcasm of the father in the person of his son.

Conference was followed by the Convocation of 1604, and the passing of the famous hundred and forty-one canons, which enforced uniformity under more rigorous penalties than ever. The Puritans beheld all their burdens bound with a double and galling force upon their necks.

Bancroft, moreover, was made primate in the same year, and they well understood the significance of this fact. Ever since the notorious sermon at Paul's Cross in 1588—a sermon, the purport of which James, then in the heat of his Presbyterian zeal, had protested against from Scotland—Bancroft was known as the leader of the extreme Prelatist party. He had announced, so far back as that year, the new ground which the controversy was destined to take up on the Church side. He had struck the chord of a hostile dogmatism, which, however strange in its first utterance, gradually passed into a general argument and watchword. Bishops, he maintained, were a distinct order from priests, and possessed superiority over them *jure divino*. Prelacy, in short, was of special divine appointment. This was a shaft into the ranks of the Puritans which could scarcely fail to excite commotion, considering the course which the argument had hitherto taken.

It was some time, however, before the new dogmatism took root in the ecclesiastical mind, and germinated into strength and consistency. It scarcely did so during the course of Bancroft's own primacy. His archiepiscopal rule was less distinguished by any intellectual change in the character of the controversy, than by its coarse and imperious system of repression. He himself proved more of an ecclesiastical dictator than anything else. Persecution was his active weapon.

In the previous reign there had no doubt been persecution, but there had also been argument—a fair field
of debate, in which the highest intellects of the respective sides were pitched against one another—by no
means to the disadvantage of the Church. But mere
offence and violence now became the order of the day.
Hundreds of ministers were suspended, and laymen as
well as clergymen imprisoned. A bencher of Gray's
Inn ventured to defend a minister who had petitioned
the House of Commons, and he himself, at Bancroft's
instance, was apprehended and immured in jail for
life. The Puritans suffered, but did not yield, and
their sufferings gradually won them popular sympathy
and respect.

Hitherto they had been only an insubordinate faction in the Church. They had constituted an active
but by no means a large party in the country. They
were respected for their conscientiousness—they were
influential from their clear convictions and their energetic combination; but there is no evidence that in
Elizabeth's reign they represented any very general
national feeling. Elizabeth herself and her policy
were more popular than anything else, while the old
Romanism was still in various districts substantially
the prevailing religion. But it was the natural tendency both of James's civil and ecclesiastical policy, to
invest the Puritan cause with a national and widely
spread interest. The indecision of the one, and the
want of magnanimity in the other, created an increasing sympathy for those who steadfastly upheld the
principles of Protestantism, and were exposed to sacri-
fices for their consistency. Such a sympathy especially
spread among the burgher or citizen class, who had
already begun to incline this way in the previous

reign. Many circumstances contributed to the growth of this spirit from the very accession of the Stuarts; but it was only in the reign of Charles that it reached its full increase.

The oppression of James's reign drove many of the more zealous Puritans from the country, first to Holland, and then to the great Western Continent, where they were destined to plant their faith as the seed of a new and powerful civilisation. In 1620 the Mayflower and the Speedwell sailed from Delft Haven, bearing the first Saxon colonists of America, the Pilgrim Fathers. Many were disposed to follow their example. To the Puritan mind, in its stern loyalty to the Bible, and love of self-government according to its own ideal, there was something peculiarly fascinating in the thought of erecting a model state on a distant and unexplored shore. Had free egress been granted, in this and the succeeding reign, to the proud spirits that groaned restlessly under prelatic tyranny at home, it may be a question whether the dangerous element would not have been eliminated from the home society, and the shock of civil war averted. The story of the eight ships that lay in the Thames, bound for New England, in the spring of 1638, on board of which were John Hampden, Oliver Cromwell, and Arthur Haselrig, may serve at least to suggest the possibility of such a result.

It was the whole aim of Bancroft's policy, as we have said, to crush the Puritans. It was inspired by the spirit of the royal saying, "I will make them conform, or else I will harry them out of the land, or else do worse." And Clarendon seems to have believed that, had Bancroft lived, he would have subdued these unruly spirits, and extinguished that

fire in England that had been kindled in Geneva ; for
" he understood the Church excellently well, and had
almost rescued it out of the hands of the Calvinian
party."

But it was the fatal destiny of the Stuarts not to
be consistent even in misgovernment. On Bancroft's
death in 1610, Abbot was appointed to the primacy,
and he, Clarendon adds, " unravelled all that his predecessors had been doing for many years. He considered the Christian religion no otherwise than as it
abhorred and reviled Popery, and valued those men
most who did that most furiously. He inquired but
little after the strict observation of the discipline of the
Church, or conformity to the articles and canons established, and did not think so ill of the Presbyterian discipline as he ought to have done. His house was a
sanctuary to the most eminent of the factious party,
and he licensed their most pernicious meetings."
Abbot, in fact, was a semi-Puritan, and it is difficult to
understand under what mistake James appointed him
to the office. It is certainly a singular circumstance
in the history of the movement, that it should twice
have received a special impulse from the very quarter
that was designed to check it. As Grindal undid the
work of Parker, so Abbot undid the work of Bancroft, or at least both of them acted as far as they could
in the same direction. The primacy was substantially
Puritan in the case of both ; and had they been permitted a free exercise of their functions, it is difficult to
say what might have been the result to the Church of
England. This, however, was not permitted to Abbot
any more than to Grindal. Like his predecessor, the
former not only soon lost the royal favour, but sank into
a pitiful and half-disgraceful obscurity, as the uninten-

tional agent in a mournful disaster. While hunting
in a park of Lord Zouch's, in Hampshire, he unwarily
let fly his arrow, and killed the keeper on the spot.
James showed him personal kindness in the circumstances ; but the primate, deeply distressed in mind,
withdrew altogether from the Council board, where
before "his advice was but little regarded."

During the ten years, however, that Abbot retained
his place at the head of ecclesiastical affairs, there was
a great relaxation in the system of prelatic oppression
inaugurated by Bancroft. The Puritan was left in
comparative tranquillity. The well-known character
of the primate, as in Grindal's time, served as a conscious support to him. He was still left to feel that
he belonged to the Church of England, and to cherish
the hope that it might one day be conformed to his
desires. In any case, while the hand of actual persecution was lifted from him, and his principles not laid
under ban, he was content to cherish them in peace,
and to wait for their triumph.

That triumph was still distant ; and new principles
and shapes of party were in the mean time springing
up in more menacing and formidable opposition than
ever. The spirit which Bancroft had introduced into
the controversy thirty years before, had been silently
taking root and growing up in many minds. It would
be absurd to ascribe too much importance to the memorable sermon at Paul's Cross ; but the echo of it long
outlived the preacher, and sentiments in conformity
with it had now begun to characterise a large portion
of the Anglican clergy. A change of spirit was gradually creeping over the Church. The deeper thoughtfulness and manlier sense of the Elizabethan age had
faded away, and given place to a theological intellec-

tualism, comparatively pedantic and formal. Andrews and Donne, Williams and Laud, mark the progress of this change. These men were sufficiently remarkable as preachers and as politicians ; but they had lost the comprehensive grasp of principles, and, above all, the robust vigour of sentiment and honest earnestness, that distinguished the theologians of the Reformation. In comparison with Hooker, or even Jewell, they had not a particle of philosophy. Their theology was a craft at which they were marvellous adepts ; but it had lost the relation to life and general thought which marked that of the previous age. The higher clergy generally were become more men of system than of thought—members of an order, rather than leaders of an advancing spiritual intelligence. It was only natural for such men, when they found themselves confronted with a defiant dogmatism like Puritanism, to seek their safety in the invention and support of an opposite dogma. Sacerdotalism, accordingly, became the contending watchword with Presbyterianism : the divine right of the bishop encountered the divine right of the Presbytery ; an Anglican *jus divinum* met the Puritan *jus divinum*. Episcopacy and ceremonialism were not merely defensible, but they were stamped with an hereditary divine sanction. The one was of apostolical succession, the other was a part of the "beauty of holiness." The external worship of the Church of England became in the hands of these men a positive divine institution, just as the Genevan discipline had been to the Puritan the handiwork of God—the very "pattern" of the things shown in the Mount. Extreme, as usual, called forth extreme.

Not only so, but along with this change in the ecclesiastical aspect of the controversy, a remarkable and decisive change of doctrinal view was rapidly proceeding. Calvinism was being abandoned by the Church, and becoming the exclusive property of the Puritan. This change had been for some time working beneath the surface, but it only showed itself prominent towards the close of James's reign. It is very significant, and lay in the conditions of the agitation from the very beginning. The remarkable thing is rather that it should have been so long delayed, than that it should at last have come so quickly and thoroughly. The Puritan was a Calvinist naturally and entirely. The well-spring of his peculiar thought and life—the original of his theology and church—were in Geneva. The Churchman was Calvinistic, not so much from conviction or affinity of sentiment, as from the mere dominance of a great system over the theological mind of his time. Calvinism, more or less definite, became the reigning expression of the religious thought of the age of the Reformation and that which immediately followed. But so soon as the character of this thought began to change, Calvinism began to lose its hold, and the very means taken to strengthen its ascendancy by a natural reaction led to its overthrow.

James had come from Scotland a zealous Calvinist; and, even after he had been some time on the throne of England, he had communicated to the States of Holland his abhorrence of the doctrines of the successor of Arminius at Leyden.* The change that was creeping over other minds, however, had not left the royal mind unaffected. It was felt and acknowledged at Court, as elsewhere, that Puritanism and Calvinism had a natural and essential affinity. The convictions of the King were waxing comparatively weak under such

* Conrad Vorstius.

an experience; the last remnant of his Scottish theological education was beginning to break up. Still the process was gradual. His mind clung to the old orthodoxy, and he sent, when requested, four representatives to the synod of Dort in 1618. He expressed himself, moreover, delighted with the decisions of that famous synod. The Calvinistic world was everywhere excited and pleased with so triumphant a result. Nothing could well have been more summary and successful; but, as in many other cases, the very excess of the triumph proved a defeat. The Arminians were rudely silenced and expelled from the synod; but the spirit of free inquiry which, in their circumstances, these men represented, lived on and took a new start, all the more surely because of the violent and unreasoning treatment with which their opinions had been encountered. The "five points" settled at Dort were debated over again in many an English parsonage, and in the halls of Oxford and Cambridge, and not always with the same result—not unfrequently with a quite opposite result. Among many of the younger and more active clergy, a strong doctrinal reaction set in. The sentiments of Arminius and Episcopius were welcomed by them as an availing counterpoise to the Calvinistic opinions so closely identified with Puritanism. They gladly caught the new "wind of doctrine," and trimmed their movement to catch its favouring gale.

The president of St John's College, Oxford, was the representative and chief of this rising party in the Church. From the time that he had taken his degree in 1598, he had been known in Oxford as a zealous, confident, and aspiring person; fond of management, and devotedly attached to all the ancient Catholic usages of the Church. He was of little stature, and

the wits had dubbed him *parva Laus*. Small he was,
beyond doubt, in all his convictions and aspirations, his
poor superstitions and scrupulosities;* a man of weak
but obstinate judgment, of cold though intense feeling, of mean yet tenacious temper, and of narrow yet
indomitable persuasions — exactly the man to initi-
ate a fanatical movement in behalf of an established
cause. In this man the new Anglican movement was
impersonated. He tells us that he was one of those
who believed in the " divine apostolical right " of Episcopacy ; that his predominant aim as a churchman
was to secure uniformity, " being still of opinion that
unity cannot long continue in the church when uniformity is shut out at the church door." The idea of
ceremonial uniformity possessed him, in fact, as a passion. It was the thought in which he lived ; it was
the cause, we may say, for which he died. The Church,
as a positive institution, divinely prescribed in every
lineament and form ; the sacraments and clergy as
the sole channels of grace ; the dresses and ritual as
the very "beauty of holiness"—these were to Laud no
mere matters of argument, but the very essence of
faith. He saw at once the meaning and value of the
doctrinal change that had begun, and set himself at
its head. Although comparatively languid in his own
dogmatic sympathies, it was he who invented the name
of "doctrinal Puritanism" to designate the opposition
to the Church, and led the reaction against Calvinism.

James was at first naturally puzzled by the new
turn which the defenders of the Church were taking.

---

* Laud's diary shows abundantly the superstitions of the man, his
regard for dreams and omens, and his scrupulous and timid anxieties.
It is a strange picture of the brooding of a narrow yet enthusiastic
nature.

He could not all at once get quit of his strongly-pronounced Calvinism. Beyond doubt he had a lurking love for the Genevan dialectics in which he had been trained, and in which he himself had been no inconsiderable adept. But he loved power still more than Calvinism ; and, identifying always more the ecclesiastical with the royal prerogative, according to his famous saying, " No bishop, no king," he soon parted with any doctrinal scruples he had, and gave the full weight of his authority to the new prelatic movement. While the miserable intrigue about the Spanish match was proceeding—to the great disgust of the old national feeling, which had not forgot its proud resentment against Spain—and the Puritan party availed themselves of the state of affairs to inveigh strongly against Popery and Arminianism, he issued *directions to preachers,* commanding them to abstain from such exciting discussions. The deep points of election and reprobation, and the universality and irresistibility of divine grace, were laid under ban, and excluded from the pulpits. The *directions* professed to be aimed against both parties alike, but they chiefly struck at the Calvinistic party. The pulpit had become the great support of this party. The system of lecturers, which attained its full growth in the succeeding reign, was rapidly spreading in the towns. It was greatly patronised by the middle classes, who could in no other way have their love for preaching gratified ; and to assail the freedom of the pulpit was really, therefore, to assail one of the most powerful influences exerted in favour of Calvinistic and Puritan doctrine.*

* We shall hear more of the lecturers as we proceed. The people delighted in them ; the High Church clergy detested them. Heylin speaks of them as being " neither birds nor beasts, and yet both of them to-

It was not only by such means, however, that James showed his deepening attachment to the semi-Romish party that was rising in the Church. This party aimed, under a totally different feeling from that which impelled the early reformers, to assimilate the religious observances of the country to those that had existed in the old Catholic times. Regular attendance in the parish church on Sundays, and the old recreations and games afterwards, was one of their favourite devices for this purpose ; and the *Book of Sports* was the consequence. There was nothing which more deeply offended the Puritan. It violated at once his profound convictions and his most sacred feelings. The May-pole and Sunday dance on the village green became a standing opprobrium to his conscience, as they were a dishonour to his religion ; and among all his incentives to violent action, none was stronger than his outraged feeling against a system identified to him with such desecrating abominations.

After the accession of Charles in 1625, the great parties in the Church and country became more definitely and widely opposed to one another. A quarter of a century's renewed and embittered conflict had left traces wholly irremovable. James's selfish vanity and pedantic tyrannies had thwarted and annoyed the popular instincts at every point, without doing anything to extinguish them. Beyond doubt, the powers opposed to Puritanism had lost during this period both in intellectual and moral strength. The proud earnestness which had distinguished the leading churchmen

gether." " The lecturers," says the more sober Selden, " get a great deal of money, because they preach the people tame, as a man watches a hawk, and then they do what they list with them."

of the age of Elizabeth, the national sense and dignity which they had represented, had passed away ; while Puritanism itself had grown, from being a mere contentious and unruly element, into a great moral and political as well as religious cause.

It is impossible to conceive any one more in contrast with this growing phase of the national life than the monarch who now succeeded to its guidance. Trained under the tutorship of Buckingham and Laud, he had attained to manhood without the slightest notion of liberty of conscience or liberty of any kind. His reason was a slave to the dogmas which he had been taught, and all his feelings and sympathies were enlisted on the same side. His judgment was narrow, and his will at once sanguine and perverse. Blameless in personal conduct, and of pure and pious affections, all that was good equally with all that was evil in his nature and education, clung to the fabric of the constitution in Church and State as it had descended to him. He cared not so much for its principles—for of principles his mind did not fit him to have any clear conception—but he admired and worshipped its forms and supposed prerogatives. He was, in short, a natural despot, with the mystic enthusiasm and deep falsehood, without the resolute energy and unscrupulous decision, of the race. He and Laud suited each other perfectly ; the same dictatorial and overbearing policy in conception, the same earnestness in details, the same love of ceremonies, the same intensity in trifles, the same suppleness of principle and the same rigour of creed, the same mysticism and the same formalism, characterised them. Their sympathies exactly met, their views coalesced, and their ambition sought the same channels of gratification. Under their united action, the question

which had so long agitated the country assumed dimensions far more serious and startling than had yet
characterised it. It became a question not merely of
ceremonialism and anti-ceremonialism, nor even of
Episcopacy and Presbytery, but of Protestant freedom and popular rights against Popery in the Church
and absolutism in the State. The principles of the
prolonged controversy had worked themselves into
this broader and more fundamental opposition. The
ground was taken up for the final conflict approaching
between the parties.

It was the political element at length mingling in
the controversy which carried it to its full height.
Charles I., in his more consistent assertion of despotic
power in the face of an increasing disaffection, was
destined to bind up the opposing forces into a fiercer
and more compact antagonism, and to precipitate
them towards their great outbreak. The gap between
the parties had gone on widening and changing its
attitude, until they fairly confronted each other in
deadly hostility. It was not so much that any new
claims were advanced on the part of the Crown—precedents might be found for the most obnoxious exercises of the royal prerogative (although scarcely for the
exact form of them)—but it was that such claims were
no longer tenable in the face of the changes in public
opinion, and the altered relations which the Crown and
Parliament, as the representative of that opinion, now
bore to one another. The absoluteness which was natural
and possible to Elizabeth, which had an excuse in the
comparatively disorganised condition of the national
sentiment, and which rested, beyond doubt, on a great
conservative interest in the State and in the Church—
which, in short, had so much national life in it, and

was sustained by such moral dignity as to enlist in its
support all the highest minds of the time—had ceased
to have the same reality and meaning in the hands of
Charles; while, by its mere continued exercise, it had
rather grown in pretension than abated any of its
severity. It had lost its weight without losing its
sting. The great interests on which it rested had disappeared, while it seemed to stand as insolently erect
as ever. The Tudor spirit had fled from it, while it
showed even an uglier face of tyranny than in the
Tudor age.

The mere continuance of the strife had helped to
aggravate its issue. Constant provocation incensed
the Crown and increased its arbitrariness, while di-
minishing its material and moral strength. The dominant party in the Church suffered from the reaction
of their uncontrolled privileges—especially from the
withdrawal of that earnest spiritual life which, naturally inclining to a freer exercise of spiritual rights
than the Church allowed, was absorbed in nonconformity. There are many painful evidences of this in
the social history of the time, as preserved in Baxter's
account of his early years, and in Mrs Hutchison's
Memoirs. Under the force of the restraint which was
everywhere laid upon the movements of the religious
life, great laxity of manners had sprung up under the
shelter of the Church—nay, within the bosom of the
Church itself. The parochial clergy, who made themselves the mere creatures of a State system, showed
not merely a lack of earnestness, but frequently a deplorable irreligion and immorality in their conduct.*
The system became still more contemptible in the men
who represented it, than oppressive in the agencies by

* See *Sketch of Baxter's Life.*

which it was enforced. On the other hand, the religious and social impulses which were confined and driven into obscurity gathered strength in their confinement. Kept under control, they got hardened and disciplined instead of extinguished. A wide, though lurking, popular feeling was gradually awakened, which began not merely to resent the old interferences with religious freedom, but to oppose itself constitutionally to the royal prerogative. Religious oppression was recognised as merely one aspect of a power which was inimical to the national freedom in all its manifestations. The old spirit of English independence was aroused, and looked abroad for its enemies on which to take a deadly vengeance.

It is a striking process of revolution by which a controversy about vestments passed into a great national struggle. The progress, the outbreaks, and the triumph of the contest are all singularly characteristic. The patience of resentment, and yet the tenacity of conviction, on the part of the people, gradually passing in the one case beyond bounds, and, in the other case, swelling into a mighty and indomitable principle ; the vacillations and contending fanaticisms in the Church ; the infatuation and blinded selfishness of the two Stuart monarchs ; the mingled heroism and caution of the Parliamentary leaders ; the disorderly humours which might have proved ruinous, and the patriotic resistance which might have been broken or wearied out, had not a great Hero stepped forward to give unity to the former, and to carry the latter forward in a splendid career of victory ; the magnanimous and apparently unselfish advance of this Hero, till, returning from the bloody glory of his

D

Irish conquest, other leaders seemed to retire, and leave him master of the field; the blended grandeur and gloom of his usurpation and rule, as they worked themselves out amid the perplexities of his Parliaments, the discontents of his old friends, the murmurs of the army, and the sorrows of his family, and yet to the glory of his country, and the renown of his name abroad as well as at home; all make a picture —dazzling in colour, yet sober in outline—brilliant with all the wonder of romance, yet shaded by the steady and softened light of duty—such as nowhere else can be paralleled.

It is our intention to sketch a few of the main figures in this marvellous picture. The great soldier-figure that stands central and conspicuous over all in the group—in whom the spirit of the movement assumed its most heroic mould, and broke forth into its grandest and most conquering passion; the proud poet and scholar whom we discern by his side—a less conspicuous, but a purer and more unworldly figure, in whom the same movement reached its height of moral and intellectual sublimity; the enthusiastic theologian, who never wearied in the service of a cause which yet often filled him with misgivings; the poet-preacher, whose experience and dreams illustrate so vividly its internal conflicts and spiritual aspirations. These are but prominent figures in a crowded canvass. Many others would find their place along with them in a history of the time; but the study of these may enable us to comprehend, although not in all its variety and extent, the real meaning and character of the movement in which they were engaged.

I.

CROMWELL.

CROMWELL.

OF all the representatives of English Puritanism, Cromwell is the most characteristic and distinguished. No country but England, no religion but Puritan Protestantism, could have produced such a Hero. In his life and character he exhibits, more completely than any other, the various principles moving the popular heart of England in the reign of Charles I.,—the political instincts, the social impulses, and the moral and Christian enthusiasms which, after smouldering as a slow fire for years—breaking out here and there into uneasy flame, and dying down again—had at length kindled into a raging heat, penetrating every home, and lighting up with sympathy or hostility every hearth in the kingdom. All that was deepest in the inward life of Puritanism—its spiritual struggles, its eager gropings after a living truth—and equally all that was most marked in its outward features—its gravity, severity, and strange mixture of Jewish-Christian forms of speech, with the cursory and direct business of the day—find in Cromwell their appropriate expression. He is Puritan in spirit, Puritan in face. The lines of his portrait have all the weighty unornamental dignity, the bluff uncourtly heroism, the dreamy and somewhat dull imaginativeness, and the

depths of devotional passion, which Puritan ambition
in its highest forms recalls. And if Cromwell was
something more than a Puritan—if he rose, in the
strength of his genius and broad worldly vision, as
well as through his active experience of military and
State affairs, to a higher point of view than Puritanism in its special character can be said to have done
—there were also other points of practical virtue, simplicity, and self-denial, in which many will say that
during his later career he fell below it. If we take
him all in all, however, he is certainly its most conspicuous, its greatest representative. The shadow of
his greatness falls across the whole course of its history. Rising from the midst of its religious influences,
nursed in the bosom of its spiritual earnestness, hardened into firmness and self-conscious strength and
triumph in its deadliest conflicts, he at length en-
throned its principles at the head of the three kingdoms, and gave them not only a national but a Euro-
pean sway.

There have been various biographies of Cromwell,
from Noble's *Memoirs of the Protectoral House of Cromwell*, to Guizot's Life; but it is not in any of these, even
in the last, that the student will find the best and
most living sources of information. These are to be
found, beyond question, in his own letters and speeches,
as elucidated by Mr Carlyle in his well-known work.*

---

* There is none of Mr Carlyle's works better, upon the whole, than
his *Letters and Speeches of Oliver Cromwell*. There is none certainly
marked by a deeper insight, or a more true and close appreciation of
fact, with less exaggeration and wantonness of descriptive statement.
Its editorial and fragmentary character admirably suits the author's
genius, which is more successful in broad and vivid effects, and dashes
of portraiture, than in carefully-drawn outlines and minutely-shaded
sketches of character.

Here, as everywhere, the man's own words are his best biography. What he really was, what he thought, what he aimed to do, what he failed to do, how he lived, and fought, and governed, we can learn more from meditation on these words than we can in any other way. We get, if not completely to understand him, yet to understand him better than we ever did before—to gather up the threads of his life into a more consistent tissue—to see what *meaning* it had, and what influence on human history it exercised.

The life of Cromwell naturally falls into three great divisions. The first extends to the close of what may be called his private life, or to the outbreak of the civil war in 1642; the second runs from this period throughout the whole of his brilliant career as a Puritan patriot and soldier, a space of twelve years or so, on to 1654; the last comprises the period of his Protectorate, when he appears as a statesman and sovereign, a brief space of scarcely four years (1654-1658). The proportion between these several periods is remarkable: the long and well-matured discipline of more than forty silent years of home thought and common business, through which the Puritan hero was prepared for his work; the struggle of twelve; the triumph of four. It is well to remember that up to middle age, the man whom we see finally ruling the destinies of England, and leading in triumph the interests of Protestantism in Europe, was a quiet farmer in the fens of Huntingdon. This of itself were sufficient to show that no mere theory of restless pride or of selfish aggrandisement will gauge his character, and account for him as an historical phenomenon. To whatever degree the desire of power may have been cherished in him by his remarkable fortunes and the ever-expanding consciousness of his genius, he must also have possessed many strongly-marked features, independently of the ambition which absorbed the later energies of his career, and drew forth the imperial pomp and passion of his character.

Cromwell was born in the spring of the last year of the sixteenth century, at Huntingdon. He was the fifth child, and the only son that survived, of Robert Cromwell, younger son of Sir Henry Cromwell, and brother of Sir Oliver Cromwell of Hinchinbrook, an excellent property in the immediate neighbourhood, now belonging to the Montague family. It was sold by this same Sir Oliver, uncle of our hero, to this family. Sumptuous living, an easy and rejoicing hospitality on the part of both the father and the son, had reduced the fortunes of the house, and rendered such a step necessary. The father, Sir Henry, was called, from his profuse expenditure, "the Golden Knight," and Sir Oliver seems to have vied with him in this respect. In 1603, immediately after the accession of James, he entertained the King and his retinue with great magnificence at Hinchinbrook. Again, in 1617, when James was on his way to Scotland, with Dr Laud in his company, intent on Episcopal innovations there, he repeated his hospitality, although, on this second occasion, with diminished splendour; and soon afterwards the property passed out of his hands. The good knight, however, continued to cherish warmly his Royalist predilections, even when his nephew had become the great Parliamentary captain. A fine old country gentleman he seems to have been, with the genuine hearty humour of the race. It is a capital trait recorded of him,* that when his eldest son—in whom the family turn for expenditure was hereditary —presented a list of his debts, craving for some aid towards their payment, Sir Oliver answered with a bland sigh, " I wish they were paid."

On his father's side Cromwell was thus of a gentle and old family†—of the same stock, in fact, from which Thomas Cromwell, Earl of Essex, came. This famous minister of Henry VIII., as Mr Carlyle has shown in detail, was nephew to Oliver's great-grand-father. On his mother's side a far higher but somewhat more imaginary descent has been claimed for him. His mother's name was Elizabeth Stuart ; she was the daughter of William Stuart of the city of Ely, "a kind of hereditary farmer of the cathedral tithes and church lands round that city ;" and the story is that this Stuart family in Ely was an undoubted offshoot of the royal family of Scotland, having sprung from one Walter Steward, who had accompanied Prince James into England, when he was seized and detained by Henry IV. This scion of the royal blood of Scotland is supposed to have married advantageously and settled in England ; and one of his race having been Popish Prior of Ely, on the dissolution of the monasteries, was made, in reward for his pliancy of character, the first Protestant dean, through whom came the mother of our hero.

Cromwell's father, according to the well-known popular story, was a brewer. This occupation does not seem very compatible with his kindred and descent, and the hero-worshipper is apt to kindle into some indigna-

---

* CARLYLE.

† " I was by birth a gentleman," he himself says.—*Speech to Parlia-ment,* Sept. 12, 1654. "Genere nobile atque illustri ortus," says Milton.

tion at the suggestion. There seems, however, a fair
foundation for the story, though Royalist calumny has
touched it with ready exaggerations. Robert Cromwell was evidently a farmer of certain lands of his own
lying round Huntingdon. His proper business was to
manage his own estate; but as his house was conveniently situated for the purpose, with the little brook
Hinchin running through its courtyard into the Ouse,
he seems to have combined brewing with agriculture,
under the laudable impulse of gain. Heath's version,
in fact, may not be very far from the truth—viz., that
"the brew-house was managed by Oliver's mother and
father's servants, without any concernment of his
father therein."

Oliver Cromwell's mother was plainly a spirited,
earnest, and industrious woman, who grudged no
labour for the good of her family. When she was left
a widow with six daughters, she gave dowries of the
work of her own hands to five of them, sufficient to
marry them into wealthy and honourable families. To
the last—and she survived to see her son raised to the
highest pinnacle of power—she cherished her simple
tastes and homely sense. She desired that she might be
buried without ceremony in some country churchyard
—a desire, however, with which her son did not comply.
There is a portrait of her, Mr Foster says, at Hinchinbrook, " which, if that were possible, would increase
the interest she inspires, and the respect she claims ;
the mouth so small and sweet, yet full and firm as the
mouth of a hero—the large melancholy eyes—the
light pretty hair—the expression of quiet affectionate-
ness suffused over the face, which is so modestly en-
veloped in a white satin hood—the simple beauty of
the velvet cardinal she wears, and the richness of the

small jewel that clasps it, seem to present before the gazer her living and breathing character." *

Cromwell was the only son of his father's family that survived. Of his numerous sisters we know little beyond the fact of their marriage. Of his relatives, however, it may be interesting to know further, that one of his aunts on the father's side was the mother of John Hampden, who was therefore full cousin to Oliver; and that another cousin, the son of an uncle Henry, was the famous Oliver St John, the ship-money lawyer. Cromwell's kindred, therefore, were on all hands sufficiently notable. He sprang from the gentry of England; and if he gave to his family name an undying distinction, it conferred upon him, from the first, credit and reputation.

Many semi-mythical stories are told of our hero's childhood and youth. There is probably some grain of truth preserved in them, with loads of calumny and falsehood. In some, the element of fact or trait of character, from which the mythical embellishment has arisen, can be clearly traced. This is particularly the case with the singular story told by Noble and Heath, of his having, during the Christmas revels at his uncle's house, "besmeared his clothes and hands with surreverence" (whatever that may particularly mean), and in this state accosted the master of misrule, and "so grimed him and others upon every turn," as to create a serious disturbance, and lead to his being thrown into an adjoining pond, and there "soused over head and ears." Such a story not inaptly corresponds with his odd and somewhat coarse turn for practical jokes in after years; and probably this well-known feature of his later character is the simple

* FOSTER'S *Lives of the Statesmen of the Commonwealth*, vol. i. p. 9.

explanation of the earlier tradition. So of his vision, in which, when laid down to sleep one day, tired with his youthful sports, he saw the curtains of his bed withdrawn by a gigantic figure, which told him that he should yet be the greatest man in England. Although soundly flogged by the schoolmaster, at the particular desire of his father, for entertaining such a piece of folly, it is said that the dream could not be driven out of the boy's head, and, according to the testimony of Clarendon, it passed into a popular tradition regarding him, "even from the beginning of troubles, and when he was not in a posture that promised such exaltation." It is even said to have had some weight with him in his decision to decline the crown, as he remembered that the figure had not mentioned the word *king*, but only that he should be the greatest man in the kingdom. Such a story can only be considered as an evidence of the ease with which the popular mind satisfies itself as to the explanation of great facts, whose real meaning it never comprehends. The best, perhaps, of all these stories of Cromwell's boyhood, is that which relates how he fought with Prince Charles at Hinchinbrook, when he was there with his father in 1604, on his way from Scotland to London. The tradition is that he gave the Prince a bloody nose— a circumstance, says Noble, which was looked upon "as a bad presage to that King when the civil wars commenced." Even Mr Foster seems struck with so notable an omen. "The curtain of the future was surely," he says, "for an instant upraised here." We may safely say that the story is a good one, and that, supposing Prince Charles and the youthful Cromwell did encounter each other, the stalwart "manchild of the brewer of Huntingdon" was no doubt very likely then, as afterwards, to prove victor, and even to leave the impress of his prowess on the face of his victim.

The young Oliver was sent to the grammar-school at Huntingdon, at the head of which was a Dr Beard, remarkable for the severity of his pedagogic discipline. As a schoolboy he is represented to have been "notorious for robbery of orchards and of dove-houses, stealing the young pigeons, and eating and merchandising of them." Likely enough the energy of his "rank nature" found vent in a somewhat riotous indulgence in all the usual sports and escapades of boyhood; and one statement we can believe to be literally true—that he would work as "a very hard student for a week or two, and then be a truant or otiose for twice as many months."

From school at Huntingdon, Cromwell went to Cambridge in the end of his seventeenth year (1616), and was entered as a commoner of Sidney Sussex College. The same wild reputation follows him here. He made "no proficiency," says one of the gossips,* "in any kind of learning; but then and afterwards sorting himself with drinking companions and the under sort of people (being of a rough and blustering sort of disposition), he had the name of a royster among most that knew him." During his short residence at Cambridge, says another,† "he was more famous for his exercises in the fields than in the schools (in which he never had the honour of, because no worth and merit to, a degree), being one of the chief match-makers and players at football, cudgels, or any other boisterous sport or game."

Whatever truth there may be in these descriptions of his irregularities, it is by no means true that he made

* SIR WILLIAM DUGDALE.　　　　† HEATH.

no progress in learning. In after years he had a fair knowledge of Latin, which he could only have acquired at this time. During his Protectorate he conversed with the Hague ambassadors in Latin;* and Waller, his kinsman, reports that he was well versed in Greek and Roman history. His was not, indeed, in any sense, a scholarly nature; but it is a mere aspersion—one of the thousand that have gathered around his name—to suppose that he was indifferent or hostile to learning. The respect which he showed in the days of his power to his old *Alma Mater*, the testimony of Milton and others, are sufficient to refute any such accusation. According to Milton, "he gathered up the literary dust of Cambridge without deepening the tracks of learning. He acquired an ordinary acquaintance with literature without being in any sense learned." He had other work to do than that of the schools. With a soaring loftiness, according to his wont, the poet-secretary continues the idea: "It did not become that hand to wax soft in literary ease which was to be inured to the use of arms, and hardened with asperity; that right hand to be wrapt up in down among the nocturnal birds of Athens, by which thunderbolts were soon after to be hurled among the eagles which emulate the sun."

Cromwell had scarcely been more than a year at Cambridge when his father died, and he returned home in consequence. So far as we can judge, this event terminated his scholastic education. The circumstances of his mother—the large charge with which she was left—the loss of her father in the same year—and an alienation which had existed for some time between Sir Oliver's family and her own—probably prevented

* Only "very vitiously and scantily," according to Burnet's sneer.

Oliver continuing his studies. He proceeded soon after to London, to commence the study of law. He is stated to have entered as a member of Lincoln's Inn, although research has failed to discover his name in the books of any of the Inns of Court.

During this period his youthful excesses are reported to have reached their height. The gossips* vie with one another in "strongly-coloured" stories of his wildness and debaucheries. It is impossible to say what amount of truth there may be in such stories. Mr Carlyle makes short work with them, but the uniformity of the tradition would seem to imply some substratum of truth. Wickedly coloured they no doubt are—embellished by all the piquant inventiveness of the slander of the Restoration—yet we can well believe that the youth of Cromwell was one of stormy and passionate excitement. A nature like his is apt to give the rein to its impulses, till some special influence or event comes to arrest and turn it in a new direction.

Such a change in his life was now at hand. While in London he had become acquainted with the family of Sir James Bourchier, "a civic gentleman" of good means and considerable property near Felsted in Essex;

---

* Heath, Anthony Wood, and almost "every contemporaneous record," says Mr Foster, "combine to give a strongly-coloured picture of his uncontrouled debaucheries at this time." One extract will suffice. "The ale-wives of Huntingdon and other places, when they saw him a-coming, would use to cry out to one another, 'Here comes young Cromwell, shut up your dores,' for he made no punctilio to invite his roysters to a barrel of drink, and give it them at the charge of his host; and in satisfaction thereof either beat him or break his windows, if he offered any show, or gave any look or sign of refusal or discontent." There is a worse story than any more personal debauchery, which represents him as attempting to obtain possession of his uncle, Sir Thomas Steward's property, on some plea of his uncle's imbecility;—but the calumny has obviously originated in a misinterpretation of some family disagreement.

and on the 22d of August 1620, when he was twenty-one years and four months old, Oliver Cromwell was married to Elizabeth, daughter of this gentleman, in the Church of St Giles, Cripplegate, London. Elizabeth Bourchier is not said to have been possessed of any remarkable personal attractions. She is not much spoken of, indeed at all, in his letters or elsewhere. Several letters, indeed, of his to her survive, written during his Scottish campaign, and one of hers to him, belonging to the same period; but they are brief and not particularly characteristic. The impression they give of her is that of a strongly affectionate and sensible woman, but somewhat narrow-minded and exacting *—more intent on her family cares than on the great concerns in which her husband was acting a part. One has said—and the description seems to suit her very well—that she was "an excellent housewife, and as capable of descending to the kitchen as she was of acting in her exalted station with dignity."

After his marriage Cromwell settled in his father's residence at Huntingdon, and during the next eight years we scarcely know anything of his history. He appears to have farmed, as his father had done before him, and spent his life in the usual manner of a country gentleman. His own means must have been

---

* She says in the single letter of hers which survives (which, by the way, is extremely wretched in its spelling), almost querulously, " I should rejoice to hear your desire in seeing me—but I desire to submit to the providence of God." But she says also beautifully, and with a touching strength of affection—"My life is but half a life in your absence, did not the Lord make it up in himself." In one of his replies, Sept. 1650, he says, characteristically, " I have not leisure to write much. But I could chide thee that in many of thy letters thou writest to me that I should not be unmindful of thee and thy little ones. Truly, if I love thee not too well, I think I err not on the other hand much. Thou art dearer to me than any creature—let that suffice."

limited, and his duties probably left him but little leisure. He had leisure, however, to think; for it was during these years, and there is reason to suppose not long after his marriage, that the great religious change passed upon him which coloured his whole life, and, more than anything else, gave consistency and meaning to it. How this change was wrought there remains no means of tracing. There is no record of his spiritual experience at this early period; and we cannot even say whether Sir Philip Warwick's reminiscences of his illness and hypochondria* refer to this or a later time of his life. At the best, these are but vague signs of the great crisis of his spiritual being, whose secret intensity can only be gathered from the fulness of feeling and energy of action which it called forth.

He soon showed the bent of his new impulses. Religious life and earnestness appeared to him all to lie with the persecuted Nonconforming party in the Church. Whether or not any of them had been instrumental in leading him to new thoughts, his sympathies at once gathered round them. His house became a refuge of the Puritan preachers; they met in it for worship, in which he not only joined, but actively participated. He became known as one of the most active of the party, and identified himself with all their movements, appearing personally in their behalf before the Bishop of Lincoln.† From being an idle and boisterous youth, he became in a few years a zealous, religious, leader.

---

* Dr Simcott, physician, Huntingdon, told Sir Philip that Cromwell was very "splenetic" about this time—that he had been sent for at midnight to see him—that he laboured under the impression he was just about to die—and had "strange fancies about the town-cross."

† Afterwards Archbishop Williams.

E

We can well understand, although we are not able clearly to trace how all this occurred to Cromwell. As soon as he began to seek a sphere of activity in connection with his new convictions, his great energy, and quick sympathies with the common social feeling around him, would naturally drive him into the ranks of Puritanism. Without frivolity, earnest and thorough-going even in his dissipations, with no reverence for conventionalities, but rather a fierce impatience of them, the Court or ecclesiastical party possessed no points of attraction to him. The only feeling that might have bound him to it—the old traditionary loyalty of his family, which had cost his uncle and grandfather so dear—had become weakened by various circumstances, even if its natural influence had not been broken by his disagreement with his uncle. Royalism had lost its old charm; it had widely alienated the national feeling. Spanish intrigues and Laudian ceremonialism had made it especially contemptible with ardent reforming young minds. Puritanism became, by mere force of contrast, the instinctive creed of such minds between the years 1620-30. To one like Cromwell, with a vague, uneasy sense of genius, and a profound feeling of the reality of religion stirring him, it opened up a field of active interest and ambition. Every one of its objects made a claim upon his sympathy and enthusiasm. The privilege of preaching the gospel with as few formalities as possible—the right to a private judgment in matters of conscience—the need of defence against the old Papal spirit of boundage over men's souls and bodies—these were things directly calculated to interest a young Protestant gentleman in the beginning of the seventeenth century. We cannot tell when the great principle of the rights of conscience first impressed Cromwell; but we shall see how early he was excited about Popery, and every attempt to reintroduce it; and how at last, in the days of his power, it was perhaps his highest honour to reach the right meaning of the doctrine of toleration, and nobly to vindicate it against the straitest sect of that very Puritanism which had first practically taught him it.

During these early years of his residence at Huntingdon, six children were born unto him, four of whom were sons, but only two of whom* survived, and afterwards reappear in history. With this family growing up around him, and amidst his farming duties, and Puritan interests and associations, he spent this quietest period of his life. Gradually he rose to repute and credit among his fellow-townsmen. Particularly he seems to have concerned himself in the scheme at this time set agoing by some of the wealthy London Puritans for buying-in lay impropriations as they were offered for sale, and from such funds providing lecturers to supply the spiritual destitution prevailing in many parts of the country. This was a favourite scheme of the Puritans; and these lecturers, we have seen, were their favourite preachers. "It is incredible," says Fuller, "what large sums were advanced in a short time towards so laudable an employment." Lecturers spread themselves over the country, especially in the market-towns, where they preached on market-days and on Sunday afternoons; and we shall find immediately how great was Cromwell's interest in their maintenance and work.

* Another son (five in all), and two more daughters, cf whom we shall afterwards hear, constituted his family.

His activity and talent were already, in 1625, so well recognised, that it was proposed in that year, when Charles called together his second Parliament, to send him up to Westminster as member for the borough of Huntingdon. The proposal, however, did not on this occasion take effect. In 1628, when Charles, needy for supplies, and unable to find them by other and less constitutional means, called together his third Parliament—the famous Assembly that drew up and passed the Petition of Right—Cromwell was returned as member for Huntingdon. His cousin Hampden was member of this Parliament, and other names no less celebrated—Selden, Elliot, Pym, and Holles. Long afterwards, when the rustic squire from Huntingdon had become the greatest man in England, it was remembered what a rough and clownish appearance he presented at this time ; and in the mad days of the Restoration the subject suggested itself to a divine, whose cleverness scarcely redeems the infamy of his sycophancy, as a telling point for a royal sermon. "Who that had beheld such a bankrupt beggarly fellow as Cromwell," says South, preaching before Charles II., "first entering the Parliament House with a *threadbare torn coat* and a *greasy hat*, and perhaps neither of them paid for, could have suspected that in the course of so few years he should, by the murder of one king, and the banishment of another, ascend the throne, be invested in the royal robes, and want nothing of the state of a king, but the changing of his hat into a crown !" *

The first session of this Parliament did not last long,

* South was not yet bishop, but only chaplain to Buckingham when he thus preached before his royal patron. "Odds fish, Lory," exclaimed Charles, after the sermon, "your chaplain must be a bishop. Put me in mind of him at the next vacancy."

but it had been distinguished by various important
movements. Among other things that it had taken in
hand, was the severe exposure of certain Popish
practices on the part of Mainwaring, one of the royal
chaplains. Pym led the way in this exposure; and the
chaplain, abandoned for the time by his master and
Laud, had to submit to the censure of the House. The
royal favour, however, was speedily extended to him
in compensation. No sooner had Parliament risen than
he was promoted. Other circumstances of ill omen had
occurred. "Tonnage and poundage" had been levied
unwarrantably without Parliamentary consent, and in
the very face of the provisions of the Petition of Right;
this great remonstrance itself was reported to have
been tampered with. Parliament reassembled in the
January of the following year, not in the very best of
tempers it may be imagined. A committee of religion
was immediately appointed, and a hot and indignant
debate ensued as to the Romanising tendencies displayed in high quarters. Hampden had spoken, and
when he sat down his cousin for the first time rose
and addressed the house. " A harsh and broken voice
of astonishing fervour," * made a strange contrast to
the mild and dignified accents of Hampden. But
energy is stamped on every word of the broken and
fragmentary record of this first speech of Cromwell.
The direction which his sympathies had been taking
—his association with Puritan lecturers, the impatience of his stern Protestant feeling, are all apparent.
He said "he had heard by relation, from one Dr Beard
(his old schoolmaster at Huntingdon), that Dr Ala-
baster had preached flat Popery at Paul's Cross ; and
that the Bishop of Winchester (Dr Neile), he had com-

* FOSTER.

manded him as his diocesan he should preach nothing
to the contrary. Mainwaring, so justly censured in the
House for his sermons, was, by the same bishop's means,
transferred to a rich living. If these are the steps to
church preferment," added he, "what are we to expect?" Cromwell's statement so impressed the House,
that it resolved on immediate action. In the Commons' Journals of the same day, there stands recorded
the following notice: "Upon question *ordered*. Dr
Beard of Huntingdon to be written to by Mr Speaker,
to come up and testify against the bishop: the order
for Dr Beard to be delivered to Mr Cromwell." *

The Protestant temper of the House was not to be
restrained. The King, by the help of the Speaker, tried
to evade its determinations. When it came to the
point, Mr Speaker Finch refused repeatedly to "put
the question," alleging that he had the King's orders to
adjourn. But at length, after an astonishing scene, in
which the Speaker gave way to tears, while the members
around menaced him if he persisted in opposing the
mind of the assembly, he was forcibly detained in
his chair until they had passed three emphatic resolutions protesting against "Arminianism, Papistry, and
illegal tonnage and poundage." Dissolution, of course,
immediately followed these proceedings; and Cromwell, after a brief Parliamentary experience, returned
to his native Huntingdon, to remain still for some years
in comparative obscurity. There can be no doubt,
however, that from this time he became a man of mark
in his party. Far more, probably, than we can now
guess, he had shown during this short period of public
life, powers fitted to raise him to influence and distinction; while, at the same time, he had entered into

* CARLYLE.

connection with the great national leaders of the movement. He was no longer merely the head of a provincial party, but one of a patriot band, representing a
powerful national feeling. In communion with such
men, he must have felt his sympathies elevated, and
his convictions enlightened and strengthened.

Cromwell returned to Huntingdon in the spring of
1629. In the course of the following year he was named
along with his old schoolmaster, and Robert Barnard,
Esq., a Justice of the Peace for that borough. Here he
remained for three years or so, still carrying on, apparently in connection with his mother, his old farming
operations. He seems, however, to have been but ill
at ease—troubled with dark thoughts as to his own
spiritual condition and the state of the country. It
is to this period that Mr Forster refers his "strange
fancies about the town-cross," and his hypochondriacal
apprehensions of death. It can be easily imagined
how his strong nature, having been called forth into
temporary excitement by the events of the Parliament
of 1628, and having sunk back into an uneasy and tormenting inaction, would prey upon itself.

In 1631 he effected the sale of the properties in
which he was interested in the neighbourhood of Huntingdon, and removed to St Ives, five miles down the
river, where he rented a grazing farm. His mother
appears to have remained at Huntingdon, as we find
that his children continued to be baptised in the old
church there. At St Ives he became still more distinguished than hitherto for his systematic and rigorous devotions, and for the religious influence which he
sought to exercise over those around him. He prayed
with his family and servants in the morning and evening. He sought to mix up religion with the work of

the fields, just as afterwards he mixed it up with the
work of fighting.   The spirit which inspired and
fashioned his famous Ironsides out of ploughmen and
graziers, was now working in him.   He continued also,
with increasing heartiness, his old concern in the Puritan lecturers sustained by the rich merchants of London.   These lecturers had been greatly persecuted during the years succeeding the dissolution of Parliament.
Laud and his accomplices had hunted them down
wherever they could, and discouraged and broken up
the system as far as in their power.   St Ives appears
to have been fortunate in possessing for its lecturer, up
to the year 1635, one Dr Wells, "a man of goodness,
and industry, and ability to do good in every way, not
short of any man of England," says Oliver, in his first
extant letter.   This letter is in every way remarkable.
It is addressed "to my very loving friend Mr Storie,
at the sign of the Dog in the Royal Exchange,
London ;" and after congratulating Mr Storie and his
fellow-citizens on their good works in "providing for
the feeding of souls," by means of the lectures which
they had instituted in the county—and speaking of the
excellence of Dr Wells, who had been so acceptable in
his calling, and since whose coming the Lord had
wrought by him much good among them—it proceeds
to regret the likelihood of the lectures' discontinuance
for want of funds.   "And surely," he urges, "it were
a piteous thing to see a lecture fall in the hands of
so many able and godly men, as I am persuaded the
founders of this are, in these times wherein we see they
are suppressed, with too much haste and violence, by
the enemies of God's truth.   Far be it, that so much
guilt should stick to your hands, who live in a city so
renowned for the clear shining light of the gospel.

You know, Mr Storie, to withdraw the pay is to let fall the lecture—for who goeth to warfare at his own cost?"—a very characteristic hint—the clear light of common sense (as always with him) shining through the most fervid expressions of religious feeling.

Amidst all his religious exercises, Oliver's farming was not prosperous. The lands seem to have been of a boggy, intractable character, yielding no return for his patient industry. It is the sneer of Hume, copying Heath as usual, that "the long prayers which he said to his family in the evening, and again in the afternoon, consumed his own time and that of his ploughman," and left no leisure for the care of his temporal affairs. No man was ever less likely than Cromwell to commit such a mistake. He had now, and always, far too practical an eye for such maundering. Yet, whatever was the cause, he did not succeed at St Ives. His crops failed, and his health became disordered. The cold and damp of the district affected his throat, producing a kind of chronic inflammation in it. It was remembered long afterwards what a strange appearance he used to make at church, as he came up the aisle—his throat rolled in flannel, his rough dress ill-arranged—and the red flannel flaunting after him.

In 1636 he is found no longer at St Ives, but at Ely. Here he had succeeded to his maternal uncle, Sir Thomas Steward, who, as his fathers before him, had farmed the cathedral tithes. He took up his residence in the old glebe-house near St Mary churchyard—a house still standing, and described by Mr Carlyle in 1845 as an ale-house, with still some chance of standing; " by no means a sumptuous mansion," he adds, "but it may have conveniently held a man of three or four hundred a-year, with his family, in those simple times. Some quaint air of gentility still looks through its ragged dilapidation." Here Cromwell spent the few remaining years of comparative inaction that still awaited him, " living neither in any considerable height nor yet in obscurity," as he told his Parliament of 1654.

The state of the country was in those years rapidly getting worse. Charles had nearly played out his scheme of self-government. The trial of Hampden, protracted for months, served to feed the popular discontent. The quiet magnanimity of the victim, the eloquence of his defence, the legality as well as righteousness of his cause, all served to stimulate the public ardour, and strengthen the rising feeling against the ministers and the Court. The bishops, too, were carrying their short-lived triumph to its most oppressive and insolent excesses. Old Palace Yard, on the 30th of June 1637, presented a spectacle calculated to move men's hearts —not to submission, nor even to despair, but to fierce impatience and rooted vengeance rather. Prynne, and Bastwick, and Burton—a lawyer, physician, and clergy-man—were there exhibited in three pillories, and had their ears cut off and their cheeks branded before a large crowd. This was what Laud's ingenious ecclesiastical devices had come to. These men had ventured to question not only the policy but the legality of these devices. Prynne had openly declared that he was prepared to prove them to be contrary to the law of England. This was the answer he and the rest received. Legal or not, they were to be enforced at the expense of the ears of all gainsayers. The threat was a vain one. " Cut me, tear me," cried Prynne, " I fear thee not—I fear the fire of hell, not thee ;" while Bastwick's wife, at the foot of the scaffold, received her husband's ears into her lap and kissed them.

This very same year, and only a month later, scenes equally remarkable in their way were transacted in Scotland. · Jenny Geddes with her stool and ever-memorable cry, " Deil colic the wame of thee, thou foul thief, wilt thou say mass at my lug ?" had made in old St Giles's a " beginning of the end." The fierceness of national indignation was rising high. It was getting "too hot to last." *

As Cromwell in his Ely home mused on such matters, his heart was deeply stirred in him. He was wrapped now, according to his wont, in deep gloom, and now excited to violent energy. His thoughts were driven inwards, and he anxiously pondered anew whether the ground of the matter was right in him. A letter of this period to his cousin, Mrs St John, the second in Mr Carlyle's list, is among the most characteristic of all his compositions that have been preserved. Amidst its wild and groping earnestness, and strange intensity of biblical language, it sheds a vivid light upon the inward man. A strongly-moved and earnest soul makes itself bare to us, just as it emerges from darkness and struggle. He writes : " Dear cousin —I thankfully acknowledge your love in your kind remembrance of me upon this opportunity. Alas ! you do too highly prize my lines and my company. I may be ashamed to own your expressions, considering how unprofitable I am, and the mean improvement of my talent ; yet to honour my God, by declaring what he hath done for my soul, in this I am confident, and will be so. Truly then, this I find, that He giveth springs in a dry barren wilderness, where no water is. I live, you know where—in Mesech, which they say signifies

* Burton's saying, as he was carried fainting from the scene of his torture.

prolonging—in Kedar, which signifies *blackness:* yet
the Lord forsaketh me not. Though He do prolong,
yet He will, I trust, bring me to His tabernacle, to His
resting-place. My soul is with the congregation of the
first-born : my body rests in hope : and if here I may
honour my God by doing or by suffering, I shall be
most glad. Truly, no poor creature hath more cause
to put himself forth in the cause of his God than I. I
have had plentiful wages beforehand, and I am sure I
shall never earn the least mite. The Lord accept me
as his son, and give me to walk in the light—and give
us to walk in the light, as He is the light. He it is
that enlighteneth our blackness, our darkness. I dare
not say He hideth his face from me : He giveth me to
see light in His light. One beam in a dark place hath
exceeding much refreshment in it. Blessed be His
name for shining upon so dark a heart as mine. You
know what my manner of life hath been. Oh! I lived
in, and loved darkness, and hated light ; I was a
chief, the chief of sinners. This is true : I hated godliness, yet God had mercy on me. O the riches of his
mercy! praise them for me. Pray for me, that He who
hath begun a good work would perfect it in the day
of Christ." *

An air of singular reality, confused but vivid, is
impressed upon every line of this letter—a reality not
suggested by the scriptural language in which it is
expressed, but which looks through all the conventional
phrases of that language. It is a poor, nay, it is an
unintelligible criticism, which can see nothing but
hypocrisy in such a letter. It ought to be remembered
that, on any other supposition than that of the downright and awful sincerity of the writer, much more

* CARLYLE, 141-2.

than hypocrisy is needed to explain it in the circumstances—addressed as it was to his cousin, and meant for her eye alone; we must suppose weakness and folly as well, of which not even a royalist theologian would venture to accuse Cromwell.

This is one side of the picture which our hero presents to us in these years—an earnest man concerned about his soul, and rejoicing that the light of Christ has dawned upon him. There is another side to the picture, in which we see him no less earnest, in a different capacity, as a leader of the popular feeling in a great movement which made much noise at the time in Huntingdon and its neighbourhood. The Earl of Bedford had some years before started a scheme for the draining of the extensive fens which covered some millions of acres in that and the adjoining counties—a project long talked of. The work had proceeded so far. The great *Bedford level*, as it was called, for carrying the river Ouse between elevated embankments into the sea, had been completed, or nearly so; when the Crown, by commissioners, interfered with the professed design of abetting the work, but in such a manner as to stir up a fierce strife in all others interested. Its spirit of encroachment here, as everywhere, was so obviously manifested as to provoke opposition on all hands. Oliver Cromwell threw himself heart and soul into the movement, headed the widespread disaffection, and by a "great meeting" at Huntingdon, and otherwise, effectually put a stop to the invasions of the Crown, and for the time defeated the completion of the great project. He was far, however, from being opposed to it in itself, and it is absurd to represent the matter as if he were so.* It was merely his

* So far from this, that when, in the year 1649, the Long Parliament

instinct here, as elsewhere, to resist the domineering spirit of the Crown in defence of popular rights and privileges. The notoriety he acquired in this commotion procured him among the people the appellation of the "Lord of the Fens." The great energy and decision of his character were quietly noted, and it was felt that he would make himself known in the times that were approaching. It was remarked that he was a man "that would set well at the mark."

Times sufficiently stirring were at hand. The attempt to re-establish Episcopacy in Scotland had produced its natural fruits. The famous Glasgow Assembly had demolished the elaborate machinery devised by Laud and his coadjutors. Charles resolved to send an army into Scotland to enforce his designs; and the long-forgotten idea of a Parliament was once more pressed upon him as the only mode of enabling him to meet his difficulties and equip his army. A Parliament was accordingly summoned in the spring of 1640; Cromwell was appointed to sit in it as member for Cambridge; but it had scarcely met when it was dismissed. The royal temper was still intractable; and a last desperate effort, to which Wentworth, now Earl of Strafford, gave all his influence, and contributed himself the large sum of £20,000, was made to raise and send forth an army without Parliamentary intervention. The attempt, however, was disastrously unsuccessful. The soldiers were ill-affected towards the cause of Episcopacy: "in various towns on their march, if the clergymen were reported Puritan, they went and gave them three cheers; if of surplice tendency, they sometimes threw his furniture out of win-

passed an Act for "draining the great level of the fens," Lieutenant-General Cromwell was among its most active supporters.

dow." *   Such an army was obviously not likely to
set up the power of the bishops. The Scottish force
in the mean time penetrated England, and forcing its
way toward Newcastle, the King's army retired upon
York, where he and Strafford were.

The war was virtually ended; and Charles returned
to his capital baffled and gloomy at the result. Summoning hastily a " Council of Peers," he concluded a
treaty with the Scots, and was compelled once more to
think of calling together a Parliament. Twelve of the
Peers petitioned him to do so. The city of London
would only advance money on condition that he would
do so. The Scots remained at Newcastle comfortably
quartered, and encouraging by its sympathy the Puritan
disaffection everywhere. Charles was in straits such as
he had never yet been ; and reluctantly he yielded and
summoned the Commons. This, known as the Long
Parliament, was the most memorable that ever sat in
England. It met on the *third* of November 1640. The
long-suppressed feelings of the country at length found
vent in a persistent course of reform. Bill followed
bill in rapid redress of grievances under which the
Commons had long groaned. Ship-money was declared to be illegal ; the Star Chamber and the High
Court of Commission were abolished ; the power of
arbitrary taxation was taken from the King, and the
bill for triennial Parliaments passed. Laud was impeached, and imprisoned in the tower ; Strafford was
struck down from his proud and oppressive elevation.
Never was monarch more hopelessly embarrassed
—more violently and yet feebly inconsistent—than
Charles. At one time he tried a compromise with the
popular party ; then he entered into plots with the

* CARLYLE.

army for the rescue of Strafford from the Tower; then,
finally, he abandoned him, and signed his condemnation on the 10th of May 1641.

After the death of Strafford a temporary reaction
set in. The secession of Hyde and Culpeper and Falkland from the popular party, served for a while to
weaken it, and strengthen the side of the King. Many
as well as these known names were disposed to think
that the royal concessions had proceeded far enough;
that the rights of the constitution had been amply
vindicated; and that the course of innovation should
be stayed. They felt that the country was trembling
on the brink of revolution; and that a further step in
advance, still more a step of violence on either side,
would precipitate matters towards a crisis which must
issue in a civil war. They shrunk from the fearful
responsibility of such an issue. That this was the
honest motive of such a man as Falkland in joining
the King there can be no doubt. Personal peculiarities
in him, as well as in Hyde, may have had something
to do with the result; his keen and sensitive nature,
delicate and classic in its aspirations, may have operated, just as Hyde's reserved dignity and coldness did,
in withdrawing him from the cause of popular agitation. But it is clear, also, that the genuine principles
of both were implicated in making the stand they did.
They had been foremost in urging on the "Bill of
Attainder," for they hated Strafford even more than
Pym and Hampden; but in his overthrow they seemed
to see the security of the constitution; and they gave
themselves to the service of the King with a sincere
desire to maintain the integrity of the Government,
and avert the revolutionary dangers which seemed
threatening.

But they mistook—even Hyde did—the character of the King, and they underrated the daring and address of the leaders of the popular cause. Following Strafford's execution, the King had gone to Scotland; and there, in the midst of many intrigues, and in contact with the ardent courage of Montrose,* he had recovered not only his spirits, but his old ideas of prerogative and kingly power. He returned, inflamed with his own importance, and a sense of his outraged rights, and threw himself far more heartily into the counsels of the Queen and her secret Popish conclave, than into the deliberations of his new supporters.

In the mean time Pym had taken a step which reopened the whole subject of popular grievances, and struck a deadly blow at the new policy of conciliation. He had prepared and was urging forward "The Grand Remonstrance." Whatever be the explanation of this move of the Parliamentary leaders—whether it proceeded from their honest convictions that the process of reform was not by any means complete—from their fears, or their ambition—it had the effect of giving a new and decisive turn to the struggle. Their victory made them more confident, and the King more desperate. The remonstrance was carried by a majority of eleven, on the 22d of November, after a long debate and a memorable scene, which, save for the firmness and presence of mind of Hampden, might have ended in bloodshed. It was on leaving the house after this exciting struggle that Cromwell is reported to have said to Falkland, that if the remonstrance had not been carried,

---

* It is doubtful whether Montrose had any personal intercourse with the King, although Clarendon alleges that he had. "He" (Montrose), he says, "came privately to the King." There can be no doubt, however, that communications passed between them.

he would have sold all that he had next day and gone
off to America.

Other events followed in rapid succession. The long-
pending attack against the bishops was unexpectedly
brought to a violent issue. Through the folly of Williams, the thirteen who had been impeached were
arrested, and eleven of them carried to the Tower,
to bear Laud company. Charles, at the same time,
intoxicated by his flattering reception in the city by
a Royalist Lord Mayor, and seduced by the evil counsels of the Queen and her creatures, was meditating
designs of a dark and aggressive character. Selecting
five of the leaders of the Commons and one in the
Lords, he demanded their impeachment and surrender
as traitors ; and when baffled in this milder effort, he
made his appearance in Westminster with an armed
guard to enforce his summons and arrest his victims.
The step was at once impotent and fatal. The members, duly warned, had disappeared into the city ; and
Parliament retreated thither also, "to be safe from
armed violence."

The crisis could now no longer be delayed. The King,
with the Queen and his family, left London, while the
five impeached members were transported in triumphal
barges from the city to Westminster. The city militia
lined the banks of the Thames on both sides. Four
thousand knights and gentlemen on horseback arrived
from Buckingham to hail their compatriots, and carrying in their hats a printed oath to live or die in defence
of the Parliament. The popular enthusiasm knew no
bounds ; and amid this display of excited patriotism,
the House of Commons took immediate and energetic
resolutions for the defence of the country. An armed
guard was appointed to watch the approaches to the

town, before a new governor of the Tower, in the confidence of Parliament, should be appointed; the governor of Portsmouth was ordered to receive no troops or ammunition into that town without the sanction of Parliament; and Sir John Hotham, a gentleman of influence in Yorkshire, was commanded to take possession of Hull, the great northern arsenal, and preserve it.

The King still professed to keep up negotiations with Parliament, but his sole aim was now to gain time to carry out the hostile measures on which he had already resolved. He retired first to Hampton Court and then to Windsor; and there, in a secret council, it was agreed that the Queen should proceed to Holland, taking the crown jewels with her, and do all she could to raise arms and ammunition, and excite sympathy for the royal cause. As Charles returned from Dover, where he had seen her embark, he was met by urgent messages from Parliament as to the command of the militia, which it claimed for men possessing its confidence. This was almost the last point on which he held out. He had yielded the governorship of the Tower; he had even, against the advice of Hyde, yielded to the tears of the Queen what his own conscience strongly repudiated—the bill of exclusion against the bishops; but he would not give way on the subject of the militia. Instead of returning to London, he met the prince with his tutor at Greenwich, and immediately set out northwards. Twelve Parliamentary commissioners overtook him on his way, and again solicited him on the subject of the militia; but he refused to alter his previous answer "in any point." A week later new messengers found him at Newmarket, and a long and excited conversation ensued; Charles urging, with something of pathetic dignity, his complaints, and Lord Holland, on behalf of the Parliament, still reiterating the question of the militia. "Might not the militia be granted, as desired by Parliament, for a time?" "No, by God," was his reply, "not for an hour. You have asked that of me which was never asked of a king, and which I would not intrust to my wife and children." And so was snapped the last feeble thread of negotiation on both sides; while parties rapidly took their sides, and the country prepared for a fierce and hitherto unexampled struggle.

During these two memorable years, Cromwell was an active although not a prominent agent. Beside Pym or Hampden, or even Strode or Haselrigge, he was not conspicuous in the Commons. He did not speak much, but he was constant on committees, zealous against the bishops, and in many ways one of the most earnest, untiring, and forward of the party. We find him moving for a conference with the Lords to stay the investiture of five new bishops which Charles was foolish enough to urge forward at such a time (October 1641, just after the reassembling of the Parliament). We find him again bringing before the House a calumny circulated by the royalists to the effect that it was offended at the entertainment given by the city to the King (27th November). But a still more important motion than either of these was made by him in the same month of November. The country had been startled and horror-struck by the news of the Papal insurrection and massacre in Ireland. It was necessary that troops should be raised for the defence of the kingdom; and it became an obvious anxiety to the popular party that these troops should not be diverted from their proper object to the furtherance of

the King's private designs. This was exactly a point
to interest Cromwell, who was already beginning to see
more deeply into the nature of the crisis than many of
those around him. To the heads of a proposed conference with the Lords on the state of the kingdom, it
was accordingly added, "upon his motion," that the
two Houses should unite in passing an ordinance to
continue the command of the "train bands on that
side Trent" in the hands of the Earl of Essex (who
had been appointed to this command during the King's
absence in Scotland), "*until Parliament should take
further order.*" The effect of this motion was really
to open the question which, in the following year,
as we have seen, became the critical and final one between the Parliament and the King.

These, as well as other incidents, are sufficient to
prove the activity of Cromwell in the early years of
the Parliamentary struggle. There have been two
sketches of him, however, preserved during those years,
which perhaps give a still more lively impression of
the part that he took, and the zealous earnestness that
he showed, in the popular cause. They are of cog-
nate origin—neither of them flattering, yet both very
graphic in their way. The one is from the garrulous
pen of Warwick, and the other from the politely-ma-
licious pen of his friend and patron, Clarendon. We
subjoin them for the reader's gratification. He will
note particularly the photographic impress of the outward features of our hero.

"The first time," says Warwick, "that I ever took
notice of Mr Cromwell, was in the very beginning
of the Parliament held in November 1640, when
I" (he was member for Radnor) "vainly thought myself a courtly young gentleman — for we courtiers

valued ourselves much upon our good clothes! I
came into the House one morning well clad, and
perceived a gentleman speaking, whom I knew not,
very ordinarily apparelled—for it was a plain cloth
suit, which seemed to have been made by an ill country
tailor. His linen was plain, and not very clean; and
I remember a speck or two of blood upon his little
band, which was not much larger than his collar.
His hat was without a hat-band. His stature was of
a good size; his sword stuck close to his side; his
countenance swollen and reddish, his voice sharp and
untuneable, and his eloquence full of fervour; for the
subject-matter would not bear much of reason, it being
in behalf of a servant of Mr Prynne's, who had dispersed
libels against the Queen for her dancing; and he aggravated the imprisonment of this man by the council-
table unto that height, that one would have believed
the very government itself would have been in great
danger by it. I sincerely profess it lessened much my
reverence unto that great council, for *he was very much
hearkened unto.* And yet I lived to see this very
gentleman, whom, out of no ill-will to him, I thus
describe—by multiplied good successes, and by real
but usurpt power (having had a better tailor, and
more converse among good company) in my own eye,
when for six weeks together I was a prisoner in his
sergeant's hands, and daily waited at Whitehall—appear of a great and majestick deportment, and comely
presence."

The other description, by Clarendon, is equally characteristic. The scene is a private committee, which
sat in the Queen's Court; the subject regarding an en-
closure of certain wastes belonging to the Queen's manors, which had been made without consent of the

tenants, and transferred by the Queen to one of her servants " of near trust," who again had disposed of his interest to the Earl of Manchester, against which the tenants, as well as " the inhabitants of other manors," had petitioned with loud complaints as a great oppression. Notwithstanding Mr Hyde's courtly language, the business does not look well—was, in fact, just a case for the interference of the " Lord of the Fens," who had already, in his own district, amply vindicated the rights of the people against royal oppression in such matters. " Oliver Cromwell being one of them," continues Hyde, " appeared much concerned to countenance the petitioners, who were numerous, together with their witnesses ; the Lord Mandeville being likewise present as a party, and, by the direction of the committee, sitting covered. Cromwell, who had never before been heard to speak in the House,* ordered the witnesses and the petitioners in the method of proceeding, and seconded and enlarged upon what they said with great passion ; and the witnesses and persons concerned, who were a very rude kind of people, interrupted the counsel and witnesses on the other side with great clamour when they said anything that did not please them; so that Mr Hyde (whose office it was, as chairman, to oblige persons of all sorts to keep order) was compelled to use some sharp reproofs, and some threats, to reduce them to such a temper that the business might be quietly heard. Cromwell, in great fury, reproached the chairman for being partial, and that he discountenanced the witnesses by threatening them ; the other appealed to the committee, which justified him, and declared that he behaved himself as he ought to do, which more inflamed him

* Not true, as we have seen.

(Cromwell), who was already too much angry. When
Lord Mandeville desired to be heard, and with great
modesty related what had been done, or explained
what had been said, Mr Cromwell did answer and
reply upon him with so much indecency and rudeness,
and in language so contrary and offensive, that every
man would have thought that as their natures and
their manners were as opposite as it is possible, so
their interest could never have been the same."

Every one has seen such portraits as that drawn by
Warwick—the "stature of a good size," the "countenance swollen and reddish," the "voice sharp and untuneable," the "linen plain and not very clean," the
"speck or two of blood upon his little band" (an ex-
panse of shirt worn over the collar of the coat, with a
view to the long hair which was then fashionable), "not
much larger than the collar itself" (that is to say, un-
fashionably narrow in the eyes of the "courtly young
gentleman"); "the plain cloth suit made by an ill
country tailor." The features are exactly such as the
photograph stamps with faithful unspirituality, while
the true portrait lies behind the outer and unillumined
lines, to be called forth by the vivifying eye of the
friendly imagination—to every other eye invisible. The
process is not difficult in the present case; it scarcely
needs, as with the reminiscent courtier, the help of "a
better tailor" to see in Warwick's literal but coarse likeness the true image of the Puritan hero, with his proud
soul lighting up his countenance, and suffusing it with
indignation; plain and bluff in his dress and manners
now as at all times, but now also, under all his external
coarseness, having a certain "great and majestical deportment, and comely presence," no less than in his
days of state. Under the exaggerations of both sketches,

and especially the vehemence and "passion" of manner
on which they dwell, it is easy to trace the keen patriot,
warmed more by excitement in other people's service,
and the sense of wrong done by the strong against the
weak, than by any regard to his own interests, or by the
impulses of his own ambition. There can be no doubt
that, although he was not yet recognised as a Parliamentary leader, those who were ostensibly leaders saw
and appreciated his great powers, and looked forward
to his future career with interest, perhaps with awe.
"Who is that man—that sloven—that spoke just now?
for I see that he is on our side by his speaking so
warmly," asked Lord Digby of Hampden, as they left
the House the same day that Sir Philip Warwick describes what he saw, and how it impressed him. Conceited trimmers like Digby, whom the snares of the
Court so soon entangled, were not likely to know anything of the blunt and uncouth member for Cambridge. "That sloven," was Hampden's reply, "if
we should ever come to a breach with the King, which
God forbid, will be the greatest man in England."

It was not, however, till the crisis of the war that
Cromwell's peculiar and unexampled powers were
shown. As soon as the King's final determination about
the militia was known, he was found in his native district
organising an incipient force among the servants and
farmers who had formerly acknowledged and been emboldened by his influence. His military genius showed
itself from the first. The sense of a great talent awoke
in him, which might for ever have lain hid in the deep
background of his nature but for the exigency which
called it forth. The nucleus of his famous troop of Ironsides may be said to date from this very commencement
of the war—from the first preparations which he made

with such zealous foresight to preserve in the midland
counties the authority of the Parliament and extend its
power. These preparations were entirely successful,
effective in proportion to the quietness and decision with
which they were carried out. The Midland, or what
were called the Eastern Associated Counties, remained
true to the popular cause throughout the struggle ;
and from their unanimity and compact organisation,
escaped comparatively the miseries of actual warfare.

Of his military activity at this time we get merely
glimpses, but they are very significant and characteristic
glimpses. The university of Oxford had already sent its
plate to the King for his service. Cambridge was meditating a similar step when Cromwell appeared, "seized
the magazine in the castle, and hindered the carrying of the plate from that university." His musketeers
were over all the country, keeping a vigilant watch
for the Parliamentary interests, "starting out of the
corn and commanding stray youths to give an account
of themselves." His uncle, Sir Oliver, had a visit from
him. The old royalist had evidently been meditating
help for the King in his straits, and his nephew and
godson "thought it might be well to pay him a visit
with a good strong party of horse." Warwick is the
gossip here, as so often elsewhere ; and there is a delightful piquancy in the story which he tells—such a
mixture of business and dutifulness—of sternness to
the cause and yet reverent affection for his uncle—
that we are inclined to own its truth, doubtful as is
the source. "During the few hours that he was there
Cromwell asked him (the uncle) his blessing, and
would *not keep on his hat in his presence ;* but at the
same time he *not only disarmed but plundered him,* for
he took away all his plate."

On the 23d of August 1642, Charles raised the royal standard at Nottingham, in an unpropitious storm of wind which blew it down again. The Earl of Essex, at the head of the Parliamentary forces, received instructions, "by battle or otherwise, to rescue the King and his sons from these perfidious counsellors, and bring them back to Parliament." The Earl of Bedford, a grave and moderate man, like Essex, was made general of the horse; and Oliver Cromwell was named captain of the 67th troop.

The King, accompanied by his nephew, Prince Rupert, lately arrived from Germany, removed to the western counties, and set up his headquarters at Shrewsbury. Essex advanced towards him slowly, and Charles dreamed of marching upon London and finishing the war by a single bold stroke. He had even proceeded some days on his march, when Essex overtook him on the borders of Warwickshire, and the first battle ensued in this great struggle—the battle of Edgehill, as it was called. The result was indecisive. Prince Rupert broke the Parliamentary horse and pursued them from the field; but, on the other hand, the royal infantry were dispersed, the Earl of Lindsay, commander-in-chief, severely wounded, and the King's standard taken.

Apparently it was after this battle, and the experience he derived from it, that Cromwell had that remarkable conversation with Hampden which he himself narrates,* as to the quality of the Parliamentary forces, and the need of an entirely different metal to meet the aristocratic gallantry opposed to them. "At my first going out into this engagement, I saw these men (the men of the Parliament) were beaten at every

* Speech to Second Parliament. CARLYLE, ii. 526.

hand, and I desired him (Hampden) that he would make some additions to my Lord Essex's army of some new regiments, and I told him that I could be serviceable to him in bringing such men in as I thought had a spirit that would do something in the work. This is very true that I tell you; God knows I lie not. Your troops, said I, are most of them old decayed servingmen and tapsters, and such kind of fellows, and, said I, these troops are gentlemen's sons, younger sons, and persons of quality; do you think that the spirits of such base and mean fellows will be ever able to encounter gentlemen that have honour and courage and resolution in them? Truly I did tell him, you must *get men of spirit.*" Hampden admitted the excellence of the notion, but deemed it impracticable. Cromwell set about converting it into a fact. He had already, in truth, made a beginning with the men he had raised in his own district. Carrying out the same plan, and seeking for men of a *religious spirit,* potent to meet the *spirit of honour* opposed to them, he formed a regiment of horse, most of them freeholders and freeholders' sons, who, "upon matter of conscience," engaged in the quarrel under his guidance; and being "well armed within by the satisfaction of their own consciences, and without by good *iron* arms, they would as one man charge firmly and fight desperately." * "They were never beaten," he himself said, proudly, of them. And "bold as lions in fight, they were in camp temperate and strict in their behaviour." "Not a man swears but he pays his twelvepence," was the current remark of the day regarding them.

The great soldier of the Commonwealth was already apparent in the captain of the 67th regiment of horse.

* WHITELOCKE.

The energy, comprehension, and success of his movements marked him out at the first from the other Parliamentary commanders. In comparison with the respectable patriotism of Essex, the ostentation of Waller, and the vacillating intrepidity of Manchester, he
was found steady, hopeful, self-possessed, victorious
in whatever was intrusted to him. None of all then
acting against the King—not even Hampden, nor
Oliver St John—saw so clearly that "things must
be much worse before they are better;" and with
this calm and strong conviction, he took his measures
and made his preparations accordingly. While Essex
hesitated, and Parliament negotiated, he acted—and
acted with a decision which never returned upon itself
nor questioned its aims. This decision is the great
secret of his success. However we may explain it—
whether, with some, as a part of a deliberate and daring
scheme of ambition, formed from the beginning, or as
the expression of his honest and deeply-felt convictions
regarding the state of England at the time—it is the
great key to the sweeping energy with which he advanced from point to point in his great career. While
the accidents of the strife removed men like Hampden
on the one side and Falkland* on the other from the
scene ; and the pressure of unforeseen and unexplainable dangers, fast accumulating, wore out and destroyed
others like Pym—more than all the others great in the
senate, and capable of directing the storms of faction ;
Cromwell seemed to grow in proud confidence and

---

* There is something very touching in Falkland's death, notwithstanding Mr Carlyle's sneer as to the " clean shirt." He courted and found
death on the field of Newbury, " weary," as he said, of the times, and
foreseeing much misery to his country. Clarendon's portrait of Falkland is one of his most perfect, and must always fascinate the historical
student.

cheerful and expanding consciousness of right as the
struggle went on. As Essex became more desponding,
and Waller more incompetent, and Manchester more
scrupulous, and the great names of Pym and Hampden
remained no longer as guides amid the darkness, the rude
determination and unconquerable heroism of this man
made him master of every successive exigency,—and
what he gained he never lost. If we could conceive
Cromwell removed from the scene of struggle, and our
view only rested on the divisions of the already diverg-
ing parties in the Commons, or the inconsistencies and
feebleness of its generalship in the field, the chances of
internal dissolution would seem far more imminent than
approaching triumph to the popular cause. And Cromwell himself was still labouring under this fear when,
more than a year hence, he openly accused Manchester
in the House of being reluctant to conquer. The rally-
ing but inconsistent forces of Puritanism, he felt, needed
a commander to unite them ; or, if this was impossible,
to carry the boldest principles of the movement to
triumph, and to bend the others into subordination
and harmony. More obscurely, perhaps, he felt even
then that he himself was that commander—that the
genius of the movement was destined to culminate in
him as its greatest hero.

In the early spring of 1643, Cromwell is for the first
time designated colonel, and shortly afterwards (*May
1643*), he obtained, to use his own words, a "glorious
victory." The scene of this victory is supposed to
have been near to Grantham, although history has
failed to give any chronicle of it save his own brief
and characteristic description.   " Advancing, after
many shots on both sides," he says, "we came on with
our troops a pretty round trot, they standing firm to

receive us : and our men charging fiercely upon them,
by God's Providence they were immediately routed,
and ran all away ; and we had the execution of them
two or three miles. I believe some of our soldiers did
kill two or three men apiece in the pursuit."

His next achievement was the relief of Gainsborough,
which he effected after a sharp and bloody struggle,
in which General Cavendish, second son of the Earl of
Devonshire, and cousin of the Earl of Newcastle, then
the great representative of, and the most successful commander for, the King in the north, was killed.* The
action was close hand to hand, " horse to horse," " when
we disputed it with our swords and pistols a pretty
time." The steadiness of Cromwell's men, however,
triumphed. " At last, they a little shrinking, our men
perceived it, pressed on upon them, and immediately
routed the whole body ; and our men pursuing, had
chase and execution about five or six miles." This
engagement was the first in which Cromwell came into
notice as a military leader. " It was the beginning of
his great fortunes," says Whitelock ; " now he began
to appear in the world."

It was in the month of July that this achievement
of Cromwell's took place. In the previous month
Hampden had fallen wounded to death in a skirmish
on Chalgrove Common, some miles from Oxford. He
was seen " to quit the field before the action was finished, contrary to his custom, with his head hanging
down." Charles, at Oxford, was greatly excited by
the news ; and with a pathetic courtesy, which touches
us even if we may doubt its sincerity, sent to inquire
for his great opponent, and to offer to send him medi-

* " My captain-lieutenant," says Cromwell, " slew him with a thrust
under his short ribs."

cal assistance if he had none at hand. All assistance, however, was vain. Hampden felt from the first that his wound was mortal, and busied his last hours in writing letters to his friends, and earnestly counselling those active measures for the prosecution of the war that he had long had at heart. He was attended by an old friend, Dr Giles, Rector of Chinnor, and his dying words were words of prayer—" O Lord, save my country."

Hampden's death, and Waller's serious reverses, gave a very gloomy turn to the affairs of Parliament at this time. On all sides save in the east they wore a disastrous look. Here, notwithstanding the backwardness of Lord Willoughby, the Parliamentary general, the vigour of Cromwell's influence was everywhere apparent. Especially he held in check the forces of Newcastle, and proved a terror to the northern Papists. He had been appointed by the Parliament governor of the Isle of Ely, and this strengthened his influence throughout the district. In this capacity he is found making a speech in Ely Cathedral, which must have astonished his auditors. An Act of Parliament had abolished the ecclesiastical usages obnoxious to the Puritans. Cromwell counted it his business to see the Acts of Parliament in this as in other things strictly enforced; and one of the canons being so foolish as to disregard the new arrangements, and proceed in the old manner of surplice and ceremony, he was saluted with the cry, " Leave off your fooling, and come down, sir"—a cry which doubtless startled the ecclesiastic in the midst of his elaborate sanctities.

In the autumn of 1643 he had a hard fight at Winceby, in which he nearly lost his life. " His horse was killed under him at the first charge, and fell down upon him; and as he rose up he was knocked down again." Afterwards, however, he recovered a "poor horse in a soldier's hand, and bravely mounted himself again."* It is evident that Cromwell had enough to do during the somewhat unhappy close of the first period of the war. There is no evidence, however, that he was for a moment desponding, or even embarrassed. His letters betray an invariable self-confidence — a steady faith.

The campaign of 1644 opened vigorously on both sides. Essex and Waller commanded for the Parliament in the midland and western counties; Manchester and Cromwell in the eastern counties; and Fairfax and his father in the north co-operated with the Scots, who had entered England to the number of 20,000, under the command of the Earl of Leven. Newcastle, who had gallantly maintained the royalist cause in the north, was now besieged in York by the combined forces of the Parliament and the Scots. Prince Rupert hastened from Lancashire at the head of 20,000 men to his relief. On his approach the Parliamentary forces raised the siege, and after an ineffectual attempt to intercept him withdrew towards Tadcaster. So far Rupert had accomplished his purpose; but, not content with this measure of success, he insisted on giving battle to the Parliamentary army. In spite of Newcastle's remonstrances, he carried his design into effect. The marquess felt himself insulted and overborne by the rude and impetuous prince. He evidently discredited the existence of a letter from the King, which the prince urged as his plea for fighting; yet he yielded, declaring that he had no other ambition than to live and die a royal subject. A somewhat

* Narrative by John Vicars, 1646; quoted by Carlyle, p. 190, vol. i.

similar dissension distracted the councils of the Parliamentarians. The Scots were opposed to battle, and their timid counsels for a while prevailed, to the great disgust and indignation of Cromwell. A battle, however, was inevitable. Eagerness on the one side was responded to by hope* on the other; and although the Scots were already within a mile of Tadcaster, and Manchester's foot were also on the march, they turned at a summons from Fairfax that Rupert had drawn out his forces to meet them on Long-Marston Moor; and there, on the evening of the 2d of July, the two armies met. After a severe and varying struggle, which at first seemed in favour of the Royalists, who broke and dispersed both Fairfax's men on the left, and the Scots in the centre under Leven, victory declared in favour of the Parliamentary army. The Royalists were driven from the field with great disaster, and chased within a mile of York; "so that their dead bodies lay three miles in length."

This decisive victory was, beyond doubt, mainly due to Cromwell, who retrieved the day with his horse, after it seemed nearly lost. There is no reason to doubt the accuracy of his own account, that "the battle had all the evidence of an absolute victory, obtained by the Lord's blessing upon the godly party principally. We never charged, but we routed the enemy. The left wing which I commanded, being my own horse, saving a few Scots † on our rear, beat all the Prince's horse. God made them as stubble to our swords." And it was after he had thus done his own share of the work on the left that he swept round

---

* "Hope of a battle moved our soldiers to return merrily," says a Parliamentary chronicler—Ash.

† Commanded by General David Loslie.

with his victorious horse to the right, where Fairfax and Leven had yielded to the Royalists, and turned there also the tide of battle.

The event was a signal one for Cromwell and the army, and more than justified Prince Rupert's eager inquiry at a prisoner who was taken on the eve of the engagement—"Is Cromwell there?" It was beginning to be felt now, on all hands, that he was the great hero on the Parliamentary side of the struggle. He and the "godly party" that he represented henceforth emerge into prominence as the genuine war-party. It was evident that they had aims beyond the Presbyterians, and that they were rapidly acquiring an influence in the army which would enable them to carry out these aims. The very extremity of their views gave them strength on the field. While Essex in the south and west, and Leven in the north, were distracted in their warlike efforts by their desires of peace, and Manchester shared in their anxieties, Cromwell and his party had no misgivings. Their minds were not set on peace. They saw the deeper turn that the revolution was taking, and they gladly gave themselves to the current. Cromwell himself more and more felt that war was his element—that his place of power was on the battle-field. It was there that his soul kindled into greatness, and that his marvellous energies for the first time had found adequate scope. The tone in which he writes, accordingly, shows how far all ideas of peace were from his mind at this period—how he was knitting himself up to a fiercer struggle than ever, and how his own side of the cause was becoming more intensely and dogmatically consecrated to his mind and imagination as the *cause of God.*

But this very determination on the part of Cromwell

and his followers, it may be imagined, filled moderate men all the more with distrust and apprehension. They seemed to awaken suddenly to a perception of the dangerous character of this powerful leader. Manchester especially, perhaps from more immediate contact with him, and a closer cognisance of his designs, became alarmed and doubtful. The old bonds of amity between the general and lieutenant of the eastern associated counties were broken—never to be repaired. The altercation which subsequently ensued between them in Parliament was merely the expression of a deep-seated misunderstanding and dislike that had been for some time springing up. The Peer resented the forward zeal and incessant interference of his lieutenant ; the latter was indignant at the indecision, and what he no doubt considered the incompetency of his general. Perhaps we may infer, from Clarendon's story of their early conflict, that there never had been any great heartiness of affection between them. On one side the moderate men drew together, and held meetings as to the critical aspect of affairs, and the dangerous prominence into which a single triumphant soldier was rising. On the other, Cromwell separated himself more definitely from the Presbyterian party, taking Fairfax with him, and bent with an unflinching heart on a more energetic and conclusive prosecution of the war.

The slight results that had followed the great victory of Marston Moor, Essex's reverses in the south-west, and the submission of his troops, helped to confirm Cromwell in his views. He and all the decisive party felt that some great stroke must be struck, before the royal power could be overthrown, and the popular cause, as they esteemed it, triumph. While these dis-

sensions were still at their height, the armies met
once more on their old ground at Newbury.* Charles,
inflated by the news of Montrose's triumphs in Scotland, made a sudden resolve to march upon London.
Parliament, however, collected its forces and waited his
movement. Essex, ill at ease and despondent, refused
to join the army and take the command ; but Manchester took his place, and Cromwell headed, as before,
the horse. After some severe skirmishing on the two
previous days, the serious fight began on the 29th of
October. It was long and bloody, and contested with
desperate bravery on both sides. At night, when the
moon rose above the field of carnage, it was unde-
cided. The Royalist troops had not suffered more than
their opponents, and still stood their ground. But
Charles, apprehensive and hopeless of victory, withdrew his forces during the night in the direction of
Oxford. The vigilant eye of Cromwell detected this
movement, and he earnestly implored Manchester to
allow him to fall with his cavalry upon the retreating
army. But Manchester refused ; and the fruits of a
virtual victory were again lost.

Cromwell returned to Parliament full of gloomy
resolves. He took Vane into his counsel, and silently
they formed their plans for a new organisation of the
army, and the subversion of the Presbyterian generals,
under whose guidance so little good had come of their
fighting. In Parliament they had to proceed cau-
tiously, as they were still there in a considerable
minority. His indignation, however, against Manchester could not be restrained ; and he had scarcely
returned, when he openly accused him of lack of zeal,
and of backwardness in the cause. Ever since the

* Where Falkland had fallen in September 1643.

taking of York, following the victory at Marston Moor,
he had seemed afraid of decisive victory, he said, "as if
he thought the King too low, and the Parliament too
high." Manchester retorted in the House of Lords, and
did not spare Cromwell, whom he in turn accused of
disrespectful and seditious language towards both the
House of Lords and the King. He did not hesitate even
to bring forward an unmeaning and absurd charge of
cowardice, which Cromwell's enemies had trumped up
against him. Great excitement and alarm prevailed
among the Presbyterians. Cromwell had become their
bugbear. They held consultations as to whether they
should impeach him. Essex's house was their rendez-
vous; and Whitelocke has preserved a very graphic
account of a meeting, to attend which both he and
Maynard were sent for in the middle of the night. It
ended in nothing, and Cromwell only grew stronger as
he took a higher courage from the baffled movements
of his enemies.

In the month of December he ventured openly upon
the first part of the scheme which he, Vane, and others
had concocted. The House of Commons was met in a
grand committee, to consider the sad condition of the
kingdom groaning under the intolerable burdens of the
war; and "there was a general silence for a good space
of time," every one waiting for the other to begin the
unpleasant subject, when Lieutenant-General Cromwell rose to speak—"it being now high time to speak,
or for ever hold the tongue," as he said. He spoke
of the miserable condition of the country, and then of
what the enemy, and even "those who had been
friends at the beginning said, that the members of
Parliament were continuing the war for their own

private interests—having got great places and commands, and the sword in their hands;" and then suggesting that all "strict inquiry" or recrimination
should be abandoned as to past oversights, of which he
admitted himself guilty as well as others; he expressed
a trust that, having true English hearts and zealous
affection towards the general weal of their mother
country, there were no members of either House who
would scruple to *deny* themselves and their own private
interests for the public good.

The result of this ingenious movement is well
known as the "self-denying ordinance," which, after
much debate, and having been rejected by the Lords,
was at length passed by both Houses.

There has been a great deal of discussion as to
Cromwell's particular relation to this ordinance. Did
he mean honestly to include himself under its dis-
qualifying clauses? And was it merely the force of
circumstances, and the necessities of Parliament, that
afterwards secured him in his military command?
Or was it part of the scheme from the first, that while
Essex and Waller and Manchester were got rid of, he
should be retained, and the way more completely
opened for his ambition? The selection of Fairfax for
general, who was known to be under Cromwell's influence, and the keeping open his own appointment of
lieutenant-general, or second in command, are pre-
sumptions in favour of the latter view. The general
facts of the case—the improbability of men like Vane
and Ludlow being parties to any scheme of mere
personal ambition on Cromwell's part—the accidental
manner in which Cromwell's services were protracted, and, with apparent reluctance, authorised by the

Commons—Joshua Sprigge's emphatic statement * on the subject—all favour the former opinion.

Any general argument on either side is beset by difficulties. It may be safely said, however, that there is no evidence that the men who assisted Cromwell to carry this measure were accomplices with him in any deliberately planned scheme of ambition to serve his interests. They acted mainly, no doubt, from an honest motive to serve their own designs, and bring the war to a successful determination. They saw that nothing but such a sweeping measure, and the reconstruction of the Parliamentary forces under new generals, who should be free from the jealousy and timidity of the old ones, could secure such a result. Vane and others knew Cromwell's great military genius and decision, without doubting at this time that his patriotic views were similar to their own. They looked, therefore, without distrust on his continuance in his command. † Their aim was to have an efficient army, and only secondarily, and with a view to this primary aim, to deprive certain officers of their command. As for Cromwell himself, we cannot believe that he contemplated his own permanent retirement from the stage of military affairs. He knew his own strength and the needs of his country too well to allow us to suppose that he could have deliberately entertained such an idea. Essex and Waller and Manchester might pass from the scene. The accidents of their lot, more than anything else, had placed them where they were; and, unambitious as

---

* See extract from his *Anglia Rediviva*, afterwards quoted, and found at length in Carlyle, vol. i. p. 206. Sprigge was chaplain to Fairfax, and has left in this work a " florid but authentic " account of the new model army, by whose exertions the war was brought to a triumphant close.

† There is evidence of this, Carlyle says, p. 208, vol. i.

both Essex and Manchester were, they laid down
their command probably with more pleasure than
they ever took it up. But Cromwell's character and position were altogether different. Of all
men he was the genius of the crisis, and he could
only pass away with it. To suppose that his retention
of his command was a result of his own elaborate
deception, consciously worked to this end, is to mistake
his character, and to contradict certain undeniable
facts ; but to suppose, on the other hand, that he
doubted that his services could be retained, is to
credit him with a dulness from which no man was
more free. He knew all the circumstances of the
case, and no doubt calculated on the issue. These
circumstances, far more than any plot or direct scheming on his part or others, had the real settling of the
business.

The story is, and it seems perfectly credible, that he
came to Windsor " to kiss the general's hand, and take
leave of him, when, in the morning, ere he was gone
forth of his chamber," certain commands were received
by him, " than which he thought of nothing less in all
the world," * to pursue and attack a convoy sent by
Prince Rupert to transport the King from Oxford to
Worcester. The commands were from the committee
of both kingdoms; and immediately on receiving them
Cromwell took horse, and not merely attacked the convoy successfully, but, after his wonted manner, performed various gallant exploits in succession. Fairfax
no doubt honestly felt that he could not want him ;
and he and other officers accordingly petitioned Parliament that he might be appointed lieutenant-general,
and commander-in-chief of the horse. The Commons

* SPRIGGE.

continued his services for " forty days," and then for
" three months," and so on, until at last, in the glory
of his exploits, and the need of his guidance, no one
challenged his position, and he assumed his natural
supremacy as the real head of the army of the Commonwealth.

After various deeds in his old district, he is found
on the memorable field of Naseby. Fairfax, who had
laid siege to Oxford, suddenly raised it at the command of Parliament to go in search of the King, and
try the new army in a decisive contest. Consciously
reliant on the stronger genius of his friend, it was then
that he sent the message to the Commons about Cromwell, and that the latter, at his invitation, hastened to
join him. They came up with the King's forces at
Naseby, a small hamlet near Northampton ; and here,
on the 14th of June 1645, after three hours' fight very
doubtful, and conspicuous deeds of bravery on both
sides, Rupert's wonted heedlessness in pursuit, and
Cromwell's steadiness, self-control, and his final charge
at the head of his dragoons, decided the fate of the day.
Never did soldiers fight better than Cromwell's troopers
on this great day, and he was not slow to improve the
occasion. " Sir," wrote Cromwell to the Speaker of the
Commons House of Parliament, on the very field of
battle, a day before the despatch of Fairfax, " this is
none other but the hand of God ; and to Him alone
belongs the glory wherein none are to share with Him.
The general served you with all faithfulness and honour ; and the best commendation I can give him is,
that I dare say he attributes all to God, and would
rather perish than assume to himself—which is an
honest and a thriving way ; and yet as much for bravery
may be given to him in this action as to a man. Honest

men served you faithfully in this action. Sir, they are trusty; I beseech you in the name of God not to discourage them. He that ventures his life for the liberty of his country, I wish he trust God for the liberty of his conscience, and you for the liberty he fights for."

The Royalist power was completely broken by the battle of Naseby. Charles in vain tried to rally new forces in Wales; he in vain looked towards Scotland, where Montrose, after a succession of brilliant skirmishes, had at length been utterly vanquished at Philipshaugh by Leslie. Discomfited and discouraged on all sides, he again withdrew into Oxford for a while. In the mean time, the Parliamentary forces under Cromwell pursued their career of victory. After having reduced the "clubmen" in the south-west—for the most part "poor silly creatures," whom the hardships in the war on both sides had goaded to an active resistance in their own behalf—he marched towards Bristol, which had been lost to the Parliament in the first year of the war. After a vigorous storm, and obstinate resistance, the Parliamentary forces made themselves masters of its outer forts, and Prince Rupert was glad to capitulate for a free exit. This may be said to have been the last great stroke of the war. With the fall of Bristol, the hopes of Royalism were extinguished. Rupert was driven forth a wanderer without an army, and Charles himself left without succour.

From Bristol the triumphant Puritans marched southward, reducing every stronghold on their way— Winchester, Basing House, Wallop. In the south and in the west, where they had hitherto been strongest, the remains of the Royalist forces were entirely crushed. Sir Ralph Hopton, one of the most honourable of all the commanders on the side of the King, was driven into Cornwall, and finally, in the following spring, compelled to surrender the wreck of his army, and betake himself to the Continent.

The King, shut up in Oxford, moodily contemplated the ruin of his adherents everywhere. Sir Jacob Astley, almost the very last of those who kept the field for him, was surrounded and captured on his way to join him at Oxford, on the 22d of March 1646. He is reported to have said, as he fell into the hands of the enemy, " You have now done your work, and may go to play, unless you fall out among yourselves." Charles saw no rescue ; and in the end of the following month at midnight, on the 27th of April, he left Oxford in disguise, and sought shelter in the Scottish camp at Newcastle.

This closed the "First Civil War ;" four years of bloody and varying struggle, in which one man, more than any other, amidst all its vicissitudes, had been seen to rise step by step. At the opening of the war his name had been little more than heard of within the precincts of Westminster,—at its close, his fame was second to none in England. The Parliament hastened to do honour to him. He was welcomed with state, and received the thanks of the House for his "great and many services." A pension of £2500 was settled on himself and family, and certain land granted to him as a security for the allowance.

It is no part of our plan to endeavour to trace the thread of movements and negotiations which followed Charles's retirement to the Scottish camp—his continued refusal to come under the conditions of the Covenant—his attempts to play off the Presbyterians against the Independents and the Independents against the Presbyterians—the failure of the treaty of New-

castle—the King's surrender into the hands of the Parliament—and the further train of negotiations which
sprang from this event. These two years' intrigues, in
all their meaning and aims, remain still very intricate
and baffling to the historical student. In all that
concerns Cromwell especially, the entanglement is
extreme ; and it cannot be said that the most recent
elucidations clear up anything here. To what extent
Cromwell deliberately encouraged and abetted the
schemes of the army—to what extent he was drawn
along unwillingly into these schemes, and forced by
the necessity of his position to act as he did—as the
only condition of saving himself and his compatriots—
it is difficult to say. The more we look at all the circumstances, the more does the idea of conscious design
on the part of Cromwell to guide the conflict to its
issue recede into the background ; and that issue itself
appear as a terrible retribution waiting on the hopeless
jealousies of rival interests, as yet inflamed rather than
satisfied by the blood that had been shed on both
sides. The result long hung in the balance. The
Parliament, backed by the city, was really bent on
settlement with the King, if he would only adopt the
Covenant and authorise the Presbyterian form of Church
government. The army, confident in its own strength,
and especially in the thoroughness and earnestness of
its fanatical convictions, had no thoughts of compromise. As between the two, Cromwell and others
seemed to mediate ; but all his sympathies and all his
convictions were with the army. He knew them and
they knew him. He himself may have been really
anxious to treat with Charles ; there may have been
even some foundation for the alleged agreement between them, whereby he was to receive an earldom

and the government of Ireland; there can be no
doubt that his frequent presence at Hampton had
nearly excited to outbreak the jealous fanaticism of
the army. But he could, nevertheless, have scarcely believed in the possibility of a reconcilement at this time;
he saw with too open an eye all the difficulties of the
position.

Whatever sincerity may have animated Cromwell in
the various projects for a settlement, there was no
sincerity on Charles's part. His duplicity strengthened as his weakness increased. It had become a
part of his nature, nay, of his religion; and while with
the one hand he professed to yield, with the other he
communicated to the Queen that she might be entirely
easy as to his concessions which he made, as he had
no intention of observing them when the time came.
The story of Cromwell and Ireton discovering the
King's secret correspondence with the Queen sewed up
in a saddle on the way to Dover, may be apocryphal,
but it is perfectly conceivable. And even, as a story,
it symbolised the universal feeling as to Charles's inveterate and hopeless falsehood. This feeling, that it
was impossible to bind him—that after all that had
been gained nothing was really secure if he was only
restored to power—coupled with the mounting fanaticism and proud resentment of the army, which had
already begun to look on the King as the great criminal
whose arbitrary ambition had been the cause of so
much bloodshed in the country, effectually rendered
all projects of treaty impracticable, and was fast preparing the way for the tragedy which was to end the
struggle.

The great meeting at Windsor, in the beginning of
1648, bears a marked significance in this point of view.

It is plain that the idea of Charles's fate had then become fixed in the minds of the leaders of the army. The picture is an awful and exciting one—lurid with the wild gleam of religious passion, and darkened by the clouds of political hatred. There is a peculiar mystery of horror, now as at all times, in the mixture of divine ideas with men's hates, jealousies, and revenges. " After one whole day spent in prayer, on the next day, after many had spoken from the word and prayed, Lieutenant-General Cromwell did press very earnestly on all present to a thorough consideration of our actions as an army, and of our ways, particularly as private Christians, to see if any iniquity could be found in them, and what it was, that if possible we might find it out, and so remove the cause of such sad rebukes as were upon us." . . . Then after another day's self-examination and prayer, and " bitter weeping, so that none was hardly able to speak a word to each other, they were led and helped to a clear agreement among themselves, not only discerning that it was the duty of our day, with the forces we had, to go out and fight against those potent enemies which that year in all places appeared against us, with a humble confidence in the name of the Lord, only that we should destroy them. . . . And we were also enabled then after sermon, seeking His face, to come to a very clear and formal resolution on many grounds at large then debated amongst us : that it was our duty, if ever the Lord brought us again in peace, to call Charles Stuart, that man of blood, to account for that blood he had shed and mischief he had done to his utmost against the Lord's cause and people in these poor nations."*

It is pleasing to turn from this unhappy picture to

* CARLYLE, vol. i. p. 313.

contemplate our hero in a different light. Of his
family we do not learn much in those years, but they
had now grown up around him. Of his five sons, indeed, only two remained. The eldest, Robert, had
died in 1639, at Felsted, where he had probably been
living with his maternal grandfather, who had his
country-seat there. The burial registers of that parish
contain a singular entry regarding him, celebrating his
piety and speaking of his father as *vir honorandus.*
He died at the age of nineteen, in the full promise of
his opening manhood (*fuit eximie pius juveniss, deum
timens supra multos,* says the register) : and there can
now be no doubt that it was to this untimely and bitter
stroke that the father alluded, in the memorable words
as to " his eldest son," that he uttered on his deathbed.[*]
Although no trace of it is to be found in any of his
correspondence, the deep sorrow had yet sunk into his
heart, to come forth to the light again in the moment
of his own approaching fate. His second son Oliver,
who lived to be a cornet in the eighth troop of what
was called " Earl Bedford's horse," was slain in battle,
but at what particular date remains unknown. His
two eldest daughters were both married in the spring
of 1646 ; the one to Ireton, and the second to Claypole, who became " Master of the Horse" to Cromwell.

His peculiar attachment to " Lady Claypole " is
well known. Writing from Scotland in 1651, he says,
with the peculiar brief pathos at times characteristic

---

[*] See FOSTER'S Essay on the *Civil Wars and Cromwell,* an admirable
piece of historical criticism, like all the other writings of the author
on this fruitful time. For the discovery of the parish register of Felsted, and the fact that Cromwell's eldest son lived to manhood—a fact
unrecognised even in Mr Carlyle's volumes—the public are indebted to
Mr Foster. Both Mr Carlyle and Guizot make the words of the deathbed refer to the death of Oliver (the second son).

of him: "I earnestly and frequently pray for her and for him [her husband]. Truly they are dear to me—very dear." We nowhere, however, trace his hand in correspondence with her.

The following remarkable letter is addressed to his elder daughter, Mrs Ireton, in the autumn of 1646, while the negotiations with the King were proceeding. It deserves to be set before the reader fully in the light which it casts upon the character of both father and daughter. The intensity of religious persuasion which animated both comes out very strongly. After excusing himself for not writing to her husband, from the laudable and considerate plea that "one line of mine begets many of his, which I doubt makes him sit up too late," he continues: "Your friends at Ely are well; your sister Claypole is, I trust in mercy, exercised with some perplexed thoughts. She sees her own vanity and carnal mind; bewailing it, she seeks after (as I hope also) what will satisfy: and thus to be a seeker is to be of the best sect next to a finder; and such an one shall every faithful humble seeker be at the end. Happy seeker, happy finder! Who ever tasted that the Lord is gracious, without some sense of self-vanity and badness? Who ever tasted that graciousness of His, and could go less in desire—less than pressing after full enjoyment? Dear heart, press on; let not husband, let not anything cool thy affections after Christ. I hope he will be an occasion to inflame them. That which is best worthy of love in thy husband is that of the image of Christ he bears. Look on that and love it best, and all the rest for that. I pray for thee and him; do so for me." Surely touching and grand words! No indifference or derision can empty them of their meaning. There is a reality

H

and weight of meaning in every sentence, beside which the common sort of religious commonplace is dim and pale. That they came from our hero's heart none can doubt, however they may try in vain to fathom the strange mystery of this heart.

The long, intermitting correspondence regarding the marriage of his son Richard, serves also to present him in a very characteristic light. It began in February 1647-8, and did not terminate till April 1649. It is marked by eminent sense and shrewdness, and a prudent forethought and care as to settlements in his son's interest. There is a swift decisive summariness in it, and a force of meaning in every sentence no less notable than in his more serious letters. It matters not what the business in hand may be, Cromwell would have it done at once and well. Richard's character also stands clearly depicted in these letters as that of a good, easy, and unambitious man, of gentle, cheerful, and strong affections, but singularly unendowed by any of his father's vigorous and aspiring temper.*

The meeting of the army leaders, we have seen, took place in the spring of 1648 ; and the Presbyterians, now finally alienated from the Independents, were already active in discontent and open tumult. In Kent, in Wales, and in the north, there were signs of renewed agitation on behalf of the King. The Scotch had at length declared in favour of Royalty, against the " Sectaries," and entered England, 40,000 strong, under the command of the Duke of Hamilton. Leaving a portion of the Republican party at St Alban's to

---

* On the 6th of April 1649, Cromwell writes to his " worthy friend, Richard Mayor, Esquire, at Horsley," thus : " Sir—My son had a great desire to come down and wait upon your daughter. I *perceive that he minds that more than to attend to business here*" [London].

overawe the capital (doubtfully Presbyterian), Cromwell marched towards Wales, and began what has been called the "Second Civil War." It was but of brief continuance. At the head of his veterans he attacked and took Pembroke Castle, and speedily subdued Wales. He then hurried northwards to encounter the Scotch under Hamilton. The battle of Preston, in the month of August, may be said to finish the campaign. Nothing could be more complete than the disaster which he inflicted on the immense and disorderly mass of the Scotch army, but imperfectly hearty in the cause for which they fought. His success was again everywhere complete. The Kirk party in Scotland, headed by Argyle, lent their influence to aid his designs. The conqueror advanced into Edinburgh, took up his abode in the "Earl of Murrie's house in the Cannigate" there; accepted a great banquet from the submissive Covenanters; and, having put things in order to his mind, returned southwards. He was again in England, busy with renewed negotiations about the King before the close of the year.

The Royalist interests were now everywhere crushed. The Presbyterians, still nominally a majority in Parliament, were in reality defeated. The army had entirely broken with them, and its leaders were already the true masters of England. They knew their power, and waited their opportunity. While Cromwell tarried in the north, extinguishing the last embers of Royalist disaffection, Parliament made one more last effort to come to an understanding with the King, and so arrest the power of the Revolution, which it felt was fast sweeping towards itself. It was in vain. The forty days' treaty of Newport came to

nothing, like all its predecessors. Charles was hopeless; long-practised craft had poisoned the very fountains of trust in him, and treaty with him was no longer
possible. The Parliament had ceased to be powerful;
the force which it had evoked in its own defence had
risen up against it; its creature had grown to be its
master. While other interests had suffered from the
continuance of the war, the army had risen on their
weakness or ruins, and it now stood the only govern-
ing power in England.

On the 20th of November we find Oliver at Knot-
tingley, writing to Fairfax as to the grievances of the
army, and his quiet determination to support them. *All*
the regiments had petitioned against the treaty of Newport, and " for justice and a settlement of the kingdom "—a sufficiently ominous petition! Cromwell
expresses his sympathy with them, and is persuaded
that the cause is a good cause—nay, a divine one.
" I find," he says, " in the officers of the regiments a
very great sense of the sufferings of this poor kingdom;
and in them all a very great zeal to have impartial
justice done upon offenders. And I must confess I
do in all, from my heart, concur with them; and I
verily think, and am persuaded, that they are things
which God puts into our hearts."

At the same time, only a few days later, he writes
to Colonel Hammond, who was in charge of the
King in the Isle of Wight, one of his most remarkable letters.* We can read in it the struggling
depths of his spirit, and the stern though confused
strength of his convictions. Undivine as these convictions may seem to us, they seemed to him to rest on
an eternal foundation. Hypocrisy is about the very last

* CARLYLE, i. 393.

word we should think of applying to them. It is not a double mind, but a too intense and absorbed mind, out of which they come. It is the madness of a fixed idea, and not the treachery of a false nature, of which they are born. The fearful *duty* towards which he points, is obviously no pretence of language, but the overmastering impress of a diseased faith, which has taken up into its supposed divine warrant all human scruples and personal interests, and sublimated them till they seem celestial in the consecrating halo through which he views them. "If the Lord have in any measure persuaded His people of the lawfulness—nay, of the duty—this *persuasion prevailing upon the heart is faith :* and acting thereupon, is acting in faith; and the more the difficulties are, the more the faith." Out of such a faith, it is not difficult to see what duties—nay, what crimes—might grow.

This letter to young Hammond never reached its destination. He had been wavering for some time in his trust, puzzled and awestruck, as well he might be, by the dire crisis gathering around him. With his scruples, "dear Robin" was not to be trusted, even to the force of such arguments as Cromwell's letter contained; and, accordingly, a more imperative argument is served upon him in the shape of an order to remove to headquarters at Windsor, while a less scrupulous Colonel Ewer, who had already distinguished himself by his forwardness in the presentation of the army remonstrance to the Parliament, beset the royal lodgings at Newport, and removed the King to a more solitary and secure confinement in Hurst Castle.

Things now rapidly approached the end which Cromwell and others had foreseen and prepared for

some time. The Commons refused to entertain the
remonstrance of the army by a large majority. The
news rekindled the military devotion which we have
already seen so ominous in its results. After a day
spent in prayer, the army resolved to march upon
London. This was on the 2d of December. On the
4th, Parliament had not only dismissed the army remonstrance, but decided, by a majority of forty-six,
that his Majesty's concessions in the treaty of Newport were a ground of settlement. On the 6th, two
regiments—one of cavalry, and one of foot—were
marched into Palace Yard, and into Westminster Hall;
and Colonel Pride, with a paper in his hand, containing a list of the obstinate majority, *purged** the Parliament of refractory Presbyterians, and left the Independents victors on the floor of St Stephen's as in
the ranks of the army.

The result is well known. The House of Commons, thinned in numbers—reduced to a mere frac-
tion of its numbers—resolved to impeach the King,
and bring him to trial. The Lords tried to interpose
some obstacles when the ordinance instituting a high
court to try the King came before them. Manchester, Denbigh, and Pembroke declared they would
have nothing to do with it. " I would be torn to
pieces, rather than take part in so infamous a business," said Denbigh. The Commons, however, determined to proceed without them, and the High Court
of Justice, with John Bradshaw at its head, began
its proceedings on the 8th of January. After three
weeks' sitting, and many strange and exciting incidents, the King was condemned on the 27th. His
lofty and quiet mien, in contrast with that of his rude

* Carlyle's picture of this famous event is very graphic--p. 399.

and stormy accusers, has stamped itself indelibly on the historical imagination. It is an impressive and touching picture. Charles appeared the hero at last, when the long web of his craft had run out, and he was thrown back upon the simple dignity of his kingly temper.

On the 29th, the warrant for the execution was signed and sealed; and on the following day, in "the open street before Whitehall," Charles Stuart, "king of England," was beheaded amid the tears of his attendants and the wonder of the multitude.

Cromwell apparently took no *special* share in these proceedings. There is no reason whatever to believe, as has been represented, that he had the King's life in his hands; and the stories as to the visit of his cousin, and other interpositions made with him on the King's behalf, are in the main mere exaggerations. What credit is due to the other and less worthy stories as to his strange, mad levity—his smearing Henry Martin's face with ink, after his signing the death-warrant, and Martin in turn smearing his, it is difficult to say. He had such a mad turn with him, beyond doubt. The terrible workings of his inner life, the tumult of principle and aspiration which often raged within him, sometimes broke out in this ungovernable manner, showing, yet hiding, the wild surging of passion within in an unintelligible uproar and folly of external manner. It is a sufficiently awful contrast—the buffoonery of the triumphant soldier, and the pathetic dignity of the fallen monarch; but even if that traditionary imagination, which is always tender to suffering and severe to successful principle, has not given much of the contrasted colouring to the two pictures, we must remember that the character of a great historical event is not to be decided by the mere beauty or offensiveness of its accidents. Crime or not, the death of Charles seemed, beyond doubt, to those who were concerned in it, the inevitable issue of the great struggle in which they had been engaged. It was the ending of the tragedy—the Nemesis of long years of suffering and tyranny. The pathos of it must ever move our pity; but even our horror of it forms no ground on which utterly to condemn it.

Cromwell was now virtually master of England. As head of the army, he was the head of the nation. It is true that Fairfax still continued nominally first in command; and that Cromwell, even some time after this, professed not only a willingness, but apparent eagerness, to serve under his old friend, saying he would rather do so than command the greatest army in Europe.* But while this nominal precedence was still conceded to Fairfax, the real power and supremacy lay with our hero. A Council of State was appointed to manage the executive in civil affairs; and Cromwell consented to go with the flower of his veterans to Ireland, and reduce that kingdom to civil order and obedience.

A stern duty, however, awaited him in the first instance. The spirit of insubordination continued to spread in the army. So far, he had yielded to this spirit, and identified himself with it. The King's death had been hastened on and accomplished under its exciting influence, sweeping all before it, and really controlling the organisation of Parliament, while the latter yet professed to act in some measure independently and according to its lawful forms. It was clear, however, that unless the spirit of agitation was checked, the bonds of all order would be dissolved, and government rendered

* RUSSEL'S *Cromwell*, vol. ii. p. 45.

impossible. Cromwell saw and appreciated the crisis ;
and, secure of the main leaders, who had been actively
concurring with him in the King's death, and whose
ambition and vengeance were fully satiated for the
time, he resolved to strike a swift and effective blow
on the first reappearance of disorder. Accordingly, a
mutiny having broken out in Whalley's regiment, the
prominent disturbers were seized, tried by court-mar-
tial, and one of the most vehement of them shot down
forthwith in St Paul's Churchyard. The disturbance
spreading to the regiments quartered in the country,
the same effective measures were adopted. Lilburne, a
particularly noisy agitator of the time, was securely
imprisoned, other ringleaders were shot, and the
" levellers " everywhere quelled. It was a moment of
imminent danger ; and what it might have come to,
save for the energy of the Lieutenant-General, it is difficult to say. But here, as everywhere, he was master
of the moment ; and while he saved his country
from anarchy, he raised his own fortunes to a higher
pedestal.

The career of victory on which he now entered—at
the head of an army that had learned respect, as well
as affection for him—first in Ireland, and then in Scotland, is written broadly in the history of his country.
The mingled glory and carnage of his Irish campaign
have formed a theme for the eulogy of his admirers,
and the detractions of his enemies almost equally.
The military genius which it displayed, the swift energy
and decision of his movements, the terrible grandeur
of his work, all admit ; while there are few who can
read without horror the indiscriminate slaughter which
he not only permitted, but encouraged and authorised.
The single defence that can be offered for his cruelty

was its *necessity*.   He had undertaken the task of paci-
fying Ireland ; and this task could only be accomplished by the exhibition of a power calculated to overawe and subdue the unruly elements which then everywhere raged in that country.   Cromwell knew this.
He knew that nothing short of an example of resistless
determination and might could effect his purpose.
This is his own excuse ; and in war it is and must
ever be held a valid excuse.   Severity is, then, truly
mercy in the end.   As he himself says, " Truly, I
believe this bitterness " (putting every man of the garrison of Drogheda to death) " will save much effusion
of blood, through the goodness of God."   One shudders
indeed to read of the goodness of God in connection with
such carnage, and still more to read the explanations
which he gives more at length in his communication
to the Speaker of the Commons.   " It was set upon
some of our hearts that a great thing should be done,
not by power or might, but by the Spirit of God.   And
is it not so clearly ?   That which caused your men to
storm so courageously, it was the Spirit of God, who
gave your men courage."   Such words breathe more than
the vengeance of the old Theocracy against the Canaanites; and it was the same spirit, no doubt, that animated
these Puritan warriors, and made them march to siege
and battle with Bible watchwords in their mouths,
and the fury of unholy wrath in their hearts.   There
is nothing to be said in defence of the spirit from any
Scriptural point of view.   Every such defence must proceed upon utterly mistaken grounds ; but if the spirit
cannot be defended, the policy which employed it, and
made it subservient, not merely to the physical subju-
gation, but the moral ordering of a kingdom, may be
excused, and even vindicated.

In the course of nine months, Ireland was all but subdued, and Cromwell, leaving the completion of the work to Ireton, hastened back to London in connection with the pressing state of matters in Scotland. There Puritanism had renewed the alliance with Royalty. Charles II. had taken, or professed to take, the Covenant; and the Scottish nation, with its religious conscience thus dubiously quieted, had armed itself to maintain his rights, and set up again the fabric of sovereign authority in the two kingdoms. The existence of the Commonwealth was seriously threatened, and a blow must be struck immediately before the threatening evil spread into England. Cromwell was the only man to strike this blow. He and the Council, indeed, professed to urge the command upon Fairfax. It is difficult to suppose that he could have been sincere in this; yet we need not suppose that he merely acted a part.* His real intention, probably, was to bring Fairfax to a point; to force him either to an active service, which he knew was far from congenial to him, or to compel him to give up his commission—a result which he accomplished. He set out for Scotland, for the first time, "Captain-general and commander-in-chief of all the forces raised, or to be raised, by authority of Parliament, within the Commonwealth of England."

No part of Cromwell's career is more exciting, picturesque, and instructive as to his character, than his Scottish campaign. His long letters to the clergy; the zeal and effect with which he criticises their arguments, and assails their position; his respect for the religious earnestness opposed to him, and yet his

---

* Ludlow, in his sneering, deprecatory way, says, "Cromwell acted his part so to the life, that I really thought he wished Fairfax to go."

scorn for its narrowness; the wisdom of many of his remarks on Christian liberty and Church policy, are all deeply interesting. Presbyterianism then, and always has, shown but a slight capacity to see through its own formulæ to the living truth beyond. With what smiling yet strong irony does the great soldier try to raise it to a higher point of view! Addressing the "Commissioners of the Kirk," he asks, "Is it therefore infallibly agreeable to the word of God all that *you* say? I beseech you in the bowels of Christ, think it possible you may be mistaken. Precept may be upon precept, line may be upon line, and yet the word of the Lord may be to some a word of judgment, that they may fall backward and be broken, and be snared and taken." * Again, a month later, in a letter to "the Governor of Edinburgh Castle," who had written on behalf of the ministers : "Are you troubled that Christ is preached? Is preaching so exclusively *your* function? Is it against the Covenant? Away with the Covenant if this be so! . . . Where do you find in the Scriptures a ground to warrant such an assertion, that preaching is exclusively your function? Though an approbation from men hath order in it, and may do well, yet he that hath no better warrant than that hath none at all. Approbation is an act of conveniency in respect of order—not of necessity to give faculty to preach the gospel. *Your pretended fear, lest error should step in, is like the man who would keep all the wine out of the country, lest men should be drunk."* † Yet again, in the same letters : "We look at ministers as helpers of, not lords over, God's people. I appeal to their consciences whether any person, trying their doctrines and dissenting, shall not incur the censure of

* CARLYLE, ii. 20.   † CARLYLE, ii. 64.

sectary. *And what is this but to deny Christians their liberty, and assume the infallible chair ? What doth he, whom we would not be likened unto, do more than this ?"*

Such is the intellectual and theological side of Cromwell, on his second memorable visit to Scotland. The military side is not less impressive. Of all his military achievements, that of his retreat to Dunbar, and subsequent battle, is perhaps the greatest, if for no other reason than because, for the first time in the course of his conquering career, we see him in straits through which he cannot get "almost without a miracle." "The enemy hath blocked up our way," he writes,[*] "and our lying here daily consumeth our men, who fall sick beyond imagination." But the force of his genius rises with the occasion. "Our spirits are comfortable, praised be the Lord, though our present condition be as it is. . . . *Whatever become of us*, it will be well for you to get what forces you can together." Nowhere does he seem more the hero. No scene in all his life is at once more striking and simple in its grandeur—the half-famished troops, lying weary and exhausted with their fruitless marches in search of an enemy that had refused to fight them, but had hung in their retreat, with a harassing tenacity, on their rear; their turning to bay in the narrow corner ("the pass at Copperspath") in which they were hemmed, with the hills before them covered by the enemy, and the sea behind; the night of storm and "hail clouds;" the quiet magnanimity of his letter to Haselrig; the eagerness with which he watched the Scottish troops descend from their vantage-ground;

---

[*] Letter to Sir A. Haselrig at Newcastle, dated "Dunbar, 2d September 1650."

the prayer and the pealing watchword—" The Lord of
Hosts"—as it rang through the English ranks in the
morning; the terrible charge upon the half-sleeping
and drenched Scotch; and the cry which Hodgson
heard burst from him as they first wavered and fled,
" They run! I profess they run!"

The Scotch, after their defeat at Dunbar, rallied at
Stirling; but their councils were divided, and their
strength effectually broken. Some of them, irrespective of the Covenant, were disposed to embrace the
Royal cause. Others, in zeal for the Covenant, dis-
trusted the King and his special adherents. There
were, in fact, three parties : a right, left, and middle—
a Royal, Religious, and Royalist-religious, or official
party — Malignants, Whigs or Remonstrants, and
" Resolutioners"—so called from their having carried
through the Parliament and Assembly a set of resolutions for the admission of Malignants to fight in the
general cause of covenanted Royalty. It was a great
satisfaction to Cromwell that, the genuine Covenanters
or Whigs having been dispersed in the west by Major
Whalley, he was left to fight it out with the two other
parties, for whom he had comparatively little respect.
His visits to Linlithgow and Glasgow, where Mr
Zachary Boyd " railed on his soldiers to their very
face in the High Church ; "* his correspondence with
the heads of the Remonstrant party; his siege of
Edinburgh Castle and its surrender, fill up the events
of the year. Then follow, his somewhat serious illness
during the winter in his old lodging, the " Earl of
Murrie's house in the Canigate;" his second visit to
Glasgow; his church-going, and personal conferences
with the clergy, who hesitated not in his presence to

* BAILLIE, iii. 119.

"give a fair testimony against the Sectaries;"* renewed operations hither and thither in the spring (1651) near to Stirling, and across to Burntisland; the breaking of the Royalist army from Stirling, and its march into England; his march in pursuit, and the great and decisive victory of Worcester on the 3d of September, the anniversary of the day of Dunbar.

The battle of Worcester was, as he wrote, his "crowning mercy;" "as stiff a contest for four or five hours as ever I have seen." The Scots fought with desperate bravery, but their efforts were of no avail. The star of Cromwell was in the ascendant. The passion of a great strength which had never been broken in battle, was upon him, and carried him resistlessly to victory. Carlyle says grandly, "The small Scotch army, begirdled with overpowering force, and cut off from help or reasonable hope, storms forth in fiery pulses, horse and foot; charges now on this side of the river, and now on that; can on no side prevail; Cromwell recoils a little, but only to rally and return irresistible; the small Scotch army is on every side driven in again; its fiery pulsings are but the struggle of death; agonies as of a lion coiled in the folds of a boa." †

Cromwell returned in triumph to London after an absence of fifteen months, during which he had more securely established his power over the army, and enhanced his fame by two great battles. It is not to be supposed that he and the other chiefs of the army would be more deferential to the "Rump" of a Parliament (little more than a hundred members) still sitting in Westminster, than they had been to the same assembly when in comparative strength and consideration. On its part the Parliament was sufficiently

* BAILLIE, 165.　　　　　　† CARLYLE, ii. 142.

deferential, four of its most dignified members having been commissioned to meet the conqueror at Ayles-bury with congratulations, and to accompany him as he entered London amid the obeisance of Lord President and Council, Sheriffs, and Mayors, and the shouting of the multitude. " In the midst of all," White-locke says, " Cromwell carried himself with much affa-bility." Afterwards, indeed, his bearing was criticised. His chaplain, Hugh Peters, told Ludlow that he discerned in his master on the occasion, a certain inward elevation and excitement of conscious greatness, as if he already saw within his grasp the crown and sovereignty of England—so much so, that he (the chaplain) had said to himself, " This man will be king of England yet." Beyond all doubt, Cromwell returned from his great successes in Ireland and Scotland, if not a changed man, yet with far higher and clearer aims for himself and his country. It was impossible that he should not feel how the reins of power had been gathered into his hand, and that if the nation was to be settled after its long and exhausting conflicts, he must himself undertake the settlement of it. It is vain for any to talk of unprincipled craft and ambition at this stage of his career.* Circumstances had made him first the hero, and now the virtual sovereign of his country.

Still, for nearly two years, he remained without any special assumption of sovereignty, while Parliament was engaged in endless debates and negotiations as to its dissolution, and the arrangements for a new repre-sentative. Such debates had commenced from the time of the King's execution, but gone to sleep during the Scottish campaign. Cromwell's return brought

* As Guizot even in his latest biography does.

them to life again, and by a majority the "Rump" agreed to its dissolution three years hence.

Many conferences were held in the mean time, at Cromwell's house at Whitehall, with the chiefs of the army and divers of the Parliamentary leaders, as to the order of government; some, especially the lawyers, arguing in favour of a limited monarchy under the King's son—others, with almost all the officers of the army, declaring in favour of a republic. While these negotiations were proceeding in London, and the soldiers of the Commonwealth were resting from their stern struggles, and enjoying the excitement of political discussion and petitioning, its sailors, under Blake and Dean, were achieving glorious triumphs over the Dutch,* and establishing its supremacy on the seas and throughout Europe. The "Rump" calmly took the triumphant course of events as its own, and seemed less disinclined than before to resign its position and influence. The army became impatient, and petitioned more vehemently; conferences increased at the Lord General's house. Parliament at length resolved on instant dissolution—a whole year earlier than it had first intended; but the bill by which the members of the "Rump" proposed to carry their resolution into effect, was clogged with such conditions as should secure their own return to the new Parliament, and their effectual influence over its composition.† Such a proposal deeply incensed Cromwell and the army, and he determined to prevent its passing.

The act by which he accomplished this was one of the most questionable, if also one of the most scenic and daring in the upward course of his ambition. Its external features stamped themselves vividly on the

---

* March 1653.   † GUIZOT's *Cromwell*, 348, vol. i.

memories of those who witnessed it, and were long afterwards remembered with a mixture of fear and laughter.

The Lord General was busy in consultation on the ever-renewed subject of the government of the country, with the officers of the army and certain members of Parliament, waiting for others who had promised to come, on the 20th April (1653), when, instead of the expected members, a message came that the House was intent on hurrying through its bill.   Deeply moved, Cromwell is yet represented as very reluctant to act, when Colonel Ingoldsby arrived, exclaiming, "If you mean to do anything decisive, you have no time to lose." Vane was earnestly pressing the measure to a vote, notwithstanding Harrison's dissuasions. It seemed likely that he should succeed in his object.   Cromwell at length made up his mind and hastened to Westminster, taking a troop of musketeers with him from his own regiment.   These he disposed to suit his purpose, and then entered himself and " sat down as he used to do in an ordinary place." His appearance and the cut of his clothes, as on former occasions, were all remembered.   He was " clad in plain black clothes and grey worsted stockings;" and the old passion and fervour, as when he had some great work to do, gleamed in his eye.   For a while he listened with apparent calmness to the debate.   Vane was still speaking, and as he urged the immediate passage of the bill, Cromwell beckoned to Harrison, saying, "This is the time, I must do it." On Harrison's representation, however, he still remained for a quarter of an hour, until Vane ceased speaking, and the question was about to be put from the chair, "That this bill do now pass," when he rose, put down his hat, and addressed the House, at first in a measured and rather complimentary manner, till, waxing hot with the burning thoughts that had been long on his mind, he changed his tone, and vehemently reproached them with their injustice, delays, and self-interest. "Your time is come," he exclaimed, as his violence increased and almost mastered him,[*] "your time is come, the Lord hath done with you; He has chosen other instruments for the carrying on of His work that are more worthy." Several members[†] interposed, "but he would suffer none but himself to speak." At length Sir Peter Wentworth found voice, and spoke for a little, upbraiding Cromwell for his unbecoming language and ingratitude as a trusted servant of the Commonwealth. But this only further kindled his passion, and, thrusting his hat upon his head, and leaping into the centre of the floor, he cried, " Come, come, we have had enough of this—I'll put an end to your prating." As he spoke, he stamped upon the floor and beckoned to Harrison, " Call them in," when the doors flew open and his musketeers made their appearance. " You are no Parliament," he exclaimed, as he wildly walked up and down, flinging taunts at the members all round. " I say you are no Parliament; begone, give way to honester men. Some of you are drunkards," and he looked on Mr Challoner. " Some of you are adulterers," and his eye searched poor Sir Peter Wentworth and Henry Martyn. He walked up to the table on which lay the mace carried before the Speaker, " What shall we do with this bauble?" he said ; "take it away. It's you that

---

[*] He spoke, says Ludlow, " with so much passion and discomposure of mind as if he had been distracted."

[†] Vane and Martyn.

have forced me to this;" "I have sought the Lord
night and day that He would rather slay me than put
me up on the doing of this; but now begone." One by
one they rose and left—a special shaft being aimed at
Sir Harry Vane as he ventured some further remonstrance on departure. "Sir Harry Vane—Sir Harry
Vane—the Lord deliver me from Sir Harry Vane."
The house was cleared, the door locked, and the key
and the mace carried away; and so ended for the time
the great Parliament of England, so glorious in its beginning, so feeble and ridiculous in its close.

This may be said to mark the conclusion of the
second period of Cromwell's career. Hitherto he has
appeared first as the Puritan patriot and man of the
people, and then as the great and successful warrior
of the Commonwealth. The transformation has been
sufficiently astonishing, from the farmer of St Ives to
the conqueror of Ireland and the victor of Dunbar and
Worcester. He is still to show himself in another and
perhaps higher character; but before proceeding, we
may pause briefly to characterise his military genius.

In no other great hero, not even in Alexander or
Napoleon, do we recognise a more intuitive military
genius, more exact appreciation of the difficulties to
be overcome, more prompt and skilful boldness in
meeting them, more decision in council, more terrible
energy in action, above all, more quiet consciousness of
strength, more effective control of himself and others,
till at the right point he could apply all his resources
and bear down opposition with an overwhelming mastery. The campaigns of other warriors, as Napoleon's
early career in Italy, may seem to be more dashing
and brilliant, but they are not really more glorious.
They may dazzle more by their *eclat*, but they do

not show, in a greater measure, patience combined
with energy, forethought with swiftness, and rapidity
with thoroughness of execution. In the highest military genius there must always be a sublime faith
amounting to passion. Mere calculations, and mere
discipline and science, may achieve great victories,
especially in modern times, but will never inspire
with enthusiasm great armies, and mould them into
conquerors. The passion of a fixed idea can alone do
this ; and Cromwell was animated from first to last
by the highest form of this passion. His faith was
no mere intensity of selfish trust—no mere personal
ambition ; it was a faith in the God of battles, a fixed
devotion to the Divine. The same theocratic consciousness which sustained David in his wars with the
Philistines, sustained Cromwell in his wars with the
cavaliers. He was the servant of God, his soldiers
were the people of God—" the godly party." So, beyond doubt, he thought. It was " principle" that
moved him and moved them to engage in the quarrel
—they made "conscience" of their cause; and it was
this lofty and intense consciousness of the Divine
which made the highest, the really prevailing element
of that military genius, which, from guarding with
stern faithfulness the eastern associated counties with
his troop of Ironsides, carried our hero in triumph to
Marston Moor, and from Marston to Naseby, and from
Naseby to Drogheda, Dunbar, and Worcester.

But henceforth it is no longer as warrior but as
statesman that we contemplate him. With the crowning mercy of Worcester his military career was ended,
and a new career of patriotic statesmanship opened to
him. The difficulties of the country, the difficulties
of his position, were immense; but he had counted the

cost, and he was not the man to flinch from the position and the work to which Providence had called him. There are few pages of history more nobly pathetic—more deeply tragical than the struggle on which he now entered, and which he sustained for five years. This concluding period of his life may not, indeed, at first sight seem a struggle, but rather a triumph. Our attention is apt to be fixed by the prosperous aspects of the Protectorate, the power which he exercised in Europe as the head of the Protestant cause, and the glory which he everywhere gave to the name of England among the nations ; but his position was, nevertheless, one of struggle almost to the last. The history of his Parliaments and the study of his speeches are enough to show this. He desired to govern constitutionally after all that happened, and this was no easy, nay, it was an impossible task in the circumstances. He relished power, but he hated injustice. He would have no interest oppressed, not even the Jews or Quakers, whom all stronger sects alike delighted to persecute. He was thoroughly tolerant in so far as he could elicit any response to his own tolerant spirit from the contending parties.* He desired, therefore, to make the basis of his government as broad as possible, compatible with the interests of religion and the cause for which he had fought. He aimed, in short, to construct in a liberal spirit the forms of the old constitution. But it was just the retribution of his career that he could not do this. The steps by which he had risen to power had so shattered that constitution ; his own position, however just in a sense deeper than all

---

* " If the poorest Christian, the most mistaken Christian, shall desire to live peaceably and quietly under you : I say, if any shall desire but to lead a life of godliness and honesty, let him be protected."—*Speeches*, CARLYLE, ii.

constitutions, was so autocratic—so arbitrary and in-
definite—that it was not possible for him to re-establish
the powers which had been cast down, and restore them
to quiet and efficient working.

His first effort at statesmanship was the famous Assembly of Puritan notables, derisively know as Barebones Parliament. Two days after the dismissal of the
"Rump," he published a "Declaration of the Lord
General and his Council of Officers," explaining the
step which he had been forced to take, and the grounds
of it; and intimating that he was about to call together an assembly of "known persons, men fearing
God, and of approved integrity, who should see to the
settling of the Commonwealth." The manner in which
this assembly was collected was sufficiently singular.
The Independent ministers throughout the country
were to take the sense of their congregations, and to
send up to the Lord General and his officers, lists of
those whom they judged "qualified to manage a trust
in the ensuing government—men able, loving truth,
fearing God, and hating covetousness." From these
lists Cromwell and his officers in council* selected one
hundred and thirty-nine representatives, and to these,
summonses were sent to appear at Whitehall on the
4th of July 1653. Only two to whom summonses
were sent did not appear.

No assembly, perhaps, ever essayed a more difficult
task than this assembly of Puritan notables—none has
ever been more vilified and ridiculed. Praise God Barebones, " the leather merchant in Fleet Street," has been
historically embalmed as its symbol of contempt; and
yet, as Carlyle says, with a scorn outmatching all the
cavalier ridicule which has been lavished on it, "Praise

* New council.

God, though he deal in leather, and has a name that
can be misspelt, is in every respect a worthy and good
man—the son of pious parents—himself a man of piety
and understanding and weight, and even of considerable private capital—my witty flunkey friend!"—as
his scorn explodes in a burst.   For all this, and notwithstanding Mr Carlyle (whose fealty to his hero, and
admiration of his actions, nothing can move), there
were plainly elements of ridicule about this assembly.
The very manner in which it was collected must have
brought together disproportionate and ludicrous elements—men, God-fearing and honest, it might be, with
a heart to do their country good, abolish its abuses,
and re-establish order and peace within its bounds,
yet men also more remarkable for piety than policy—
more fitted to legislate in their respective parishes
than in the Parliament of England, and presenting,
in the nature of the case, many external features
moving to mirth rather than to respect, and to a suspicion of wide incongruity between their capacity and
their aims.   Such an impression has certainly stamped
itself on the national mind, and perpetuated itself in
an inveterate association of ridicule surrounding the
" Barebones Parliament."

Cromwell's speech to this assembly is the first of
the now well-known series.   He told them, that by reason of the " scantiness of the room and the heat of the
weather" he would "contract himself;" but he spoke,
nevertheless, for more than two hours.   He reminded
them of all the remarkable events by which, since the
opening of the civil war, they had been brought to the
point at which they now stood.   " Those strange turn-
ings and windings of Providence—those very great
appearances of God in crossing and thwarting the pur-

poses of men, that He might raise up a poor and contemptible company of men into wonderful success."
He reviewed the recent conflict of the army and Parliament, and defended the course which he had taken
in dissolving the latter as a *necessity* laid upon him for
the defence of those " liberties and rights" for which he
and others had fought. *Necessity* was his great argument, and his only valid argument. "It has come by
way of necessity—by the way of the wise providence
of God through weak hands," he urged. He then
counselled them to tolerance in memorable words,*
and to *owning* their call. "You have been passive in
coming hither, being called. Therefore own your call !
I think it may be truly said that there never was a
Supreme Authority consisting of such a body, above
one hundred and forty, I believe ; never such a body
that came into the supreme authority before under
such a notion as this, in such a way of owning God,
and being owned by Him."†

The assembly, among its first acts, assumed the
name, insignia, and privileges of Parliament. It also
manifested great activity in practical measures of reform, collection of taxes, and consolidation of the
revenue ; but so soon as it essayed the higher task of
reforming the church and the law, it fell into intermin-
able divisions. Opposition assailed it from all sides ;
and the more moderate, alarmed and wearied at the
wild projects of the extreme gospel party, led by Harrison, tendered their resignation, and the assembly was
broken up.

Cromwell was moved by this first legislative failure;
but he took courage. He and his officers adopted more
decided measures than they had yet done to strengthen

---

* Quoted in foregoing note.   † CARLYLE, ii. 211.

his power. They met and drew up an "Instrument of Government," conferring upon him the office of *Lord Protector of the Commonwealth of England, Scotland, and Ireland.* This was on the 12th of December 1653; and on the 16th Cromwell was formally installed in the "Chancery Court in Westminster Hall." The ceremony was simple but impressive: he was dressed in a "rich but plain dark suit—black velvet, with cloak of the same; about his hat a broad band of gold." Mr Lockier, his chaplain, gave an exhortation. Lambert presented him, on his knees, with a civic sword, while he laid aside his own, denoting his exchange of military for civil rule.

The "Instrument of Government" by which Cromwell now ruled was in many respects a wise and liberal measure. It made provision for the calling of a new Parliament on a broader and fairer basis of representation than hitherto.* It decreed that without the sanction of Parliament no taxes could be raised, and that its laws were to have effect within twenty-one days, whether they received the assent of the Protector or not. Further, Parliament was not to be prorogued without its own consent during the first five months of its sitting; and all officers of state were to hold their appointment subject to its approval. All this sufficiently proves how eager Cromwell was to rest his power on the old forms of the constitution, liberalised in the spirit of the great conflict which had closed. He was not disposed, as afterwards he declared, on any account to abandon his cause and the position to which he had been raised, which he considered neces-

---

* It antedated the reform of Parliament, in short, by more than a hundred and fifty years, cutting off small and "rotten" boroughs, and giving members to large and growing towns that had recently sprung up.

sary for the vindication of this cause—" he would be rolled in blood in his grave rather ; " but supposing his position granted, he would far rather govern constitutionally than otherwise.

Cromwell was no sooner installed than he set himself, in conjunction with his Council, earnestly to the task of government. His most urgent and important work was to introduce some order into the confused religious influences surrounding him, whose ferment had borne him on triumphantly to power, but whose mere anarchic developments no man was less disposed to countenance, even if they had not directly provoked his hostility by their attacks upon his position. He prized Christian liberty in his heart, and freely conceded it to all peaceable citizens ; but he had no hesitation in putting the rein upon men " who forgot all rules of law and nature," and made " Christ and the Spirit of God a cloak for all villany and spurious apprehensions." So he quietly checked the excesses of the Anabaptist leveller, Feak, and his colleagues ;* and despatched Harrison, the head of the Fifth-monarchy men, to his home in Staffordshire. What to do, however, with the general ecclesiastical arrangements of the kingdom, was a more difficult question. Episcopacy was abolished ; Presbytery had not taken its place ; and great disorder and much inefficiency in the Christian ministry prevailed throughout the country. Cromwell very wisely did not attempt to set up a consistent form of church government. He did not trouble himself with the mere machinery of Christian instruction ; but he determined to carry a thorough reform into the spirit and character of the instruction itself. He did not care particularly whether the

* See Feak's message to him. CARLYLE, p. 234.

clergy were Presbyterians, or Independents, or even Anabaptists—(Episcopacy, as identified with malignancy and royalism, was not embraced in his system)—so that they were faithful, peaceful, Christian men. With the view of securing such a result, he appointed a commission for the trial of public preachers, composed of the most distinguished Puritan clergy, with certain laymen added to them. He further appointed, in the same spirit, commissioners in each county to inquire into "scandalous, ignorant, and inefficient" ministers, and have their places supplied with faithful men. Arbitrary as such commissions were in their constitution, there exists undoubted evidence of the fairness and tenderness as well as thoroughness with which they executed their task, and the widely beneficial influence which they exerted.* Able and serious preachers who lived a godly life, of what "tolerable opinion soever they were," multiplied throughout the land, so that many thousands of souls blessed God for what had been done.†

The foreign relations of the country were at the same time triumphantly ordered by him, and his power universally acknowledged abroad. Treaties were concluded with Holland, Denmark, and Sweden. The Dutch, humbled by the splendid victories of Blake, were glad to conclude a peace. France and Spain sent embassies, and so far acknowledged the new government.

But the great test of the government was still to come. A new Parliament, elected on the reformed basis of representation laid down in the "Instrument," met on the

---

* BAXTER's *Unprejudiced Evidence*.

† No doubt, also, hardships were inflicted under such a system, which, in its natural arbitrariness, could not fail of such results. Fuller's case has been often cited.

3d of September 1654, the anniversary of the day of Dunbar. It was to be a "free Parliament," as Cromwell himself said, or at least as free a Parliament as could then be in England. Catholics were excluded, and those who had served in the late war against the Commonwealth ; but otherwise, Republicans and Presbyterians, as well as adherents of the government, were freely chosen. There were to be 460 members—400 for England, 30 for Scotland, and 30 for Ireland. The Parliament had scarcely met, when it showed symptoms of disaffection. Cromwell addressed it long and powerfully. His three speeches to this Parliament are his greatest oratorical efforts, less involved and confused in their outline than his speeches commonly are, more heated with genuine feeling, and rising to easier and higher touches of eloquence. In the first, he impressed upon them the importance of their meeting, and the great end of it, "healing and settling." He then described the wild religious fanaticism which he had been obliged to put down, and the measures of reform which the government, himself, and his Council had accomplished. He narrated how he had made peace with Swedeland, with the Danes, and with the Dutch, and how he was in treaty with France. The whole speech was luminous with political wisdom, and ably designed to smooth into practical working order the diverse tempers before him.

He had miscalculated, however, the men with whom he had to deal. Instead of setting themselves to the quiet work of legislation on the assumed basis of the government which had called them together, they set themselves to discuss the validity of this government, and the question of the " Instrument " by which it was constituted. This refractory and captious spirit roused

Cromwell to instant action. He had them summoned to the "painted chamber," and addressed them again at length, above all insisting that the government was settled in its "fundamentals," and that these were beyond their question. This truly grand speech contains the clearest enunciation of his great principle of religious liberty,* and is touched here and there with a noble tenderness of feeling. "There is, therefore," he concluded, "something to be offered to you ; a promise of reforming as to circumstantials, and agreeing in the substance and fundamentals—that is to say, in the form of government now settled." They were to be required to give their assent and subscription to this promise and agreement, as the condition of their continuing to sit in Parliament.

The more stern of the Republican leaders—Bradshaw, and Scott, and Haselrig—refused the subscription, and quitted London. A majority, however, acceded to the condition, and began anew the work of legislation ; but they made little of it. While admitting the fundamental article of the "Instrument" of government, they quibbled over the details, and, by the end of their five months, they had made no progress in voting supplies or reforming circumstantials. Accordingly they received their dismissal, in a speech flaming high with a proud resentment, that they had been unjust to him, and insensible to the great opportunity offered them of benefiting their country. Some had spoken of his creating necessities that he might exalt himself and his family. Such a charge brought down the whole thunder of his wrath. " I say this, not only to this assembly, but to the world, that the man liveth not who can come to me, and charge me with having

* CARLYLE, ii. 298.

in these great revolutions made necessities. I challenge even all that fear God. And as God hath said, 'My glory I will not give to another,' let men take heed, and be twice advised how they call His revolutions, the things of God, and His workings of things from one period to another—how, I say, they call them necessities of man's creation."

This Parliament, beyond doubt, was a great disappointment to Cromwell. It destroyed his hopes of constitutional government; it served, by its captious stubbornness and disaffection, to revive everywhere the spirit of discontent; it proved to him his weakness in the midst of his power. He felt bitterly that he could not set up what he had cast down. His own faction he might maintain, but the old forms of the constitution—free and settled in their working—with which he desired to surround himself, seemed intractable in his hands. All his activity was needed, immediately on the dissolution of Parliament, to crush the plots, Royalist and Republican, which had gathered new life during its sittings, and were everywhere ready to burst forth. Ludlow and Alured, in Ireland, Overton and others, in Scotland, needed to be looked after. Fleetwood was instructed to deal with the one, and Monk with the others. Various other leaders of the "Anabaptist levelling party," Harrison, Carew, and Lord Grey of Groby, were seized and confined in various prisons. With these, his old allies, he dealt as tenderly as possible, consistently with the safety of his position and government. With Penruddock, and the leaders of the Royalist insurrections in the north and west, he dealt far more severely. They expiated their rashness on the scaffold; or, what was almost worse, they were shipped to the West Indies and sold as slaves. Everywhere he crushed out the embers of disaffection with a firm yet considerate hand. Viewed in the light of his own postulate as to his position, his acts were necessary, and by no means cruel, as a whole; viewed in any other light, they must, of course, be judged arbitrary, and cruelly oppressive.

Now for some time he remained more absolute in his single authority than ever. Throughout the country he established a species of military despotism—his famous system of major-generals. It was divided into districts, and a military chief appointed in each, whose duty it was to put down all anarchy, and keep the Royalists quiet, by levying heavy fines upon them for the support of the State. The system was an unmitigated tyranny, both politic and social. Nothing can be said for it except its stern necessity as a temporary provision for the maintenance of order. The peace it secured, and the confidence it re-established, are said to have proved in many respects beneficial.

Having thus quieted the aspect of affairs at home, he had leisure to direct and extend to still more splendid results than hitherto his foreign policy. Identifying himself with the interests of free religious opinion, and proudly vindicating them as the champion of Protestantism, he assumed towards foreign nations an attitude of controlling influence. It is at this time we contemplate him, along with Milton, writing on behalf of the persecuted Piedmontese, and refusing to sign the treaty with France till it had promised to see with him to the rights of these poor people. He ordained a day of fasting and a public collection to be made for them, while Milton represented their case in letters to all the Protestant powers.

The same principle which made Cromwell thus stand forth as the representative of Protestantism in Europe, plunged him into war with Spain, as the natural enemy of Protestant England. This is the express ground on which he himself defended the Spanish war. "The Spaniard is your enemy; and your enemy, as I tell you, *naturally*, by that antipathy which is in him,* and also providentially, and this in divers respects." The armament which he fitted out against their West India possessions, while it failed in its substantial objects, took possession of Jamaica, which has ever since remained a British possession. This, at the time supposed to be a barren conquest, was the only trophy of an expedition which had evidently been one of great interest and hopes to him. It is the single failure of his career, and he resented it by throwing the commanders of the expedition into the Tower on their return home.

Strengthened by the reduction of his enemies at home, and by the glory of his power abroad, Cromwell was induced once more to summon a Parliament for the 17th of September 1656. After adressing them (as usual) in a lengthened speech† explaining the position of affairs, and the grounds on which he was

---

* Elsewhere, in the same speech: "Why, truly your great enemy is the Spaniard. He is a natural enemy. He is naturally so; he is naturally so throughout—by reason of that enmity that is in him against whatsoever is of God."

† The conclusion of this speech is in his grandest strain; as, indeed, the whole is wonderful—"rude, massive, genuine, like a block of unbeaten gold." In the end he says,—"If God give you a spirit of reformation, you will prevent this nation from 'turning again' to those fooleries ['horse-races, cock-fightings, and the like!' which had been abolished as having been made the occasion of Royalist plots, &c.]; and what will the end be?—Comfort and blessing. Then Mercy and Truth shall meet together. There is a great deal of 'truth' among professors, but very little 'mercy.' They are ready to cut the throats

prepared to maintain the government, he purged them according to a rule which had been agreed upon between him and his Council. A hundred members out of the four hundred were prevented from taking their seats. This violent act, only justifiable, like many others, by the necessities of his position, excited great indignation; but it was carried quietly through; and Haselrig (his old friend), and Ashley Cooper, and other disturbing spirits, sent back to their homes to nurse their discontent in private.

Parliament thus purged and approved, showed itself more subservient to his wishes. It wasted its time, indeed, in fruitless and absurd discussions as to the opinions of a poor wandering fanatic of the name of Naylor, and the punishment with which he should be visited—evidence enough how far it was from appreciating those noble expressions of the doctrine of toleration which he addressed to it. But at length, after some five months' work and many negotiations, it drew up a new "Instrument of Government," by which it provided for the Protector assuming the office of king, and appoint-

---

of one another. But when we are brought into the right way, we shall be merciful as well as orthodox : and we know who it is that saith, ' If a man could speak with the tongues of men and angels, and yet want *that*, he is but sounding brass and a tinkling cymbal.'

"Therefore I beseech you, in the name of God, set your hearts to this work. And if you set your hearts to it, then will you sing Luther's Psalm [the 46th, of which Luther's hymn, *Eine feste Burg ist unser Gott*, is a paraphrase]. This is a rare psalm for a Christian !—and if he set his heart open, and can approve it to God, we shall hear him say, ' God is our refuge and strength, a very present help in time of trouble.' If Pope and Spaniard, and devil and all, set themselves, though they should ' compass us like bees,' as it is in hundred-and-eighteenth psalm, yet in the name of the Lord we should destroy them. And, as it is in this psalm of Luther's, ' We will not fear, though the earth be removed, and though the mountains be carried into the middle of the sea ; though the waters thereof roar and be troubled ; though the mountains shake with the swelling thereof.' "

ing his successor. The interviews and debates to which
this proposal led, the strange and apparently inconsistent veerings in Cromwell's own mind, make a deeply
interesting but perplexing study. Suffice it to say that
they ended in his rejecting the proposal of Parliament.
On the 8th of May 1657, he finally decided not to
adopt the title of king; and the issue was, that he was
again, and more formally, inaugurated as Protector,
amid the joyful huzzas of the people. The same Parliament abolished the system of major-generals; and
in the new instrument reconstituting the Protectorate,
it provided for the institution of a House of Lords.
Piece by piece, he would fain have surrounded himself with all the old machinery of the constitution.

After an adjournment of six months, Parliament reassembled, and of the fifty-three Peers nominated by
Cromwell, forty appeared to take their place. Scarcely
any of the old Peers, however—not even Lord Warwick
—came. He declared that he could not sit in the same
assembly with Hewson the cobbler and Pride the dray-
man. The Protector, by reason of "some infirmities
upon him," made them but a short speech ; probably
he was somewhat despondent and hopeless. The position of affairs was once more critical ; his own health
was failing—the old factions were noisy and gathering
strength again. The members excluded in the previous
session now professed their willingness to take the oath
of the new constitution, and there was no longer any
valid reason for insisting upon their exclusion. Haselrig, one of the most persevering and violent, had been
prudently nominated by Cromwell a Peer, but he declined to take his seat, except in the House of Commons. He insisted upon having the oath administered
to him, and took his place in the Commons as the

leader of the old Republicans. As may be conjectured, dissensions speedily sprang up in such an assembly. Only two days after the opening of the session, a message was sent from the House of Lords, inviting the Commons to unite with them in an address to his Highness to appoint a day of fasting and humiliation. This was enough to kindle the embers of unappeasable dissatisfaction. The Republicans fired at the title which the so-called Peers had given themselves. " We have no message to receive from them as Lords," they exclaimed—" they are but a swarm from ourselves." In vain Cromwell summoned them to attend him in the Banqueting Hall, at Whitehall, and addressed them in earnest and solemn words, as to the dangers that were threatening at home and abroad, and his determination to stand with them in the old cause—the interests of the Commonwealth which he had sworn to maintain. They returned, only to renew with more eagerness their faction fight as to the title under which they should recognise the other House ; and after a five days' debate, they decided by a majority, not to recognise it under the name of the House of Lords.

This decision stirred the Protector to the very depths of his stormy nature. Without consulting with any one, he went, accompanied by only a few guards, to the House of Lords, and summoned the Commons to attend him. Fleetwood, his son-in-law, here joined him, and tried to dissuade him from his plans, which, he urged, would take even his friends by surprise. But laying his hand upon his breast, he swore by the living God, that he would do it, and that they should not sit another hour. His speech was short, and betrayed the depth of his emotion. We feel a noble pity for the giant bending beneath the pressure of his difficul-

ties, resolute not to yield, and yet unable to bear solitary the heavy burden. "To be petitioned and advised
by you to undertake such a government— a burden
too heavy for any creature—certainly, I did hope that
the same men who made the frame, should make it
good unto me. I can say in the presence of God, in
comparison with whom we are but poor creeping ants
upon the earth, I would have been glad to have lived
under my woodside, to have kept a flock of sheep,
rather than undertake such a government as this."
A magnanimous pathos, surely, in this thought of his
old quiet former life at such a time ! He reproached
them with their moving the question of a "Republic,"
as opposed to the government already settled—with
their tampering with the army—with their even, some
of them, "listing persons by commission of Charles
Stuart," to join with any insurrection that might be
made. "And what is like to come upon this," he concluded," the enemy being ready to invade us, but even
present blood and confusion? And if this be so, I do
assign it to this cause—your not assenting to what
you did invite me by your petition and advice, as that
which might prove the settlement of the nation. And
if this be the end of your sitting, and this be your
carriage, I think it high time that an end be put to
your sitting. AND I DO DISSOLVE THIS PARLIAMENT !
And let God be judge betwixt you and me."

Parliament was accordingly dismissed—its endless
debatings suddenly stifled ; but not sooner than necessary; for Royalist discontent was everywhere active,
breaking out in ever-renewed flame. "If the session
had lasted but two or three days longer," says Har-
tlib, Milton's friend (to whom his tractate on education was addressed), "all had been in blood, both in

city and country, on Charles Stuart's account." Cromwell was fully conscious of his perils. And now, as ever, he took his resolutions swiftly, and followed them up with prompt and unflinching action. Two ringleaders* in the Royalist plots were seized, condemned, and summarily executed—notwithstanding the influential connections of the one, and the earnest entreaties of his own daughter in the case of the other. Once more he crushed, by his terrible yet considerate vigour, his enemies on all hands. His arms on the Continent were at the same time triumphant. Dunkirk was gloriously taken, and its keys deposited in his hands. Splendid presents were exchanged between him and Mazarin, and splendid embassies sent to him. He received them in kingly state, rising from his throne and advancing two steps to meet the Duke of Crequi, the head of the embassy, and seating him on his right hand, while his son Richard sat on his left. His power seemed more consolidated, his position more triumphant, than ever; but in reality the shadow of his fate was rapidly closing around him; he was pressed by pecuniary difficulties; calamity had attacked his prosperous family; and his own health was breaking under the harassing burden of his anxieties.

His two eldest daughters, we have seen, were married in the outset of his career. The eldest was by this time married a second time, to Fleetwood (one of Cromwell's stanchest friends), Ireton having died in Ireland. Both his sons were busily engaged in various duties of office. Henry, the younger, unlike his brother, was of bold and enterprising spirit, and shared his father's genius for government. His administration of Ireland, under great difficulties, showed a vigilance,

* Sir Henry Slingsby, uncle to Lord Faulconbridge, and Dr Hewit.

capacity, and energy, which have won the commendation even of Royalist critics of the time. The impression we gather of Henry is almost more cavalier than
Puritan ; a dashing, gallant, and generous fellow he
appears to have been, of careless temper though strong
will, and, if Mrs Hutchison and other sources are to
be believed, somewhat dissolute.* His two younger
daughters, Mary and Frances, were now grown up.
Both, especially " the Lady Frances," suggest a pleasing picture of beautiful, vivacious, and happy youth.
The one was wedded to Viscount Faulconbridge, " a
person of extraordinary parts," and strongly attached
to the Protector's person and government ; the other
to Mr Rich, grandson of the Earl of Warwick, and
heir to his estates. This last † marriage was a subject of anxiety to Cromwell. The "settlements," as
before, in the case of Richard, were hard to make,
and yet the " little Fanny " (she was only seventeen) was resolved to settle. It came right in the
end, and both sisters were married within a week
of each other (November 1657). Cromwell had great
pride in all his daughters. His family feelings were
strong, and tenderly affectionate. But his heart, above
all, clung to the Lady Claypole. She was "dear
to him—very dear." It was the tragedy of his lot,
as he now seemed to stand at the pinnacle of his
power — his enemies at home and abroad crushed
and silent, and the incense of foreign flattery surrounding him on his perilous seat of sovereignty—to have

---

* See a remarkable and very interesting letter of remonstrance from
his sister Mary (7th Dec. 1655), which suggests the same conclusion.

† " And truly, I must tell you privately, they are so far engaged that
the match cannot be broken off. She, Frances, acquainted some of his
friends with her resolution when she did it." So writes her sister Mary
to Henry in June 1656.

darkness sent into his house, and the desire of his eyes removed. The prosperous glory of his family underwent sudden eclipse; and, at the very height of his fame and power, he died broken in heart, nursing deeper than all state anxieties the sorrows of his home.

Only twelve days after the dissolution of Parliament, his son-in-law, Mr Rich, took ill and died. Wedded only in the previous November, his death took place in February (1657-8); and the removal of one so young and beloved, leaving a still younger widow, cast the first shadow over his household. Only two months after, the Earl of Warwick, one of the Protector's oldest and most prudent friends, followed his young grandson to the grave. Severe as these blows were, they did not touch him so acutely as to interfere with his activity. He was plunged in cares of foreign policy and negotiations with Thurloe and others. A new Parliament, rendered imperatively necessary by the state of the finances, was talked of; the French embassy, with its glittering show, had to be received; and, amidst all, the Lord Protector bore himself with what spirit and show of sovereign unconcern he could. But while these State affairs were being transacted, a deeper sorrow than he had yet known was preparing for him. "The Manzinis and Ducs de Crequi, with their splendour and congratulations," had scarcely withdrawn, when all his thoughts were absorbed by the news of the serious illness of his daughter Elizabeth (the Lady Claypole). Weak and invalid for some time, he had sent her to reside at Hampton Court; but the internal disease under which she suffered rapidly increased. Pain of body alternated with anxiety of mind regarding her beloved father. "She had great sufferings, and great exercises of spirit." For fourteen days the Protector watched by her bedside, "unable to attend to any public business whatever." The stormy world in which he had so long lived was far removed, as he sat, during these silent days and nights, watching the ebbing life of his darling child. "It was observed that his sense of her outward misery in the pains she endured took deep impression upon him."

On the 6th of August she died, and on the 7th he himself was reported ill in a letter of Thurloe to his son Henry. About this time it was that he called for the Bible, and desired them to read to him in Philippians iv. 11-13. "'Not that I speak in respect of want: for I have learned, in whatsoever state I am, therewith to be content. I know both how to be abased, and I know how to abound: everywhere and in all things I am instructed, both to be full and to be hungry, both to abound and to suffer need. I can do all things through Christ which strengtheneth me.' This Scripture did once save my life when my eldest son* died, which went as a dagger to my heart—indeed it did." After this he partially recovered, and made an effort to resume his labours. George Fox records how he met him in these few days riding into Hampton Court Park at the head of his life-guards; "and, as he rode," says the garrulous self-conscious Quaker, "I saw and felt a waft of death go forth against him."

On the 24th of August he left Hampton Court and returned to Whitehall. A sudden visit of Ludlow to town filled him with some disquiet, and he sent Fleetwood to inquire after him. He was himself again ill, and his disease rapidly gained ground. At length he was confined to bed. His physicians stood around, with sad faces, and his wife sat anxious by him. A strange

* Robert (as before explained).

excitement, however, buoyed up his own heart; and, taking his wife's hand, he said, "I tell thee I shall not die of this bout. I am sure I shall not." The strong spirit was reluctant to yield; and his chaplains fancied that they heard the voice of God, in answer to their prayers, saying, "He will recover." The days passed, however, and there was no sign of recovery. On the 2d of September, the eve of his fortunate day, he asked, in a lucid interval of his delirious sufferings, "Is it possible to fall from grace?" "It is not possible," the ministers replied. "Then I am safe," he said, "for I know that I was once in grace;" and he poured forth an earnest confession and prayer to God.* During the night his voice continued to be heard in snatches of prayer. "God is good—truly, God is good," he often repeated. Amid the wild storm of the autumn night,† the voice of the dying hero rose in these still and grand accents. At length he muttered, when desired to take some refreshment, "It is not my design to drink or sleep; but my design is to make what haste

---

* There are few prayers more touching, more truly Christian, in all the annals of devotion. "Lord, though I am a miserable and wretched creature, I am in covenant with Thee through grace. And I may, I will, come to Thee for Thy people. Thou hast made me, though very unworthy, a mean instrument to do them some good, and Thee service; and many of them have set too high a value upon me, though others wish and would be glad of my death. Lord, however Thou dispose of me, continue and go on to do good for them. Give them consistency of judgment, one heart, and mutual love; and go on to deliver them, and with the work of reformation; and make the name of Christ glorious in the world. Teach those who look too much upon Thy instrument, to depend more upon Thyself. Pardon such as desire to trample on the dust of a poor worm, for they are Thy people too. And pardon the folly of this short prayer, even for Jesus Christ's sake. And give us a good night, if it be Thy pleasure. Amen."

† "The usual representation is here followed, which makes the night of the 2d of September (1658) 'such a night in London as had rarely been.' The height of the storm, however, is stated by some to have been on Monday the 30th of August."—CARLYLE, ii. 665.

I can to be gone." When morning dawned he lay insensible; and between three and four of the afternoon of his *fortunate day*, he heaved a deep sigh and expired.

In attempting to sketch the character of Cromwell, it is especially necessary to get some central point of view from which we can survey it in its whole outline. The complexities which it presents—its deep and involved shades—its confused and apparently conflicting features—render this all the more necessary. For, otherwise, his character becomes unintelligible—a mere mass of inconsistencies, in which we can see no coherence or meaning. He is great, and yet base; religious, and yet a hypocrite; a demagogue, and yet a despot; a dissembler, and yet a trifler; a man of vast and imperial schemes, and yet a man of low and paltry interests. This is something of the blurred and contradicting picture which Cromwell presents in many of our histories. It may be safely said that no great character can be explained in this manner. We must seek for some inward unity out of which the character has grown—for hidden threads of consistency running through it, underlying all its more obvious appearances, and binding up its complicated structure into an intelligible whole.

The secret of Cromwell's character appears to lie where he himself supposed—in the depth and power of his religious sentiment. This we must either admit, or hold him throughout to have been a hypocrite. Only one of these two alternatives can possibly remain after the careful study of his letters. This man was either from the first a conscious hypocrite, *acting a part*, as has been maintained—deliberately forecasting schemes of glorious yet fraudulent ambition, the perfidy of which he sought to conceal by the most elaborate and unwearying pretensions to piety; or he was at first and throughout a man in whom the sense of the Divine predominated—whose rooted and most ruling instinct was to do God service; and who, amid all his actions, deeply censurable as some of these may have been, never entirely lost sight of this principle or purpose. Religion so filled his life that it either held him or he held it as a mere tool in his service. And there are few who will read his correspondence and speeches from beginning to end, with any understanding of them—with any intelligent sympathy with the time and its modes of religious feeling—and doubt which of these views is the correct one.

The alternative of hypocrisy in the face of his letters involves a series of suppositions so incredible, as to compel every candid student to part with it.* These letters are written in all circumstances—when as yet he was but a Puritan farmer and friend of persecuted ministers, when first the great contests of the Parliament began to stir his tumultuous energies on the eve of battle, and when the excitement of

* In evidence of this, allusion may be made to the different view of Cromwell's character suggested by Mr Foster in his "Life," written for the *Cabinet Cyclopædia* more than twenty years ago—in many respects an admirable life—and that suggested in his recent paper, *The Civil Wars and Oliver Cromwell.* The "inimitable craft and skill, assuming the garb of sanctity," which explains so much in the "Life," has entirely disappeared in the later sketch. The result of Mr Carlyle's labours, he says, "has been to show conclusively, and beyond further dispute, that through all these [Cromwell's] speeches and letters one mind runs consistently. In the passionate fervour of his religious feeling the true secret of his life must be sought, and will be found. Everywhere visible and recognisable is a deeply interpenetrated sense of spiritual dangers, of temporal vicissitudes, and of never-ceasing responsibility to the Eternal, ' Ever in his great Taskmaster's eye.' "—FOSTER'S *Essays,* i. 312.

victory was yet on him—regarding the most ordinary
domestic details, and the most broad general principles
of religion and policy. They all bear a natural impress ; they show the man, the politician, the warrior,
the father, the husband, and patriot, and not merely
the religionist. The religious ideas and phraseology
in which they abound are in no sense factitious ; they
are the living essence of his common thought ; they
are mixed up with everything he says and does. The
same tone pervades the letters throughout—the same
cast of earnest, grave, and tender feeling—the same
air of *reality*. As we read them, and try to purge our
minds of all remembrance of the traditionary Cromwell
with his hypocrisies and grimaces, there is nothing
whatever that could excite such an image within us.
His character rises before us plain, massive, and grand ;
rude in its features, irregular in its outline, but glowing
with an intensely concentrated meaning; radiant with a
divine fire in every feature—an earnest, practical, strong
man, " in the dark perils of war, and in the high places
of the field : hope shone in him like a pillar of fire when
it had gone out in all others." The confidence of a
divine cause—the light of a divine trust—the soaring
passion of a faith mighty to subdue mountains,—these
are the grand elements of his character. He un-
covers his most familiar thoughts, he writes of the
most ordinary details as to the marriage and settlement of his son, and the same earnestness meets us—
the same practical spirit and aim show themselves.
No expression escapes from him that suggests ostentation or mere effect, or double dealing. If this be
hypocrisy, it is difficult to conceive what more the
most natural and downright sincerity could have been.
We recognise in Cromwell, therefore, above all, the

reality of religious conviction. He lived *by faith.* It was the firm perception and hold of the Divine that carried him forward through all his difficulties and amidst all his triumphs. God he felt to be with him and to be his God; and his firm persuasion of this it was that strengthened his heart and consecrated his sword, and bore him erect when weakness or blindness left others struck down or groping helplessly amidst the confusion and darkness. The spirit of Puritanism found in him its most thorough expression as well as its greatest representative. He was penetrated to the very core of his being by the thought that God was ever near to him and guiding him, "ordering him and affairs concerning him," and that the cause which he served was His cause. He "seldom fought without some text of Scripture to support him." And as he fought, he lived. He was an "unworthy and mean instrument," to do some good, and God some service. To doubt or deny the leading of God in the great events of his time, was to him the deepest impiety—the most ungodly malice. "Is it an arm of flesh that hath done these things?" he says, writing from before Waterford in 1649. "Is it the wisdom, or counsel, or strength of men? It is the Lord only. God will curse that man and his house that dares to think otherwise. Sir, you see the work is done by a divine leading. God gets into the hearts of men, and persuades them to come under you. . . . These are the seals of God's approbation of your great change of government—which indeed was no more yours than these victories and successes are ours; yet let them with us say, even the most unsatisfied heart amongst them, that *both* are the righteous judgments and mighty works of God."

This spirit may be called fanaticism. The identification of the Divine, not merely with a great moral cause, but with the accidents of that cause—the interpretation of success as a token of the divine favour, and the reverse—all this is of the essence of the fanatical. Puritanism itself was a fanaticism, in so far as it merged the spiritual in the temporal, and made its own dogmas and ordinances the measure of the divine. And the impartial critic cannot refuse to admit that fanatical elements mingled in Cromwell's character. The presence of these elements made him pre-eminently the man of his time—the great impersonation and power of it. But while we can everywhere trace in him the capacities of fanaticism, and while these show themselves now and then in startling and even shocking expressions, we see also at every turn of his life how far he was above them—how the native greatness of his mind, the breadth of his spirituality, as well as the shrewdness of his sense, raised him beyond the limits of the enthusiast. Destitute of intellectual cultivation, and without any of the checks that come from æsthetic sensibility or refinement, his mind was yet too enlightened, sound, and sagacious, and his sympathies too direct, broad, and vigorous, to permit him to be absolutely swayed by any theories whatever. It was this that made the difference between him and many of the men like Harrison, or even Vane, who at one time surrounded him, and with whom he acted. It was this that made the difference between him and the Scotch ministers and generals with whom he argued. The Divine was never to him this or that institution or covenant. The external never enslaved him, however it guided him. The great hero of Puritanism, he yet rose above its narrowness. Its faith never left him, and its hopes never died out of him, but its forms fell

away from him when they were no longer serviceable.
Moving in an atmosphere of the wildest fanaticism,
and having " sucked its very dregs," as Mr Hallam will
have it, yet Cromwell was himself no fanatic. The
Divine mastered him, but did not prostrate him. It
inspired, and guided, and blessed him—it carried him
to triumph and power ; made him a tower of strength
to the persecuted Protestant abroad, and a protection
to the peaceable Protestant at home. But even when
its highest passion swayed him, and the very hand
of God seemed upon him and his ways, his own
eye was clear, and his heart sound, and his hand
steady ; and while the whispers of the Divine were in
his ear, there was no intoxication nor delusion in his
soul.

Cromwell, then, was no hypocrite and no mere enthusiast. He was simply the greatest Englishman of his
time ; the most powerful, if not the most perfect, expression of its religious spirit, and the master-genius
of its military and political necessities. This is the
only consistent and adequate explanation of his career.
Every such time of revolution must find its representative and hero, the mirror and minister of its necessities,
but at the same time the master of them. Had Cromwell been less religious, he could never have become
a centre of influence in such a time. Not even the
subtlest and most profound dissimulation could have
made him so. Had he been merely religious—had the
Godward tendency absorbed his being, and become a
disease of fanaticism, rather than a stimulant of patriotism, then his incipient influence would have crumbled
to pieces in his grasp, and his power have gone from
him so soon as he tried to exercise it. It was not
merely because he represented his time, but because he

rose above it—because religion was in him the nurture of transcendent abilities, the baptism and ever-renewing life of heroic energies—that he became what he was, and accomplished what he did. Religion formed him, but the original materials were of the grandest and most powerful character. "A larger soul, I think, hath seldom dwelt in a house of clay than his was." *

This largeness of soul was everywhere seen in Cromwell's actions. His mind heaved with the burden of his thoughts at every great crisis of his life. He saw the wide issues stretching out before him—issues quite unseen and unappreciated by many with whom he acted; and the absorption of thought and semi-prophetic rapture which sometimes came from this dreamy and far-reaching foresight,† appears to be the true explanation of many supposed instances of his profound dissimulation. He has been credited with elaborate and hidden scheming, when in fact he was rather dreaming, seeing in vision before him the great outline of the future. A certain exaltation of spirit, lofty, ardent, and uncalculating, was apt to sway him like a divine afflatus, betraying itself in his face and manner, sometimes in a radiant majesty and kingly presence, and sometimes in a wild and boisterous humour. It was this that, suffusing his whole being, and giving to his steps an "uncontrollable buoyancy" when he entered

---

* MAIDSTONE.

† His supposed words to M. de Bellièvre, President of the Parliament of Paris, who had seen and known him before his assumption of power—words upon which Mr Foster has dwelt so much in his recent essay—that *"one never mounts so high as when one does not know where one is going"*—are not inconsistent with the gift of foresight attributed to him, even if the words were anything more than a confused memory on the part of M. de Bellièvre. Cromwell's foresight was not the foresight of worldly prudence, but the vision of his destiny as in God's hands, to do some great work, to *mount as high* as he could.

L

London in state, after the battle of Worcester, led his
Republican chaplain to murmur to himself, "That man
will yet be king of England." It may have been the
same rapt excitement that made him jest so wildly with
Ludlow and Martin on the eve of the King's death, and
pursue the former down stairs with the cushions of the
council-chamber in which they had met, and where,
while talking with them, the curtain of the future had
risen before him. Ludlow, with his "wodden head,"
could only see the tomfoolery of this; but there was
a fulness of bursting thought, of inarticulate emotion,
in our hero that may be conceived exploding in such
a riotous and absurd manner, as this and many stories
impute to him. Many of these stories, indeed, are mere
lies—the concoctions of the mean cowards that dared
to slander him after the Restoration for a piece of bread.
Yet it was of the very character of Cromwell's greatness
—substantial and massive, without classical dignity or
harmony or delicacy — to be indifferent to outward
polish and calm restraint of demeanour. Some elements of his rude farmer life—of that disorderly appearance which, on his first becoming known in Parliament, so stamped itself on the minds of his contemporaries—probably remained in him to the last, under all
his "great and majestical deportment."

For mere forms of any kind he evidently cared little.
He appreciated and made use of them in public, and
wherever the national honour was concerned in him as
its representative; but he was also glad to lay them
aside, and descend from formality to simple familiarity.
"With his friends," says Whitelock, "he would be
exceedingly familiar, and by way of diversion would
make verses with us. He would commonly call for
tobacco, pipes, and a candle, and would now and then

take tobacco himself. Then *he would fall again to his serious and great business."* Obviously a plain and simple man among his fellows, with no airs and no grandeurs about him when he had no stately work to do, no national splendours to represent, and no Manzinis and Ducs de Crequi to overawe. This genuine simplicity, amidst all his extravagances and assumptions, we cannot help thinking had more to do than anything else with his refusal of the title of king. With the reality of sovereignty in his possession, the mere name and insignia could have but few attractions for him. And confused and unintelligible as those interviews and speeches between him and the Parliamentary chiefs and lawyers on the subject are—suggesting now his wish for, and now his indifference to, the title—the prompting of his own manly and simple nature had probably as much to do with the result as the apprehension of the army or any other cause whatever. To represent him as merely dallying with the Parliament and the lawyers, while he had made up his mind to accept, and as having been at length only prevented from carrying out his wishes by the threatenings of the army chiefs, is more consistent with a character of craft and intrigue than with one of principle, tact, and energy.

The student of this part of English history is everywhere driven back upon a broad interpretation of facts. He has always the same problem before him—to explain the culmination of a patriotic and religious revolution by the triumph of mere force and perfidy, planned with long deliberation, and executed with consummate skill; or, on the other hand, to regard the power and Protectorate of Cromwell as the inevitable issue of successive national exigencies, understood and seized as they came by a master—by the one man in the kingdom who had a real discernment of the course of events, and real capacity to guide and order them. There are, no doubt, circumstances on the mere surface that favour the former explanation. It was the one which necessarily sprang up and became part of the national creed after the Restoration. But the more all the inner history and details of the time are studied; the more the temper of the religious influences, which then more than all other influences moved the English people, is apprehended; the more, above all, the great central character is probed and examined in the light of his own sayings and doings, apart from the scurrilous exaggerations of Royalist pamphleteers,* or the envious misinterpretations of Republican zealots,†—the more will the latter view gain ground as the only consistent and intelligible, as well as enlarged and liberal interpretation of all the circumstances. Selfish and despotical as may still be judged many of the acts of Cromwell; puzzling and obscure as must remain some of the shades of his character; perilous as may be the very glory claimed for him—such as no other in our national liberty can ever share, and none without crime could ever again dream of;—yet his true parallel will be found not in the vulgar despot, who triumphs by terror and rules by the bayonet, but in the divine hero who, interpreting the instincts and necessities of a great people, rose on their buoyancy to the proud position which, having seized by his commanding genius, he held, upon the whole, with a beneficent influence, as he did with an imperishable glory.

* Heath and others.　　　　† Ludlow and others.

II.

MILTON.

MILTON.

It may seem questionable to assume Milton as a representative of Puritanism; and in the narrower sense of that word, the question would be a fair one; for Milton was certainly a great deal more than a Puritan. His mind and culture show elements even anti-Puritan. His youth and early manhood were academic and literary. Classical and poetical studies moulded his taste, and disciplined and refined his intellect. The Cambridge student of the years 1625-1632 — the youthful poet at Horton—and the leisurely *dilletante* traveller at Florence, Rome, Naples, and Geneva, during the seven following years—seems far enough from participation in the religious spirit which was then spreading throughout England, and beginning to move it to its centre; then, again, the later spiritualist of the years of the Restoration, Arian in doctrine, and latitudinarian in practice, who owned no church, and nowhere joined in public worship—the blind old poet—the divine dreamer of a Paradise Lost and a Paradise Regained—" who used to sit in a grey, coarse cloth coat at the door of his house near Bunhill Fields, in warm sunny weather, to enjoy the fresh air," may seem equally removed from the nonconformity that was still active and zealous under all its renewed oppressions—that lived in jails or flourished in corners beyond the scrutiny of the Five-mile Act.

It is nevertheless true that, in all the higher and more comprehensive meaning of the word, Milton was a Puritan. Even in his early years, his sympathy with its spirit of ecclesiastical reform, the polemical hatred against Episcopacy which it nourished, prevented him from entering the Church. On his return to England from his travels abroad, he plunged into the very heart of the religious contention that was then brewing on all sides. His first prose writings are as distinctively Puritan in their dogmatic spirit as any writings in all the century. During the years of his controversial manhood, he was identified closely with every great phase of the movement. He was the advocate of its triumphs—of its excesses. He stood forth before the world as its literary genius and apologist. And, finally, his two great poems, while classical in their structure and in the severe and felicitous majesty of their style, are intensely Puritan in their spirit —in the intellectual ideas, and even the imaginative scenery through which their great purpose is worked out and impressed upon the mind of the reader.

There is no picture of Puritanism, therefore, that would be at all complete which did not embrace John Milton as one of its prominent figures. The very fact that his relations to it are in some respects exceptional —that he stands so much alone, and above the movement, while intimately connected with it—makes it all the more necessary to introduce him ; for there is no other character can be a substitute for him ; there is no one else that did the same work as he did, and in the same spirit. He remains the single great poet that Puritanism has produced ; and while we shall see abundantly how much more went to his formation than Puritanism—how broader sympathies and affinities were necessary to nurse and educate his genius—we shall see at the same time what a peculiar consecration its religious spirit gave to that genius—to what unearthly heights it carried it "above the Olympian hill," "above the flight of Pegasean wing;" and what richness, and strength, and mystery of grandeur all his high powers derived from communion with those biblical thoughts and biblical forms of expression on which the Puritan spirit exclusively fed and delighted to clothe itself.

The life of Milton is in itself a sort of Puritan Drama, severe, earnest, sad, yet with the bright lights of an irrepressible poesy irradiating it. The spiritual discontent and unrest of his youth hiding itself beneath a widely sympathetic and varied culture of his intellect, taste, and feelings, of which his early poems continue the ever beautiful expression ; his stormy and contentious manhood, mingling pride and sternness, and even cruel harshness, with the assertion of the most noble principles, both political and religious ; and then the mournful close of all, " the evil days and evil tongues "—

> " In darkness, and with dangers compassed round,
> And solitude,"

in which his high hopes for human freedom and the triumph of divine truth expire—the picture is a grandly impressive one, the heroic lesson of which is only the more conspicuous from the apparent failure, the sacrifice of the hero.

His life divides itself conveniently for our purpose into three main epochs—the first extending to his

return from his travels abroad and settlement at home
on the eve of the outbreak of the civil war (1608-40);
the second running throughout the memorable twenty
years of the civil war and the Commonwealth (1640-60);
and the third reaching from the Restoration to his
death in 1674.   The first of these is the period of
his education and early poems—the classical period, so
to speak, of his life; the second marks the era of his
controversial activity—the Puritan phase of his career;
the third is the age of his later great poems, and of
his contemplative speculations in Christian doctrine.
The first period is the most crowded with external
incidents; the second and third derive their chief interest from the splendid intellectual monuments that
so thickly mark them, and the preparation of which
constituted their chief occupation.

Milton's father was a scrivener in Broad Street,
London, and there the poet was born on the 9th of
December 1608.   Besides himself, there were four
children, three sisters and a brother.   Two of the
sisters died in infancy; but his brother Christopher
and his sister Ann both meet us in interesting relations as we trace the career of the poet.   The original
seat of Milton's family was in Oxfordshire; and the
reputed grandfather of the poet, by name also John
Milton, is said to have held the office of under-ranger
of the royal forest of Shotover, in the immediate vicin-
ity of Oxford.*   Recent researches† cannot be said to

* " His grandfather was of Holton in Oxfordshire, near Shotover,"
says Aubrey.   " He was," says Wood, " an under-ranger or keeper of
the forest of Shotover, near to the (said) town of Holton, but descended
from those of his name who had lived beyond all record at Milton, near
Holton and Thame in Oxfordshire."

† Mr Hunter and Mr Masson.

have thrown any clearer light on the pedigree of the
poet. That his grandfather's name was Richard and
not John, and that he was of Stanton St John's instead
of Holton, have been suggested with some degree of
probability, but without any satisfactory clue of evidence. It is more clearly known that he was a Roman
Catholic, and rigidly devoted to his faith; so that when
his son John, the father of the poet, embraced the Reformed doctrines, he disinherited him, and would never
again receive him into favour. To this event, probably, it was owing that he settled in London as a
scrivener, a business very much resembling that of a
modern attorney.

Under the sign of the Spread Eagle in Bread Street,
Milton's father throve in this capacity. He was a
" man of the utmost integrity," his son says, with
some degree of pride; eminently successful in his profession, but by no means merely a man of parchments
and law, for he found leisure to devote himself to literature, and especially to music, in which he became
highly proficient, and one of the best composers of his
time. The name of the poet's mother is commonly
supposed to have been Bradshaw, of the same family
as the famous John Bradshaw, President of the Council of State in the Commonwealth, although, somewhat
strangely, her own grandson Phillips gives the name
as Caston. Of her character there is not much known,
save what her son says in the same treatise in which
he characterises his father. " She was a most approved
mother," he says, " and widely known for her works of
charity."*

Milton's home appears to have been a very happy

* " Matre probatissima et eleemosynis per viciniam protissimam
nota."—*Defensio Secunda.*

one—a grave and earnest Puritan home, in which
prayer was daily offered, in which the minister of the
parish, the Rev. Richard Stoke, a "zealous Puritan,
and constant, and judicious, and religious preacher,"
was a frequent visitor, but where no gloom reigned.
His father's devotion to music must of itself have
lightened any tendency to domestic austerity, and
his son's tastes in the same direction proved a constant source of entertainment. The Poet gave very
early promise of his wonderful gifts, and this, combined with his singular beauty, made him an object
of very fond and proud interest to his parents. In
evidence of this, we have his portrait taken by Cor-
nelius Jansen when he was only ten years of age,—
the well-known picture of the little boy-poet, with his
auburn hair not yet clustered round his neck, but lying
in soft gentle waves on his forehead ; the face, dreamy
and solid rather than bright and vivid, set above a stiff,
broad, and elaborate frill, and light-fitting tunic, enve-
loping his person more like a casing of armour than a
soft and fitting child-raiment. According to Aubrey,
he was even now a poet. The verse-making tendency
had begun to show itself in him, fostered by his father
and his father's friend John Lane, whose "several
poems, if they had not had the ill fate," says Philips,
" to remain unpublished, might have gained him a
name not much inferior, if not equal to Drayton and
others of next rank to Spenser." Not only Lane's
poems, but his very name has perished in the great
current of English literature.

Milton's special education seems to have been conducted at home in those early years, under the direction
of a tutor of the name of Thomas Young, a Scotchman
by birth, and a student of St Andrews. He afterwards

became a prominent Puritan divine, and Milton retained
for him a strong feeling of gratitude and respect.*

When about twelve, the young poet was sent to St
Paul's grammar school, founded by Dean Colet, and in
the poet's time under the charge of a Mr Gill and his
son, the former of whom was really a man of superior
worth and learning, "a noted Latinist, critic, and divine."
The son was also a man of considerable accomplishment—a poet in his way, but of an erratic and troublesome disposition.   Milton, in after years, preserved
somewhat intimate relations with both of them, and
various Latin letters passed between him and young Gill,
for whom he seems always to have felt a warm interest,
notwithstanding his vanity and recurring unsteadiness.
Here he laid the foundations of his Latin scholarship,
although none of his compositions in that language
can be referred to so early a date.†   Here also his
mind opened to the great world of thought.   He himself tells us that "before he left school he had acquired
various tongues, and also some not insignificant taste
for the sweetness of philosophy."   He pursued his
studies with great ardour, strongly encouraged by his
father, whose name he never ceases to mention with
affectionate esteem, when he alludes to the subject of
his education, which he often does in his writings.   His
ardour was in fact over-stimulated; and late hours and
undue application as a boy laid the foundation of
weakness in his eyes, and otherwise injured his health.
"The study of humane letters," he says, "I seized
with such eagerness that, from the twelfth year of my
age, I scarcely ever went from my lessons to bed be-

* He was one of the Smectymnuan divines that Milton defended.

† The earliest is a letter to his old tutor Young, dated March 26,
1625, immediately after he had left school and entered at the university.

fore midnight; which, indeed, was the first cause of injury to my eyes, to whose natural weakness there were also added frequent headaches."

Along with his classical studies he found leisure to cultivate his native literature, and his poetic vein had already begun to flow freely in his own language. The poetry of the Elizabethan age, in its outburst of splendid production, could not but fascinate a youthful imagination such as his. His own admiring language, as well as the tastes of his schoolmaster,* admit of little doubt that he studied Spenser with delighted enthusiasm. But a poet of far less name—scarcely, indeed, remembered now—appears to have exercised the most direct influence over Milton at this time, and even permanently to have imbued his poetic thought with certain forms of imaginative suggestion. This was Du Bartas, a famous French poet of his day, whose *Divine Weeks and Works* had been translated by Sylvester and become widely popular. Du Bartas was a particular friend of King James, and had visited him in Scotland.† His popularity at Court had probably helped the circulation of his poem; but it had in itself also many claims to the interest of such an age, when intellectual excitement was running so strongly on religious topics. The high-sounding breadth and magnificence of its descriptions, the vague though barren grandeur of its conceptions—its bastard sublimity, in short—were just what was

---

* Old Gill evidently knew Spenser and admired him. See MASON'S *Milton*, p. 62.

† The readers of James Melville's Diary will remember a famous intellectual skirmish in St Mary's College, St Andrews, between Andrew Melville and Archbishop Adamson, at which Du Bartas and the King were present, and the judicious criticism of the former upon the encounter of the rival theologians.

likely to seize on the mind of a schoolboy,* even such
a schoolboy as Milton. In the two specimens which
have been preserved of his political genius at this time,
we can trace distinctly the influence of his study of
Du Bartas. These are two translations of Psalm 114
and 136, which were afterwards published by himself,
with the inscription that "they were done by the
author at fifteen years old." Johnson's somewhat
disparaging criticism of these pieces is well known;
but they are spirited and harmonious, showing the true,
clear, firm tone of genius, although the echo of Du
Bartas lingers in them.

Milton was entered, on the 12th of February 1624,
as a " lesser pensioner " at Christ's College in Cambridge.† His tutor was the Rev. William Chappel,
who became Provost of Trinity College, Dublin, and
afterwards Bishop of Cork. Chappel was a man of
great distinction in his college, especially as a disputant. He had displayed his powers with singular
triumph before King James in 1615, and even against
the King himself when he ventured, with his accustomed vanity, to take up the subject, and enter the
lists with the theological champion. James, with
unwonted good-nature, after getting the worse of an
argument, " professed his joy to find a man of so great

---

* Mr Masson has quoted a saying of Dryden's, in which he owns to the
same influence. " I can remember," he says, " when I was a boy,
I thought inimitable Spenser a mean poet in comparison of Sylvester's
Du Bartas, and was rapt in ecstacy when I read these lines :—

  ' Now when the winter's keener breath began
  To crystallise the Baltic ocean,
  To glaze the lakes and bridle up the floods,
  And periwig with wool the bald-pate woods.' "

† " Admissus est pensionarius minor, Feb. 12, 1624, sub Mro Chappel, *solvitque pro ingressu*, 10s.," says the catalogue of students for the
year.

talents, so good a subject." No tutor, according to
Fuller, "bred more or better pupils than Mr William
Chappel, so exact his care in their education." However this may have been, Milton and he did not suit
each other; for towards the end of his second academic
year they had a quarrel, so inveterate and disagree-
able as to necessitate Milton's removal from the university for some time. This is the famous incident
of his "rustication," of which Johnson has made such
unfavourable use. The incident, when looked into,
seems to have been of a comparatively trivial character,
not involving the loss of a term, if it partook of the
character of "rustication" at all; while the insinua-
tion, introduced with such an air of rotund reluctance,
but with such real relish—"I am ashamed to relate,
what I fear is true, that Milton was one of the last
students in either university that suffered the public
indignity of corporal correction"—does not rest on any
satisfactory evidence.*

To the close of the same year we are indebted for
the verses "On the Death of a Fair Infant Dying of a
Cough." The infant was his niece, the daughter of his
sister, who, just before the poet left home for college,
had been married to Mr Edward Philips, of the Crown
Office. The little one had scarcely come to excite its
parents' hopes when it was snatched away :—

> "O fairest flower ! no sooner blown than blasted—
>   Soft silken primrose, fading timelessly—
>   Summer's chief honour—if thou hadst outlasted
>   Bleak winter's force that made thy blossom dry."

There is, with some youthful pedantry, great sweetness

---

* The reader is referred to Mr Masson (pp. 135, 136), who has examined with the most conscientious care this as every other incident of
the poet's youthful career.

in the verses, and a lingering softness, very touching, as in the concluding verse—

> " Then thou, the mother of so sweet a child,
> Her false-imagined loss cease to lament,
> And wisely learn to curb thy sorrows wild,
> Think what a present thou to God hast sent,
> And render Him with patience what He lent.
> This if thou do, He will an offspring give,
> That till the world's last end shall make thy name to live."

In the remaining years of Milton's academic career he established a high reputation for scholarship; and whereas, at first, he seems to have been but little liked,* he became at length, if not popular, yet highly esteemed in his college. His nephew says, " He was loved and admired by the whole university, particularly by the fellows and most ingenious persons in his house." And he himself, in reply to an opponent, who, on the commencement of his controversial activity, when he had begun to stir the powerful dislike of the Prelatic party, accused him of having been " vomited out " of the university "after an inordinate and riotous youth," derisively thanks him for the slander; "for it hath given me," he continues, "an apt occasion to acknowledge publicly, with all grateful mind, that more than ordinary respect which I found above any of my equals at the hands of those courteous and learned men, the fellows of that college, wherein I spent some years: who, at my parting, after I had taken two degrees, as the manner is, signified many ways, how much better it would content that I would stay; as, by many letters full of kindness and loving respect, both before that time and long after, I was assured of their singular good affection towards me." †

* JOHNSON.   † *Apology for Smectymnuus.*

M

It was Milton's intention, on proceeding to Cambridge, to qualify himself for the Church. His father and his friends seem to have considered this the natural employment to which his great powers called him, and he himself entered into their intentions. " By the intentions of my parents and friends, I was destined, of a child, to the service of the Church, and in my own resolutions." When precisely his own mind began to waver in this resolution, we cannot say. His university experience had something to do with it; but the real cause was deeper, and lay, beyond doubt, in the profound opposition of his temper and character to the spirit then prevailing in the heads of the Church. Laud had been appointed Bishop of London in 1628, and during the next three years —coinciding with the concluding years of Milton's university course, when his mind would be naturally busy with his prospects, and he was perfectly competent to appreciate the full bearing of all that was going on around him—the new Court favourite, bishop, and privy councillor, was carrying out his schemes for the more Catholic remodelling of the Church with a high hand. These schemes were such as a mind like Milton's could only contemplate with disgust. The proud consciousness of genius which he already cherished, his lofty sympathy for all that was great and noble in moral sentiment, his intense seriousness of thought, and his contempt for mere forms and niceties of detail, must have made him regard such a system as Laud's with the whole dislike of his high and sensitive nature. This is sufficiently apparent in his own language, in the same passage from which we have already quoted. " Coming to some maturity of years, and perceiving what tyranny had invaded the

Church, that he who would take orders must subscribe
slave, and take an oath, without which, unless he
took with a conscience that he would relish, he must
either straight perjure or split his faith, I thought
better to prefer a blameless silence before the sacred
office of speaking, bought and begun with servitude
and forswearing." The subscriptions and oaths required from candidates for holy orders, he says here,
expressly repelled him; but it was not these formalities merely in themselves—for, in point of fact, he had
already, by his entrance into the university, complied
with all that they involved; it was such signs of bondage, viewed in the light of the dominant system, whose
aim was to exterminate all individuality and freedom
of conscience, and the nobleness of thought that alone
comes from these; it was the Prelatic "tyranny," in
short, which more than ever, and in worse forms,
had invaded the Church, that really moved him to
abandon it.

He does not seem, however, to have made up his
mind definitely before he left the university. The
process of struggle and dislike had begun, but it had
not yet terminated; for it is in the last year of his
university course that he is supposed to have written
to a friend as if he were still slowly carrying on his
preparations for the Church, "not taking thought of
being late, so it give advantage to be more *fit*." His
friend, who is unknown, had remonstrated with him
on his "too much love of learning, and his dreaming
away his years" in the arms of studious retirement,
rather than actively bestirring himself for the duties
of life; and he defends himself in a strain half-play-
ful, half-serious. Although he does not clearly explain, he hints that he had far deeper grounds than

any mere "endless delight of speculation" for his hesitation—grounds which had not yet turned him from his resolution, but were evidently in course of doing so.   In this same remarkable letter he encloses the well-known beautiful sonnet " On his being arrived at the age of twenty-three : "—

> " How soon hath Time, the subtle thief of youth,
>   Stolen on his wing my three-and-twentieth year !
> My hasting days fly on with full career,
> But my late spring no bud or blossom showeth.
> Perhaps my semblance might deceive the truth
> That I to manhood am arrived so near ;
> And inward ripeness doth much less appear
> Than some more timely-happy spirits endueth.
> Yet be it less or more, or soon or slow,
> It shall be still, in strictest measure, even
> To that same lot, however mean or high,
> Towards which Time leads me, and the will of Heaven.
> All is, if I have grace to use it so,
> As ever in my great Taskmaster's eye."

There is beneath the deprecating tone of the sonnet the same quiet consciousness of strength as in the letter, and especially the same grave moral seriousness.   His " inward ripeness" might much less appear, considering his years, than in the case of others; but even while his modesty suggests this thought, his heart tells him that the ripeness is there, and will show itself in full time ; and his proud integrity, and climbing earnestness, he knows, are equal to any task that may be assigned him.   There is now, and at all times, in Milton, a sustained self-conscious strength and dignity of purpose which shrinks from no inspection.

On leaving Cambridge, after taking his Master's degree in July 1632, Milton retired to his " father's country residence" at Horton, in Buckinghamshire. Hither the scrivener had sought a pleasant retreat

in which to spend his old age. The world had prospered with him; his daughter was well and happily
married, and his sons nearly educated, and looking
forward to settlement in the world; and so he sought
repose, in his declining years, from the cares of business, amidst the rural delights whose memory had
lingered in his heart from the days that he left the
village home in Oxfordshire. Horton is pleasantly
situated, not far from Windsor, in the district familiarly known in our political history as the Chiltern
Hundreds. A fertile landscape, well wooded and
watered, "russet lawns and fallows grey," and the
quiet rich meadow-pastures, such as the English eye
delights to look upon, formed the scene then as well
as now—the noble towers of Windsor, "bosomed high
in tufted trees," rising over it, and crowning it with
their magnificence. Here Milton spent the most part
of the next five years of his life, varied by occasional
journeys to London for the purpose of purchasing
books, or of "learning something new in mathematics
or in music."

There is no period of our poet's life that fixes itself
in such a fitting and felicitous picture before the mind
as these five years at Horton. It is the eminently poetical period of his life—poetical not merely in the luxuriant inspiration of the "Allegro" and "Penseroso," the
"Arcades," "Comus," and "Lycidas," but in the circumstances in which we image him to ourselves; for
without drawing upon our mere fancy, we cannot but
conceive him as a loving and delighted student of nature
in those years. He himself, indeed, says nothing of his
conscious delight in nature. In his allusions to this
period he speaks rather of his hard and continued
studies. "In continued reading, I deduced the affairs

of the Greeks to the time when they ceased to be
Greeks." But, however busy with his historical studies,
his imagination must have been also intensely quickened by the outward world around him. At every
pore of his sensitive being he must have drunk in
deep draughts of natural beauty, and through every
sense garnered up treasures of imagery for exquisite
use ; for his poems of this period, especially the
"Allegro" and "Penseroso," show a pure, full, and
unrestrained abandonment to outward impressions,
quite singular with him. The most charming complacency in Nature is united to the most vehement
and passionate sympathies with it. His soul goes
forth in revel with its moods—now gay with its smiles,
now sad with its gloom, now singing in a clear heaven
of light, and now "most musical, most melancholy."
There is little or none of the self-conscious restraint,
reflective subtlety, and elaborate application that may
be traced in his muse both before and afterwards.
For example, in his ode on the "Nativity," composed
before leaving college, as well as in his college exercises, we see strongly at work the didactic elements
of his mind forecasting a high and solemn lesson in
every play of thought ; and this moral intent—this
divine aim—was deeply implanted in the very heart
of Milton's genius, and gives its complexion to all
his most characteristic writings. But now, for a while,
in his fresh and free communion with nature, he is
able to forget this moral spirit, and to surrender himself to the mere wayward impulses of sensuous feeling
as they stir him. It is as if he had made a pause in
the serious and thoughtful purposes of his life, and
given himself up for a season to an entranced enjoyment of external life and beauty.

The sonnet on "May Morning," which opens this series of his poems, strikes the key-note of the whole:—

> "Now the bright morning star, day's harbinger,
> Comes dancing from the East, and leads with her
> The flowery May, who from her green lap throws
> The yellow cowslip and the pale primrose.
> Hail, bounteous May ! thou dost inspire
> Mirth and faith, and warm desire.
> Woods and groves are of thy dressing,
> Hill and dale doth boast thy blessing ;
> Thus we salute thee with our early song,
> And welcome thee, and wish thee long."

The song of the nightingale warbling at eve, "when all the woods are still ;" the night raven singing beneath the "jealous wings" of the "brooding darkness ;" the lark beginning her flight and "startling the dull night" "from her watch-tower in the skies ;" the "dappled dawn," "the frolic wind," "breathing the spring," and "the rocking winds piping loud ;" the great sun

> "Robed in flames and amber light,
> The clouds in thousand liveries dight ;"

the morn "riding near her highest noon ;" and

> "as if her head she bowed,
> Stooping through a fleecy cloud ;"

the "upland hamlets, with many a youth and maid

> "Dancing in the checkered shade ;"

and the evening stories when the dance is done, spiced by the "nut-brown ale ;" the whistle of the ploughman o'er the furrowed land ; the blithe song of the milk-maid ; the mower whetting his scythe, and the shepherd telling his tale,

> "Under the hawthorn in the dale."

Such are mere fragments of the series of imagery that

meets us in "L'Allegro" and "Il Penseroso," all gathered
from the daily scenes and sounds surrounding the poet
in Horton, filling his heart with gladness, colouring
his imagination with the most varied hues, and moulding his utterances to the most perfect music. There
are nowhere in our language such charming nature-
pieces—such breathings of harmonious responsiveness
to the checkered influences of the external world as
they play over the soul, and draw it now to mirth and
now to melancholy, now to rapture and now to sadness. It requires an effort of thought to realise the
Milton of later years in those effusions, with scarce a
plan, without the least trace of moral lesson; like the
continuous snatches of a melodious spirit swayed by
the sensitive impulses of the hour, and catching up,
by the mere affinity of imaginative contrast—by the
links of mere vagrant association—the successive pictures that evoke and express its feeling. They have
none of the classicality of his "Ode"—of its severe
majesty, its spiritual aim. They are the mere war-
blings of a rich-souled child of nature, giving forth, in
bursts of lyrical sweetness, the natural impressions
which have sunk into his being and wakened it to
song.

In the "Comus" and the "Lycidas" we have the
same full, vivid, and rich appreciation of nature, but
not the same degree of abandonment to its impulses.
There is much more of ethical and didactic seriousness
in both. The moral austerity of the lady in "Comus"
rising in "sacred vehemence" against the "unhallowed"
suggestions of the Bacchanal—the whole idea of the
poem, which is essentially ethical, notwithstanding its
light lyrical structure and the sensuous fulness of its
imagery—remind us of Milton's more characteristic

spirit; while the pensive grandeur of the "Lycidas," with all its lingering and softened music, has its almost perfect harmony and blended pathos of feeling broken by a passage where we catch loudly the voice of the stern Puritan moralist :—

> " Last came, and last did go,
> The pilot of the Galilean lake :
> Two massy keys he bore of metals twain ;
> The golden opes, the iron shuts amain.
> He shook his mitred locks, and stern bespake :
> ' How well could I have spared for thee, young swain,
> Enow of such, as for their bellies' sake
> Creep, and intrude, and climb into the fold !
> Of other care they little reckoning make
> Than how to scramble at the shearers' feast,
> And shove away the worthy bidden guest.
>
> .   .   .   .
>
> And, when they list, their lean and flashy songs
> Grate on their scrannel pipes of wretched straw :
> The hungry sheep look up and are not fed ;
> But, swoln with wind and the rank mist they draw,
> Rot inwardly, and foul contagion spread.' "

The difference between the stern strength, the vehement and even harsh earnestness of these lines, and the gentle natural pathos, the sweet-tempered tenderness of those almost immediately following—

> " Bring the rathe primrose that forsaken dies,
> The tufted crow-toe and pale jessamine,
> The white pink, and the pansy freaked with jet,
> The glowing violet,
> The musk-rose, and the well-attired woodbine,
> With cowslips wan that hang the pensive head,
> And every flower that sad embroidery wears :
> Bid amaranthus all his beauty shed,
> And daffodillies fill their cups with tears,
> To strew the laureat herse where Lycid lies "—

presents in interesting connection the two main and contrasted features of Milton's genius—severe, self-

contained seriousness, and surrendering passionateness
—the conscious reflectiveness of the moralist, and the
rich abounding sensitiveness of the poet.

During those happy years at Horton we see him
almost entirely as the gentle poetic dreamer. His imagination, fed by the rural sights and sounds amidst
which he lived, burst into its most beautiful bloom.
The joyous fulness of his ripening manhood, as it
were, filled up his whole activity. But we detect in
such a passage as that from the " Lycidas " how the
austere and polemical side of his nature was vigorous
and working beneath all the rich manifestations of the
imaginative and poetical. The Milton of Horton, as he
apparently dreams away his years in studious leisure
and the love of nature, is still the Puritan, although
we can just trace, as it were, the grave Puritan eyes
looking forth from a face of bright natural beauty, and
tresses of luxuriant culture. The eyes are Puritan
eyes as we steadily gaze into them, though all else is
artistic, imaginative, unpuritan.

On the 3d of April 1637 Milton's mother died, and
in the spring of the following year he set out for the
Continent. He had probably for some time cherished
this project, and his mother's death, by breaking the
tie which bound him to Horton, may have set him
free to carry it out. He arrived in Paris in May 1638,
furnished with a letter of advice—an " elegant epistle,"
he terms it—from Sir Henry Wotton. Through Sir
Henry or others he was introduced to Lord Scudamore,
the English ambassador, who received him very cour-
teously ; and what was still more gratifying to him,
took pains to make him acquainted with Grotius, then
ambassador in Paris for the Court of Sweden. The
great Dutchman was naturally an object of regard to

Milton ; and Grotius, on his part, seems to have recognised the worth and genius of the young Englishman. "He took," says Phillips, "the visit kindly, and gave him entertainment suitable to his worth and the high commendations he had heard of him." Grotius was then busy with a great scheme of comprehension for the Lutheran and English Churches. He had broached the subject to Laud, but with little success. No doubt he would discourse of its advantages with Milton—we may please ourselves at least with this thought; but he was not likely to receive much more encouragement from him than he had done from the English primate, though from very opposite reasons. The mild latitudinarianism of the Dutch jurist and divine, his Arminian sympathies and spirit of ecclesiastical indifference, were not likely at this date to commend themselves to one moved with disgust at Prelatic tyranny, and who, even in Italy, could not hold his tongue on the subject of Popery.

Milton's stay in Paris was short—only " for some days," according to his own statement. He took his departure towards Italy, furnished with letters of introduction to English merchants along his proposed route. He seems to have taken his journey leisurely, probably by way of Lyons and the Rhone to Marseilles, and thence to Nice, where he took packet for Genoa. From Genoa he went, also by sea, to Leghorn, and thence to Pisa and Florence. Here he remained for " two months."

It is easy to imagine the delighted enthusiasm with which Milton would enter Italy. And, coming after his sojourn amid quiet English landscapes, the change to its brilliant skies, and the southern luxuriance of its natural life, may have been among the most fruitful

and enriching sources of his enjoyment. His poetic
culture certainly bears traces of the one influence, no
less than of the other. Yet, so far as we can gather
from his own statement,* which is the only basis of
our knowledge of his Italian journey, it was the Italy
not so much of natural beauty as of scholarly and historical association that interested Milton. Florence,
as the great centre of Italian culture, was the first place
where he tarried. In this city, which he says he had
always regarded above others for the elegance of its
language and the distinction of its men of genius, he
found himself for a while in a congenial home ; and
he recalls as an imperishable memory the pleasant intercourse he had there with its great scholars.   " There,
immediately," he says, " I contracted the acquaintance
of many truly noble and learned men, whose private
academies (valuable alike for the cultivation of polite
letters, and the preservation of friendships) I constantly
frequented. The memory of you, Jacopo Gaddi ; of you,
Carlo Dati ; of you, Frescobaldi, Coltellini, Bonmattei,
Chementelli, Francini, and of several others, always
grateful and pleasant to me, time shall never destroy."
With these worthies he entered into the most free and
unreserved literary associations. At their meetings or
academies he gave specimens of his poetical powers
by reciting some of the Latin poems he had already
composed.†   They complimented him in return.
Count Carlo Dati eulogised him in a Latin address,
and Francini wrote an Italian ode in his praise. Another litterateur, Antonio Malatesti, whose name does
not occur in his enumeration, presented him with a

---

* *Defensio Secunda.*

† " Under twenty, or thereabouts," he says. He shows a singular
anxiety at all times to claim any merit arising from the youthfulness of
his compositions.

manuscript copy of his poems, inscribed with a flattering dedication to himself. What probably interested
Milton still more than these literary pleasantries of
intercourse—he seems to have talked freely and fully
with these friends on the subject of religious and intellectual liberty. In his "Areopagitica," he says,
in allusion to this, " I could recount what I have seen
and heard in other countries, where this kind of inquisition tyrannises ; where I have sat among their
learned men (for their honour I had), and been counted
happy to be born in such a place of philosophic freedom as they supposed England was, while themselves
did nothing but bemoan the servile condition into
which learning amongst them was brought ; that this
was it which had damped the glory of Italian wits ;
that nothing had been there written now these many
years but flattery and fustian."

An allusion in the same passage lets us know that
he also visited, while in Florence, the famous Galileo,
grown old and blind, and a " prisoner to the Inquisition for thinking in astronomy otherwise than the
Franciscan and Dominican licensers thought." The
impression made upon his mind was evidently a strong
and lasting one,* and served to deepen his hatred of
ecclesiastical tyranny.

The glory of Italian literature, as well as of Italian
art, had perished before the time of Milton's visit, as
the above passage indicates to have been the feeling of
the Italians themselves. With the death of Tasso in
the end of the previous century (1595), their last

---

* His remembrance of Galileo remained to suggest an image in *Paradise Lost*, Book I., 289, 290—

> " The moon, whose orb
> Through open glen the Tuscan artist views,
> At evening from the top of Fesole."

great poet had passed away ; and if something more
than " flattery or fustian " still lingered, the real life of
Italian genius was yet gone.　The very picture suggested by the allusions of Milton—the literary academies which everywhere prevailed—the sonnet-writing,
and panegyrising, and epigrammatical embellishing,
which were the great staple of literary produce, all
point to a period of intellectual decadence.　Amidst
these small and rather wearying flatteries, it is interesting and touching to think of the genius of England,
still in its lusty youth, and ripening into one of its
noblest expressions, offering its homage in Milton's
person to the weakened and departing genius of
Italy.

From Florence Milton proceeded by way of Siena
to Rome, where he remained about the same time that
he had done at Florence.　The "antiquity and ancient
fame" of the city detained him, although he does not
seem to have formed so many friends here, or to have
lived a life of such free literary and social intercourse
as at Florence.　He makes special mention, however,
of one friend, from whom he experienced such kindness as to draw from him afterwards a long letter in
acknowledgment.　This was Lucas Holstein, a German,
and Protestant by education, but who had entered
into the service of the nephew of the Pope, Cardinal
Francesco Barberini, and become one of the librarians
of the Vatican.　Milton describes in his letter how,
going to the great library without any introduction, he
was received by Holstein, who had heard of him, with
the "utmost courtesy," and conducted by him to the
museum, and allowed to inspect the splendid collection of books and MSS.　Nor did Holstein's kindness
stop here.　By his influence Milton was invited to a

great entertainment and concert at the house of the
cardinal, his patron, who honoured the poet on the
occasion by waiting in person at the door of the saloon
to receive him, and, *almost* laying hold of him by the
hand, introduced him in a "truly most honourable
manner."

It was probably on this occasion, as his biographers
have conjectured, that he heard the famous Leonora
Baroni sing, to whom he has addressed Latin epigrams,
expressive of the delight with which he heard her.
Her "very voice sounds God," he says, in language
more grand than reverential.

Having completed his stay at Rome, he set out for
Naples. On his way he met a "certain eremite,"
who, evidently captivated by the intelligence of the
young Englishman, introduced him, on his arrival at
Naples, to John Baptist Manso, Marquis of Villa, the
most distinguished of Neapolitans, the friend and biographer of Tasso, now nearly eighty years of age, but
as keenly interested as ever in genius and poetry.
Milton warmly expresses his obligations to him. "As
long as I stayed," he says, "I experienced from him
the most friendly attentions. He accompanied me
to the various parts of the city, and took me over the
viceroy's palace, and came more than once to my
lodgings to visit me. At my departure he excused
himself for not having been able to show me the
farther attentions he desired in that city, because that
I would not be more silent in the matter of religion."
A kindly, judicious old man! who would fain have
been of more service to the young poet, whom he
evidently admired and liked, if he had only been more
cautious with his tongue. Milton fully appreciated
his kindliness, and showed his appreciation, after the

accustomed manner, by an address in Latin hexame-
ters, in which, in the name of Clio and of great Phœ-
bus, he wishes his "Father Manso a long ago of
health," and prays that it may be his own lot to have
such a friend as Manso had been to Tasso, should he
ever be able to carry out his aspirations to write, as
the Italian poet had done, a great epic.* Manso
repaid the compliment by the present of two richly
ornamented cups, with an affixed epigram, quaint and
graphic, in allusion to the old story of the beautiful
Anglic youths and Gregory the Great.†

It was Milton's original intention to have prolonged
his journey to Greece, but the news of affairs in England stayed his farther progress. "While I was desirous," he says, "to cross into Sicily and Greece, the
sad news of civil war coming from England called me
back; for I considered it disgraceful that, while my
countrymen were fighting at home for liberty, I should
be travelling abroad at ease for intellectual purposes."
Accordingly he retraced his steps to Rome, unheeding
the warnings which had been conveyed to him by the
English merchants at Naples, who had learned by
letters that "snares were being laid for him by the
English Jesuits if he should return to Rome." His
freedom of speech seemed likely to prove dangerous
as well as inconvenient to him. Some of the bold
sentiments that he had vented on his former visit had
probably been repeated in ecclesiastical ears. Threat-

* Not *Paradise Lost*, however, of which, as yet, he has no thoughts,
but an epic calling back "our native kings and Arthur's stirring wars."

† "Joannes Baptista Mansus, Marquis of Villa, Neapolitan, to John
Milton, Englishman.

"Mind, form, grace, face, and morals are perfect. If but thy head were,
Then not Anglic alone, but truly angelic thou'dst be."

MASSON'S *Milton*, 708.

enings had been heard against him, and his friends
took the alarm; but the Jesuits, after all, did not
take the trouble to molest him. He was allowed to
enter Rome again and depart safely, although he takes
care to assure us that he made no concealment of his
opinions. "What I was, if any one asked, I concealed from no one. If any one in the very city of
the Pope attacked the orthodox religion, I, as before,
for a second space of nearly two months, freely defended it."*

He returned also to Florence to regale himself
once more with the congenial society that he had
left behind him there; and it is supposed to have
been on this second visit to the fair Tuscan city, or,
as some conjecture, as he passed through Bologna on
his way to Venice, that he made the acquaintance of
a Bolognese lady, "young, gentle, loving," from whom
he had great difficulty in tearing himself away. We
know nothing of this love affair save what he himself
tells us in his five Italian sonnets and single canzone
on the subject; and these give the inner history more
than the external circumstances of his passion. From
one of these sonnets, however (that addressed to his
friend Diodati), we learn that the lady was a genuine
Italian beauty, "with no tresses of gold, or cheeks of
vermeil tincture, but the new type of a foreign beauty,
of carriage high and honourable, and in whose eyes
there beamed the serene splendour of a lovely black,
while her song was so bewitching that it might lure
from its middle hemisphere the labouring moon." He
who used to "scorn love and laugh at his snares," had
now fallen and become entangled in them. The wonder

---

* This was his rule, he says; but he did not, of his "own accord,
introduce into these places conversation about religion."

N

is that, with his poetic heart and florid fulness of manly beauty, he had escaped so long; and, indeed, it may be doubted whether this be the first gleam of a tender interest in his life.* Unhappily he was destined to become too reflectively conscious of this interest, and of the relations and consequences which spring out of it.

Having visited Venice, and shipped homewards there a collection of books and music which he had been diligently making in the course of his journey, he returned across the Alps to Geneva, where he remained for some time. Of this stage of his tour we know less than of any other, although the home of Calvinistic Protestantism must have had singular attractions for Milton. To what extent his residence in it may have served to develop his ecclesiastical views, and to deepen his increasing dislike to the Church of England, it would be difficult to say. The great minds to whom he would most naturally have deferred had all gone by this time. Even the elder Turretin was dead some years before.† His chief associate was John Diodati, one of the professors of theology, and the uncle

---

* See MASSON's *Life*, p. 160. Every one, too, knows the story of the young foreign lady who, passing in the neighbourhood of Cambridge a spot where Milton had lain down and fallen asleep under a tree, was so struck with his beauty that she approached to look at him, and left in his hand unperceived (as she thought) some Italian lines written in pencil expressive of her admiration; and how Milton, on awaking, and being informed who had placed the lines in his hand, conceived a violent passion for the fair unknown, and afterwards went to Italy in quest of her, and dreamed of her to the last as his vanished ideal. The story, of course, is mythical, as in the case of many other poets, of the visit of the Spirit of Truth and Beauty to our poet, and his unattainable search after its full enjoyment. The later facts of the Bolognese lady and his Italian visit probably gave some of its colouring to the story.

Milton's delicate and blonde beauty, it may be added, was a common topic of remark while he was at the university, so much so that he was called "The Lady of his College."   † 1631.

of the young friend to whom one of his Italian sonnets
was addressed. Diodati was an able and accomplished man, but there is no trace of his having exercised any peculiar influence upon Milton. The nephew
had been his form-fellow at St Paul's school. Their
souls had been knit together as those only of young
men are at school and college ; and he now learned
with deep grief of his friend's death during his absence
in Italy. The friendly heart* had been cold in death,
even while he had been recalling its sympathy with
him in his love anxieties.

From Geneva Milton returned by the " same route as
before" to Paris, and reached England about mid-
summer 1639, having been absent "a year and three
months, more or less." He closes his own brief narrative of his journey with the memorable words, " Here
again I take God to witness that I lived in all those
places where so much license is permitted, free and
untouched by any kind of vice and profligacy, having
this thought constantly before me, that though I
might escape the eyes of men, I could not escape
those of God."

On his return, he settled in London. Of Horton
we learn no more, and are left to conjecture that his
father had disposed in the interval of his pleasant
residence there, the *paternum rus*, and gone to live
with his second son, Cristopher, with whom we find
him some time after this at Reading. At first Milton
lived in lodgings, but very soon he removed to a house
of his own, " sufficiently large," as he says, " for himself and his books." This house was in Aldersgate
Street, and stood at the end of an entry. It was one
of many houses of the sort at this time in London,

---

* *Pectus amicus nostri*, says Milton to Diodati in one of his letters.

called "garden houses," removed by their position
from the noise of the streets, and was, as his nephew
says, "the fitter for his turn, by the reason of the
privacy, besides that there were few streets in London
more free from noise than that." Here our poet
settled with his books, delighted to resume his "inter-
mitted studies," * and with a cheerful feeling that the
national excitement, now running at its height in the
metropolis, was working out ends dear to his sense
of liberty and his convictions of religion. His own
time of action had not yet come.

In betaking himself to a life of studious retirement
and educational activity, Milton did exactly what became him; for it was not in outward activity, but
in the realm of thought, that he was destined to influence the development of the revolution. He knew his
own function sufficiently; and Johnson's sneer, therefore, about his "vapouring away his patriotism in a
private boarding-school," is as inapplicable as it is ill-
natured. He took his two nephews to live with him,
and received a few more pupils, sons of his friends,
to whose education he devoted himself. It was an
employment in which he himself never could have
felt any shame, whatever some of his biographers
may have done; and Johnson only betrays his own
soreness of feeling in connection with his early and
less happy employment in the same capacity, by
the manner in which he speaks of this portion of
Milton's life.

The course of study which he travelled over with
his pupils was a very extensive and somewhat remarkable one,—the principle of which was to com-
municate useful information, along with the know-

* *Def. Secunda.*

ledge of Greek and Latin. He read with them accordingly, with a few exceptions, not what are usually called the classics, but such writers as the four Scriptores, *Rei Rusticæ*, Cato, Varro, Palladius, and Columella; Pliny's natural history and Celsus; and in Greek, such poets as Aratus and Apollonius Rhodius.* In addition, he instructed them in mathematics and astronomy, and entered with them on a course of theological study in Hebrew and Chaldaic, "so far as to go through the Pentateuch, and gain an entrance into the Targum;" and in Syriac, so far as to read some portions of St Matthew's Gospel in that language. On Sundays he read with them in the Greek Testament, and dictated parts of a system of divinity, mainly extracted from the Dutch theologians. Whatever we may otherwise think of such a system of instruction, it shows a reach and comprehensiveness quite Miltonic. It has an air of independence too, that in this, as in other matters, was very characteristic of him. Looking back with some degree of contempt upon parts of his own scholastic training, and proudly confident in his own judgment, he was exactly the man to carry out a new system, without any regard to the opinions or prejudices of others. In education, as in social life and government, Milton was naturally a theorist, reasoning out his plans with consistent and dogmatic earnestness from certain main principles.

Aubrey describes him, in his intercourse with his pupils, as "severe on the one hand," yet also "most familiar and free in his conversation;" exacting, so far as application on their part was concerned, yet freely

---

* These works, Cato, Varro, &c., it will be seen, reappear in his own *Tractate on Education.*

according to them the benefit of his advice and assistance. He worked hard along with them, and shared
the frugality of their meals. Once in three or four
weeks, however, he gave himself a "gaudy day,"
which he spent with some young friends, the chief of
whom were Mr Alphry and Mr Miller, "the beaux of
those times," says Phillips, "but nothing nearly so
bad as those nowadays."

But Milton had scarcely begun his studies with his
pupils when he felt himself also called to other and
more important work. Although his patriotism had
not prompted him on his first return to enter actively
into the contest between King and Parliament, yet he
was far too deeply interested in the contest, and had
far too thorough a penetration of its real causes, long
to remain silent. As he himself afterwards said, in
the noblest of his early prose writings on the subject,[*] his knowledge was a "burden" to him. He
felt that God had given him, "in more than the
scantiest measure," to know something distinctly of
him and of his true worship, and that the obligation
lay on him to speak out what he knew. It was the
condition of the Church that now, as before, chiefly
occupied his attention. He and many others felt
that it was the prelatical tyranny of recent years that,
more than anything else, had afflicted the country.
The ecclesiastical clique that had ruled the King, and,
by its base and petty tyrannies, insulted the national
Protestant feeling, had long been the object of his
detestation. This detestation had been augmented
into an anti-Episcopal feeling of the strongest character, due in some degree, perhaps, to his residence
in Geneva. At length his convictions became so

* Second Book of the *Reason of Church Government against Prelaty.*

urgent on the subject that he could no longer forbear
to utter them. He thought how miserable an account
he would be able to give of himself, "what stories he
should hear within himself all his life after, of discourage and reproach," if he did not assist the Church
of God in her struggle with her enemies. The voice
of rebuke would be heard by him saying, "Thou hadst
the diligence, the parts, the language of a man, if a
vain subject were to be adorned or beautified; but
when the cause of God and His Church was to be
pleaded, for which purpose that tongue was given
thee that thou hast, God listened if He could hear thy
voice among his zealous servants, but thou wert dumb
as a beast."

Under the influence of such feelings, Milton prepared himself for the long course of polemical warfare
in which he was to spend the most part of the next
twenty years of his life. With regret he quitted temporarily the high intentions which he had nourished,
of doing something for his country's literature which
it would "not willingly let die." Proudly, and with
that grand consciousness of "his own parts," which was
always remarked in him, he speaks of his plans and
the divine consecration of his genius. "That which
the greatest and choicest wits of Athens, Rome, or
Modern Italy, and these Hebrews of old, did for their
country, I, in my proportion with this, over and above
of being a Christian, might do for mine." This had
been his thought; but for the present these intentions
were "plucked from him by an abortive and fore-
dated discovery." His "garland and singing-robes
must be laid aside for a time;" he must clothe himself
with the garments of controversy; but he promises to
resume his higher function as far "as life and free

leisure will extend," when the land shall have "en-
franchised herself from this impertinent yoke of prelaty, under whose inquisitorious and tyrannical duncery
no free and splendid wit can flourish." He was, indeed, to keep his promise to resume the singing-robes,
long laid aside, and " soaring in the high reason of his
fancies," to take a loftier poetic flight than he had yet
done, but in far other circumstances from those he
fondly anticipated!

The polemical writings which Milton now published
in rapid succession against Episcopacy, constitute the
first of the three divisions into which his controversial writings divide themselves. A bulky pamphlet
in two books, addressed to a friend under the title of
*Reformation in England, and the causes that hitherto
have hindered it*, opens the series in 1641. This is a
vehement attack upon Prelacy as unscriptural and
unprimitive. All his long-harboured hatred to the
system comes out in it. The comparison of the early
church of Ignatius, and even of Cyprian, is pointed
by him to the disadvantage of its later Popish and
prelatic assumptions. "Then did the spirit of unity
and meekness inspire and animate every joint and
sinew of the mystical body; but now the gravest and
worthiest minister, a true bishop of his fold, shall be
reviled and ruffled by an insulting and only canon-
wise prelate, as if he were some slight, paltry companion; and the people of God, redeemed and washed
with Christ's blood, and dignified with so many glorious titles of saints and sons in the Gospel, are now
no better reputed than impure ethnics and lay dogs.
Stones, and pillars, and crucifixes, have now the honour and the alms due to Christ's loving members.
The table of communion now becomes a table of sepa-

ration, stands like a walled platform upon the brow
of the quire, fortified with bulwarks, and barricaded
to keep off the profane touch of the laics; while the
obscene and surfeited priest scruples not to paw and
mammoc the sacramental bread as familiarly as his
tavern biscuit." Such an extract will convey to the
reader a sufficiently lively impression of the strength
and vehemence of spirit which distinguish this first
polemical writing of our author.

Bishop Hall entered the lists as the champion of
his order, and published, in the same year, *An humble
Remonstrance in favour of Episcopacy.* To this an ·
immediate reply appeared, the joint production of five
Puritan ministers,[*] the initials of whose names formed
the word *Smectymnuus,* under which appellation the
work appeared.

Archbishop Usher joined in the fray, and devoted
his great learning and patience of inquiry to the investigation of the right government of the Church, and
the defence of Episcopacy against the writers who
had attacked it. The five Puritan ministers were no
match for the tolerant and enlightened prelate, whose
calm wisdom and profound information left them far
behind in the discussion. This consciousness, besides
his own interest in one of the Smectymnuans (his old
tutor, Thomas Young), is supposed to have drawn
Milton again into the field. He felt that he had
thrown down the gauntlet in his first treatise, and
that it behoved him to come to the rescue in a strife
which he had provoked, and regarding which he felt
so deeply. Two further writings accordingly appeared
from his pen still in the same year—the first entitled,

[*] Stephen Marshall, Edmund Calamy, Thomas Young (Milton's tutor),
Matthew Newcome, and William Spenston.

*Of Prelatical Episcopacy, and whether it may be de-
duced from the Apostolical times by virtue of those
Testimonies which are alleged to that purpose in some
late Treatises, one of which goes under the name of
James, Archbishop of Armagh ;* the second, *The reason
of Church Government urged against Prelaty,* in two
books. The latter is a somewhat extended treatise,
discussing the various points of the argument under
successive heads and chapters, and containing, in the
preface to the second book, that noble and touching
account of his early studies and literary aims, which
has been so often quoted.

Even these works, however, did not exhaust Milton's
labours for the year. He published, further, *Animadversions upon Bishop Hall's Reply to Smectymnuus.*
Having once taken up the pen, he did not let it rest
in his hands. The labour was congenial to him,
although he says he did it "not without a sad and
unwilling anger, not without many hazards." In the
present case he appears to feel that he has gone somewhat beyond the bounds of grave controversy. But
a bishop acts upon him for the present with a magical
force of indignation. His invective dilates, and his
scorn lashes itself into a wilder fury, whenever the
object crosses his intellectual vision. Even a man
so worthy as Hall, is only "an enemy to truth and
his country's peace," and this all the more that "he
is conceited to have a voluble and smart fluence of
tongue." "I suppose, and more than suppose," he
adds, "it will be nothing disagreeing from Christian
meekness to handle such a one in a rougher accent,
and to send home his haughtiness well besprinkled
with his own holy water."

His freedom and roughness of speech called forth

a swift and unsparing reply, written, as was supposed, by a son of the bishop. This reply bore the title of *A Modest Confutation against a Slanderous and Scurrilous Libel*, and retorted Milton's animadversions by a vehement and somewhat disgraceful attack upon his character. Stung by the "rancour of an evil tongue," he published his *Apology for Smectymnuus*, the most elevated of all his writings on this subject, especially in the introduction, where he replies to the assault upon his character, in a tone of disdainful magnanimity very characteristic. Whenever he strikes the chord of his own feelings, and the personal or moral interest of his theme sways him, it is observable how his tone rises, how his thoughts attain a loftier sweep, and his language shows a richer and grander strength. In fair argument,—in detailed rejoinder,—he is frequently weak and coarse. His weapons are, as it were, too heavy for him; and he makes rough and aimless gashes at his adversary, rather than adroitly disables him. His inferiority to Hall in light fence, in a "coy and flirting style," as he contemptuously calls it, was evidently rather conscious to himself, although it was a consciousness far from humiliating to him. With the proud scorn of a great mind, he knew that, right or wrong, on small matters, he had the highest and most comprehensive view of the moral bearings of the question.

Upon the whole, these earlier prose writings of Milton, although of little critical value in the determination of the special controversy, are grand specimens of Puritanical argument. Puritanical they are to their very core,—in the style of their reasoning,—in the intensity of their feeling,—in the harsh bitterness of their assault upon the catholic forms of the Church,

—in their almost total want of historical appreciation—in everything save, perhaps, the magnificent
luxuriance and swell of style, with gleams of the
old Horton radiance upon it. The fundamental principle of Puritanism as to Church government—that
it is "platformed in the Bible,"* is almost everywhere
assumed by him as beyond question; or when it is
argued, as in the two opening chapters of *The Reason of Church Government*, — argued as if it were a
foregone principle upon which little time need be
wasted. He says expressly in his first pamphlet of
Reformation in England, " If, therefore, the constitution of the Church be already set down by divine pre-
script, as *all sides confess*, then can she not be a hand-
maid to wait on civil commodities and respects,"—a
singular enough statement in the view of Hooker's
great work, with which he shows his acquaintance in
a later writing† of the same year. But while pro-
fessedly adhering to this principle, the very language
in which he expounds it rises above it. The formal is
continually running with him into the moral—the
technical into the spiritual‡—and the latter element, as
may be easily imagined in a mind like Milton's, by-
and-by gained the ascendancy, and left far behind his
earlier visions of a definite church polity " taught in
the Gospel."

More even than the argumentative principles of
these treatises, the intense anti-prelatical bitterness
which they display, and the dogmatic unhistorical
tone in which they estimate Catholicism, mark their
Puritanism. The harsh and intemperate coarseness of

* *The Reason of Church Government*, chap. i.

† *Ibid.*, chap. ii.

‡ *Ibid.*, chaps. ii. and iii.—in the latter, when he replies to Usher's
argument drawn from the Pattern of the Law.

language in which Milton almost uniformly speaks of "bishops" is a singular illustration of the times. They are a "tyrannical crew, and corporation of impostors that have blinded and abused the world so long." * Their "mouths cannot open without the strong breath and loud stench of avarice, simony, and sacrilege, embezzling the treasury of the Church on painted and gilded walls of temples, wherein God hath testified to have no delight; warming their palace kitchens, and from thence their unctuous and epicurean paunches, with the alms of the blind, the lame, the impotent, the aged, the orphan, the widow."† Their supposed greed and gluttony is a special and constantly recurring subject of attack. ‡ "What a plump endowment," he says, "would brotherly equality, matchless temperance, frequent fasting, incessant prayer and preaching, be to the many-benefice-gaping mouth of a prelate! what a relish it would give to his canary-sucking and swan-eating palate!"§ "A race of Capernaïtans," he elsewhere exclaims, "senseless of divine doctrine, and capable only of loaves and belly-cheer!" ‖ "A man shall commonly find more savoury knowledge in one layman than in a dozen of cathedral prelates."

This coarse vehemence of tone, wherever the image of well-endowed Prelacy crosses his argument, can only be understood or at all excused when we remember that it was Prelacy that seemed to Milton, more than anything else, to have "filled the land with confusion and violence." The Laudian bishops seemed to him

* *Of Reformation*, book i.　　　　† *Ibid.*

‡ It is remarkable how constantly this line of attack runs through the anti-Episcopal polemics of the seventeenth century. Some of the expressions in which it is conveyed, in the Scottish Presbyterian writings, are equally ludicrous and nauseous in their plainness and strength.

§ *Of Reformation*, book i.　　　　‖ *Animadversions, &c.*

all that he painted them. The institution with which they were identified looked to his eyes a mere " tyrannical duncery," a mere " tetter of impurity," without ancient dignity or catholic beauty. Calvin* does not take a more extremely polemical view of the rise of Catholicism, or manifest more incapacity in appreciating the circumstances of its historical growth, and its conservative fitness for great practical ends. He can only see fraud, avarice, faithless and tyrannical ambition, in the picture which history brings before him. The dogmatic present obscured all fair and discerning appreciation of the Catholic past. In this respect Milton was a Puritan, scarcely, if at all, above the popular level of his age. The same spirit shows itself in his scornful contempt of the Liturgy, and his abuse of what he calls " Antiquity,"—the Patristic writings, namely, of the fourth and fifth century. The one still " serves to all the abominations of the antiChristian temple," and " while some men cease not to admire its incomparable frame, he cannot but admire as fast what they think is become of judgment and taste in other men, that they can hope to be heard without laughter ;"† the other is an " undigested heap and fry of authors." " Whatsoever time, or the heedless hand of blind chance, hath drawn down from of old to this present in her huge drag-net, whether fish or seaweed, shells or shrubs, unpicked, unchosen, those are the fathers." ‡

In all this Milton shows that while he had imbibed the moral spirit and Christian earnestness of Puritanism, he had also learned its dogmatic narrowness. The reaction against Laudism had driven him to an excess

---

* *Institutes*, book iv. cap. 6, 7.
† *Apology for Smectymnuus*, sect. xi.   ‡ *Of Prelatical Episcopacy*.

of opinionativeness, and of passionate and resentful feeling on the other side. He had lost the balance of candid judgment on the great topics in dispute: few men had it in his day. In knowledge and argumentative clearness he must be placed below such men as Usher or even Hall. There is a wild unfairness in him that provokes sympathy for his opponents, and which is felt to be but ill sustained by his irregular and loosely-compacted masses of argument. Yet there is also in his very unfairness a strength of moral indignation, and crowning his most straggling reasonings a light of principle, that carries him into higher regions of discussion than any of his contemporary controversialists.

The *Apology for Smectymnuus* closed the series; and an important incident of his life requires to be narrated before we can understand the origin and character of the second phase of his controversial career.

Milton had now attained his thirty-fifth year, and save his passion for the fair unknown Bolognese, his heart had remained untouched—so far as is clearly known. There is no evidence that he was now seized with any sudden and romantic passion: all the circumstances of the case rather seem to show the contrary. The fact is, that in his new mode of life he felt the want of some one to assist him in his household cares and duties; and this probably more than anything else suggested the thought of marriage to him. It is a poor ideal of a poet's marriage, but it is the one that most exactly suits the circumstances. All that is really known is, that " about Whitsuntide of the year 1643, Milton took a journey into the country, nobody about him certainly knowing the reason, or that it was more than a journey of recreation. After a month's stay, home he returns a married man who set out a bachelor—his wife being Mary, the eldest daughter of Mr Richard Powell, then a Justice of the Peace, of Forest Hill, near Shotover, in Oxfordshire." Such is the statement of his nephew Phillips; and none of his biographers have been able to add any clearly ascertained details to the story, * however ingeniously and happily it may have been filled up by the pleasant conjectures of the authoress of *The Maiden and Married Life of Mary Powell.* There is reason, indeed, to believe that he had some previous acquaintance with the Powells. This is suggested by the story itself, as well as by the discovery of certain pecuniary relations long pending between the families. † The Miltons, it will be remembered, came from this very district. It is very probable, therefore, that Milton's unexplained journey about Whitsunday 1643, was by no

---

* Mr Masson has not yet reached this stage of his task, and his power of research may throw some clearer light upon the story.

† The researches of Mr Keightley have discovered that a loan of £500 had been made by Milton's father, in his son's behalf, to Mr Powell. So far back as the year 1627, the third year of his university course, this debt is found to have been contracted to Milton by his future father-in-law. In whatever way we explain this circumstance—even if we suppose it to have been a pure business transaction on the part of the scrivener with one who, belonging to his native district, had naturally applied to him for the money—it serves as a point of connection between the families. Milton could not help feeling some interest in a family, the head of which stood indebted to him in such a sum, especially as it is evident that difficulties arose regarding the payment of the debt. We can well imagine, therefore, that the journey into Oxfordshire in 1643 was by no means Milton's first visit to the Powells. We may even suppose, with Mr Keightley, that, while staying at Horton, he had "taken many a ride over to Forest Hill, and that on his return from the Continent he may have gone down more than once to try to get his money." Setting up house, as he then was, the money must have been an object to him, and such occasional journeys to Forest Hill seem exceedingly natural in the circumstances. The attachment may have thus grown up more gradually than has been supposed. On such visits he may have seen and admired Mary Powell, and, forgetful of the debt, courted and won the daughter.

means his first visit to "Forest Hill, near Shotover." But, whether it was so or not, there is too good reason to conclude that his courtship and marriage were hasty and ill-considered.

Mrs Milton had scarcely settled in her new residence when she returned on a visit to her parents, and, notwithstanding her husband's entreaties, refused again to leave them. Michaelmas, when she promised to be back, came, but she remained at home ; her husband's letters remained unanswered ; and a special messenger, at length despatched by him to escort her back, was dismissed with "contumelious treatment." Such are the well-known facts of this unhappy affair in our poet's life. Into these bare facts we must read the best meaning we can.

Incompatibility of temper and character is the natural explanation, and the one suggested by Milton's own allusions to the subject. A young girl, the daughter of a devoted royalist family, married on a sudden to one whom, at the best, she had more learned to respect than to love—transported from the happy country, and a romping household of eight children, where, Aubrey tells us, there was a "great deal of company and merriment, as dancing," &c., to the dull and studious retirement of Aldersgate Street, where "no company came to her, and she often heard her nephew cry and be beaten ;" it is easy to understand how rapidly the elements of incompatibility might develop themselves in such a combination of circumstances. It was a sufficiently harsh change for the young wife, and it would have required a character of more firmness and elevation than she seems to have possessed to resist the depressing influences of the change, and to adapt herself to her new duties.

And Milton was not likely to do his utmost to smooth and lighten her new lot for her. Probably he never thought of such a thing. There is nothing in his writings that suggests that he would have much delicacy or considerate tenderness in such a matter. In all his allusions to the subject—even in his poetry—there is a harshness of tone, and a cold austerity of feeling, that shows a man more disposed to stand on his rights than a heart wounded in its most sacred feelings. He could speak, for example, of his wife as a "mute and spiritless mate," and exclaim, "who knows but that the bashful muteness of a virgin may ofttimes hide all the unliveliness and natural sloth which is really unfit for conversation!" Nay, in still stronger language, with evident pointing to his own marriage, he deplores the case of one who "finds himself fast bound to an uncomplying discord, or, as it oft happens, to an image of earth and phlegm, with whom he looked to be the copartner of a sweet and gladsome society." Such expressions no doubt escaped from him under strong provocation; but even in such a case they show, as well as his whole tone on the subject of matrimony, a want of forbearing gentleness and reserve of feeling. He was capable of the deepest affection, of the most genuine kindness—his after-conduct proved this; but that bright and delicate courtesy, which seeks to please woman apart from duty, and which acknowledges devotion to the sex, as an imperial sentiment ruling the necessities of social existence—this is not found in Milton. It is foreign to his deliberate theory of life; it is no part of the radiant investment with which he surrounds his Eve, or ideal woman.

How far the fact of his wife being a royalist * may

* "The family," Phillips says, "being generally addicted to the cava-

have had to do with the unhappy result, it is difficult to say. Such an opposition of feeling would not be without its influence, as in the contrasted and not less unhappy, although less notorious, case of Hooker. Hooker's wife was inclined to Puritanism,* and her temper certainly partook of its less amiable characteristics. None can ever forget the depressing picture given in Walton's *Life*, of "Richard being called to rock the cradle," when his two old pupils paid him a visit at his parsonage. Milton's royalist wife forsook him; Hooker's Puritan wife tormented him; and, beyond doubt, the great antipathy which they represented cut deeply into the heart of society—in many families setting brother against brother and wife against husband. The Puritan and the Anglican were far more separate than the Anglican and the Catholic had ever been. The schism of the former represented the true disunion produced by the Reformation in England; that of the latter, powerful as it was politically, did not spring out of any equally wide or clearly marked divergence. The undertone of sentiment in the Elizabethan Church was, after all, much the same as in the old Catholic days. Although the monasteries were suppressed and the power of the Pope denied, the intellectual and moral spirit of the Church was but little changed, and the old festivals and order of service remained very much the same. But with Puri-

lier party, and some of them possibly engaged in the King's service, who by this time had his headquarters at Oxford, and was in some prospect of success, they began to repent them of having matched the oldest daughter of the family to a person so contrary to them in opinion; and thought that it would be a blot on their escutcheon whenever that court should come to flourish again."

* There is good reason to believe this, for her Puritan friends seem to have made free with his MSS. after his death. See Keble's Preface to Oxford edition of Hooker.

tanism arose a fundamental difference of opinion,
and this difference soon worked itself into all the
forms of religious service and all the relations of social
life.   In the very cut of the hair and the mode of
dress it showed itself; and such an influence, penetrating the whole framework of society, could not fail
to operate extensively upon the family relations—in
certain cases harmonising and strengthening them, but
in certain other cases embittering and weakening them.
It suggests a striking enough reflection, that the two
intellectual chiefs of the rival systems, Hooker and
Milton, should have tasted in their domestic life the
bitterness of the great schism which, in its opposite
sides, they represented.   Standing intellectually in
the van of the struggle, they were made to feel how its
mighty agitations touched their own hearths, and its
unhappiness pierced to their own hearts.

The series of publications which the unfortunate
result of Milton's marriage called forth, are among the
least interesting and valuable of his writings.   They
bear too obviously the trace of the special circumstances which called them forth, and are, throughout,
far too arbitrary and personal in their attempt to settle
a practical question of grave and difficult import.
He has himself sought to vindicate for them a place in
the great intellectual plan which he set before him, of
maintaining the cause of liberty in all its essential
bearings.   "I perceived," he says, "that there were
three species of liberty which are essential to the happiness of social life—religious, domestic, and civil; and
having already written concerning the first, and the
magistrates being strenuously active in obtaining the
third, I determined to turn my attention to the second,
or the domestic species.   As this seemed to involve

three material questions—the conditions of the conjugal tie, the education of children, and the right of free speculation—I undertook the examination of each of them, and began by explaining my sentiments, not only concerning the matrimonial rite, but concerning its dissolution, should this become necessary."* Such a task may very well have presented itself to a mind like Milton's. The question of divorce, as merely one aspect of the great question of liberty, may have previously interested him; but it is, nevertheless, plain that his writings on the subject, which followed one another in quick succession from 1644 to 1645, sprang directly out of his own case, as they everywhere bear the stamp of it. The general principle which they each and all maintain was the one involved in his own marriage—the principle, namely, "that indisposition, unfitness or contrariety of mind, arising from a cause of nature unchangeable, hindering, and ever likely to hinder, the main benefits of conjugal society, which are solace and peace," is a sufficient reason of divorce. In four treatises,† published within little more than a year, he advocated this principle, now and then, in its statement and illustration, rising into an elevated strain of moral reflection or of indignant sentiment; but, as a whole, in a manner tedious, minute, and unsatisfactory. His tendency to theorise and carry out

---

* *Defensio Secunda.*

† "The Doctrine and Discipline of Divorce restored to the good of both Sexes from the Bondage of Canon Law" (1644)—in which year two editions appeared, addressed to "The Parliament of England with Assembly."

"The Judgment of Martin Bucer touching Divorce" (1644).

"Tetrachordon; or Expositions upon the Four Chief Places in Scripture which treat of Marriage or Nullities of Marriage," (1645); also addressed to the Parliament. And,

"Colasterion; a Reply to a nameless Answer concerning the Doctrine and Discipline of Divorce," 1645.

his deductions arbitrarily from a single point of view,
is especially conspicuous in these writings ; and, coming
in contact with a subject which obstinately resists its
application, it often leads him into great weakness of
argument.

Viewing the subject ideally and in the abstract, all
would admit the force of Milton's argument, that a
marriage which is not one of heart and sympathy,
securing to the husband and wife respectively, "against
all the sorrows and casualties of this life," " an intimate
and speaking help, a ready and reviving associate," is
no true marriage, but " a perpetual nullity of love and
contentment — a solitude and dead vacation of all
acceptable conversing. "   " When love finds itself
utterly unmatched and justly vanishes,—nay, rather
cannot but vanish,"—then, though the artificial bond
may subsist, a union, such as alone becomes two rational beings, is already dissolved.   The outward relation
may continue, but "not holy, not pure," not beseeming
the sacred character of marriage. ("For in human
actions the soul is the agent."   "Intellective principles" must form their spring, else they "participate
of nothing rational, but that which the field or the fold
equals.")* In the region of mere idea and moral principle this is incontrovertible, but, unhappily for the
argument, the question is not an ideal, but an entirely
practical one.   In so far as marriage is an object of
legislation, it cannot be dealt with in the abstract, or
on any principle of sentiment.   Society can only take
cognisance of a tangible bond, constituted by obvious

---

* The whole of this passage from the *Tetrachordon* gives a very good
idea of Milton's main argument.   In its mixed beauty and coarseness of
expression it is also interesting, in a literary point of view, as a specimen of his style and of that of his age in such matters.

sanctions, and subsisting so long as certain plain conditions involved in the bond are fulfilled, or may be
fulfilled. The State cannot, apart from all higher views
of the question, provide for the operation of the varying
influences of human temper and feeling, or, as our author
would have it, show "some conscionable and tender
pity for those who have unwarily, in a thing they never
practised before, made themselves the bondmen of a
luckless and helpless matrimony." * Men and women
must protect themselves in the first instance ; and if it
be true that "the soberest and best governed men are
least practised in these affairs, and that, for all the
wariness that can be used, it may yet befall a discreet
man to be mistaken in his choice," society is, nevertheless, not bound to make allowance for such mistakes,
where they would clearly tend to interfere with its
order and stability. It is only when a greater injury
and disturbance to this order would arise from the
maintenance of the marriage tie than from its dissolution—as in the case of adultery—that society can consent to its dissolution. It is only by some abnegation
of man's absolute rights that he enjoys the benefits of
social intercourse at all ; and a man cannot be free to
consult his own mere inclination—which is what is
really implied in his argument—in the disruption of
so vital a bond as marriage, so long as he remains
a member of the community whose sanctions guarantee
the sacredness and security of the bond while it lasts.
He cannot have the privileges of civilisation and at the
same time the license of an unfettered individuality.
Milton would, no doubt, have repudiated such an interpretation of his theory—in fact, he does so ; still, it
seems impossible to distinguish his principle logically

* *Doctrine and Discipline of Divorce.*

carried out, from that of an absolute individual liberty
to retire from the marriage-contract so soon as any
distaste of mind or of nature may spring up between
married persons. To a great extent, moreover, the
question is argued by him all on one side—that of the
man ; marriage is regarded especially with a view to
his advantage, and its breach with a view to his convenience. There is a haughty and cold indifference to
the rights on the other side, as well as to all the grave
difficulties and anxieties connected with children,
which adds to the unsatisfactoriness of his argument
while weakening its interest.

In these few remarks we have merely looked at
Milton's argument in its relation to the rights and
obligations of society. Its relation to Scripture suggests another view, which he is far from having
evaded, but the difficulties of which it cannot be said
that he has any more satisfactorily met and resolved.
The truth is, that the question was one of too delicate
and practical a character for his genius, which ranged
freely among principles, and possessed a grand power
of theoretic and eloquent deduction, but which was
unaccommodating and unyielding in its application
to the problems of practical life.

We see the full force of his genius at this time
displayed in a writing of a very different character—
viz. his famous *Areopagitica, or Speech for the Liberty
of Unlicensed Printing*, published and addressed to the
Parliament in the same year, 1644. The subject obviously fell within his great plan of discussing the
whole question of liberty, and he had long reflected
on it accidentally, as the *Areopagitica* was called
forth by a special Act of the Parliament to which

it was addressed.* Far less complicated than the subject of divorce, and admitting of a far more direct
and conclusive appeal to the great principles which
lie at the foundation of human freedom, Milton's task,
in the present case, if not more congenial to his feelings,
was far more suited to his intellect. Starting on that
elevated key which was natural to him, which was the
appropriate expression of the lofty pitch at which his
ideas mostly ranged, he scarcely drops this key throughout the treatise. His thoughts march, from beginning
to end, at the same high level, only swelling here and
there into a richer and more felicitous fulness. Nothing
can be grander or more expressive than many of the
separate sayings † which enrich the style of this treatise,
and give to it dignity, force, and pregnancy, condensing
into a massive gem-like pith wide trains of advancing
argument. There are none of his prose writings less
temporary, less imbued with the narrowness and accidents of his own personal feeling, or less bound to the
mere temper and tendencies of his time; and this is
shown in the mere fact of its continued popularity (if
we can use such a word in Milton's case at all), while
his other prose writings, for the most part, are forgotten and unread, save by the student.

* The Parliament, under the influence of the Presbyterians, had set
forth an order " to regulate printing : that no book, pamphlet or paper,
shall be henceforth printed, unless the same be first licensed by such, or
at least one of such, as shall be thereto appointed."

† As, for example, when he defends the reading of all sorts of books
by the example of holy Chrysostom, who nightly studied Aristophanes,
and " had the art to cleanse a scurrilous vehemence into the style of a rousing
sermon ;" or again, when he says, that a " man may be a heretic in the
truth, and if he believes things only because his pastor says, or the
'Assembly' so determine, without knowing other reason, though his
belief be true, yet the very truth he holds becomes a heresy ; " or, when
again he tells us that "opinion in good men is but knowledge in the making."

The great principles expounded in the *Areopagitica* are as true and as needful now as they were in Milton's own day; the very illustrations by which he enforces them have, with a slight change of colouring, a vividness of application that, after two centuries, and all our boasted Protestantism, is perfectly startling. Take merely one as a specimen in which he pictures certain "Protestants and professors" in his day : "They live and die," he says, "in as errant and implicit a faith as any lay Papist of Loretto; men who, unable themselves to bear the burden of their religion, find out some factor, to whose care and credit they commit it — some divine of note and education, to whom they assign the whole warehouse of their religion, with all the locks and keys ; so that a man may say his religion is no more within himself, but comes and goes according as that good man frequents his house. He entertains him, gives him gifts, feeds him, lodges him ; his religion comes home at night, prays, is liberally supped, and sumptuously laid to sleep ; rises, is saluted, and, after the malmsey, or some well-spiced brunge, and better breakfasted than he whose morning appetite would have gladly fed on green figs between Bethany and Jerusalem, his religion walks abroad at eight, and leaves his kind entertainer in the shop, trading all day without his religion." There are few things more exquisite than this, both in its descriptive truth, and its broad yet covert sarcasm ; while it paints to the life the spirit which still infests much of our Protestantism. There are many passages equally felicitous, clothing the deepest truths in a diction of mingled luxuriance, sweetness, and power.* The treatise claims

* It is impossible to give an anthology of such pieces ; but we may instance that in which he speaks of the knowledge of good and evil in

the ever-renewed study of the friends of Protestant
freedom. Nowhere are its principles more fairly and
eloquently expounded; and even the germ of all that
is really just and good in the most recent discussions
of "Liberty" will be found in it.

Still, in the same year, he published his "Tractate on Education," addressed to Master Samuel Hart-
lib, in which he advocates a plan of instruction similar
to that which he had conducted with his nephew.
There are some features of the plan narrow and erroneous; but there are others, such as the transference
of logic and literary composition from the beginning
to the close of the scholastic career, and the advantages
which he attributes to a musical training, eminently
suggestive. The "Tractate" is brief and pleasing in
its style, with much of the same pungent richness of
thought and observation that distinguishes the *Areopagitica.*

The publication of these writings, with those on the
subject of divorce, all during a space of eighteen
months,* while Mrs Milton remained with her friends
at Forest Hill, must have left Milton little leisure to
seek for any other solace in his solitude. According
to the story, however, he is represented as at length

the world as leaping forth "out of the rind of one apple tasted as two
twins cleaving together," and breaks forth into the strain—"I cannot
praise a fugitive and cloistered virtue unexercised and unbreathed, that
never seeks out and sees her adversary, but slinks out of the race where
that immortal garland is to be run for not without dust and heat."
Elsewhere he says grandly, and in the highest spirit of freedom,
"Though all the winds of doctrine were let loose to play upon the
earth, so truth be in the field, we do injuriously, by licensing and pro-
hibiting, to misdoubt her strength. *Let her and falsehood grapple. Who
ever knew truth put to the worse in a free and open encounter? Her confut-
ing is the best suppressing.*"

* The first edition of his Poems—those of the Horton period, with a
few others, also appeared in 1645.

desirous of carrying his principles of divorce into practice; and, as accordingly, paying his addresses to a
young lady, daughter of a Dr Davis. Whether the
rumour of such an event had any effect in piquing the
jealousy of his wife, we cannot say. Other and better
known circumstances—the ruin of her family with
that of the Royal cause, and the surrender of Oxford in
1646—led her to think of the possiblity of a reconciliation, notwithstanding the apparent gulf which his writings had placed between them. Milton's own friends,
probably alarmed at the practical turn which his
speculations seemed about to assume, concurred in her
intention, and did what they could to bring it to a prosperous issue. One day when he was visiting a rela-
tive, named Blackborough, in the lane of St Martin's-le-
Grand, his wife, who had concealed herself in an inner
room, came forth, and threw herself at his feet implor-
ing forgiveness. The sternness of his anger at first
restrained the boon; but at length he relented,* and
took her again to his home and heart. She returned,
not to the house in Aldersgate Street, but to a larger
house which he had taken, and was then preparing at
Barbican.

Here Milton continued his old vocation, and we are
left to infer that his reconciliation with his wife continued cordial. It is not likely that he could have

---

* The following lines from the tenth book of *Paradise Lost* almost
certainly point to, if they do not really describe, the scene which occurred on this occasion between Milton and his wife :—

> "She ended, weeping; and her lowly plight,
> Immovable till peace obtain'd from fault
> Acknowledged and deplored, in Adam wrought
> Commiseration: soon his heart relented
> Towards her, his life so late, and sole delight,
> Now at his feet submissive in distress:
> Creature so fair his reconcilement seeking,
> His counsel, whom she had displeased, his aid;
> As one disarm'd, his anger all he lost."

found his ideal of matrimony realised in one whose sympathies and tastes were evidently in many respects opposed to his own. He made the best of his position, however, and in the issue he proved himself a warm friend to his wife's family. When the disasters of the civil war drove the Powells from their Oxfordshire home, and entirely ruined them for the time, he received the whole of them into his house, where, in the course of a few months, his father-in-law seems to have died.

This addition to his household must have partially interrupted his scholastic labours, or at least interfered with their privacy and efficiency. Phillips indicates as much when he tells us, that after their removal the house looked again "like a house of the Muses only." The accession of scholars, he confesses at the same time, had not been great; and this probably led to Milton's removal in the end of the year 1669 to a smaller house in Holborn, "with its back opening into Lincoln's-Inn-Fields." Before this removal his eldest daughter Anne was born on the 29th July 1646; the second daughter, Mary, was born in the house in Holborn on the 25th of October 1648.

Phillips has some absurd story of a plan of making Milton, at this time, an officer in Waller's army. "He is much mistaken," he says, "if there was not about this time a design of making him an adjutant-general in Sir William Waller's army; but the new modelling of the army proved an obstruction to this design." This story is improbable, both in relation to Waller and to Milton, the former of whom was a Presbyterian, and not likely therefore to have courted the assistance of one whose wider sympathies with the revolutionary movement were rapidly carrying him beyond Presbyterianism; while the latter was not very likely to have thought of such a position. It labours under the farther improbability of not answering to the circumstances, for the new modelling of the army was by this time completed, or nearly so, and Waller superseded in his command.*

From the time of his removal to Holborn, Milton seems to have gradually abandoned his scholastic function and confined himself to his studies. His pupils either fell of, or, on his father's death in March 1647, he may not have had the same occasion to employ himself in this manner. His literary activity is not found to correspond with his supposed leisure. The three years from the commencement of 1646 are entirely barren in authorship, although he is supposed during this period to have written the four first books of his *History of England*. Probably several of the compilations† which he afterwards published, and of which he seems to have been fond, owe their origin to this period.

In the beginning of the year 1649 we find him busy with his first treatise regarding the King, which opens the third series of his controversial writings. It was intended to bear upon the position and fate of Charles, but it was not published till a week or two after his execution. Its extended title sets forth in full its object: " *The Tenure of Kings and Magistrates, proving that it is lawful, and hath been held so through all ages, for any who have the power to call to account a tyrant or wicked King, and, after due conviction, to de-*

---

* Phillips fixes the time, in Mr Keightley's notes, to have been " not long after the march of Fairfax and Cromwell through the city" (August 1647).

† For example, besides his *History of England*, his *Accidence Commenced Grammar*, and his *Brief History of Moscovia*.

*pose and put him to death, if the ordinary Magistrate
have neglected or denied to do it; and they who of late
so much blame deposing* (i.e. *the Presbyterians*) *are the
men that did it themselves."*

The general tone of this treatise shows how completely Milton had identified himself with the extreme
movement party in the revolution. His mind was not
one to shrink from the obvious course of events; its
convictions were too stern, and its impulses too confident; it rose, rather, and felt itself stronger in the
face of so great a crisis. He has no patience with the
Presbyterians, who, having brought affairs to such a
conclusion by their conduct to the King, refuse to concur in his condemnation, and "begin to swerve and
almost shiver at the majesty and grandeur of some
noble deed, as if they were nearly entered into some
great sin." To him, as to the great leader of the movement, the *course of affairs* was their own justification.
The Parliament and army needed no other vindication
than the "glorious way wherein justice and victory
had set them; the only warrants through all ages,
next under immediate revelation, to exercise supreme
power."

He argues the theses with which he has inscribed
the treatise from two points of view; first, from the
nature of the kingly office, as being "only derivative,
transferred, and committed to the holder in trust, from
the people, to the common good of them all, in whom
the power yet remains fundamentally, and cannot be
taken from them without a violation of their natural
birthright;" and, secondly, from such historical "examples" as seemed to him to justify it. The argument,
conducted from the first point of view, where he
handles principles, is, as usual, far more true and

effective than the historical argument to which the necessities of the case, as regarded by his adversaries more than his own inclination, compelled him. The former (barring its iterations of a hypothetical formal covenant between people and their rulers, which so long continued a staple theory of political writers) is one of the most clear and consistent arguments in Milton's controversial writings, unembarrassed by any trace of passion, and free from that generalising vagueness and rigour of statement with which he generally covers any weak position.

The treatise had but little effect in its intended direction of " composing the minds of the people." It had, however, a decided effect upon the Council of State, with Bradshaw, Milton's kinsman, at its head. It is even possible that Bradshaw may have had something to do with the suggestion of the defence of the conduct of the army and Parliament. In any case, such a defence could not pass unacknowledged by those whom it so deeply concerned. Its author was a man whose services could be obviously turned to good account. He had both the heart and the ability to aid them as few had. The office of Foreign or Latin Secretary to the Council of State, was accordingly offered to Milton, and accepted by him, at a salary of about £290 per annum. The date of his appointment is the 18th of March 1649.

His special business in this capacity was to prepare, in Latin, the foreign correspondence of the Council; and forty-six letters, which were published after his death, so far represent his labours in this direction. With a view to these labours, and in order to be near their scene, he removed from Holborn to lodgings at Charing Cross ; and by the end of the year

(1649) he was established in lodgings at Whitehall,* where he remained for a year and a half.

Milton's ordinary duties, however, as Secretary to the Council of State, formed the least notable part of the work which devolved upon him in his new vocation. Of all his remaining prose writings,† the most elaborate and important are directly connected with his office, and grew out of it. These writings, more than anything else, identify him with the events of his time. They are in a manner national documents, in which he professed not merely to expound his own sentiments (he never allows the reader, in any of them, to forget his own lofty personality), but, moreover, to represent the nation and people of England. We see in them the greatest intellect of the age dealing with its greatest problems—contemplating the great revolutionary movement still sweeping its widening course in these memorable years, when the highest authority of the State having been struck down, the master that was to seize the slackening reins of government had not yet taken them in hand—and from the very heart of the

* His residence at Whitehall appears to have been a subject of dispute between the Parliament and the Council, as indicated by various orders of Council in the course of 1651. By one of these, of date the 11th of June, a Committee is instructed to go to the Committee of Parliament for Whitehall, to acquaint them with the case of Mr Milton, "in regard of their positive order for his speedy remove out of his lodgings in Whitehall; and to endeavour with them that the said Mr Milton be continued where he is in regard of the employment which he is in to the Council, which necessitate him to reside near to the Council." This negotiation, however, does not seem to have had a favourable issue; for we find Milton's household again "soon after," transported to a "pretty garden house in Petty France, in Westminster, next door to the Lord Scudamore's opening into St James's Park." Here he remained till the Restoration.

† His observations on the Articles of Peace between the Earl of Ormond and the Irish were published before his appointment to the office.

movement directing its agitations, and vindicating its excesses.

There can be no doubt of the grandeur of the intellect thus employed, and of the deep interest attaching to its reflections. The views of Milton are valuable in virtue of the mere compass and earnestness of his powers; it is something to know what the highest genius in England thought of the mighty events amidst which he was living. But with the fullest admission of this, there are few who will recognise in him any adequate title to represent and interpret the mixed feelings of the people of England at this crisis. Isolated in the very greatness of his powers, dogmatical in his convictions, austere in his sympathies, and self-concentrated and proudly independent in all his moral impulses, we feel as we read these apologetic writings that their author is as ever intensely one-sided. Not merely does he not do justice to any opposite point of view from his own, but he shows the most rude and violent contempt for it. He speaks as one who, standing amid a crowd, and professing to represent it, yet takes counsel only with his own heart, and in the very act of representation asserts his solitary and sublime personality. He could not be sympathetic with the common hearts around him; he could not understand the varying pulses of the popular feeling, as it veered lately in high resentment against the King, and now in deep and pathetic sorrow over his tragic end. This was to him the evidence of a mere " voluntary and beloved baseness," which could not appreciate the reality of a national mission nor the glory of a great cause.

This one-sidedness, frequently weak in its bitterness, is especially characteristic of his *Iconoclastes*, in answer to the famous defence and description of the King in his sufferings, entitled *Eikon Basilikē.* There is none of Milton's writings less pleasing than this. The subject was unfortunate, and scarcely to be handled save with a delicacy of criticism, and a point of grave and pathetic satire, of which he was no master. The ingenious misrepresentations of the book to which he was replying, and the attempt which it makes to cover Charles's delinquencies by an appeal to his personal virtues and diligent pietisms, might have been successfully met by an exposure, respectful yet keen, and tender while just ; but Milton is simply insulting in the harshness and bitter frigidity of his invective. He assails the memory of the "martyr" with a savage intemperance, which excites our pity far more than it convinces our judgment. The description given of him in the *Eikon*, is "a conceited portraiture drawn out to the full measure of a masking scene, and set there to catch fools and silly gazers." "Its quaint emeblms and devices" are " begged from the old pageantry of some Twelfth Night's Entertainment at Whitehall." Ridiculing the affectionate cares of Charles's attendants, his only grief is "that the head was not shook off to the best advantage and commodity of them that held it by the hair." The prayer which he delivered to Bishop Juxon, immediately before his death, is alleged to be stolen, word for word, from the mouth of a heathen woman praying to a heathen god, and that in no serious book, but in the "vain amatorious poem" of Sir Philip Sidney's *Arcadia,** "as if Charles and his friends thought no better of the living God than a buzzard idol, fit to be so served and worshipped in reversion with the polluted oils and refuse of Arcadias and romances."

* The prayer of Pamela in the *Arcadia.*

There is throughout the whole of the treatise a wanton vein of personal criticism upon the King,—his character,—his religion,—"the superstitious rigour of his Sunday's chapel, and the licentious remissness of his Sunday's theatre,"—even his family relations. The Presbyterians, as sharing in the lamentation for the death of Charles, come in, as constantly in this series of writings, for the lash of a vehement scorn. "Their pulpit stuff, from first to last, hath been the doctrine and perpetual infusion of servility and wretchedness to all their hearers, and their lives the type of worldliness and hypocrisy, without the least true pattern of virtue, righteousness, or self-denial in their whole practice." This is sufficiently sweeping, and well shows the one-sidedness and passionate depth of Milton's polemical nature. By the mere force of big abuse, and the heavy march of a reviling rhetoric, he tries to crush his adversaries, never seeking any points of appreciating or tolerant interest with them, never sparing in tenderness any feature of apparent excellence, but dealing his blows with indiscriminating roundness, as if he delighted in the havoc and pain that he inflicted.

His two great Latin works—his first and second *Defences for the People of England*—are of a higher character than the *Iconoclastes.* In them he deals with the King's deposition and death more on the broad and general grounds of the first elements of government. On such grounds Salmasius was no match for him; and the literary world of his day did not present his match. Even Grotius, if we could conceive him engaged in the controversy, could not have brought to it a more enlarged, comprehensive, and enlightened grasp of the great principles of political science than our author. He is found, like all the writers of his time, mingling up the discussion of these principles with scriptural precedents, and trying to prop his cause on the dogmatic authority of the biblical text, as well as on the clear basis of natural reason and justice. This, which the controversial methods of his time required, does not add value to his treatise; it is the weak and failing point in it. Its real force arises from the degree in which it carries the discussion beyond such formal pedantries of the schools and the details of theological sophistry into the free atmosphere of moral and political argument. In this higher region, as always, lies his strength. Here was his real triumph against Salmasius, who — a mere scholar and grammarian — nowhere ventured beyond the shallow dogmatisms of scholastic tradition, and sought to defend the excesses of tyranny by the worn-out falsehoods of literary pedantry and scriptural assumption.

The genius and force of Milton's *Defence* were universally acknowledged. He himself tells us that he received the congratulations of all the foreign ministers in London upon its publication. Queen Christina could not help complimenting it to the face of Salmasius; and the veteran grammarian is said to have sickened and died with chagrin at the triumph of his rival. It may have been that his opponent's unsparing invective did touch him to the heart, and shorten his days. On both sides the amenities of controversy were unknown; and with all our respect for Milton's genius, and admiration for the magnificent argument which his *Defence* embodies, it must be confessed that the coarse scurrility in which it abounds is often very trying and offensive. " Rogue," " puppy," " foul-mouthed

and infamous wretch,"* are among the epithets he
applies to the scholar at Leyden, whose ears had been
long accustomed to the incense of flattery and the en-
comiums of disciples. In the very preface he attacks
with ridicule what Salmasius and all his friends no
doubt considered his strong point—his latinity. Salmasius had used the word *persona* in the modern sense
of person; Milton exclaims, "Quæ unquam latinitas
sic locuta est," and then makes heavy mirth over the
idea of murder being committed on the mask of a
king.†

This tone of personal abuse rises in the second *Defensio pro Populo Anglicano* into a still higher and more
vehement key; but in this case Milton received special
provocation. His own character had been maliciously
and disgracefully attacked; and although that "meek
silence and sufferance," and the eloquence of deeds
"against faltering words," of which he elsewhere speaks,
would now, and always, have better become him, yet
we cannot wonder that when he felt himself so bitterly
aggrieved he should have poured forth the vials of his

---

* These are merely specimens. His vocabulary of abuse is tremen-
dous— directed not only against Salmasius himself, but against his wife.
"Domi Lyciscam habes," he says, "quæ tibi misere dominatur," c. iii.

† *In persona regis.* Salmasius had complained that executioners in
vizards (personati carnifices) had cut off the King's head. "Quid hoc
homine facias?" exclaims Milton; "questus est supra 'de paricidio in
persona regis admisso;' nunc in persona carnificis admissum queritur"—
(What sort of a fellow is this? having complained above of murder per-
petrated on the mask of a king, he now complains that it was committed in the mask of an executioner.) In the reply which Salmasius left
behind him, and which was not published till the Restoration, he eagerly
defends his latinity, and retorts Milton's scurrility with reproaches on
the subject of his blindness. It is a sufficiently sad spectacle; and
Johnson's blunt comment upon it brings out all its odium and absurdity.
"As Salmasius," he says, "reproached Milton with losing his eyes in the
quarrel, Milton delighted himself with the belief that he had shortened
Salmasius's life; and both perhaps with more malignity than reason."

most noisome wrath in reply. The unfortunate issue of the affair was, that he happened to be mistaken in the object upon whom he poured his opprobrium. His defence against the work of Salmasius appeared in the end of 1650. Immediately in the following year a reply appeared, which he attributed to Bishop Bramhall, and which he did not consider worthy of calling forth any confutation from his own pen. This he left to his nephew, John Phillips, whose work he corrected and sanctioned. In the course of the following year, however, a work appeared abroad, bearing the title *Regii Sanguinis Clamor ad Cœlum adversus Paricidas Anglicanos,* in which his character, and even his personal appearance, were held up to infamy. The real author of this attack was a Frenchman, Peter Dumoulin, afterwards rewarded with a prebendal stall in Canterbury; but Milton got somehow persuaded that its author was a Scotchman of the name of More, who was Greek Professor at Geneva when he visited it in 1639. All the personal rancour of the *Defensio Secunda* is suggested by this idea of More's authorship, and never was poor wretch so impaled on the horns of a wild but lofty abuse. Nothing can exceed the proud bitterness—the sublime scurrilousness of the tone. His name is played with — *morus* being the Latin for a mulberry-tree; his amours are depicted; his whole history is set in the light of the most cutting sarcasm. It is amusing yet pitiful to see a genius like Milton's dragged through the mire after an unknown libeller, and missing its aim after all. Nor was he contented with this defence; in the following year (1655) he returned to the subject, and penned a pamphlet expressly in self-defence, under the title *Auctoris pro se Defensio contra Alexandrum Morum Ecclesiasten;*

and this having called More himself more prominently into the field,[*] he aimed at him a further *Responsio.* A controversy which had begun in a noble instinct of patriotism, and the principles involved in which had tasked his great powers to the utmost, unhappily degenerated into an obscure squabble as to character, in which our author could only win a triumph by calling names with a more lusty and powerful tongue, if also with more reason, than his antagonist.

After these labours, which carry us on to the year 1655, Milton appears to have rested from authorship for some time. There is reason to think that he had exhausted himself in these arduous preparations, and that his impaired health needed rest and recreation. Already, in the preface to his *First Defence,* he complains of his bodily indisposition; that he is so weak in body as to be forced to write by piecemeal, and to break off "almost every hour," while the subject was one that required all his stretch of mind. The special " bodily indisposition" to which he alludes was probably the increasing failure of his sight. He himself believed that his blindness was accelerated by his labours on that occasion; and the reproaches of Salmasius and of the author of the attack upon him, which he attributed to More, seem to indicate that the public had the same feeling. He was totally blind in the year 1653, if not previously. His blindness arose from paralysis of the optic nerve, and was the result of his intense habits of study, induced upon original weakness. It did not affect the appearance of his eyes, which remained free from all speck or discolouring,—the same dark grey orbs looking forth into the world of life and nature, al-

* More had also replied to the first attack. See KEIGHTLEY's *Life,* p. 49.

though no longer able to flash forth the rich meanings in which they pictured themselves to his imagination.

About the same period that his decaying sight became blindness, another calamity overtook him in the loss of his wife. There is no reason to think, after all that happened, that this was not a calamity to him. During eight or nine years of wedded life, those two hearts, bitterly as they had been alienated, and mortifying as many of the associations connected with their rupture had been, must have yet contracted many ties of affectionate union, the dissolution of which could not but bring sharp grief to the survivor. Milton was left alone in his blindness, with three little girls, the eldest of whom was only a child. It was a pitiful position for the blind and lonely man, and we cannot wonder that he sought ere long another helpmate. His home must have been but a poor and uncomfortable one, without some one to superintend it and look after his daughters; and to this period may be traced the seeds of those evil and careless dispositions in them of which he afterwards complained. With something of the proud spirit of their father, and the pettish coy nature of their mother,* and without affectionate vigilance to guard them from evil, no wonder if the little creatures became disorderly and impatient in their manners, and grew up into some hardness of nature. After about two or three years of widowhood, Milton married for his second wife, Catherine, daughter of a Captain Woodcock of Hackney. The marriage was performed by civil contract on the 12th of November 1656, by Sir John Dethicke, "knight and alderman,"

* Milton's complaint of his wife's muteness and reserve was probably in a great degree the more coyness of her youthful simplicity in the view of his superior powers.

after the publication of their agreement and intention on three market-days. There is nothing known of the relatives of this lady, although Mr Keightley has hazarded a conjecture that, on this occasion also, Milton married "out of his own tribe" (as he says). He presumes that the lady was a Royalist or Presbyterian. In any case the marriage was a happy one, only too swiftly broken. This second wife died in childbed about fifteen months after their union. In a beautiful sonnet, bearing the date of 1658, the poet has commemorated her virtues and his affection for her :—

> " Methought I saw my late espoused saint
> Brought to me, like Alcestis, from the grave.
>
> .   .   .   .   .
>
> Her face was veiled ; yet to my fancied sight
> Love, sweetness, goodness, in her person shined
> So clear, as in no face with more delight :
> But O ! as to embrace me she inclined,
> I waked ; she fled ; and day brought back my night."

Notwithstanding his blindness, Milton remained as Latin secretary throughout the Protectorate. He received an assistant, and a colleague * was also joined with him, who, latterly, was his friend Andrew Marvell. He still continued himself to prepare all the higher and more important State papers, many of which, in the shape of letters written in the name of the Protector, are published along with his other works.

It will not appear unnatural to those who understand the men and the circumstances, that he should have willingly acquiesced in the Protectorate, and

---

* An order in council, dated April 17, 1655, reduces Milton's salary from £288 to £150, to be paid to him *during his life;* from which circumstance some have inferred that this was virtually a *retiring pension:* but he continued in active service long after this ; and in 1689 there is an order for the payment of John Milton and Andrew Marvell, both at the rate of £200 a-year.

rendered its great master his services. Milton was
a republican; and to the very last, when all may be
said to have lost faith in a free Commonwealth, he
wrote in the same high and confident admiration of
it as ever. But while he was a republican, he was
no democrat. So far from this, his nature and all his
sympathies were intensely aristocratical. It was not
for the government of the people, the "credulous and
hapless herd begotten to servility," but for the government of the *wisest*, that he cared. This is the express
ground on which he defends, in his *Defensio Secunda*,
the authority of Cromwell. "In the state of desolation,"
he says, "to which the country was reduced, you, O
Cromwell, alone remained to conduct the government
and serve the country. We all willingly yield the
palm of sovereignty to your unrivalled ability and
virtue, except the few among us who, either ambitious
of honours which they have not the capacity to sustain,
or who envy those which are conferred on one more
worthy than themselves, or else who do not know that
nothing in the world *is more pleasing to God, more
agreeable to reason, more politically just, or more generally useful, than that the supreme power should be vested
in the best and wisest of men.*" * Like Cromwell himself, the author of the *Defence* despised incompetency
and hated disorder. The incapacity and factiousness
of the Rump sufficiently justified, to his mind, their
violent dismissal ; and, if we may judge from the way
in which he alludes to the circumstance, even Colonel
Pride's purge secured his sympathy and approval.

With such sentiments, it can be no matter of
surprise that he not only accepted the Protectorate,
but cordially approved of it. It did not appear to

* P. 945.

him in the light of a usurpation, but only as a necessary means of consolidating the liberty which England
had achieved for herself. He cherished no fear of
Cromwell tyrannically betraying the interests of the
country; he admired the heroic grandeur of his character, and he gladly and proudly served under him.
To what extent these two great minds came into
closer contact we have no means of knowing. There
was, of course, much in Milton of which Cromwell
could have no appreciation; and, absorbed in the
urgent duties of practical government, the Protector
may have scarcely penetrated beneath the surface of
the mighty genius that worked beside him in the
Council office at Whitehall, and gave itself with such
willing capacity to do his service. He may have
been to Cromwell, after all, but his blind secretary,
possessing a rare and serviceable gift of expression
in the Latin tongue; a man of marvellous and ready
powers, but little more. We would fain cherish a
different idea, and believe that two such minds could
not come together as they did without reciprocal admiration, and insight into each other's deeper spirit;
and that, as Milton saw and appreciated the great
qualities of the only man fit to govern England in
those years,* so Cromwell discerned in his blind companion the traces of a genius, the mightiest that then
swayed the realm of thought and of imagination. There
were moments certainly, as in the preparation of the

* SONNET TO THE LORD GENERAL CROMWELL, May 16, 1652.

" Cromwell, our chief of men, who, through a cloud,
    Not of war only, but detractions rude,
    Guided by faith and matchless fortitude,
    To peace and truth thy glorious way hast ploughed,
    And on the neck of crowned fortune proud
    Hast reared God's trophies, and His works pursued."

great state papers in vindication of the war with Spain, and the writing of the letters to the King of France in behalf of the persecuted Piedmontese, when they must have come very near to each other in intellectual sympathy, and their hearts flashed high together in proud resentment over religious wrongs. The great Puritan warrior and poet, in high converse respecting the rights of free thought and the necessity of vindicating the Protestant cause and the name of England abroad as well as at home—stirred into indignant pity —with the one, overflowing in commanding remonstrance ; with the other, rising into a sublime appeal to the great Avenger—suggests one of the most noble and touching pictures which even that heroic age presents.

After Cromwell's death Milton still acted in his official capacity under the brief Protectorate of Richard, and then in the name of the restored Parliament that succeeded on his abdication. His last official document bears the date of May 15, 1659. His pen was unusually busy during the troubled months that followed. His apprehensions in regard to religious liberty and the purity of the Church were all renewed, and he addressed Parliament at length on both subjects. The first he handled in a *Treatise of civil liberty in ecclesiastical causes, showing that it is not lawful for any person on earth to compel in matters of religion.* The latter he set forth in *Considerations touching the likeliest means to remove hirelings out of the Church, wherein is also discourse of tithes, church fees, and church revenues, and whether any maintenance of ministers can be settled by law.*

The first of these treatises is in his best style, enlarged and profound in argument, and animated and

nervous in expression, with almost none of that minute
and reiterated appeal to scriptural and historical re-
ferences which so often breaks the force and clear
coherence of his reasoning.   It is an exposition of the
fundamental principles of Protestantism, and the doctrine of toleration which arises out of them.   He was
always happy and powerful in this field of argument.
The comprehensive and expressive sweep of many of
his statements have the same pregnant bearing as
in the *Areopagitica* upon the general state and relations of religious and speculative opinion.   There is
nothing, he shows, that many professed Protestants
less understand, than the ground on which they stand,
and which alone gives any consistency to their position.   There is nothing they are so slow to yield to
one another as perfect liberty of opinion—nothing
even that they seem more afraid to claim for themselves; while yet there is, and can be, no other basis
of Protestantism than this perfect freedom whereby
every man judges the truth for himself in the light
of Scripture.   That "no man, no synod, no session
of men, though called the Church, can judge definitely the sense of Scripture, is well known to be a
general maxim of the Protestant religion, from which
it follows plainly, that he who holds in religion that
belief or these opinions which to his conscience and
actual understanding appears with most evidence or
probability in the Scriptures, though to others he
seem erroneous, can no more be justly censured for
a heretic than his censurers, who do but the same
thing themselves which they censure him for doing."
And in reference to this principle he points out
how far more reprehensible is the conduct of the
persecuting Protestant than the Papist.   "The Papist

exacts one belief as to the Church due above Scripture, . . . but the forcing Protestant, although he
deny such belief to any Church whatsoever, yet takes
it to himself and his teachers, of far less authority
than to be called the Church, and above Scripture
believed."

In this treatise, and that on *True Religion, Here-
sie, Schism, and Toleration*, published only the year
before his death, we have our author's mature views
on the subject of toleration. His point of view is as
comprehensive in the earlier as in the latter treatise.
The principles announced in both cover every latitude
of doctrinal opinion—Popery and idolatry excepted;
the latter as being "against all Scripture, and therefore a true heresy, or rather an impiety, wherein a
right conscience can have nought to do;" the former
as being not so much a religion as a usurped political
authority, "a Roman principality rather endeavouring
to keep up his old universal dominion under a new
name and mere shadow of a Catholic religion." Milton, in short, had worked out the intellectual principles of toleration thoroughly, but under the pressure
of traditionary modes of thought, which were of the
very religious framework of Puritanism (his view of
idolatry, for example), he did not see his way to the
universal practical application of these principles.
The course of opinion has helped to work the subject
free from the obtruding elements of dogma which refused to concede to a conscientious idolatry its free
rights of sufferance; but it cannot be said that it has
yet disembarrassed it of all the difficulties connected
with the political assumptions of Popery.

In the second treatise whose title we have given,
Milton's Protestantism may be said to reach its fur-

thest point of development. Its aim is substantially
to vindicate the separation of Church and State. The
question of tithes is discussed as quite inapplicable
to the Christian ministry, and the necessity of any
legal maintenance for this ministry is strongly repudiated. Recompense is to be given to ministers of the
Gospel " not by civil law and freehold, but by the
benevolence and free gratitude of such as receive
them."

Besides these treatises devoted to the subject of
religion, the political state of affairs engaged his
interest and occupied his pen at this time. He
penned in October (1659) *A letter to a friend concerning the ruptures of the Commonwealth,* which was
not, however, published at the time. A public pamphlet followed *On the ready and easy way to establish
a Free Commonwealth, and the excellence thereof, compared with the inconveniences and changes of readmit-
ting kingship into this nation.* In this publication
Milton drew a strong picture of the evils of a return
to the royal authority. He painted the difference between a commonwealth freely served by its greatest
men " at their own cost and charge, who live soberly
in the families, walk the streets as other men, may be
spoken to freely, familiarly, friendly, without adora-
tion ; and a kingdom whose king must be adored like
a demi-god, with a dissolute and haughty court about
him, of vast expense and luxury, masks and revels,
to the debauchery of the prime gentry." He recommended that the supreme power should be vested
in a perpetual grand Council of ablest men, chosen
by the people, to consult of affairs for the public
good. The model of the Council that seems to have
run in his mind was the Jewish Sanhedrim ; and,

after all the dreams and new models of government that had occupied men's minds, there was nothing new or specially practicable in that which he proposed. Men's minds were wearied of change and unsettlement; there were but few with the same proud heroic convictions as himself; the course of affairs, with General Monk at their head, was drifting rapidly into the old channel of royalty, with scarcely less fanatical enthusiasm than it had drifted away from it, and the republican pamphlet in the circumstances made no impression. He addressed a brief summary of it to Monk in a letter intended for his own special perusal; but the old and wary soldier had made up his mind, and Milton was left to mourn in darkness and silence the infatuation of his countrymen. A sermon by a Dr Griffiths on the "Fear of God and the King," in which the miserable trash so common in previous and after reigns as to the inviolable right of kings, was openly vented, yet once more called our watchful patriot into the field. He published notes upon this sermon; and with this closed what we may call his public and political career.

The main thought that occurs in review of this period of Milton's life, is the extent to which he represented, in his single person, the intellectual strength and aspirations of triumphant Puritanism. If Milton could be conceived removed from the scene during the decade that followed the death of Charles, the great interpreter of all that was most characteristic and powerful in English political and speculative thought would be gone. It is very true that there were whole sections of the national feeling during this time that he did not, and could not, represent. From what re-

Q

mained of the old Royalism and Anglicanism, and no
less from the strong though subdued Presbyterianism
which had so long contended side by side with the
freer Protestantism which itself had evoked, he was
entirely separated. He did not try to understand
either, and was incapable of doing them justice. But
this did not disqualify—nay, it only qualified him the
more to stand forth as the prominent defender of that
bolder spirit of political and religious thought, which
was the natural development of the great movement
of the century. The special dogmas, both constitutional and biblical, in which the movement began,
could not, in the nature of things, bind the national
mind as it rapidly expanded under its new consciousness of freedom. The current of opinion soon broke
into a wider and freer course. Puritanism enlarged
its conceptions, till it left behind it its Royalist timidi-
ties, and, in a great measure, its doctrinal narrowness.
It was this higher and more thorough spirit—this
progressive phase of the Revolution,— its extreme
right, so to speak,—that really governed England in
those years ; and Milton was its intellectual leader.
His great genius was wholly given to the service, the
exposition, and defence of its political, social, and religious claims. While Cromwell was in his Government its practical expression, he was in his writings
its argumentative expositor ; and as the one stands
alone in his capacity, so does the other. As Cromwell had no political, so Milton had no intellectual,
compeer. Together they represent the highest advance
to which the great revolutionary wave of the century
surged before it fell back again for a time into the
muddy and confused channel of the Restoration.

Because Milton and Cromwell outlived, in many

respects, the original narrowness of Puritanism, it would be absurd to say that they are not to be classed as Puritans. Puritanism was not merely a mode of theological opinion, such as we discern in the Westminster Confession and the prevailing theological literature of the time. It was a phase of national life and feeling, which, while resting on a religious foundation, extended itself to every aspect of Anglo-Saxon thought and society. Its distinguishing and comprehensive principle was the adaptation of State and Church to a divine model. In all things it sought to realise a divine ideal. But it was not so much the unity and consistency of a particular ideal, as the aim towards some ideal, and the dogmatic, positive, and formal manner in which this aim was carried out, that characterised it. The creed of Puritanism, therefore, both theological and ecclesiastical, might and did vary. Cromwell, Milton, and others soon pushed through the narrow bonds of Presbyterianism into a broader religious atmosphere. And Milton especially—gifted with that innate intuition of the divine which has a constant tendency to ascend above forms, and seek its ideal ever higher in the region of the contemplative—not merely abandoned Presbyterianism, but rose, in many respects, above the dogmatic basis to which it was so strongly welded. His was not a mind like that of Owen, or even Baxter, to rest set in any mould of dogmatic opinion prepared for it, or to busy itself with merely working out this mould into more complete and profound expressions. He was himself a *vates*—a divine seer—and no mere theological mechanic.

Yet while Milton rose above the hardening forms of Puritanism, its spirit never left him. He never out-

lived the dream of moulding both the Church and
society around him into an authoritative model of the
divine.   In all his works he is aiming at this.   He is
seeking to bring down heaven to earth in some arbitrary and definite shape.   If there is anything more
than another that marks his mode of thought, it is
this lofty theorising, which applies its own generalisa-
tions with a confident hand to all the circumstances
of life, and, holding forth its own conceptions, seeks
everywhere in history and Scripture for arguments to
support them, and to crush out of sight everything
opposed to them.   Even when he is least Puritan,
in the limited doctrinal sense of the word—as in his
writings on divorce—he is eminently Puritan in spirit.
Whatever may be his special opinions, he is everywhere a dogmatic idealist—not merely an interpreter
and learner of the divine—but one who, believing himself confidently to be in possession of it, does not hesitate to carry out his ideas into action, and square life
according to them.   The varying and expansive character of his opinions does not in the least affect the
unity of his spirit.

The epithet or the quality of Eclectic, therefore,
which some have applied to Milton, is more mislead-
ing than in any sense characteristic.   " He was not a
Puritan," Macaulay says; " he was not a free-thinker;
he was not a Royalist.   In his character the noblest
qualities of every party were combined in harmonious
union."   So far as this is true at all, it is true merely of
the superficial qualities of his nature.   If by a Puritan
he meant one who wore long hair, who disliked music,
who despised poetry, then Milton certainly was no
Puritan.   But it is only to a very material fancy that
such qualities could be supposed to constitute Puritan-

ism. It would never for a moment have struck our poet himself that his love of music, or of poetry, or even his wearing his hair long, separated him in any degree from his own party, or assimilated him to that of the Court. With the latter party he had not a single element of intellectual affinity. He and the Royalist writers of the time stood at entirely opposite poles. The whole circle of his ideas, political, poetical, and theological, was absolutely opposed to theirs. He would have abhorred Hobbes, as he despised and ridiculed Charles I. His intellect was as little eclectic as any great intellect can be. It sought nurture at every source of cultivation, and fed itself on the most varied literary repasts; but after all it remained unchanged, if not uncoloured, by any admixtures. He was direct, dogmatic, and aspiring, but never broad, genial, or dramatic. "His soul was like a star, and dwelt apart." He outshone all others. But while elevated in his grandeur, he was not comprehensive in his spirit. Even when he soared farthest beyond the confines of contemporary opinion, he carried with him the intense, concentrated, and Hebraic temper which characterised it. Puritanism was in many, perhaps in most, a very limited, while, at the same time, a very confident and unyielding, phase of thought. In Milton it loses its limits, but it retains all its confidence and stubbornness. It soars, but it does not widen; and even in its highest flights it remains as ever essentially unsympathetic, scornful, and affirmative. It lays down the law and the commandments. It is positive, legislative, and authoritative. This is the temper of our author everywhere, and this was the Puritanical temper in its innermost expression.

As to Milton's prose writings themselves, regarded

from an intellectual and literary point of view, it is
difficult to give any summary estimate of them,—they
are so great, and yet so unsatisfactory. Putting out
of view his two Latin treatises in defence of the people
of England—which in the very fact that they were
written in Latin may be said to have prepared their
own oblivion after the first excitement and admiration
caused by them were past—it is doubtful whether the
neglect into which his English prose works have fallen
is not to a large degree merited. Controversial in
their aim and structure,* they are not generally fair,
consistent, and impressive as arguments. No one
would think of consulting either Milton's anti-prelatical or divorce writings, still less perhaps his writings
against Charles I., for a candid statement of the difficulties involved in the questions which they discuss.
It was not the tendency of his mind to see difficulties,
or to admit objections. He goes right at his point in
the ideal-dogmatic manner characteristic of him, seeing only his own side, and disdaining or putting out
of sight any other; or where he is sometimes brought
face to face with a hard fact, or an embarrassing text,
cutting them asunder, and scornfully casting them
away.† They are consequently incomplete and inef-
fective; their polemics weary while they fail to convince; and the reader who seeks in them for the
weapons of argumentative victory, or for the solution
of his own perplexities, leaves them dissatisfied and
unconvinced. For after all there is nothing stronger

* This, of course, has no application to his *History of England*, and
other historical and educational compilations. But these works, whatever merits they have, do not furnish any grounds for an independent
estimate of Milton as a prose writer.

† As the way, for example, in which he deals with our Lord's statement about adultery as the only valid plea of divorce.

in argument, and nothing which serves the purpose
better in the end, than candour—the honest wish to
deal fairly and rise above obstinate prejudices. It may
not secure a ready triumph, nor a party triumph, but
it secures the only triumph that the reason acknowledges, when the passions of the hour have died down,
and the heats of violent zeal are gone out. It is
this quality more than anything else—this lofty and
rational fairness—that makes Hooker, as a reasoner,
so satisfactory. The "Books of Ecclesiastical Polity,"
in virtue of their calm, candid, and elevated philosophical spirit, form almost the single text-book of the
controversy that retains a living and instructive interest.

But unsatisfactory as Milton's prose writings are in
their controversial features, whenever he passes, as he
often does, from historical or scriptural polemic to
general discussion, intellectual reference, or personal
description, he is luminous, impressive, and powerful. His large and earnest genius moves at ease in
this higher atmosphere. His thoughts have scope to
expand to their natural dimensions, and his style rises
into corresponding majesty. While the mere details
of controversy fret and irritate him, degrade his
ideas, and lumber his style, wherever he gets above
them under the sway of moral passion or the buoyancy of his proud intellect, his prose no less than his
poetry becomes very grand. There are many passages
in which his austere enthusiasm, swelling into lyrical
rapture, breaks forth into wondrous symphonies of
language. In these fits of eloquence, neither Hooker
nor Bacon equal him. The one is more simple and
expressive in detail; the other rolls long sentences
into a sweeter and more sustained melody; but neither

rises into such voluminous and crashing bursts of music. And these passages of apostrophic grandeur and elevation, where the controversialist sinks out of sight, and the seer or poet alone appears, are more numerous in his earlier and anti-prelatical writings than might be imagined. They suggest strongly the idea of one who is naturally above the work he has in hand —whose native element is far above the din of controversy, and the temporary strife to which he lends himself. In this manner of writing, he was inferior to himself, and had the use but of his "left hand," as he said. The "genial power of nature" led him to quite another task ; and it is this genial power, constantly becoming restive and breaking forth into prose-poetry wherever the subject will permit, that gives their highest interest to these writings. The slightest catch or allusion is enough to set him off; as when, in the *First Book of Reformation*, the mention of the fathers and the martyrs of the English Church leads him to exclaim: "And herewithal I invoke the immortal Deity, Revealer, and Judge of Secrets, that wherever I have in this book plainly and roundly (though worthily and truly) laid open the faults and blemishes of fathers, martyrs, and Christian emperors, or have otherwise inveighed against error and superstition with vehement expressions, I have done it neither out of malice, nor list to speak evil, nor any vainglory, but of mere necessity to vindicate the spotless truth from an ignominious bondage," &c. Again, in his *Animadversions upon the Remonstrants' Defence,** so dry and plain a subject as the alleged novelty of the Puritanical re-

---

* Macaulay has noticed the elevated strain into which Milton rises in this treatise, when it might have been least expected, and whose general structure is not particularly interesting or forcible.

forms makes him break forth into a rapture of reply, in which he invokes the " One-begotten Light and perfect Image of the Father." " Thou," he says, " hast discovered the plots and frustrated the hopes of all the wicked in the land, and put to shame the persecutors of Thy Church ; Thou hast made our false prophets to be found a lie in the sight of all the people, and chased them, with sudden confusion and amazement, before the redoubled brightness of Thy descending cloud, that now covers Thy tabernacle. Who is there that cannot trace Thee now in Thy beamy walk through the midst of Thy sanctuary, amidst those golden candlesticks which have long suffered a dimness amongst us through the violence of those that seized them, and were more taken with the mention of their gold than of their starry light ? "

The conclusion to the *Second Book of Reformation* forms one of the most heightened and prolonged of these lyrical apostrophes, into which Milton so naturally bursts. It is, moreover, peculiarly characteristic in its combination of strength and rugged invective, with the most charming sweetness of tone, as in the following single sentence, which is all for which we can afford space. Addressing God, and inveighing in most denunciatory terms against the bishops who as " wild boars have broke into Thy vineyard, and left the print of their polluting hoofs on the souls of Thy servants," he continues : " O let them not bring about their damned designs that stand now at the entrance of the bottomless pit, expecting the watchword to open and let out those dreadful locusts and scorpions, to reinvolve us in that pitchy cloud of infernal darkness, where we shall never more see the sun of Thy truth again, never hope for the cheerful dawn, never more hear the bird of morning sing." How exquisitely the fine sense of the poet here seduces the almost raving polemic, and under its influence the tone of blustering and rude invective sinks into a softened cadence, and the fresh music of the dawn!

Altogether, Milton's prose writings, while they can never acquire, as they can never be said to have possessed, popularity (in the ordinary sense), must always remain a favourite resource to the student of our political and literary history, and among the highest enjoyments of every lover of ennobling thought, and of combined magnificence and beauty of expression. Like many other massive but irregular compositions, the more they are studied, and the more familiar we become with them, the more will we see and appreciate their real power and interest. All that is coarse, weak, and temporary, falls away as we gaze upon their grand outlines; while the broad basement and aspiring pillar, graced by the most rich and curious touches of an exquisite art, comes forth in bold and finished impressiveness.

Milton's life, after the Restoration, sinks away into quietness and obscurity. We have some characteristic facts from one or two gossipy admirers,* who were proud to recall their recollections of him. We know it chiefly by its splendid fruits in *Paradise Lost* and *Paradise Regained*.

He continued to the end to hope in a Republic. Shut up in his own world of political idealism, he calmly sketched in his letter to Monk the "brief delineation of a free Commonwealth," while the whole machinery of the Revolution was tumbling to pieces

---

* Ellwood the Quaker, and (at second hand) Richardson the painter.

around him, and the Restoration was already impending. After the re-establishment of the monarchy, he withdrew into seclusion, and was glad if he could only escape notice. His writings against the late King were seized, and, along with Goodwin's *Obstructors of Justice*, burned by the hands of the common hangman. He was himself in custody after the Act of Indemnity was passed, on what ground is not known; but it does not appear that any serious designs were entertained against him. There is a story that he owed his safety to the poet Davenant, who requited in this manner Milton's interposition on his behalf, when taken captive during the civil war and condemned to die. The tale is so pleasing, as Johnson says, that we could wish to believe it; but there seems no satisfactory evidence that Milton's life was ever really in danger. Whatever may have been Charles's faults, vindictiveness was not one of them. He had too little seriousness even to cherish resentment for his father's death; he left the punishment of the regicides to Parliament; and there were men such as Marvell, Morrice, and others, there, who were good friends of Milton, and who would do what they could to throw the shield of their protection over the blind patriot.

During the fourteen years which he outlived the return of royalty, he resided chiefly in London; and latterly, for the final nine years of his life, in a house in Artillery Walk, leading into Bunhill-fields. "This was his last stage in the world," as Phillips says. It is with this residence that Richardson's reminiscences connect him. Here he was remembered sitting in "a small chamber hung with rusty green, in an elbow-chair, and dressed neatly in black; pale, but not cadaverous, his hands and fingers gouty, and with chalk stones. . . . He used also to sit in a grey coarse cloth coat at the door of this house, in warm, sunny weather, to enjoy the fresh air, and so, as well as in his room, received the visits of people of distinguished parts as well as quality." He had many illustrious visitors, especially strangers of distinction. " He was much more admired abroad," Aubrey says, " than at home ; " although there were those at home too, such as Dryden, who, after the publication of *Paradise Lost*, learned to look with reverent and admiring eyes towards the great recluse.

Two years before his retirement to this house (1662-3), he married a third time, an event which proved happy in its issues for himself, but which served to reveal a very unpleasant picture of strife and misery in his home. At the time of his marriage his eldest daughter, who was lame and "helpless," was about seventeen, and his youngest about eleven years of age. From whatever cause, they had grown up without fondness or respect for their blind father. We have his own statement that they were "unkind and undutiful." His brother reported that he had heard him complain that " they were careless of him being blind, and made nothing of deserting him ; " that they combined together with the maid to cheat him in his marketings, and that " they made away with some of his books, and would have sold the rest to the dunghill woman." * These statements were elicited in evidence in the trial respecting his will that followed his death. They suggest a very miserable

* Mary, the second one, is even reported to have said, when she heard of his intended marriage, that " that was no news to hear of his wedding, but if she could hear of his death, that was something."

state of things; but the shadow of the picture by no means falls exclusively on the daughters, when all the facts are regarded. The wilful and hoyden blood of their mother, her dislike of retirement, and indifference to literature, they appear to have shared; but, let it be remembered how young they were. Most fathers do not look for any special amount of gravity and filial consideration and housekeeping accomplishments at such an age as even the eldest had reached. It was in Milton's nature to be exacting; not sparing himself, he had no idea of sparing others. It was his nature, moreover, not to allow for the position of others. With all his nobleness, he was deficient in forbearance of spirit and sympathy with weakness. He could no more understand the natural frivolities of girlhood than he could understand the deeply-stirred affections of royalism after the execution of the King.

Milton, accordingly, mismanaged his daughters as he had mismanaged their mother, although with more excuse in the one case, from the helplessness induced by his blindness. He required the two youngest to assist him in his studies, in a manner in which some daughters might be proud to assist their father, but which no mere sense of duty—nothing but a strong love and a congenial taste—could sustain day by day. He made them his amanuenses and readers. He expected them to be always ready to write to his dictation, and to read to him, not merely in English, but in languages of which they themselves did not understand the meaning.* This was part of their training; and there are few who will not be prepared to sympathise with

* This is the account of Phillips, so far corroborated by Aubrey. Deborah's own account to Dr Ward, of Gresham College, substantially agrees with it.

them in its irksomeness. Subjected to the rule of a step-mother, whose temper towards them at least appears to have been harsh, although Milton says she was " very kind and careful of him"*—it is little wonder that they found their father's home uncomfortable, and that one after another they should have left it. Deborah, the youngest, and who was most of a favourite with her father, was the last to leave ; but she, too, at length quarrelled with Mrs Milton, and about the year 1669 all the three daughters had gone, according to Phillips, " to learn some curious or ingenious sorts of manufacture that are proper for women to learn, particularly embroidery in gold and silver." Two of them subsequently married—the eldest and youngest—the latter of whom survived to a good old age, and was reverently sought out and assisted by Addison.

Milton's third wife was of good family, being the daughter of Mr Randle Minshull, of Wistaston, near Nantwich, in Cheshire. The marriage was one of convenience, arranged for him by his friend Dr Paget, who

---

* Phillips, who strongly takes the side of the children in the domestic quarrel, says with brief vigour, that his uncle's third wife "persecuted his children in his lifetime, and cheated them at his death." Considering how difficult it is in contemporary life to ascertain the truth in such matters, it is no wonder that we should meet with discrepancy in the long-past story of Milton's family disagreements. Aubrey says of this wife, that "she was a genteel person, of a peaceful and agreeable humour ;" and Aubrey knew her personally. Milton's own account of her kindness to him is given in the text. On the other hand, Richardson calls her a *termagant*, and represents her as worldly, and rather grasping. Such varieties in the domestic portraiture of the same person, seen from different points of view, are not uncommon. The truth probably is, that as a wife, Elizabeth Milton was affectionate and useful, a good and managing housekeeper, with the somewhat imperious temper which is apt to distinguish that character, and the chief effects of which naturally fell upon her husband's disorderly and hoyden daughters.

was connected with the lady; and the arrangement, whatever its disadvantages to the daughters, proved a blessing to himself. "Betty," as he called her, appears to have well understood the austere and high nature with which she had to deal, and to have smoothed, with a clever fitness and tender hand, his declining years.

The same solicitous medical friend (Dr Paget) who had provided Milton with a wife, shortly after found him also a companion, more suited to be his reader, and more proud of being so, than any of his daughters had been. This was a young Quaker of the name of Ellwood, who stands in interesting association with these last years of the Poet, and to whom, particularly, we are indebted for certain well-known information as to the connection between *Paradise Lost* and *Paradise Regained*. Ellwood felt an honourable pride in this association, and has recorded certain characteristic traits of the great man. "I was admitted to him, not as a servant, which at that time he needed not, but only to have the liberty of coming to his house at certain hours when I could, and to read to him what books he should appoint me, which was all the favour I desired. . . . I went every day in the afternoon, except on the first day of the week, and, sitting by him in his dining-room, read to him such books, in the Latin tongue, as he pleased to hear me read. At my first sitting to read to him, observing that I used the English pronunciation, he told me, if I would have the benefit of the Latin tongue, not only to read and to understand Latin authors, but to converse with foreigners, either abroad or at home, I must learn the foreign pronunciation. To this I consenting, he instructed me how to sound the vowels. This change of pronunciation proved a new difficulty to me; but *Labor omnia vincit improbus*, and so did I, which made the reading more acceptable to my master.   He, on the other hand, perceiving with what earnest desire I pursued learning, gave me not only all the encouragement but all the help he could; for having a curious ear, he understood by my tone when I understood what I read, and when I did not; and accordingly would stop me, examine me, and open the most difficult passages to me."

In these simple and garrulous traits, we can read an interesting and pleasing picture of the great scholar and his young Quaker friend and pupil.   After all his political and ecclesiastical excitements, it had come to this quiet retirement, and the perusal of his old favourite authors.   The country which he had faithfully served might be ungrateful, but he certainly bore no loss; not only so, but, with the magnanimity of a great spirit, he requited his country's neglect by a nobler and far more lasting service than any he had yet rendered.

The first years of his enforced retirement saw the preparation of his great epic.   *Paradise Lost* was certainly complete in the spring of 1667—probably a year before this; * but there is abundant evidence that he had been working at it long before.   According to Aubrey's statement, he had commenced it as early as 1658, when there may have seemed to him, under the settled rule of Cromwell, the prospect of a period of literary ease and culture.†   So early an

---

* Ellwood says that he had seen the MS. in the beginning of 1666, while visiting Milton at Chalfont, Buckinghamshire.

† It deserves to be noticed that literature did seem rising into renewed prosperity under the rule of Cromwell, who showed in this, as in other

origin, however, is not sufficiently substantiated, and
is in itself unlikely. If his mind were then busy with
the subject, it was probably in the earlier and cruder
shapes in which it is presented in the Cambridge
MSS. These MSS. show two plans of a sacred mystery or drama, on the subject of the Fall of Man, in
the second and more perfect of which " Lucifer appears
in an aspect exactly corresponding to that in which
he is presented in *Paradise Lost*, bemoaning himself,
and seeking revenge upon man." * It is interesting
to think of him working at his great conception in
this tentative manner ; but there is every reason to
believe that it was not till after the " evil days and
evil tongues" of the Restoration had forced him into
privacy and solitude, and driven his mind back upon
the lofty plans and ideas of his earlier years, that
he really entered upon the composition of *Paradise
Lost*. We can easily conceive with what enlarging
joy his mind, freed from the political cares that had
so long encumbered it, would revert to those half-
forgotten plans, and with what pride he would once
more take to himself, in his " darkness" and sheltered
solitude, the " garland and singing robes" so long
laid aside. The old thought to do something in
his country's literature such as " the greatest and
choicest wits of Athens, Rome, and Modern Italy, and
those Hebrews of old, did for their country"—" something so written to after-times as they should not wil-

matters, a wide toleration, and extended his patronage to royalist as
well as anti-royalist writers. Cowley and Hobbes returned from exile.
Butler "meditated, in the house of one of Cromwell's officers, his grotesque Satires against the Sectaries ; " and Davenant, on his liberation
from prison, received permission to open a theatre.—See GUIZOT's
Cromwell, ii. 167.

 * KEIGHTLEY, p. 400.

R

lingly let it die"—would then return upon him with
a zest and consciousness of strength all the greater
that he had felt how "inferior he was to himself"
in that "cool element of prose"—"a mortal thing,
among many readers of no empyreal conceit"—to
which he had been so long confined. His higher
genius had never ceased to stir him to some higher
and more enduring work; and now, when all the
public objects for which he had cared and laboured
were overthrown—when his ideal schemes of ecclesiastical and civil liberty were shattered and destroyed
—with what eagerness would he recall his vanished
dreams of poetry, and from the very depths of his patriotic despair make to himself a higher and brighter
vision of contemplation! The idealising grandeur
which in great spirits often comes from weariness and
disgust at practical life—the reaction of a mind like
his—thrown back upon its original foundations, and
congenial intuition of the "bright countenance of
Truth in the quiet and still air of delightful studies"
—such seems the natural explanation of the sublime
conception which now built itself up under his imaginative touch.

In contemplating Milton's resumption of the Muse,
it is particularly interesting to notice the change of
spirit that had come over him in the long interval of
controversy through which he had passed. The characteristics of his early poetic genius survive in his
later poems in all their richness and strength, but
they are mellowed as with a riper flavour; they are
more mature, more lofty, and, if not more instinct with
emotion, yet of a grander and more encompassing
power of feeling. The sweetness lingers, but it is of
a grave and more earnest cast; the old sensitiveness

to natural beauty has retired behind a new swell and
fulness of moral passion, such as no other poet but
Dante has ever reached, or even approached. It is this
increase of reflective and moral interest which marks
the peculiarity of his later poetic powers. The reader
sees at once what a world of hard experience the poet
has passed through, and how his nature has at once
deepened and expanded under it. It has struck its
roots far more firmly into the enduring rock of the
Divine; it has reared its natural majesty far more
nearly into the very light and glory of Heaven. A certain gaiety of heart and nimbleness of fancy has gone
from him; the inspiration of *L'Allegro, Il Penseroso*,
and the *Comus* is there, but chastened and checkered,
—lying like patches of charming spring sunshine on
the broadened current of his genius—while he has gathered in the course of twenty years of toilsome and
agitating disputes a strength of intellectual fibre, a compass of intellectual treasure, a reach of spiritual conception, and an intensity of spiritual imagination, which
amount almost to a new faculty of poetic accomplishment. The traces of harmony and of varied culture
in his early poems, the fulness of historical allusion
and local memory, and descriptive minuteness and fidelity that creeps out in them, are now everywhere manifest in an accumulated degree; while the religious
and speculative interest which was in them subsidiary,
has taken the foreground, and sublimed by its exalting
and consecrating power, all his other gifts to a higher
and more potent capacity. Many a poetic genius
would have sunk and gone out under such an experience as that through which Milton had passed.
It would have been weighed down, if nothing more,
by the very accumulation of its intellectual resources.

It was the peculiarity and greatness of his genius to
become only more buoyant under all its load of
wealth—to rise with it on more triumphant wings,
and to harmonise and mould the whole so as to give
more splendour, variety, compass, and majesty to his
poetic conceptions.

Any mere literary criticism of Milton's later poems
is beside our purpose. It concerns us, however, to
point out the influence of the puritanical spirit and
mode of thought upon the great productions which
mark this period of his life. In reference to *Paradise Lost*, in particular, in which all his powers are
seen in their most concentrated vigour and harmony,
this becomes a somewhat interesting task. The more
attentively the whole argumentative plan of this poem
is studied, and the more the lines of religious thought
which underlie it, and bind it into a grand epical
unity, are brought into view, the more will there be
recognised in them the puritanical impress—the seal
of a genius moulded after the great type of Genevan
thought, however richly diversified and enlarged.

It was and remains an essential characteristic of this
thought to conceive of the struggle between good and
evil in the world in the light of a great scheme definitely concluded in the Divine Mind, and finding its
highest warrant in the wise appointment of the Divine
Will. The mysterious facts of sin and redemption are
not merely recognised as they exist and operate in the
world, or as many conceive them to be revealed in
Scripture, but they are further apprehended and recognised as parts of an ideal economy or system of
decrees which explains them, and with a view to which
they were divinely preordered. Divine truths are not
merely accepted by Calvinism in their obvious import,

but they are reasoned backwards into a great speculative conception, embracing them all, and giving to
each its appropriate meaning and explanation in regard
to the rest. It is the aim of all Christian thought,
more or less, no doubt, to do the same thing : thought
cannot become active on the facts of revelation without trying to unite them into some ideal scheme or argument. But it was the ambition of Puritan theology to
have done this more completely than any other in its
great system of divine decrees. The mysteries of the
world lay unravelled in all their outline before the
spiritual vision of the Puritan, and his mind acquired
a dread familiarity with the divine in its supposed
workings and ends. The author of *Paradise Lost* is
everywhere such a Puritan. The conception of the
divine decrees lies at the basis of his poem. The
whole plot is wrought out from it. The fall of the
rebel angels, the creation and fall of man, are merely
successive exigencies by which the divine mind carries
out its preconceived plans. There is no mystery behind, lurking shadowy in the abyss of the Godhead.
All is prearranged and clear, setting out from a definite
decree, thus disclosed to the angelic intelligences :—

"Hear, all ye angels, progeny of light,
  Thrones, dominations, princedoms, virtues, powers,—
  Hear my decree, which, unrevoked, shall stand :
  This day have I begot whom I declare
  My only Son.
                    To him shall bow
  All knees in heaven, and shall confess him Lord."

From this absolute act the whole argument of the
epic unfolds itself. Beginning in an arbitrary and authoritative assertion of will, it advances along the same
line of conception. Satan erects his will in opposition to

the divine decree.   Assertion calls forth assertion, and
the conflict of good and evil proceeds as a conflict of
naked power on both sides.   Device in Satan is met
by device in heaven; the craft of hell seems to triumph
for a while, and man falls ; but it is only by prear-
rangement to a greater rising.

It is not merely the general scheme of thought here
presented which is Puritan, but, above all, the mode
of the thought.   There is no attempt to invest the
primal decree of the Godhead, out of which the
whole action of the poem may be said to spring, with
rational interest. Notwithstanding the often quoted
verses in the opening of the poem, the mind is not
made to rest on any moral vindication—the assertion
of eternal justice, truth, or righteousness—but on the
bare contemplation of power, the promulgation of an
absolute decree, and the maintenance of that decree in
the face of the antagonism which its very absoluteness
provokes—

> " New laws from Him who reigns, new minds may raise
>   In us who serve,"

argues Satan.   It is the mere command to submit,

> "Law and edict upon us, who, without law,
>   Err not,"

that calls forth the spirit of rebellion.   The contest is
a contest of will against will, and the ideas of right
and wrong only spring out of it—they are not pri-
marily obtruded upon the reader. This sufficiently
shows the origin of the conception. This naked pro-
trusion of will, irrespective of moral intent, as in itself
an adequate spring and explanation of action in the
Divine, is eminently characteristic of the school of
theological thought to which Milton belonged.

The perception of this enables us to analyse an

impression, to which there are few who do not own in reading the poem—admiration of the character of Satan. Irresistibly we feel our thoughts raised as we contemplate this wonderful creation; and a certain vastness of heroic interest gathers around the scarred and mighty form of the "Archangel ruined"—

> " Above the rest
> In shape and gesture proudly eminent."

It is not sympathy, it is not mere admiration, but it is the blended feeling of pathos, wonder, and awe, that surrounds a once mighty foe overthrown and laid in the dust. All readers confess to some share of this feeling. The degree in which it is raised is the great triumph of the poem as a work of art. The interest radiates from Satan as the central figure, without which, in its peculiar combinations of fallen grandeur, all would be comparatively tame. In immediate connection with this figure the poet reaches his loftiest sublimities; and as we recede from it in the later books, his power does not hold us in such thrall. Now the main secret of this strong interest in Milton's Satan is the peculiar character of the conflict in which he is represented as engaged. He falls before a higher power; he is crushed down to hell; but, from the prominence that is given to mere force in the contest, our moral sympathies, so far from being directly outraged by his rebellious spirit, are greatly enlisted on his side. It was necessary, for the purposes of his poem, that Milton should take up this view; the poem otherwise would have been no epic, and possessed no source of excitement. But it may be seriously questioned how far this triumph of art is a triumph of truth. The Puritan spirit here helped the poet; it fed the mighty creation which had seized his ima-

gination ; but, as this spirit disappears, it is felt that
the limitations which have given an epical intensity
and grandeur to the poetic conception, have narrowed
and emptied of its fulness the spiritual thought.

One of the most remarkable results of Milton's poem
is the manner in which it has added to the Protestant
conceptions of the spiritual world. The antecedent
drama of conflict in heaven, the fall of the rebel
angels, their resentment in hell, and plot against man
—are all amplifications beyond the scope, yet in the
very spirit, of the Puritan theology with which his
mind was imbued. He not only ascends to the postulate of this theology — the absolute decree of the
Divine—and weaves it into his whole plan ; but he
fills up the ante-human space which precedes the realisation of the divine plans on earth by an array of
spiritual machinery, fitting, with a singular unity and
effect, into these plans, and explaining them. Between
the decree which sets up the throne of the Messiah,
and the fall of man, which necessitates the interposition of Messiah's power, he introduces a series of
events transcending Revelation, yet so admirably developing its hints, and so completely harmonising
with the general scheme of its thought, that there
are many minds that have lost all sense of distinction
between what is merely imaginative and what is dogmatic in the representation. The epical agencies and
scenery of the early books have not merely coloured
the religious imagination, but they have, so to speak,
become a part of the creed of Protestantism. They
have replaced in it, in higher and more beautiful forms,
the medieval beliefs of celestial and anti-celestial hier-
archies, and given to them such a vividness of impression and force of theological truthfulness, that with

many they seem to be only natural and coherent parts of the Christian system. Nothing can more show how entirely congenial Milton was with the prevailing type of Christian thought in his day, than this fact of his having not only taken up its scheme into his poem, and organised the whole from it, but of his having, moreover, stamped his own imaginative enrichments of it upon the minds of succeeding generations as really parts of the same great outline of thought.

The same thing is shown by many special characteristics of the poem; the daring boldness, for example, with which long trains of argument are put into the mouth of God, and of the Son of God, and the marked forensic or juridical structure of some of these arguments. No parts of the poem are more wonderful, or show more marvellously the elastic sublimity of the author's genius. With what a rare skill he triumphs over masses of unpoetic material, and fuses them into living idea and sentiment! But he also sometimes greatly fails; and the bald structure of the argumentative dialogue or monologue reveals the hardness of the theologian rather than the plastic ease and richness of the poet.

In *Paradise Regained* this baldness of theological structure is more conspicuous. There is a comparative timidity and want of grasp in the conceptions of the poet; while the moral spirit is more narrow and stern—as especially in the manner in which he speaks of heathen wisdom in the Fourth Book. The didactic character of the poem, its want of action, and the argumentative character of the conflict carried on between the Saviour and the tempter—all serve to bring into stronger relief, or, at least, into a more complete view, the formal peculiarities of Milton's thought. *Paradise Lost* is a far grander illustration of this thought; but *Paradise Regained* is, as a whole, a more select pattern of it. The one soars in its sublime action and wealth of imaginative idea far beyond all mere schemes of argument; the other scarcely travels beyond a very definite line of intellectual conception. The dogma of his great epic, however essential to its structure, and however significant of his own spirit and creed, is, after all, a mere skeleton on which the majestic form of the poem is hung. The dogmatic import of *Paradise Regained* fills up the whole outline, and makes the whole story of the poem.

The origin of *Paradise Regained* is related by Ellwood as follows. During the time of the plague, in 1665, Milton quitted London, and took up his abode at Chalfont, in Buckinghamshire, where his Quaker friend, with that untiring and cheering kindliness which distinguished him, had provided for him, as he says, a "pretty box" about a mile from his own residence. On Ellwood paying him a visit here "to welcome him to the country," Milton called for a manuscript, which he gave to him, with a request that he should take it home, and, after carefully reading it, return it with his judgment thereupon. This was the manuscript of *Paradise Lost.* On returning it, with a "due acknowledgment of the favour he had done me in communicating it to me," continues the Quaker, "he asked me how I liked it, and what I thought of it, which I modestly and freely told him; and after some further discourse about it, I pleasantly said to him, 'Thou hast said much here of Paradise lost—but what hast thou to say of Paradise regained?'"

Supposing Milton to have commenced the composition of *Paradise Regained* soon after this conversation with Ellwood in the summer of 1665, it was probably finished in the course of the following year. It was not published, however, till six years later, in 1671, when it appeared, along with *Samson Agonistes*, in one volume.

This latter poem, classical as it is in form, is the most Puritan of all Milton's poems in sternness of spirit and concentrated and rigid outline. There is less of the "genial power of nature" in it—less of that soft brightening spirit of beauty which relieves the graver cast of his thought elsewhere, and touches his higher moods with a happy tenderness and exquisitely pleasing grace. The Hebraic temper is diffused and unbending throughout, not only mournful, but harsh, breathing the vengeance of the theocratic hero—fallen, despairing, and impatient. It is difficult not to believe that Milton has allowed to escape in this poem something of the proud bitterness of feeling which, beneath all the quiet surface of his later years, he yet cherished, as he remembered the great cause with which he had been identified, the heroes who had adorned it, and the miserable overthrow in which all had sunk and gone to ruin. Even his own domestic misfortune casts its deep and painful shadow over the picture which he draws; and in the vehement objurgations of his deceived hero we catch the very strain of the author of the *Doctrine and Discipline of Divorce.** Save for this poem, we could somehow suppose Milton to have been a happier man than he really appears to have been in those later years of his life.

Besides his great poems, this period is generally credited with the preparation of his treatise on " Chris-

* There is almost an identity at times in the language, as between the famous passage in the *Doctrine*, &c., regarding " an uncomplying discord

tian Doctrine." The history of this treatise is now well known. It was discovered in 1823 in the State-Paper Office by Mr Lemon, and edited and translated by the Rev. Mr Sumner, now Bishop of Winchester. It had been deposited in the State-Paper Office under the following circumstances : Milton, apparently designing that it should be published abroad, had intrusted it before his death to a certain Daniel Skinner, of Trinity College, Cambridge, supposed to be a nephew of his friend Cyriac Skinner. This gentleman carried it to Amsterdam, and there offered it to Elzevir for publication ; but after examining the manuscript, the Dutch publisher declined the undertaking. The English Government, in the mean time, had heard of the existence of the manuscript, and, apprehensive that it might contain writing "mischievous to the Church or State," was desirous of securing possession of it. With this view, Dr Barrow, Master of Trinity, wrote to Skinner, warning him of the danger he was incurring in his attempts to have it published. Skinner, instigated by this warning, again obtained possession of the manuscript, and transferred it to the custody of the Secretary of State, by whom it was deposited in the office, where Mr Lemon found it undisturbed in 1823.

A question has been raised as to the right relation of this treatise to Milton's theological views. Does it

of nature," and a "bondage now inevitable," where one looked for "sweet and gladsome society," and the following lines :—

> " Whate'er it be to wisest men and best,
> Seeming at first all heavenly under virgin soil—
> Soft, modest, meek, demure :
> Once found, the contrary she proves, a thorn
> Intestine, far within defensive arms
> A cleaving mischief—in his way to virtue,
> Adverse and turbulent,"

really represent his later convictions? This has generally been assumed as beyond question; but an argument has been lately raised on the subject. One thing must be admitted, that it was certainly commenced at an early period. When he first engaged in the education of his nephew, on his return from Italy, Phillips tells us that it was a part of his system on the Sundays to dictate portions of a "tractate which he thought fit to collect from the ablest of divines who had written of that subject, Amesius and Wollebius," &c. The *Treatise on Christian Doctrine* is found exactly to answer to this description. Large portions of it are not only taken from these two Dutch theologians, but the whole arrangement of the work, not only under two main divisions, entitled the *Knowledge of God* and the *Worship of God*, but in its special chapters, is found to be borrowed from them. At whatever time of his life, therefore, the Treatise may have been completed, it was evidently begun early in the second or controversial stage of his career. It has been contended, very much on this presumption, that it really represents his early and not his later theological opinions—that its Arianism was the faith of his comparative youth, from which he departed as his Christian experience deepened, and his Christian knowledge expanded.* There is some plausibility in this conjecture, but it is certainly not borne out by any conclusive facts—while, as a theory, it rests on a mistaken view of Milton's mind and character. That

---

* See *Bibliotheca Sacra*, July 1859 and January 1860, where this view is defended at great length, and with a very elaborate examination of all the facts bearing upon the point. It does not appear to me, however, after the most candid attention to his argument, that the writer has made out his case.

Milton should be an Arian is supposed to be incompatible with his Puritan spirit and the tenor of the theological systems which moulded his thought in so evident a manner. But this is to judge Milton in far too arbitrary and summary a manner. He was a Puritan, but he was also more than a Puritan. He had studied the Genevan and Dutch systems of theology until his habit of thought had become quite attempered to them, and he carried their most abstract theories into the composition of his great poems; but he was also far more than a student of any theological theories. He was a thinker on his own behalf: he had a natural largeness and independence of mind, combined with the strongest confidence in his own judgment, and something like contempt for mere Catholic tradition, whether in doctrine or church discipline. Such a mind was exactly the one to venture on new paths of theological deduction, and, amid the contemplative quietness of his later years, to elaborate views, which seemed to him to arise from his own free sense of inquiry. It is absurd, as we have already said, to identify Puritanism with any uniform series of doctrinal conclusions. It represents a mode of theological thought, rather than a definite sum of theological results; and Milton's Arianism, so far from being at variance with this mode of thought, might be argued to be only a consistent issue of it. The spirit of logical analysis which insists upon definition at every point, and carries its formal argumentativeness into the highest mysteries of spiritual truth, would find nothing uncongenial in Milton's speculations on the nature of the Godhead.

It appears to us, upon the whole, beyond doubt, that the *Treatise of Christian Doctrine* represents Milton's

most mature theological opinions. Its Arianism need
not puzzle any student of *Paradise Lost*. Its latitudinarian tone in regard to polygamy and the obligation of the Sabbath, need not even surprise any one
who rightly understands his mind and character.
Unpuritan as the sentiments on these subjects are
— more characteristically so than his Arianism —
they are merely the natural development of that
spirit of free-thinking which, in Milton as in some
others, struggled all along with the dogmatism of
their time. When, in the very heat of his controversial career, he showed, both in his *Areopagitica* and
his divorce writings, the strength of this tendency,
and his willingness to enter into conflict with the prevailing orthodoxy; and in the retirement of his later
years, and the quiet evolution of his own opinions, he
was not likely to yield less to the impulses of his own
bold inquiry and his ready and confident opinionativeness. There may seem, on a superficial view,
considerable inconsistency between such parts of the
Christian Doctrine, and especially between the liberal rationalising spirit which distinguishes them, and
the narrow Hebraic spirit, for example, of *Samson
Agonistes;* but such an inconsistency, even if it was
more marked than it is, is only the difference between
the poet yielding himself up to the mood of long-che-
rished feelings, and the intellectualist following out
the thread of his own reasoned convictions. Apparent
inconsistencies of this kind may be found in all great
minds; and in a mind like Milton's, it is only the
natural expression of its largeness and diversity, at
once poetic and concrete, and speculative and theoretic. It seems exactly to suit the character of Milton, to conceive of him in his later years embalming

in his poetry the spirit of the great movement in which he had been engaged, and yet freely criticising and holding himself above its special dogmatic conclusions.

The three years during which Milton survived the publication of *Paradise Regained* and *Samson Agonistes* are marked by various publications. In the year 1672 he published a scholastic work,* which had probably been prepared for some time. During the next year he republished his poems, English and Latin, with some additions, and also his *Tractate on Education*. His treatise on *True Religion, Heresy, Schism, Toleration*, &c., already noticed in connection with his views on the latter subject, belongs to the same year. In the succeeding and last year of his life he was still busy publishing. He collected together his Latin *Epistolæ Familiares*, the letters which he had written to friends from 1625 to 1666, and also his *Prolusiones Oratoriæ* which he had delivered at Cambridge, and gave them to the world. He appears to have carefully treasured all his literary efforts, not merely his original and independent works, but his scholastic and other compilations. Mr Keightley has remarked on his fondness for compilation. Besides his treatise on *Christian Doctrine*, he left behind him a short account of Russia or Moscovia, founded on the narratives of persons who had visited the country.

During these years the tenor of Milton's life was of an even peacefulness. Study, music, and quiet recreation filled up his days. The notices of his manners and appearance that have been preserved by Aubrey and others, chiefly refer to this time. He was an early riser: in his youth he used to sit up late, but

* *Artis Logicæ plenior Institutio ad Rami Methodum Concinnata.*

he had long since changed this practice, and he now retired to bed early, and rose in the morning at four in summer, and five in winter. Sometimes he would lie in bed awake, and have some one to read to him, or to write to his dictation. After he rose, a chapter of the Hebrew Bible was read to him, and the whole of the early part of the day employed in reading or writing—"the writing," Aubrey says, "was as usual as the reading." He used to dictate sitting at ease in his chair, with his leg thrown over the arm of it. He dined at one o'clock, and took exercise for an hour, often also in a chair, in which he used to swing himself. His dinner was frugal, and he drank little but water. But he had a quiet relish for the comforts of the table, and commended his wife for her attention to his tastes. There is a pleasing, and yet a painful sense of dependence in the remark attributed to him. "God have mercy, Betty. I see that thou wilt perform according to thy promise, in providing me such dishes as I think fit, whilst I live ; and when I die, thou knowest that I have left thee all." His poor daughters! They had no doubt, among their other neglects, kept their father's table but poorly supplied, and he had not forgotten their negligence. The afternoon was devoted to music. He played on the organ or bass viol; and either sang himself or made his wife sing. His wife had a good voice, he said, but no ear. Renewed study and conversation with his friends brought the evening to a close, when, after a light supper, a pipe of tobacco, and a glass of water, he retired to rest about nine o'clock.

His conversation, according to Aubrey, was "extremely pleasant," with a vein of satire. His daughter Deborah also says that he was "delightful com-

S

pany, the life of conversation, and that on account of a flow of subject and an unaffected cheerfulness and civility." His powers of composition varied, he has himself told us, with the season. "His views never happily flowed but from the autumnal equinox to the vernal, and whatever he attempted (at other times) was never to his satisfaction, though he courted his fancy never so much."

His beauty of person in youth and manhood has been already remarked. He was evidently not unconscious of it, as may be gathered from the manner in which he expresses himself in his *Defensio Secunda* in reply to the vulgar abuse of the anonymous libeller who attacked him. "I do not believe," he says, "that I was ever noted for deformity by any one who ever saw me; but the praise of beauty I am not anxious to obtain. My stature, certainly, is not tall, but it rather approaches the middle than the diminutive." The florid and delicate complexion of his youth he retained till advanced in life, so that he appeared to be ten years younger than he was; and the smoothness of his skin was not in the least affected by the "wrinkles of age." His eyes were grey, and never lost their hue, blind as he became. His hair was light brown, or auburn; it remained in profusion to the last, and he wore it parted evenly on his forehead, as seen in his portraits. "He had a delicate tuneable voice, and pronounced the letter *r* very hard"—"a certain sign," Dryden said to Aubrey, "of a satirical wit." "His deportment was affable, and his gait erect and manly, bespeaking courage and undauntedness."

It has been noticed that Milton attended no church, and belonged to no particular communion of Christians. His blindness was probably to some extent the explanation of this, although it requires but a slight knowledge of his mind and writings to understand what little importance he himself would attach to such things. His religious consciousness, in its very strength, did not easily conform to external modes of worship. " His having no prayers in his family" is a somewhat unmeaning accusation, seeing that he began every morning with the reading of the Scriptures, and that his wife and he, in his later years, were all the family.

Of his last days we know little. He suffered some time from gout ; yet in the end of the autumn of 1674 he appears to have been in fair health and cheerfulness. He is described by one of the witnesses in the suit regarding his will, as dining in his kitchen on a day of October, along with his wife, when he "talked and discussed sensibly and well, and was very merry, and seemed in good health of body." On Sunday, the 8th of the following month, he expired, so painlessly and quietly, that those around were unconscious of the moment of his departure. His remains were laid beside those of his father, in the Church of St Giles, Cripplegate.

Our view of Milton's character and influence has been fully indicated in the course of our sketch. But a few touches may be added to sum up our estimate. Of the two great types of human character, the broad, humane, and sympathetic, and the narrow, concentrated, and sustained, Milton belongs to the latter. His greatness awes us more than it delights us. It is like an isolated, solitary, and majestic eminence, which we never approach without reverence, but beneath the shadow of which few men dwell familiarly. Something similar to what Johnson said of his great poem, that while we read it, we are carried along with excited admiration, but when we have laid it down, we do not willingly recur to it, is true of his character. While we look on him we see and admire how lofty, and pure, and true he was; but his very goodness is not attractive. It wants ease, freedom, and sweetness, and, above all, breadth and life of sympathy. It is cold, if not stern, in its severe harmony and goodness. His goodness is almost more stoical than Christian in its proud, self-sustained, and scornful strength.

The pride of conscious power is everywhere conspicuous in him. His very manner carried force with it. He had an air of "courage and undauntedness," as Wood said. A hard adversary with his pen, he was also well exercised in the use of the small-sword, and in his youth was quite a match, he tells us, for any one, though much stronger than himself. The same "honest haughtiness and self-esteem" mark him as a scholar, as a controversialist, as a poet. From the lonely height of his own lordly genius and virtue he looked down on others. His genius was a prized possession from his youth, raising him (he felt) above his fellows, and consecrating him to a high mission. His virtue never trembled before temptation; it flung aside all ordinary seductions as easily as the strong rock drives back the idle summer waves that play around it. From such an imperial height of nature, he contemplated society around him with a somewhat disdainful interest, and sought to rectify its disorders, civil and ecclesiastical, with a high and resentful hand. He felt that he was born to rule, and so he was; but in the world of ideas rather than in the world of

reality. He wanted tact and skill, and appreciation of
the thoughts and feelings of others, and of any range
of ideas beyond his own to enable him to be a practical reformer. He remains a great theorist. And the
same sublime ideality that is the chief attribute of
his genius, is the prominent feature of his character.
Contemplating him from first to last as a student at
Cambridge, as a visitor in the academies of Italy, as
the enemy of bishops, and the secretary of Cromwell,
as the blind old poet of Bunhill-fields, we are struck
by his soaring grandeur, and the elevation which he
reaches above his contemporaries. "His natural port,"
as Johnson says, "is gigantic loftiness." In an age
of moral greatness, where heroic religious principle
swayed the lives of public men around him, the character of Milton is seen to rise majestic in its moral
strength, and his life to be conformed with a rare
consistency to a divine ideal. All is throughout as,
at the age of twenty-three, he resolved it should be—

"As ever in his great Taskmaster's eye."

The impression he left upon his contemporaries was
plainly of the kind we have described. He could be
cheerful in conversation; there was a rich liveliness
in some moods of his genius; but he was mainly of a
grave, lofty, severe spirit. "He had," Richardson says,
"a gravity in his temper, not melancholy, or not, till
the latter part of his life, sour—not morose or ill-
natured; but a certain severity of mind—*a mind not
condescending to little things.*" These last words are
full of truth. Milton's greatness wanted condescension; his goodness was without weakness; his magnanimity without sweetness. Not only what he
makes Samson say, "All wickedness is weakness,"

but the converse he seems to have believed. Had he been less strong, and less disdainful in his strength, we could have loved him more and not admired him less. Had pity mingled with his scorn, and gentleness with his heroism, he could have presented a more pleasing if not a more imposing character.

But if there are other characters that more elicit our affection, there is none in our past history that more compels our homage. We behold in him at once the triumph of genius and the unwavering control of principle. He is the intellectual hero of a great cause ; he is also the purest and loftiest, if not the broadest, poetic spirit in our literature. If there is harshness mingling with his strength, and a certain narrowness and rigidity in his grandeur, the most varied tastes and the widest oppositions of opinion have yet combined to recognise in John Milton one of the highest impersonations of poetic and moral greatness of which our race can boast.

III.

BAXTER.

BAXTER.

THE three great theologians of English Puritanism are Owen, Howe, and Baxter. They are very distinct in character and mind, and the first and last were conspicuously opposed in various points of principle and doctrine; yet together these three names form the highest representatives of the theological type of thought and feeling which sprang from, or rather accompanied and animated, the Puritanical movement. They are, if we may use the word in reference to such writers, the *classics* of Puritan theology. In them its spiritual life reached its most elaborate expression, and took its most characteristic intellectual forms. Their lives—those of Owen and Baxter especially—were intimately blended with its varying fortunes, not merely as the leaders of its thought, but as among the most active of its counsellors, and the ablest of its politicians; they shared in its triumphs, and directed its ecclesiastical and educational aims in the interval of its power; they mingled in the disasters of its fall, and bore in their persons the effect of its sufferings. The Puritan Christianity of later times has always looked back to them with a peculiar reverence, and united their names in a community of hallowed respect.

Owen is, of the three, the most perfect example of

the Puritan Theologian. The main interest of his life
and all the interest of his writings is theological.
Whatever is most essential and characteristic in Puritan divinity is to be found in his works. Its leading
ideas of *covenants, decrees,* and *federal relations,* compose the substance and structure of his thought. The
spiritual world appears to him moulded on a rigid
outline, which is not merely convenient and suggestive,
but which has become to his mind the very constitution and reality of that world. His reasonings run in
great lines, or mass in blocks of system, which fill up
for him the whole sphere of truth, and leave nothing
behind. The profoundest mysteries are measured and
weighed in the cool balances of his logic ; the most
awful secrets are handled as if mere pleas in debate.
Gifted with a logical faculty, both keen and comprehensive, he cuts through the deepest questions, and
lays side by side, in order, the most involved and
hardest subtleties. Loving, like all genuine Puritans,
argumentative amplification and detail, proceeding from
a few settled principles, and wholly undisturbed by
any of those deeper questionings which draw the mind
back upon first principles in their universal relations,
he is, of all theologians, scarcely excepting Calvin
himself, the most consistent, definite, and exhaustive,
on his own assumptions. A bolder and more unflinching theorist never trod the way of those sublime revelations that "slope through darkness up to God." He
is a Calvinist beyond Calvin. He explains, and de-
fines, and sums up, in his theological arithmetic, what
even the great Genevan did not venture to do. The
atonement is with him not merely a "sacrifice to satisfy
divine justice," but a "full and valuable compensation
made to the justice of God, for all the sins of all those

for whom Christ made satisfaction." It is only the Puritan divines of America, such as Edwards and Hopkins, who have approached or rivalled Owen in analytical boldness, and far-reaching, undeviating, and comprehending theological deduction.

Along with scholastic earnestness, profound devotion to scriptural studies, and a life of eminent spirituality, we find in Owen a like combination of practical sense and faculty for business as in his prototype Calvin. He had the same administrative power, the same coolness and patience of purpose, with a far higher courtesy and tolerance of feeling. This latter feature of Owen's character deserves particularly to be noticed. Hard and dogmatic in intellect, he was genial and gentle in his temper. Resolute in his own views, and ever ready to contend for them with his unresting pen, he had none of the meanness of bigotry which refuses to honour those who differ from him. He protected Pockock in his Hebrew professorship from the vulgar interference of the Parliamentary Triers, and left the Prelatists unmolested who assembled opposite his own door in Oxford to worship according to the Prayer-book.

His government of the University of Oxford as vice-chancellor was a striking proof both of his administrative ability and his equable and happy disposition. Looking at all the difficulties that surrounded him, it may be considered a masterpiece of policy. His learning and talents commanded respect; his firmness and kindness won him authority, and enabled him to preserve peace amidst the distracting elements. No other Puritan divine probably could have been intrusted with the task, or, if intrusted with it, could have executed it with the same success.

It was the felicity of Cromwell to detect this gift of government, and turn it to account. Of all the religious men the Protector had about him, he found none more useful than Owen.   He may have liked others more, and found in men like Hugh Peters, far inferior in sense and character, points of greater spiritual affinity; but, as a statesman, he trusted none so much, and he had good reason for his trust.   The strong convictions of the vice-chancellor, his earnest, yet calm faith, his activity and zeal, and yet his moderation and sense, made him one of the most conspicuous representatives, and at the same time one of the most powerful supporters of the Protectoral cause.

While Owen was the great dogmatist of the Puritan theological movement, Howe was its contemplative idealist.   Possessing a far less acute and discriminating mind, he excelled in grandeur of imagination and depth of feeling.   His conceptions rise into a freer independence of logical forms, and a loftier harmony of moral speculation.   This majestic and luminous elevation, and a certain tenderness and freshness of spirit, make him more congenial to the modern student than Owen, or even than Baxter.   The latter is more popular, and his directness and force are more fitted to impress the common reader; but Howe far more frequently soars into the sphere of contemplative reason, and fills the mind with the imagery of thought.   Among so many men of logic and of action he was the Christian philosopher.   His spirit certainly more nearly approaches the philosophic than that of any other Puritan divine.   Puritan formalities cling to him, and the tedium of his style, and the prolixity of his divisions and subdivisions, never allow us to forget the age to which he belongs; but he also often rises above it, and, by the lustrous fulness of his calm intellect, pierces far beyond its intellectual and spiritual machinery.

The life of Howe, like his writings, was comparatively quiet, and removed from the bustle of his times. He was one of Cromwell's chaplains, it is true; but the unworldliness of his character, his unambitious temper, and the spirituality of his devotions, kept him apart from the stir that surrounded him. It is a remarkable evidence of the comparatively undisturbed repose of his life, and the philosophical cast of his mind, that amidst the endless controversies in which his contemporaries were plunged, there is none of his writings that can be said to be directly polemical. The *Living Temple* is a vindication of Christian truth, but not of his own peculiar views of it against any of the sectaries and heretics of the day. It is more akin to the apologetical literature of a later time than to the controversial theology of his own. His vision ranged, as it were, over the hot fray of combatants immediately around him, and only descried in Spinoza an opponent worthy of his pen. Controversy then only assumed an interest for him when it ascended into the region of first principles, and left behind the formal details of ecclesiastical and theological warfare.

It is pleasant to contemplate such a man as Howe amid the fierce passions and rude and often petty conflicts of his age. He could not but bear their dint, living, as he did, in the very midst of them; but they touch him as little as possible. His countenance shows the traces of a refined and elevated nature, and of the same largeness and tenderness of soul that mark his writings. It would be difficult to conceive a more noble, spiritual, or gentle set of features. A native dignity of manner and character shine in them. The court of Cromwell may not seem the most fitting nursery of such a nature; but the presence of one who, like Howe, combined earnestness with refinement, and all the glow of the Puritan religious feeling with a chastened taste and a radiancy of imagination, is enough to show that we are not to judge this court according to any mere vulgar estimate. It must have been a pure and high atmosphere in which Howe moved freely and exercised influence. One who lived so much above the world, and on whose spirit dwelt so familiarly the awe and grandeur of the Unseen, would be a constant monitor, both of high principle and duty, in circumstances sufficient to try the one and seduce from the other.*

As a preacher, he must have favourably contrasted with most of the Court chaplains. Others may have roused more by their vehemence, and delighted by their highness of doctrine; but none approached him in dignity, and a certain mixture of sweetness and sublimity of sentiment, that still captivates the reader. Especially when he descants of the glories of heaven, and his large but lazy imagination finds room to expatiate amidst its felicities, he rises into a pictured eloquence that is wonderfully impressive amidst all the prolixities that encumber his style.

Of our three theologians, Baxter was the most energetic, and in some respects the most prominent; the

---

* Howe represented the highest religious aspect of Cromwell's court. It was not all that he wished it to be; and his sensitive uprightness and faithfulness sometimes brought him into conflict with the ruder and more fervent notions of the Protector. Preaching on one occasion of the fallacy and pernicious pride apt to be generated by the idea of a *particular faith* in prayer, Cromwell was observed to "knit his brows and discover great uneasiness:" and afterwards the chaplain thought for some time that the Protector was "cooler in his carriage toward him."

most active sharer in the events of his time, and one
of the most zealous representatives of its spirit; not
merely theologian, but preacher, politician, and nego-
tiator to the very last, when the powers of Puritanism
had again sunk under oppression. He is more comprehensive than Owen, and rises more above the
technical bondage of his system; while its spirit
pervades as completely, if not more completely, every
form of his mental life, and shows itself in him in a
greater variety of mental forms. He was more in the
world, more mixed in its conflicts, and more moulded
by them than Howe. He appears, therefore, the most
interesting representative of theological Puritanism:
others bear its doctrinal stamp more definitely and
precisely; but the very freedom of Baxter's doctrinal
sentiments, which brought him into contact at almost
every point with the religious activity of his age, in-
vests his theological career with a greater attraction,
and makes it richer in lessons of varied meaning and
importance.*

Richard Baxter was born at the village of Eaton-
Constantine, "a mile from the Wrekin-hill," in Shropshire, on the 12th of November 1615. His father was
a freeholder in this county, originally of some substance. His mother's name was Beatrice, and she is
designated as "the daughter of Richard Adeny of
Rowton, a village near High Ercall, the Lord Newport's
seat in the same county." His father had lived a

* Baxter has written his own life—a portly folio, under the name of
Reliquiæ Baxterianæ. It contains the most ample details of his history,
and will be our chief guide and authority throughout. There is also a
painstaking and creditable work by Mr Orme, entitled *The Life and
Times of Richard Baxter*, in two volumes, the second of which is devoted
to a review of his works. The same author has a similar work on Owen.

wild and jovial life in his youth, and squandered a great part of his estate in gaming; but about or shortly before the time of his son's birth a great change passed upon him. He became severely and strictly religious, and spent much of his time in pious meditation and study. This change had arisen from reflection, and the "bare reading of the Scriptures in private, without either preaching or godly company, or any other book than the Bible." Godly company and religious instruction, in fact, were not to be had in the district. The picture which Baxter draws of the clergy and their assistants is of the most melancholy description. As we read it, and think that the men whom he describes were not exceptions, but ordinary specimens of the parochial clergy of King James, the ardour of local Puritanism becomes strongly intelligible. The people, according to his description, were like their pastors—rude, ignorant, and irreligious. With such a clergy, it is remarkable that any moral or spiritual life subsisted among them at all. It is not remarkable that such as did subsist should have been called *Puritan*, and that its adherents, at first not at all disaffected, should have become gradually alienated from a Church that knew not how to respect the semblance of piety.

The incumbent at Eaton Constantine was eighty years of age. He had never preached, and yet he held two livings twenty miles apart. He repeated the prayers by heart; but, unable to read the lessons from his failing sight, he got first a "common thresher and day-labourer," and then a tailor, to perform this duty for him. At length a kinsman of his own, who had been a stage-player and a gamester, got ordination, and assisted him. The clergy of the neighbourhood were no better. In High Ercall there were "four readers successively in six years' time—ignorant men, and two of them immoral in their lives." A neighbour's son, "who had been a while at school, turned minister," and even ventured to distinguish himself from the others by preaching; but it was at length discovered that his orders were forged by the "ingenious" kinsman of the old incumbent, who had been a stage-player. "After him, another neighbour's son took orders, who had been a while an attorney's clerk, and a common drunkard, and tippled himself into so great poverty that he had no other way to live; it was feared that he and more of them came by their orders the same way, with the forementioned person." These, he adds, were the schoolmasters of his youth. They "read common prayer on Sundays and holy days, and taught school and tippled on the week days, and whipt the boys when they were drunk, so that we changed them very oft." *

The people he has described more particularly in another work.† "The generality seemed to mind nothing seriously but the body and the world: they went to church, and would answer the parson in responds, and thence go to dinner, and then to play. They never prayed in their families; but some of them, going to bed, would say over the Creed, and the Lord's Prayer, and some of them the ' Hail, Mary.' All the year long, not a serious word of holy things, or the life to come, that I could hear of, proceeded from them. They read not the Scripture, nor any good book, or catechism. Few of them could read, or had a Bible. They were of two ranks. The

* _Life_, p. 2.
† _The True History of Councils, Enlarged and Defended_, pp. 90, 91.

T

greater part were good husbands, as they called them,
and savoured of nothing but their business, or interest
in the world; the rest were drunkards : most were
swearers, but not equally.   Both sorts seemed utter
strangers to any more of religion than I have named,
and loved not to hear any serious talk of God, or duty,
or sin, or the gospel, or judgment, or the life to come;
but some more hated it than others.—The other sort
were such as had their consciences awakened to some
regard to God and their everlasting state ; and, according to the various measures of their understanding, did
speak and live as serious in the Christian faith, and
would much inquire what was duty and what was sin,
and how to please God and to make sure of salvation.
They read the Scriptures, and such books as *The Practice of Piety*, and Dent's *Plain Man's Pathway*, and
Dod on the Commandments.   They used to pray in
their families and alone—some on the book, and some
without.   They would not swear, nor curse, nor take
God's name lightly.   They feared all known sin.
They would go to the next parish church to hear a
sermon when they had none at their own ; would read
the Scriptures on the Lord's day, when others were
playing.   There were, where I lived, about the number of two or three families in twenty, and these by
the rest were called *Puritans*, and derided as hypo-
crites and precisians, who would take on them to be
holy.   Yet not one of them ever scrupled conformity
to bishops, liturgy, or ceremonies, and it was godly
conformable ministers that they went from home to
hear."

There is no reason to think that these pictures of
the state of religion in Baxter's youth are overcharged.
We can trace here and there the colouring of the Puri-

tan. The "good husbands, as they were called," who, although they might have no prayer in their families, said devoutly the Creed and the Lord's Prayer, or even the "Hail, Mary," before going to bed, may have been decently religious people, with some higher thoughts than he attributes to them. But making all allowance, the picture is sufficiently gloomy. The common life, clerical and laic, is of a very coarse and gross kind; and men who had been awakened to a sense of religion like Baxter's father must have felt a strong repulsion to it. He was specially marked out as a Puritan; and on Sundays the devotions of the good man in his family were interrupted by the merrymaking around the Maypole, which was erected beside a great tree near his door. Here "all the town" collected on Sunday afternoons, after a brief reading of the common prayer, and danced till dark. Although the "piper" was one of his own tenants, he "could not restrain him, nor break the sport." Baxter honestly confesses that his heart was frequently with the merry-makers; he could have joined them and participated in their sport, but the reproach of *Puritan* which they addressed to his father served to deter him. He reflected that his father's quiet study of the Scriptures must be after all better than their merriment, and the workings of conscience helped to check the vagrancies of the heart. The same thoughtfulness convinced him thus early that the name of *Puritan* was applied to others as well as his father in mere malice, for nothing else than "reading Scripture and praying and talking a few words of the life to come," instead of joining in the ungodly habits of those around them. Devout as his father was, in no other sense was he a Puritan; he never "scrupled common prayer nor ceremonies, nor spake against bishops, nor even so much as prayed but by a book or form."

Touched as Baxter was by such serious thoughts from his youth, he was yet far, as he afterwards considered, from being truly religious. Though his conscience would trouble him when he did wrong, yet he was addicted to divers " sins," which he has catalogued as follows :—1. Lying, that he might escape correction; 2. "Excessive gluttonous eating of apples and pears," to which he attributes the habitual weakness of stomach which cost him so much trouble and pain through life ; 3. Robbery of orchards ; 4. Fondness for play, and that with covetousness for money ; 5. Delight in romances, fables, and old tales ; 6. Idle and foolish chat, and imitation of the scurrilous talk of other boys ; 7. Pride in his master's commendations of his youthful learning ; 8. Irreverence towards his parents. The catalogue is somewhat Puritan in its amplification and severity. Boyhood would be scarcely boyhood without its play, its idleness, its love for romances, and even its fondness for apples.

Baxter's early education was very interrupted, as may be supposed, from the character of his tutors. From six to ten years of age he was under the four successive curates of the parish—"ignorant men, and two of them immoral in their lives." These years he had spent at his grandfather's residence near High Ercall. On his return to his father's house in his tenth year, he was placed under a more competent tutor, who possessed in his library the Greek New Testament and Augustin's *De Civitate*. But this teacher also neglected his trust. During two years he gave his pupil little or no instruction, and chiefly occupied himself in railing against the Puritans. After this he went to the free school at Wroxeter, under the charge of Mr John Owen, a diligent and respectable man, who did his duty. Here he had for his school-fellows the two sons of Sir Richard Newport, one of whom became Lord Newport in his day, and Richard Allestree, who afterwards became canon of Christ Church and provost of Eton College, and was distinguished for his adherence to the Royal cause. He recounts a significant trait of his boyhood in connection with his class-fellows : "When my master set him up into the lower end of the highest form where I had long been chief, I took it so ill that I talked of leaving the school, whereupon my master gravely but very tenderly rebuked my pride, and gave me for my theme *Ne sutor ultra crepidam.*"

It was about his fifteenth year that he considers himself to have awakened to a more clear and lively sense of religion. With some other boys he had been robbing "an orchard or two," and being under some convictions of wrong-doing, he fell in with an old torn book which a poor day-labourer in the town had lent to his father. The book was called Bunny's *Resolution;* it had originally been written by a Jesuit of the name of Parsons, but adapted by Bunny to the Puritan taste and standard.* The volume made a deep impression upon Baxter's youthful mind. It showed him the folly and misery of sin, and the inexpressible weight

---

* This is a singular enough fact—one of those instances which meet us everywhere of the secret links of connection between religious feeling in all sects and under the most diverse forms of manifestation. It is the same sensitive conscience which is touched in Jesuit and Puritan, the same feeling of guilt calling for the same remedy. The Jesuit (Parsons) not unnaturally considered Bunny to have used unwarrantable liberties with his book, and the latter wrote a pamphlet in his defence. The same book was useful to others among the Nonconformists as well as Baxter.--*Owen's Life and Times*, p. 6.

of things eternal; it excited in him the fervent desire
of embracing a holy life; yet it remained doubtful
to him whether his sincere conviction began now, or
before, or after. He had still but too little sense of
the love of God in Christ to the world or himself. The
treatise of the Jesuit dwelt upon this too slightly.
But another volume that came to his hand in the
same accidental manner, disclosed to him the mystery of divine love. A poor pedlar brought to his
father's door, among his other wares, Gibb's *Bruised
Reed*, and in this he found what was lacking in the
Resolution. It " opened" the love of God to him, and
gave him " a livelier apprehension of the mystery of
redemption, and how much he was beholden to Jesus
Christ." Various other books, such as Perkins *On
Repentance*, and the *Right Art of Living and Dying
well*, and also Culverwell's *Treatise of Faith*, were
highly useful to him. More than to any others was
he indebted to these silent teachers; and the fact was
never forgotten by him. He remarks that the use
which God made of books above ministers to the
benefit of his soul, made him exceedingly in love with
good books, so that he amassed as great a treasure of
them as he could.

It is interesting to notice the volumes which in successive ages are associated with the conversion of eminent religious men. Every age has its own peculiar
literature of conversion. It needs spiritual stimulants
especially adapted to it. There is something, as it
were, in the atmosphere of religious thought and feeling from time to time that requires to be condensed
and exhibited, so as to bear with a touching effect upon
the minds that are growing up under it. The tones
of Bunny's *Resolution*, or even Gibb's *Bruised Reed*,

would now fall but feebly on the youthful inquiring mind ; and even Baxter's own more memorable and powerful *Call to the Unconverted,* whose piercing earnestness has reached so many hearts, may have lost something of its force and interest to the modern reader. As the thoughts of men are widened, or at least altered in religious range, as in everything else, the argument and appeal fitted to tell most powerfully must be reflected from some new point, and made to bear with a fresh life upon changed feelings and views.

When Baxter was ready for higher studies he was induced, by the persuasion of his teacher, to place himself under the tuition of Mr Richard Wickstead, chaplain to the Council at Ludlow, instead of proceeding directly to the university. The inducement to do this was that the chaplain was permitted to have a single pupil, to whom he could give his undivided attention. But in this case also Baxter was unfortunate ; the chaplain paid little or no attention to his pupil. " His business was to please the great ones, and seek preferment in the world ; and to that end he found it necessary sometimes to give the Puritans a flirt, and call them unlearned, and speak much for learning, being but a superficial scholar of himself. He never read to me nor used any savoury discourse of godliness ; only he loved me, and allowed me books and time enough ; so that as I had no considerable helps from him in my studies, yet I had no considerable hindrance." He mentions with gratitude that he was preserved from the temptations that surrounded him in the town. An acquaintance which he formed with a young man was of great service to him. They became fast companions. " We walked together," he says, " we read together, we prayed together, and when we could

we lay together; he was the greatest help to my seriousness of religion that ever I had before, and was a
daily watchman over my soul; he was unwearied in
reading all serious practical books of divinity; he was
the first that ever I heard pray extempore (out of the
pulpit), and that taught me so to pray. And his
charity and liberality were equal to his zeal; so that
God made him a great means of my good, who had
more knowledge than he, but a colder heart." The
sequel of all this fervency is sad. Baxter's companion
fell, in course of time, into habits of drunkenness and
even of scoffing. The last he heard of him was that he
had become a "fuddler, and reviler of strict men." It
is kindly of Baxter to chronicle at length the good he
got from one who lived so to disgrace his Christian
profession. The reader of Bunyan's life may remember a somewhat similar incident in his early religious
career.

On his return, after a year and a half, to his father's
house, he found that his old master, Owen, was dying
of consumption; and, at the desire of Lord Newport,
he undertook the management of his school, "for a
quarter of a year or more." His studies were there-
after continued with Mr Francis Garbet, the "faithful
learned minister at Wroxeter." He read logic with
him, and entered upon a more severe course of intellectual application than he had yet attempted. His
weak health broke down in the attempt. He was
seized with a violent cough and spitting of blood;
his end seemed near at hand; and anxiety as to his
spiritual condition greatly increased. He mourned
over his "senseless deadness;" he felt as if he knew
nothing of the "incomparable excellency of holy love
and delight in God;" and he groaned and prayed for

more "contrition and a broken heart," and most for
"tears and tenderness." This was a time of painful
and sad experience, but also of great spiritual improvement. It made him realise more the power of redeem-
ing love, and destroyed in him the promptings of mere
intellectual and literary ambition, the *sin* (as he supposed) of his childhood!

From this time his studies were mainly confined to
divinity; his idea of going to the university was abandoned; and he gave himself to an active and direct
preparation for the Christian ministry, to which he
meant to devote himself. The clear direction thus
imparted to his studies gave them importance, and
stimulated his intellectual interest. But he was in
the habit of regretting his loss of a university education. He esteemed himself but a poor scholar. "Besides the Latin tongue, and but a mediocrity in Greek
(with an inconsiderable trial at the Hebrew long after),
I had no great skill in languages." "And for the
mathematics," he adds, "I was an utter stranger to
them; and never could find in my heart to direct any
studies that way." Logic and metaphysics were his
peculiar labour and delight. Both his natural aptitude
and his opportunities turned his main studies in this
direction. By inborn intellectual tact Baxter was a
metaphysician, and the hardest subtleties of the school-
man were to him but natural aliment. He united in
his youth, as in after years, that singular mixture of
practical fervency and intellectual dryness, which we
find in not a few of the schoolmen, and in their Protestant exemplars of the sixteenth century.* "Next to
practical divinity," he says, "no books so suited with

* This is a fact deserving of some psychological study—the intense
and lawless flow of feeling in some of the schoolmen and divines of the

my disposition as Aquinas, Scotus, Durandus, Ockham, and their disciples; because I thought they narrowly searched after truth, and brought things out of the darkness of confusion; for I could never, from my first studies, endure confusion. Till *equivocals* were explained, and *definition* and *distinction* led the way, I had rather hold my tongue than speak; and was never more weary of learned men's discourses than when I heard them long wrangling about unexpounded words or things, and eagerly disputing before they understood each other's minds, and vehemently asserting *modes* and *consequences* and *adjuncts* before they considered of the *Quod sit*, the *Quid sit*, or the *Quotuplex.*"

He continued for some time in great weakness of body, and in great anxiety as to his spiritual condition. His inward tremors reflected his outward debility. His spiritual fears and hypochondria, though not induced, were greatly increased by the disorders of his constitution. Not only now, but throughout life, he was in ill health. Amid all his labours he bore a weakened and diseased frame; it lasted long, but it never ceased to trouble him;. and in his writings everywhere we may trace something of the restlessness and morbid colouring of the Invalid.

About his eighteenth year, his views of life underwent a temporary diversion. Persuaded by his old tutor, Mr Wickstead of Ludlow, to lay aside his pre-

seventeenth century, combined with a logic, not merely hard, but arid and barren in its hardness. Among the latter, an example occurs in Samuel Rutherford, who, in his Latin theological polemics, and in his famous letters, shows this singular conjunction of mental qualities—logical aridity and sentimental fluidity. Polemics more hard and technical than those of Rutherford (as in his *Disputatio Scholastica de Divina Providentia*, &c.) not even the seventeenth century has bequeathed to us —letters kindling with a more intense and. even unhealthy fervour are scarcely to be found in the records of mysticism.

paration for the ministry, he went to London " to get acquaintance at Court, and get some office, as being the only rising way." He says that he himself consented reluctantly to this step ; he had no great confidence in his tutor's judgment, who had done his part but ill towards him ; but his parents entered heartily into the proposal, and to please them he agreed. Accordingly, he went to town, and stayed at Whitehall with Sir Henry Herbert, then "Master of the Revels," about a month. It is a strange conjunction, Baxter and the Master of the Revels ! He does not explain the conjunction, or by what chance his friend selected such an abode for him. If it was meant to give him a taste for Court life, it had, as might be expected, the very opposite effect. He was disgusted with what he saw. He felt quickly that he had " enough of the Court." " When I saw a stage play instead of a sermon on the Lord's-day in the afternoon, and saw what course was then in fashion, and heard little preaching but what was, as to one part, against the Puritans, I was glad to be gone. At the same time it pleased God that my mother fell sick, and desired my return ; and so I resolved to bid farewell to those kind of employments and expectations."

On his return home, Baxter found his mother seriously ill, and in the following May (1634) she died.* He describes the severity of the snow storm on his way home, and throughout the winter. His horse stumbled with him on his journey, and he was nearly crushed under the wheels of an approaching waggon. The home-bound youth, the cheerless season, and the

* His father married a second time " a woman of great sincerity in the fear of God." The connection appears to have been a happy one for Baxter, who speaks of his stepmother in terms of high commendation.

dying mother, make a sadly impressive picture. The storm began about Christmas-day, and lasted till Easter, the snow lying, in some places, "many yards deep;" many who went abroad in it perished. "Shut up in the great snow" through all the dreary winter, he was the witness of his mother's piteous sufferings till death released her in the spring.

He now approached manhood, but his health had not strengthened. From the age of twenty-one till near twenty-three, his debility continued so extreme that he did not expect to live. Under this experience of suffering, he became more impressed than ever by the interests of religion, and the folly of those who neglect it; and the desire to enter into the Christian ministry (should his life be spared) grew stronger than before. He so felt the unspeakable greatness of the soul's salvation, that he thought if men only heard of it as they ought, they could not live careless and ungodly lives; and "he was so foolish as to think that he himself had so much to say of such convincing evidence for the truth, that men could scarcely be able to withstand it." This was the genuine instinct of the Preacher. The triumphant faith that he would move others by what so deeply moved himself, bespoke in Baxter thus early the true spring of all pulpit eloquence. It is pleasant to think of his nursing, amidst all his weakness, and when he seemed near to die, the impulse which was to give its highest distinction and energy to his life.

It was natural that in his circumstances he should give special attention to the controversy then agitating the Church of England. The presence of this controversy has been seen more or less in every turn of his boyhood, in relation to his father, and the villagers

amongst whom he lived—his teachers, and his brief
visit to Court. His father, deeply religious as he
was, and called a Puritan by the rioting villagers, because he would not countenance their Sunday sports,
was yet a Conformist. He never "scrupled common
prayer nor ceremonies, nor spake against bishops."
Baxter had grown up with the same feelings and habits
of worship. He "joined with the common prayer
with as hearty a fervency as afterwards he did with
other prayers." Not only so, but as far as he was able
at this time to examine the subject for himself, and
consider the fair grounds of argument on either side,
he clearly inclined to the side of the Conformists. It
appeared to him that their cause was "very justifiable,
and the reasoning of the Nonconformist weak;" and
he candidly confesses that the superior learning of the
Church writers impressed him. Among these writers,
he has mentioned in his life Downham, Sprint, and
Burgess, and elsewhere he has mentioned Hooker,
with whose great work, as well as with his sermons,
he frequently shows his familiarity. He had also
"turned over Cartwright and Whitgift." On the
whole, he takes a fair and discriminating view of the
controversy at this date. In ceremonies such as kneeling, and the ring in marriage, he saw no ground for
scruple. The surplice and the cross in baptism seemed
to him less lawful, and the latter he never once used.
A form of prayer and liturgy he judged to be un-
doubtedly lawful, and in some cases lawfully imposed;
but there appeared to him much disorder and defec-
tiveness in the Church of England liturgy in particular. He also became doubtful about subscription, and
greatly deplored the want of discipline in the Church.
These were his mature convictions after ordination,

which he received when he was about twenty-three
years of age. He confesses that there were some subjects which he had not, at this date, examined with
the care that he ought to have done. He had never
once read over the Book of Ordination or the Book of
Homilies, nor did, he sufficiently understand certain
controverted points in the Thirty-nine Articles.

Following his ordination, he was, about 1638, appointed to be head-master of a school established at
Dudley. Here, in the parish church, he preached his
first sermon. Here, also, he studied more at length
the subject of Conformity, and became a zealous advocate for it. He "daily disputed against the Nonconformists," whose censoriousness and inclination
towards separation he judged to be a threatening evil
—as much contrary to Christian charity on one side,
as persecution was on the other.

He continued in Dudley about a year, when he received an invitation to Bridgenorth, the second town
in Shropshire, to be assistant to the incumbent there.
He considered it his duty to accept the invitation;
the employment exactly suited him, as he was left at
liberty in certain particulars, in regard to the obligation of which he was beginning to feel uneasy.
The minister of the place, Mr William Madstard, is
described as "a grave and severe ancient divine, very
honest and conscionable, and an excellent preacher,
but somewhat afflicted with want of maintenance, and
much more with a dead-hearted unprofitable people."
Here he preached with great zeal and to a very full
congregation; but he complains that, although his
labours were not without success, the people generally
were very ignorant, and given to "tippling, ill company, and dead-heartedness." The freedom which

he enjoyed from all restraint in the discharge of his duty greatly pleased him; he used the Common Prayer, but he never administered the Lord's Supper, nor ever baptised any child with the sign of the cross, nor ever wore the surplice. This freedom of action, combined with his youthful fervour of feeling—for he never anywhere " preached with more vehement desire of men's conversion "—evidently made his work in Bridgenorth pleasing to him, notwithstanding the small results that seemed to follow it.

The first thing that disturbed him, and led him to renewed reflection on Church government, was the *Et cætera* oath, as it was called, which required the clergy to swear that they would " *never consent to the alteration of the present government of the Church by Archbishops, Bishops, Deans, Archdeacons, &c.*" The attempt to enforce an obligation of this nature, it may be imagined, made a great commotion. Many, even of the Conforming clergy, were not disposed to bind themselves thus arbitrarily and blindly; only the Laudian section, who maintained that Episcopacy was *jure divino*, and that the royal will in itself was absolutely authoritative in ecclesiastical government, could honestly subscribe it. The measure was equally ignorant and outrageous—like many other acts of Laud's administration. It compassed no adequate purpose, while it called forth the strongest animosity, and rallied in opposition the intelligence and the conscience of the nation.

A meeting of clergy was held at Bridgenorth to " debate the business," and Baxter distinguished himself by his vigorous hostility to the oath. His renewed investigation and discussion of the subject shook his faith in Episcopal government altogether, or

at least in the "English diocesan frame." A system
which admitted of such tyrannical action, and which,
for practical purposes of moral discipline, was so power-
less, he at length became satisfied was a "heterogenial
thing," quite unlike the primitive Episcopacy. And
so it was, as he himself says, that the *Et cætera* oath
became the means of alienating him and many others
from the moderate conformity in which they desired
to spend their lives, and rousing them "to look about
them, and understand what they did."

This occurred on the eve of the Scottish war, when
the Covenant excitement had broken forth, and the
noise of the successful opposition made in Scotland to
the royal authority was spreading into England, and
kindling into flame the discontent arising from the
exaction of *Ship-money*. The national agitation was
extreme. Years of misgovernment had embittered the
country, and the most arbitrary interferences outraged
the rights of the people and the Church, without com-
pacting the interests of Government. The spirit of
loyalty and reverence was wearing out, while the rising discontent was only met by insolence and violence.
The Scottish army at length marched into England ;
and, pressed on all hands, the King was forced to call
a Parliament.

After a temporary delay, the dismissal of the Parliament, and the renewed invasion of the Scotch, the
Long Parliament met in 1640 ; and it had no sooner
done so than it showed of what spirit it was. The
Ship-money and the *Et cætera* oath mark the two lines
of civil and ecclesiastical reform into which it immediately launched; the impeachment of Strafford and of
Laud proved the stern spirit in which it was prepared to
vindicate the national rights, and avenge the national

injuries in both directions. The speeches of Falkland, Digby, Grimstone, Pym, and Fiennes were printed and greedily purchased throughout the country. The clergy, and the bishops in particular, were the objects of loud-voiced indignation. A special committee of Parliament sat to receive complaints and petitions against them; and the chairman, Mr John White, published, as a specimen of the reports made to it, *One Century of Scandalous Ministers*, showing a picture of "ignorance, insufficiency, drunkenness, filthiness, &c.," such as all good men were ashamed of.

Baxter viewed all this commotion with sympathy, and yet without any cordial or partisan interest. He nowhere shows any warm feeling on the Parliamentary side. There is now and at all times a lack of political heartiness in him. He speaks of the great movement as from a distance, as if he were an outside spectator of it, and held his mind in a fair and critical balance between the parties. This gives a certain value to his statements; but we could have wished that he had shown a warmer tinge of enthusiasm, and expressed his mind more fully regarding the great public events of his day.*

The ecclesiastical changes arising out of the Parliamentary investigation soon affected his position. The town of Kidderminster, with many other towns, sent up a petition against their vicar, as unlearned and quite unfit for the ministry. It stated that he preached

---

* He implies, indeed, that he was more zealous and decided at the time than the line of his remarks and reflections long afterwards might lead us to suppose he was. "Herein," he says, "I was then so zealous, that I thought it was a great sin for men who were able to defend their country to be useless. And I have been tempted since to think that I was a more competent judge upon the place, where all things were before our eyes, than I am in the review of those days and actions so many years after, when distance disadvantageth the reflection."

U

only once a quarter, and that "so weakly as to expose himself to the laughter of the congregation; that he, moreover, frequented ale-houses, while his curate, in this respect, was worse than himself, being a 'common tippler and drunkard,' and an 'ignorant insufficient man,' who understood not the common points in the children's Catechism. The vicar, with a conscious feeling of incompetency, sought to compound the busi- ness with the petitioners. He offered to withdraw his present curate, and make a respectable allowance for a preacher or lecturer, to be chosen by a committee of the people. The inhabitants agreed to this, and after trial of another person, at length selected Baxter to the office. He himself was inclined to the place, and after preaching one day, he was chosen, as he says, "*nemine contradicente.* And thus I was brought by His gracious providence to that place which had the chiefest of my labours, and yielded me the greatest fruits of comfort. And I noted the mercy of God in this, that I never went to any place among all my life, in all my changes, which I had before desired, designed, or thought of (much less sought), but only to those that I never thought of, till the sudden invitation did surprise me."

Kidderminster attracted Baxter from the large field of usefulness that it opened to him. There was a full congregation and "most convenient temple;" and, although the people, for the greater part, were igno- rant, rude, and riotous, like those at Bridgenorth, there were among them a small company of converts — humble and godly folks — of good conversation, who were a sort of leaven among the rest of the community. He was encouraged also by the fact that there had never been any "lively serious" preaching in the place, for his experience at Bridgenorth had made him resolve that he would never go among a people who had been "hardened in unprofitableness under an awakening ministry." His ultimate success corresponded to the heartiness of his zeal and the affection and earnestness with which he entered upon his duties. It is not till his second settlement at Kidderminster, however, that we are invited to consider his pastoral relations there. He had to submit to a temporary exile from it, and during this period we are carried with him into the midst of more exciting scenes.

The immediate cause of Baxter's retirement from Kidderminster was the extreme hostility between the Royalist and Parliamentary parties in the town. An order had been received from the Parliament to demolish all statues and images in the churches and churchyard; he approved of the order, but did not interfere, he says, in the execution of it. The multitude, however, fixed the blame upon him, and he only escaped from assault by being absent from the town at the time. When the excitement was beginning to quiet, it was renewed by the reading of the King's declaration and the preparations for war. The mob of the town was strongly Royalist; they had got the cry, "Down with the Roundheads!" which they vociferated whenever any stranger appeared in the streets with "short hair and a civil habit," and followed up their insolence by personal violence. Baxter was advised to withdraw till the excitement died down. He proceeded to Gloucester, where he remained a month, and where he made acquaintance with the new forms of religious zeal which were everywhere springing up in the country. A small party of Anabaptists were

labouring with great keenness in this city to promote
their views; while the minister, a hot and impatient
man, tended, by his opposition, to harden, rather than
convince them.   Other sects were likewise spreading,
and Baxter gazed with amazement on the dogmatic
conflicts that surrounded him.   After a short residence here, he returned to Kidderminster, and made
an effort to settle once more among his people; but
the contentions continued so violent that he was
under the necessity of again withdrawing; the fury of
faction was such in the town and neighbourhood as to
interrupt all useful discharge of his duties.

This was in October 1642, on the eve of the battle
of Edgehill.   He had retired to Alcester, and, while
preaching there for his friend Mr Samuel Clark, on
the morning of the 23d, "the people heard the cannon
play."   He has given a graphic description of what
he heard and saw.   "When the sermon was done in
the afternoon the report was more audible, which
made us all long to hear of the success.   About sun-
setting many troops fled through the town, and told
us that all was lost on the Parliament side, and that
the carriages were taken, and the waggons plundered,
before he came away.   The townsmen sent a message
to Stratford-on-Avon to know the truth.   About four
o'clock in the morning he returned, and told us that
Prince Rupert wholly routed the left wing of the Earl
of Essex's army; but while his men were plunder-
ing the waggons, the main body and the right wing
routed the rest of the King's army, took his standard, but lost it again; killed General the Earl of
Lindsay, and took his son prisoner; that few persons
of quality on the side of the army were lost; that the
loss of the left wing happened through the treachery

of Sir Faithful Fortescue, Major to Lord Fielding's regiment of horse, who turned to the King when he should have charged; and that the victory was obtained principally by Colonel Hollis's regiment of red-coats, and the Earl of Essex's own regiment and life-guard, where Sir Philip Stapleton, Sir Arthur Haselriggs, and Colonel Urrey, did much." Next morning Baxter visited the battle-field, while the two armies still remained facing one another "about a mile off." There were about a thousand dead bodies in the field between them; and many, he supposes, had been already buried.

His plans were now very uncertain. He was unable to live at Kidderminster, with soldiers of the one side or the other constantly among the people stirring up tumult, and the city exposed to the fury of the contending parties. He had neither money nor friends, and he knew not where to turn. At length he was induced to go to Coventry, where he had an old acquaintance, and here he proposed to stay till one of the parties had obtained the victory, and the war was ended, which, he thought, must happen within a few days or weeks, in the event of another battle. This idea of the speedy termination of the war was a prevailing one at its commencement. In this expectation, however, he was soon undeceived; and when he was thinking anew what he should do, he received very opportunely an offer from the Governor of Coventry to take up his abode with him and preach to the soldiers. He embraced the offer, but refused to receive any commission as a chaplain in the army. He continued during a year to discharge this duty, preaching once a-week to the soldiers, and once on the Lord's day to the people. He then removed to Shrop-

shire for two months, in order that he might be of
assistance to his father, who had suffered amidst the
troubles of the time; after which he returned to Coventry, and continued in the discharge of his former
duty for another year.

Here, upon the whole, he lived a peaceable life, considering the distractions in which the country was
plunged. His only trouble was the Sectaries. Some
of Sir Harry Vane's "party from New England" had
arrived in the place, and "one Anabaptist tailor,"
by his restless heresy, disturbed the whole garrison.
Baxter courted encounter with them, and, by his constant vigilance, and ready powers of argument, met
them at every point, so that they did not succeed with
the Coventry soldiers as with the rest of the army.
He preached over "all the controversies against the
Anabaptists first, and then against the Separatists;
and, in private, his neighbours and many of the foot
soldiers, were able to baffle both Separatists, Anabaptists, and Antinomians."

It was during this period of his second residence
at Coventry that he took the Covenant, and openly
declared himself on the side of the Parliament, both
of which steps, but the first especially, he afterwards
regretted. His idea of the Covenant was that it was
mainly intended as a test for soldiers and garrisons;
he did not anticipate that it should be exalted, as it
was, into a national badge.

While he continued at Coventry in comparative
peace, every day brought him the news of the progress of the war,—of some fight or another,—or some
garrison or another,—lost or won. "Like men," he says,
"in a dry house, who hear the storms abroad," he
heard from his retreat the sounds of siege and battle.

The "two Newbury fights, Gloucester siege, the marvellous sieges of Plymouth, Lime, and Taunton, Sir
William Waller's successes and losses, the loss at
Newark, the slaughter at Bolton, the greatest fight of
all at York" (Marston Moor), came in rapid succession, so that every morning he looked for the news of
some fresh triumph or disaster. It was a terrible
time, he confesses: "miserable and bloody days, in
which he was the most honourable who could kill
most of his enemies."

During the same period those great changes in the
leaders and the character of the war took place which
are marked by the self-denying ordinance. The Earls
of Essex and Manchester, and Sir William Waller, disappeared from the scene, and Fairfax and Cromwell
took their place. Baxter throws no light on these
movements. Sir Harry Vane in the Commons, and
Cromwell in the army, appear to him to explain all.
Both of those leaders, and Cromwell especially, he
heartily detested. It is difficult to say to what extent the traditionary view of Cromwell's character as
a deeply-designing hypocrite, who planned the whole
issue of events to serve his selfish aggrandisement, has
been owing to Baxter's strong and unhesitating representations. His statements are certainly very confident,
and must have had great influence on many minds.
There seems to have been a natural antipathy between
the two men. Cromwell's conduct, when Baxter visited
the army, is significant of his feeling; Baxter's com-
ments on the character and motives of the General show
a vein of personal dislike, as well as misunderstanding.
His whole description of the army and its leaders is,
on the face of it, strongly coloured by the hues of his
own discontent. It deserves consideration as being

that of an eyewitness and an honest man, who would report nothing but what strictly seemed to him the truth. But its querulous and dogmatic tone, and the wounded self-esteem which it betrays, are enough to caution us against the accuracy of its representations.

It was the noise of the great victory of Naseby, which sounded loud in the ears of the Coventry garrison, not far off, and a wish to see some friends whom he had not seen for years, that carried Baxter to the quarters of the army. He does not seem to have had any intention of remaining; but he felt great curiosity as to the state of religious feeling among the soldiers and their leaders, and some anxiety as to his own reception. He was astonished at the one and disappointed at the other. "We that lived quietly at Coventry," he says, "did keep to our old principles; we were unfeignedly for King and Parliament; we believed that the war was only to save the Parliament and kingdom from Papists and delinquents. . . . But when I came to the army among Cromwell's soldiers, I found a new face of things which I never dreamed of : I heard the plotting heads very hot upon that which intimated their intention to subvert both Church and State. Independency and Anabaptistry were most prevalent; Antinomianism and Armenianism were equally distributed. Abundance of the common troopers and many of the officers I found to be honest, sober, orthodox men, and others tractable, ready to hear the truth, and of upright intentions ; but a few proud, self-conceited, hot-headed sectaries had got into the highest places, and were Cromwell's chief favourites, and by their very heat and activity bore down the rest, or carried them along with them, and were the soul of the army, though much fewer in num-

ber than the rest. I perceived that they took the King
for a tyrant and an enemy, and really intended absolutely
to master him or ruin him ; and that they thought if
they might fight against him, they might kill or conquer him. . . . They were far from thinking of a
moderate Episcopacy, or of any healing way between
the Episcopal and the Presbyterians. They most honoured the Separatists, Anabaptists, and Antinomians ;
but Cromwell and *his Council took on them to join themselves to no party, but to be for the liberty of all.* Two
sects, I perceived, they did so commonly and bitterly
speak against, that it was done in mere design to make
them odious to the soldiers and to all the land ; and
that was—1. The Scots, and with them all Presbyterians, but especially the ministers, whom they called
Priests and *Priestbyters*, and *Dryvines* and the *Dissembly*
men, and such like ; 2. The committees of the several
counties, and all the soldiers that were under them
that were not of their mind and way."

Baxter was deeply concerned by this state of things.
It opened to him suddenly a new view of the prospects
of the struggle and of the dangers to which the country
was exposed. He blamed himself and others for their
inattention to the religious condition of the soldiers ;
and particularly accused himself for having declined
an invitation, which he had received some time before,
from Cromwell, to join his famous troop of horse as
their chaplain. The men of the troop, he says, had
all subscribed the invitation, but he had not only sent
them a denial, but a rebuke of their way of thinking.
Afterwards he had met with Cromwell at Leicester,
who had personally remonstrated with him on his
refusal. He says nothing more of this meeting ; but
it seems pretty clear that it had been a testing one on

Cromwell's part. He had scanned Baxter with his penetrating eye, and ascertained that they would not suit each other. Whether it was his scrupulous sensitiveness, or his restless self-confidence, or some other cause, it is difficult to say ; but there can be little doubt that Cromwell decided that the zealous preacher was not likely to prove a man after his heart. Accordingly, when he made up his mind to join the army, as chaplain to Whalley's regiment, Oliver bade him " coldly welcome," and " never spake one word more" to him. He was excluded from headquarters, " where the councils and meetings of the officers were," and soon found himself out of place. "Most of his design," in joining the army," as he confessed, " was thereby frustrated." And not only was he destined to inactivity, at least on the scale he desired, but he was made the subject of scoffs on the part of the soldiers. Cromwell's secretary " gave out that there was a reformer come to the army to undeceive them, and to save Church and State, with some such other jeers." Baxter attributes all this coldness and insolence of the Independent party to their having been made privy to his designs against the Sectaries. This may have had some effect, but his self-confidence exaggerates when he supposes that Cromwell was likely to have any dread of his influence. The simple truth seems to be, that they did not like each other, and that the great leader, while not interfering with the preacher's activity, carefully shunned his counsel.

According to Baxter's own confession, he had no dealings with Cromwell during his whole stay in the army ; he was left to infer his designs from his own general observations and suspicions. The following is his statement :—" All this while, though I came not near Cromwell, his designs were visible, and I saw him continually acting his part. The Lord-General suffered him to govern and do all, and to choose almost all the officers of the army. He first made Ireton Commissary-General ; and when any troop or company was to be disposed, or any considerable officer's place was void, he was sure to put a Sectary in the place ; and when the brunt of the war was over, he looked not so much at their valour as their opinions " (an accusation certainly inconsistent with the character of Cromwell and even with Baxter's own subsequent statement as to Cromwell's disguise of his own opinions. No man was less likely than Cromwell to prefer opinions to character) ; " so that by degrees he had headed the greatest part of the army with Anabaptists, Antinomians, Seekers, or Separatists at best. All these he led together *by the point of liberty of conscience,* which was the common interest in which they did unite. Yet all the sober party were carried on by his profession that he only promoted the universal interest of the godly, without any distinction or partiality at all ; but still when a place fell void it was twenty to one but a Sectary had it ; and if a godly man of any other mind or temper had a mind to leave the army, he would secretly or openly further it. Yet he did not openly profess what opinion he was of himself, but the most that he said for any one was for Anabaptism and Antinomianism, which he usually seemed to own."

The companion picture of Harrison is very good, and well worth quoting. There is much less ill nature in it. " Harrison, who was then great with him (Cromwell), was for the same opinions. He would not dispute with me at all " (he knew his disputant obviously too well) ; " but he would as good discourse very fluently from out himself on the excellency of free grace, though he had some misunderstandings of free grace himself. He was a man of excellent natural parts for affection and oratory, but not well seen on the principles of his religion ; of a sanguine complexion, naturally of such vivacity, hilarity, and alacrity, as another man hath when he hath drunken a cup too much ; but naturally, also, so far from humble thoughts of himself, that pride was his ruin.''

Baxter, it is clear, had no sympathy with the party rising into power. Slow to identify himself with the revolution in its earlier stages, it soon outran, in its course, all his views as to the need of change. If not in all things formally a Presbyterian—for he objects strongly to various points of their discipline (the institution of lay elders, for example), and was "not of their mind in any part of the Government which they would have set up "—he was yet more of a Presbyterian than he was anything else ; and politically his opinions did not go at all beyond theirs. He was " unfeignedly for *King and Parliament,*" against Papists and Schismatics. So he "understood the Covenant ; " and he felt at a loss to understand the deeper and more implacable form which the war gradually assumed. To him, it represented nothing but the machination of selfish and unprincipled men. He had no perception of the deeper currents of national feeling, growing out of the reaction from long years of disgraceful oppression, which were finding vent with the continued course of the struggle, and bearing men on they scarcely knew whither.

The same narrowness of apprehension and sympathy prevented him from understanding the various parties in the army, and the diverse sects which had sprung up in the country. He has given us descriptions of these parties and sects ; but there is a want of discrimination in his colouring, and a lack of charity in his judgments. Especially, he shows a defective insight into the character of the spiritual atmosphere around him—the teeming source of the conflicting opinions on which he looked with amazement.

The relaxation of the bonds of religious authority which had so long weighed upon the religious conscience of England, brought with it an upheaving of the elements which had been not merely suppressed, but treated with scorn and insult. In the first rise of the English Reformation, the principle of *individual* responsibility had no scope : it took little or no part. The course of reform was arranged by the wisdom of the State, and the policy of certain Church leaders. And when the principle of religious liberty began to show itself in the earlier manifestations of Puritanism, it was thwarted and crushed at every point. Authority held its own powerfully against it, not merely by the right of possession, but beyond doubt also, as we have seen, by the influence of learning and talent, impersonated in Hooker, Downham, and others. The result of this was, that the spring of religious liberty was driven inwards to nurse itself upon its own discontent, and to rebound, when the opportunity came, with a more violent and lawless effect than it would otherwise have done. For it is not to be supposed that a principle which has its root in the religious conscience, can be defeated by any arguments, however ingenious and powerful, against some of its manifestations. Even if we allow Hooker's great argument to be triumphant against the Puritan tenet of his day, which sought to erect the text of Scripture

into an absolute standard of ecclesiastical government
and policy, it had not and could have no effect against
the deeper principle of the movement, which testified
to the indefeasible right of the human conscience to
judge for itself in matters of religion.   And this principle, accordingly, under protracted restraint, only continued to gather a more heated intensity,—destined to
break forth into the wildest forms as soon as the hand
of authority was relaxed.   The same spiritual force
which, at the time of the Reformation, relieved itself
in such religious excesses as Anabaptism in Germany,
and Libertinism in France,—having been longer confined in England,—at length burst forth in a greater
excess, corresponding to its maturity, and the embittering restraints in which it had been held.   The element of religious liberty, cast suddenly loose, broke
out into the most lawless and extravagant forms.   The
individual conscience, rioting in its sense of freedom,
knew not its own weakness.

This is the natural explanation of the numerous
sects which now sprang up in England.   The successive manifestations of the religious excitement show
a constant advance, a progressive outburst, of the
principle of individual liberty in religion.   Presbyterianism was the first expression of the principle, and
long continued its only noticeable expression.   During
the whole reign of Elizabeth, and even of James, the
religious restlessness of the country scarcely vindicated
for itself any free movement save in this direction.
The Presbyterian platform of Church government, with
its recognition of the popular voice in preaching and
discipline, as opposed to the authoritative rule of bishops and archbishops, and a mere service of prayer and
homily—this was all the aim of Puritanism in its

primary forms. The Presbyterians were so far from letting go the element of authority, that they gave it, in the hands of the clergy, as the interpreters of Scripture and the special administrators of discipline, a peculiar prominence. It was the lack of discipline and of Church authority, in controlling the lives and opinions of clergy and laity, as may be seen from our present sketch, and many other sources, which was one of their chief complaints against the prelatical system of the time. Baxter never advanced beyond Presbyterianism. The element of clerical authority which it embodied, and its machinery of ecclesiastical inquisition, continued always to be of great value in his eyes.

It was not to be expected, however, that the religious feeling of the country, when once fairly let loose, should stop at this point. The exchange of the authority of Bishops for that of Presbyters was not likely to content the popular conscience. Accordingly, so soon as the war commenced, and all bonds of ecclesiastical control were dissolved, the excited religious feeling gave itself full vent, and burst forth in a great variety of forms. Independency, Anabaptism, and the whole brood of sects depicted by Baxter—Vanists, Seekers, Ranters, Quakers, and Behmenists—rapidly arose, jostling one another for pre-eminence, and filling the country with their discordant din.

The two first of these forms of religious opinion show the growth of religious liberty on the ecclesiastical side. The doctrinal peculiarities of Independency differed, as they do to this day, but slightly from those of Presbyterianism; and the Anabaptists (who were as different as possible from their name-

sakes of the previous century in Germany) differed
from the Presbyterians and Independents, according
to Baxter's own statement, only "in the point of baptism, or, at most, in the points of predestination, free-
will, and perseverance." Many of the most eminent
of Anabaptists, such as Bunyan, were strict Calvinists. So far as the idea of the Church, however, was
concerned, they popularised the principles of the Independents, as they in their turn had done those of the
Presbyterians. In each case the element of external
Church authority sunk more out of sight, and the con-
gregational or individual element took its place. A
hierarchy of priests and a diocesan framework had
gradually passed through Presbyteries, and a regular
order of the ministry into the absolute independence
of the Christian people, and the free call and privilege
of every one possessing the gifts to assume the pas-
torate. Still, in all these great parties the idea of
authority and of the Church was so far preserved that
the Bible was recognised as the absolute source of
religious truth, and the absolute standard of practical
morality, to be enforced upon their members by due
appliancies of discipline.

The five remaining sects noticed mark the expan-
sion of the principle of religious individualism in a
new and far deeper direction. They attacked not
merely the external ecclesiastical authority against
which the others rebelled, but the very substance of
the religious truth which all these upheld. Each of
them, though in different degrees, and with a varying
excess, sought to find the standard of religion *within*,
rather than without—in the heart, rather than in Scripture. The objective principle of authority disappeared,
and religion resolved itself into a mere subjective

feeling, asserting an absolute independence, and containing its own sufficient warrant.

The circle of religious liberty completed itself, as it will always do when traditionalism is entirely cast aside, in an unrestrained *freedom of the spirit*, which appeared to Baxter and Bunyan, and their dogmatic contemporaries, mere licence and impiety. Wild enough extravagance much of it was, but we must be careful frequently not to accept their colouring, whatever credit we give to their facts. Many men, evidently of deep piety and of a wide spiritual comprehension, as our theologian was forced to confess, were amongst the number of these sectaries.

Baxter's idea of their origin is scarcely worthy of his common sense, not to speak of his penetration. Nothing will satisfy him but that they chiefly sprung from the machinations of the Papists. We will condense his account of them severally, so far as it appears interesting. The "Vanists" were, according to him, the followers of Sir Harry Vane, and "first sprung up under him in New England, when he was governor there." Their chief characteristic was an obscure mysticism, which tended to exalt the spiritual and internal character of religion. "Their views were so cloudily formed and expressed, that few could understand them." They claimed universal liberty of conscience, and the entire independence of religion from the interference of the civil magistrate. Lord Brook, and Sterry and Sprigge, both men of name and fame in their day, belonged to this party. Of Sterry, Baxter speaks in his life with great ill-nature, punning somewhat wretchedly upon his name in conjunction with that of Vane ("vanity and sterility were never more happily conjoined");

X

while, in his *Catholic Theology*, on the other hand,
after having perused a treatise of his on Free Will, he
commends him in high terms. "I found in him," he
says, "the same notions as in Sir Harry Vane; but all
handled with much more strength of parts and rapture of highest devotion and candour towards all
others than I expected. His preface is a most excellent persuasive to universal charity. Love was never
more extolled than throughout this book. Doubtless
his head was strong, his wit admirably pregnant, his
searching studies hard and sublime, and, I think, his
heart replenished with holy love to God, and great
charity and moderation and peaceableness towards
men; insomuch that I heartily repent that I so far
believed fame as to think somewhat hardlier of him
and his few adherents than I now think they deserve."
This retractation is worthy of Baxter's heart, as it
teaches a universal lesson. If rival theologians would
try to understand, rather than to *overcome*, one another,
what increase of truth and charity might be the issue!
How many a logical Baxter still assails an intuitive
Sterry in the Christian world, and even by poor wit
tries to cover him with ridicule, while the same "holy
love to God" may really be warming the heart of each,
and all the difference between them be some wretched
convention of language, covering no life of meaning,
but only hiding the one from the appreciation of the
other, and both, it may be, from a more comprehensive
appreciation of the truth!

One is glad to record this piece of repentant charity
on Baxter's part. The only regret is that it was so
much needed, and not so comprehensive as it ought
to have been. Vane, no less than Sterry, claimed
some apology. His whole conception of Vane is an

unworthy one, and the language in which he speaks of him harsh and unjust.

The second sect he describes as Seekers. "These maintained that our Scriptures were uncertain; that present miracles are necessary to faith; that our ministry is null and without authority, and our worship and ordinances unnecessary or vain; the true church, ministry, scripture, and ordinances being lost, for which they are now seeking. I quickly found that the Papists principally hatched and actuated their sect." They were as nearly connected, probably, with the Presbyterians as with the Papists. Their origin must be sought in the disorganised condition of religious feeling. Where all was unfixed, these men were in search of a satisfying truth. In the absence of any authoritative church, they were seekers after one. They were therefore the extreme reactionists from Popery.

"The third sect was the Ranters. These also made it their business, as the former, to set up the right of nature in men, under the name of Christ, and to dishonour and cry down the Church, the Scripture, the present ministry, and our worship and ordinances. They called men to hearken to Christ *within them;* but in that they enjoined a cursed doctrine of libertinism which brought them all to abominable filthiness of life. They taught, as the Familists, that God regardeth not the actions of the outward man, but of the heart, and that to the pure all things are pure (even things forbidden); and so, as allowed by God, they speak most hideous words of blasphemy, and many of them committed whoredoms commonly."

There were many facts in the social life of the period that unhappily bear out Baxter's description of the

Ranters. Bunyan, we shall find, had a Ranter friend, who rapidly passed from a high state of religious exaltation to a state of moral libertinism. It was one of the characteristics of the time, just as it had been among the Zwickau fanatics of Germany, and the Libertines of Switzerland and France, to run from extreme religious fervour to the wildest practical licence. At the same time, it is not history, but calumny, to regard the whole sect as nothing less than immoral fanatics, who wilfully revelled in blasphemy and licentiousness. Some who had been strict professors of religion * allied themselves to it, and were influenced to do so, beyond doubt, by some real element of spiritual life which it embodied. Any such spiritual life, however, soon vanished in the midst of so much excitement, and in the entire absence of all dogmatic control; and the sect rapidly fell into degradation and contempt. Their " horrid villanies," Baxter says, " speedily extinguished them ; so that the devil and the Jesuits quickly found that this way would not serve their turn, and therefore they suddenly took another."

" And that," he continues, " was the fourth sect, the Quakers, who were but the Ranters turned from horrid profaneness and blasphemy to a life of great austerity on the other side. Their doctrines were mostly the same with the Ranters : they made the light which every man hath within him to be his sufficient rule ; and consequently the Scripture and the ministry were set light by. They spoke much for the dwelling and the working of the Spirit in us, but little of justification and the pardon of sin, and our reconciliation with God through Jesus Christ. They pretend their dependence on the Spirit against set times of prayer,

* *Baxter's Life*, p. 77. Folio.

and against sacraments. They will not have the Scriptures called the Word of God; their principal zeal lieth in railing at ministers, and in refusing to swear before a magistrate, or to put off their hat to any, or to say *you* instead of *thou* or *thee*. At first they did use to fall into tremblings and sometimes vomitings in their meetings, and pretended to be violently acted upon by the Spirit, but now that is ceased. They only meet, and he that pretendeth to be moved by the Spirit speaketh; and sometimes they say nothing, but sit an hour or more in silence, and depart. Their chief leader, James Nayler, acted the part of Christ at Bristol, according to much of the history of the Gospel; and was long laid in Bridewell for it, and his tongue bored as a blasphemer by the Parliament. Many Franciscan friars and other Papists have been proved to be disguised speakers in their assemblies, and to be among them; and it is like as the very soul of all these horrible delusions."

There is not much to criticise in this picture of the Quakers; its separate features are historically true, as they are lifelike, but the general impression is exaggerated and ill-natured. Baxter's belief of the connection of this sect with the Papists was no doubt strengthened by the accidental political relations into which the two bodies were thrown towards each other in the latter part of his life. Disowned alike by Episcopalians and Presbyterians, an affinity of persecution drew them together, and they became, in the latter years of Charles, and again in the reign of James, the joint objects of royal favours. In such facts Baxter saw the confirmation of his theory of their origin.

The Behmenists are the last sect enumerated by him Their opinions "go much towards the way of the former, for the sufficiency of the light of nature, the salvation of heathens as well as Christians, and a dependence on revelations, &c. ; but they are fewer in number, and seem to have attained to greater meekness and conquest of passion, than any of the rest. Their doctrine is to be seen in Jacob Behmen's books by those that have nothing else to do than to bestow a great deal of time to understand him that was not willing to be easily understood, and to know that his bombastic words signify nothing more than before was easily known by common familiar terms."

These sects were all more or less represented in the army, which was the hot-bed of the prevailing extravagances of opinion. The Antinomianism which so largely characterised the religious feeling of the time found its chief support and strength among the daring soldiers that surrounded Cromwell. The doctrines of free grace, in the extreme reaction which took place against the Laudian sacramental tenets, were apprehended by many irrespective of their moral influence. An unbridled opinionativeness, and a consequent contempt for all authority, political and moral, as well as religious, were fostered by hosts of pamphlets, written by such men as Overton, and the pretended Martin-Mar-Priest,* and others. The most fierce expression of this spirit was among the Levellers, headed by Lillburne and Bethel, who not only denied every rule of church government, but denounced all civil order as tyranny. "They vilified all ordinary worship; they were vehement against both king and all government except popular. All their disputing was with as much firmness as if they had been ready to draw

* These were in imitation of the Martin-Mar-Prelate pamphlets of the Elizabethan Puritanism. Overton is supposed to have been an infidel.

their swords upon those against whom they disputed."
"They would bitterly scorn me," Baxter adds, "amongst
their hearers, to prejudice them before they entered
into dispute.   They evaded me as much as possible ;
but when we did come to it, they drained all reason in
fierceness, and vehemency, and multitude of words."
Here again the idea of the Papists haunts him.   " I
thought they were principled by the Jesuits, and acted
all for their interest and in their way.   But the secret
spring was out of sight"—far below the surface of
Jesuitical intrigue certainly.

Baxter remained with the army so long as to be present at several of its operations.   Shortly after joining
it, he marched with it to Somerton ; and as he had
preached with the cannon of Naseby sounding in his
ears, so now he actually saw from the brow of a hill
on which he stood the engagement at Langport.   Bethel
and Evanson, with their "troops, encountered a select
party of Goring's best horse, and charged them at
sword's point, whilst you could count three or four
hundred, and then put them to retreat."   The dust was
so great, being in the very height of summer, that the
combatants could not see each other ; but he saw all
clearly from the eminence on which he stood.   There
were no troops engaged but Bethel's and Evanson's,
and " a few musqueteers in the hedges."   After their
repulse, Goring's army seemed to show fight again,
but on the steady advance of the Parliamentarians,
they broke and fled "before they received any charge."
" I happened to be next to Major Harrison," he adds,
"as soon as the flight began, and heard him with a
loud voice break forth into the praise of God with
fluent expression, as if he had been in a rapture."

The army proceeded to Bridgewater, whither Goring's

army had fled, and thence to Bristol, during the siege of which Baxter was taken seriously ill. He recovered just in time to see the city taken, at the cost of Bethel's life, who "had a shot in his thigh, of which he died, and was much lamented." He was successively present at the sieges of Sherborne Castle and of Exeter ; but before the completion of the latter siege, he departed with Whalley's regiment, which was sent to watch the royal garrison at Oxford. Whalley wintered in Buckinghamshire, and there laid siege to Banbury Castle, and afterwards to Worcester, where "he lay in siege eleven weeks," till the main army under Cromwell again joined him, and together they attacked Oxford. During the winter-quarters in Buckinghamshire, at a place called Agmondesham, Baxter had a famous tilt with the sectaries of Bethel's troop. Establishing himself in the reading-pew at a church where they had come together to propagate their opinions among the simple country people, he disputed against them alone from morning till almost night—"for I knew their trick," he says, " that if I had but gone out first, they would have prated what boasting words they liked when I was gone, and made the people believe that they had baffled me, or got the best : therefore I stood it out till they first rose and went away."

At Worcester he again fell ill, and having visited London for medical advice, he was sent to Tunbridge Wells to recruit. He was able to join the army once more : but his health was unequal to his exertions and anxiety of mind in the discharge of his duties, and on a renewed attack of illness at Melbourne, near Ashby-de-la-Zouche, he was glad to return to the hospitable house of Sir Thomas Rous, where he had been welcomed and cared for during a previous illness. "Thither I made shift to get," he says, "in great weakness, where I was entertained with the greatest care and tenderness while I continued to use the means of my recovery; and when I had been there a quarter of a year, I returned to Kidderminster."

Thus closed Baxter's connection with the army, which had lasted about two years *—years of trouble and perplexity to him, aggravated by ill health and the contrary spirit of those amidst whom he lived. The connection was not a happy one in any respect. He appears to have exercised but little influence over the unruly soldier-saints with whom he came in contact, while his naturally disputatious temper received an undue and almost morbid development in constant conflict with their pertinacity, "disputing from morning till almost night." On the other hand, it is probable that he learned thus early some of the experience to which, in later life, he gives frequent expression—that truth is not to be found in "a multitude of controversies." Certainly, if ever a man learned this by solemn and even dire experience, it was Baxter. His growing conviction of it could not change his nature; to the last he was accustomed to fight it out with every adversary that challenged him; but with a noble inconsistency his aspirations for peace rose above the din of battle in which he was engaged, and he felt it to be the weary and useless uproar it often really was.

It was while resident at Rous Lench that he began his career as a writer. Here he wrote the first part of the *Saints' Rest*, as he tells us in an address to

---

* He appears to have settled in Coventry in 1642, where he stayed, according to his own statement, *two* years. He seems to have left the army in 1646.

"Sir Thomas Rous, baronet, and the Lady Jane Rous, his wife," which he prefixed to the work. It is pleasant to reflect that it was at this time—the close of a period of turmoil in his life, and when his own weakness kept him face to face with death*—that he composed the most beautiful part of the best of all his works. How ardently must he have turned to the contemplation of the heavenly rest ; and, amidst the lofty raptures with which it inspired him, how poor and dim must have seemed the world of raging sects from which he had emerged! Well might he say, "How sweet the Providence which so happily forced me to that work of meditation which I had formerly found so profitable to my soul, and hath caused my thoughts to feed on this heavenly subject, which hath more benefited me than all the studies of my life." It is remarkable, also, that the very fact which partly led Baxter to begin this treatise—the want of books—has given to the first part of it, which was all that he now completed, a unity, life, and interest wanting in many of his other writings. His tendency to digression was checked from the lack of subjects to feed it, and obeying merely the instinct of his own meditative feeling and imagination, his thoughts arrange themselves into a far more harmonious and effective shape than they generally do. It would have been lucky for Baxter as a writer had he more frequently composed without access to books, and the natural vein of meditative and hortatory rhetoric, which was his strength, been left to flow freely, without the incumbrances of an argumentative prolixity, which set all patience at defiance. The second part of the

* "Living in continual expectation of death, with one foot in the grave," he himself says.—*Pref.*

Saints' Rest shows the comparative disadvantage of
scholastic leisure, and his habitual turn for polemical
discursiveness.   It is tedious and out of place.   It
might be omitted, and the work improved.   But as it
is, there is a touching harmony of tone in the *Saints'
Rest.*   There are few with any solemn feeling of religion who can read it unmoved ; the fervour and passion of its heavenly feeling, blending with the scenes
of glory which it depicts, the pathos of its appeals,
the ardour of its description, the enraptured sweetness of some of its pictures, the affection, force, and
hurry of its eloquence when he gives free rein to
his spiritual impulses, and brushes unheeding and
headlong past the tangled brakes of logic that lie
in wait for him—all render it one of the most impressive religious treatises which have descended to
us from the seventeenth century.   Much of its impressiveness flows from the intensity of the Puritan
feeling which it everywhere reflects, and the vivid
realisation of the unseen, in which this feeling lived
and moved.   The colouring of its heaven is steeped
in the intense hues of the religious imagination of the
time—Brook, Hampden, and Pym* were among the
saints whom he rejoiced he should meet above.   The
definitions, the arguments, many of the descriptions,
are Puritan ; yet the highest charm of the treatise is
the fulness with which it reflects the catholic ideas
of the eternal rest—the love, life, and fervour of tender-hearted and universal piety that it breathes.

After a retirement of some months Baxter settled

---

* Baxter, it is true, cancelled those names from a subsequent edition,
after the Restoration ; but this he did merely to avoid offence to the
authorities, and not "as changing his judgment of the persons." It was
a pity, at the same time, that he did it, especially as he tells us, "this
did not satisfy" these authorities.

once more at Kidderminster: he declined the vicarage which the people " vehemently urged upon him," but he gladly returned among them in his old capacity. In this, as in every other relation of his life, he showed, so far as money was concerned, a most unselfish spirit; he might have secured himself in legal title to the parish, but he did not care to do so ; his position was legal in every substantial sense of the term, and the treatment to which he was subjected after the Restoration, when he wished to return and minister to his old people, was equally harsh and injurious.

Baxter remained in Kidderminster fourteen years, during which the great events of the King's trial and death, the war with Ireland, the triumph of Cromwell, his difficulties, victories, and death, were all transacted. Busy with his never - ceasing labours of preaching, catechising, and writing, Baxter looked forth upon these events of his time with a spirit saddened and displeased, yet not so vexed and irritable as before. He details the events with strong reflections on Cromwell and his party, their " rebellion, perfidiousness, perjury, and impudence ;" but the peace which he enjoyed during so many years to labour in his calling, the pleasures of activity and success in which his life was spent, exerted their natural influence of contentment upon his mind. During the war with Scotland, he bestirred himself, according to his own confession, strenuously on the side of the King ; he sympathised in the aims, if he did not share in the plans, of Love and others. But while Cromwell, according to his policy of making an example, took a swift and fatal vengeance on poor Love, he never even deigned to notice Baxter's factious movements. Convinced that he could not bend him to his will, he had too much magnanimity to interfere with him violently, still more to submit him to any punishment. He respected him, although he did not like him. This Baxter is forced to acknowledge, although he ascribes the conduct of the Protector to "policy" rather than magnanimity. "When Cromwell was made Lord Protector," he says, "he had the policy not to detect and exasperate the ministers and others who consented not to his government. Having seen what a stir the engagement made before, he let men live quietly without putting oaths of fidelity upon them, except members of Parliament."

Yet Baxter's opposition, according to his own statement, might well have provoked some mark of censure. "I did seasonably and moderately," he says, "by preaching and printing, condemn the usurpation and the deceit which was the means to bring it to pass. I did in open conference declare Cromwell and his adherents to be guilty of treason and rebellion, aggravated by perfidiousness and hypocrisy." This, too, while he is forced to admit the beneficent aim of Cromwell's government in point of fact. Honesty compels from him this admission, and it is of peculiar value in the circumstances. "I perceived that it was his design to do good in the main, and to promote the Gospel and the interests of godliness more than any had done before him, except in those particulars which were against his own interest. The *powerful means that henceforth he trusted to for his establishment was doing good*, that the people might love him, or, at least, be willing to have his government for that good, who were against it because it was usurpation."

It was clear from the beginning that these two men did not suit one another. Yet Cromwell was more

tolerant and just than Baxter. In the very height of
his power, and after all Baxter's hard words, we find
the Protector courting the stern and implacable Divine.
He had avoided him in the heat of the struggle ; he
had borne with him in the crisis of his ascendancy
when his intractable temper was really dangerous : but
after the " Instrument of government" was arranged,
and power seemed settled in his hands, he sought an
interview with him, and endeavoured to impress upon
the refractory Presbyterian his views of the course of
events and of God's providence in the change of government. The proceeding, even in our author's invidious account of it, is highly creditable to Cromwell,
while it certainly proves the high esteem in which
he himself was held, and the influence of his position.
It was no sign of weakness on the Protector's part.
He had sufficiently shown by his magnanimous conduct that he had nothing to fear from men like Baxter.
He designed it, no doubt, for what it really was, a
mark of respect to his character, and an acknowledgment due to his sincere convictions. Baxter, however,
remained obstinate in these convictions.

He had been sent for to London by Lord Broghill
to assist in the determination of certain " Fundamentals
of religion," with a view to the arrangements of the new
government. His opinions on this subject were very
sensible, and stand in favourable contrast to those of
the " over-orthodox doctors"—Owen, Cheynell, and
others.* While they insisted on many minute and
absurd points being introduced as fundamental, he

* Among the advantages of Baxter's visit to London at this time, and
his conferences with other divines on the subject of " Fundamentals,"
was his introduction to Archbishop Usher. Of all men of this troubled
time, Usher was one of the most catholic and peaceable in his views.
Baxter and he were very friendly, and in their notions of Church govern-

would have had the brethren to offer Parliament the *Creed, Lord's Prayer,* and *Decalogue* alone as Essentials or Fundamentals (he preferred the former expression). "These, he held, contained all that is necessary to salvation," while they had been taken by all the ancient churches " for the sum of their religion." While the negotiation as to Fundamentals was proceeding—for, as Baxter anticipated, it proved a "ticklish business"—he was brought by his friend Lord Broghill to preach before Cromwell. The occasion was too tempting, and Baxter, preaching from 1 Cor. i. 10, regarding divisions, gave the Lord Protector very plainly a piece of his mind. " My plainness," he adds, " I heard, was very displeasing to him and his courtiers, but they felt it after. A little while after, Cromwell sent to speak to me, and, when I came, in the presence of only three of his chief men, he began a long and tedious speech to me of God's providence in the change of government, and how God had owned it, and what great things he had done at home and abroad in the peace with Spain and Holland. *When he had wearied us* all with speaking thus slowly about an hour, I told him it was too great condescension to acquaint me so fully with all these matters which were above me ; but I told him that we took our ancient monarchy to be a blessing and not an evil to the land, and honestly craved his patience that I might ask him how England had ever forfeited that blessing, and unto whom that forfeiture was made? Upon that question he was awakened into some passion, and then told me it was no forfeiture,

---

ment they could have perfectly united. It was Usher's scheme of reduced Episcopacy, we shall see, which he and the other Presbyterian
divines made the basis of their proposed compromise with the prelates
of the Restoration.

but God had changed it as pleased Him ; and then he
let fly at the Parliament which thwarted him ; and
especially by name at four or five of those members
who were my chief acquaintances, whom I presumed
to defend against his passion, and thus four or five
hours were spent." A few days after, Cromwell had
another interview with our divine, to hear his "judgment about liberty of conscience," but with an equal
want of success. Again Baxter complains of his "slow
tedious speech," and still more of the speeches of two
of his company, "in such like tedious, but more ignorant." He offered to tell him more of his mind "in
writing in two sheets, than in that way of speaking in
many days." There is an amusing gravity in this
offer. Cromwell was confessedly tedious and slow of
speech; but Baxter, of all men, professing brevity in
writing! Two sheets! Two hundred sheets would
have been a more likely result, and that "preface on
the subject," which he had "by him," we make no
doubt that Cromwell never found time to read it. He
received the paper. "I scarcely believe," its author
confesses, "that he ever read it, *for I saw that what
he learned must be from himself.*"

The view in which Baxter is now presented is almost the only public glimpse that we get of him
during the eventful fourteen years he spent at Kidderminster. His time was mainly filled up with nobler
labours than any he was capable of rendering in the
career of political action. His zealous opinionativeness prevented him from entering into hearty and harmonious co-operation with others in carrying out any
line of practical negotiation. In this respect he was no
leader. The politics of Puritanism could never claim
him as a warm ally or representative. It is its reli-

gious thought and pastoral earnestness, and not its civil ambition, that he impersonated.

He has left us details of his pastoral labours during these years—details which represent a life of unceasing activity and vigorous and joyous earnestness. He was indeed a "workman not needing to be ashamed;" and such work as he had at Kidderminster, and the free scope in which he had to do it, were entirely to his heart's content. There is no part of his life of which he writes with such zest: his constitutional querulousness rises almost into buoyancy of spirit, as he dwells upon—1. His employment; 2. His successes; and, 3. The advantages which he enjoyed.

1. Before the wars—that is, during his first stay—he preached twice each Lord's-day; but after the war " but once, and once every Thursday, besides occasional sermons." Two days every week (Mondays and Tuesdays), he and his assistant took fourteen families between them for private catechism and conference. He spent about an hour with a family, and admitted no others to be present. He devoted the afternoons to this work, the forenoons to study. On the evening of Thursdays he met with his neighbours at his house, when one of them repeated the sermon, and then they propounded any doubt or inquiries that occurred to them, and he "resolved these doubts." On the first Wednesday of every month he held a meeting for parish discipline; and every first Thursday in the month the clergy met for discipline and disputation; and in those disputations it fell to his lot to be " almost constant moderator," when he usually prepared a "written determination." All this he recalls as his " mercies and delights, and not as his burdens." Such was his "sweet and acceptable employment."

2. He next recounts his successes. And he will not suppress his satisfaction, he says, with a joyous elation, "though I foreknow that the malignant will impute the mention of it to pride and ostentation. For it is the sacrifice of thanksgiving which I owe to my most gracious God, which I will not deny Him for fear of being censured as proud." His preaching became very popular after the first "burst of opposition" which he had experienced from the "rabble" before the wars. The congregation increased greatly, so that they were fain to build *five* galleries to the church, which in itself was very capacious, and the most commodious and convenient that he was ever in. The private meetings also were full. On the Lord's-day there was no disorder, "but you might hear an hundred families singing psalms and repeating sermons as you passed through the streets. In a word, when I came thither first there was about one family in a street that worshipped God and called on His name ; and when I came away, there were some streets where there was not found one family on the side of a street that did not do so." Although the administration of the Lord's Supper was so ordered by him as to displease many, he had 600 communicants, of whom he says, "There were not twelve that I had not good hopes as to their sincerity." "Some of the poor men did competently understand the body of divinity, and were able to judge in difficult controversies. Some of them were so able in prayer, that very few ministers did match them in order and fulness and apt expressions, and holy oratory with fervency. Abundance of them were able to pray very laudably with their families, or with others. *The temper of their minds and the innocency of their lives were much more laudable than their parts.*"

And while Baxter was thus successful with his own parishioners and flock, his relations with his brethren of the ministry were also of a happy and useful character. This was a source of more likely difficulty to him than any other, from the peculiarity of his temper; but the felicity of his position at Kidderminster seems to have triumphed even here. "Our disputations," he says, "proved not unprofitable. Our meetings were never contentious, but always comfortable; we take great delight in the company of each other, so that I know that the remembrace of those days is pleasant both to them and me."

3. The thought of his successes suggests that of his "advantages." There were certain accidents of his position which appeared to him of great service in promoting his usefulness at Kidderminster, upon which he reflected with gratitude, and which he details chiefly with a view to other men's experience in managing ignorant and sinful parishes. The first advantage that he appears to himself to have enjoyed was the peculiar condition of the people, who had not before been hardened under an awakening ministry, as he considered the people of Bridgenorth to have been. "If they had been sermon-proof," he says, " I should have expected less." His next and main advantage was his own effective preaching. "I was then," he adds, " in the vigour of my spirits, and had naturally a familiar moving voice (which is a great matter with the common hearers); and doing all in bodily weakness, as a dying man, my soul was the more easily brought to seriousness, and to preach ' as a dying man to dying men.' For drowsy formality and customariness doth but stupify the hearers and rock them asleep. It must be serious preaching

which will make men serious in hearing and obeying it."

With the recommendation of a "familiar moving
voice," it is easy to conceive how impressive and
powerful Baxter must have been as a preacher. There
is a simplicity, directness, and energy in his sermon-
style, that goes to the heart even now, and which
must have told with a wonderfully stimulating effect
upon his Kidderminster hearers. In the pulpit he
was raised above the scholastic medium of thought
and definition on which his mind was otherwise apt
to dwell. As a " dying man," face to face with " dying
men," he became vehemently practical. The flame of
an overpowering conviction burning in his own soul,
communicated life and ardour to all his words. His
sermons are certainly digressive and tedious according
to our modern notions. But we must remember that
what would now be intolerable tedium, was not only
borne cheerfully, but expected and welcomed in his
age. The thoughts of all men of the time, at least
of all that Baxter was likely to address, were intensely
theological. What now seem to many mere abstrac-
tions, were to his generation living realities,—forces
moving men to fight and die. Discussions, whose
irrelevancy offends us, and digressions over which we
weary, were instinct with meaning to his audiences.
Prolixity, which we contemplate with a shudder, may
have excited in them enthusiasm. A vanished charm
must have lain in division and subdivision—in the
mere ringing, in varied cadences, of the same note of
exhortation, alarm, or consolation. Beyond doubt,
there was in all this something peculiarly consonant to
an age in which, while there was a pervading and keen
excitement about religion, there was evidently much

ignorance and dulness of religious apprehension. In
no respect is the age more remarkable. The very
rapidity with which sects arose on all hands, shows
how narrowness of religious intelligence mingled with
excitement of religious feeling.

The key to much of the characteristic literature of the
time lies in this peculiar combination. A time of intense faith, with little speculative or historical enlight-
enment, was necessarily one of endless religious controversy and sermonising. Men who were moved to
the depth of their hearts by religious convictions—the
interest of whose life was centred in the character of
their theological belief—and yet who had only very
dim and confused ideas of the past course of Christian
opinion and history, were necessarily cast afloat on the
preaching of the time to feed their religious cravings.
Shut within their own limited sphere, the conflicting
tenets around them acquired a novelty and supposed
potency which made them subjects of ever-renewing
attraction; and the sermons, which were almost their
only means of theological instruction, could scarcely be
too long,—so greedily did they thirst after a knowledge
which was to them of such vital moment. While we
may object, therefore, to the length and verbosity of
these sermons, and mourn over a dulness which seems
to argue in us a lost faculty of attention, we may yet
understand how the very elaborateness and digressive
impertinences of their structure constituted, in their
own time, a chief source of their influence.

But we must also remember that many of Baxter's
sermons, as we have them, are really expansions of
what he preached, intended for being read rather than
being heard. The *Saints' Rest* itself, which in its complete shape is an elaborate treatise, in four parts, filling

a goodly octavo, was originally written as a sermon, and the *Reformed Pastor* equally so. We must judge Baxter's preaching, therefore, rather from parts of such treatises than from the whole; and it is easy to trace in them all places where the preacher only or mainly is to be recognised—passages of rapid and overpowering practical energy, in which every word is lit with the passion of concentrated oratory, and which hurry the reader with something of the same glow of feeling which they must have kindled in those who heard them. Such passages tell more than anything else what Baxter's oratory must have been, when he was in "the vigour of his spirits." Some, like Howe, may have excelled him in grandeur and elevation of conception, or in pathetic tenderness of feeling, as in *The Redeemer's Tears over a Lost World ;* others, like Flavel, surpassed him in piquancy and pith of idea, and homely expressiveness of language, acting on the hearer like a series of unexpected surprises, always stimulating and rewarding attention; but none approached him in sweep and fulness of emotion, and in that sustained and prolonged rush of fiery appeal, earnest pleading, entreaty, or rousing alarm which constitute the most characteristic elements of pulpit eloquence. Baxter communes *soul to soul* with his hearers; every other interest is withdrawn; no colouring medium of fancy or of mere literary effect distracts the impression; only the Gospel, in the urgency of its claims or the pricelessness of its treasures, is made to fill the mind and heart. It is this fulness of the Gospel animating every sermon, and the conscious responsibility of proclaiming it—of "beseeching man in Christ's stead to be reconciled to God"—that gives to his highest flights that mixture of awe and passion, of rapture and yet of sense and reality, which makes him unequalled as an evangelical preacher.

Baxter's labours at Kidderminster were continued till the eve of the Restoration. With his preaching and pastoral visits, and clerical disputations, it might have been supposed that his time would have been fully occupied. But in addition to all these labours, he published a great variety of treatises during this period. Having once entered upon the field of authorship, his pen never rested. He wrote a treatise against infidelity,* one on *Christian Concord*, and another on *Universal Concord;* also disputations on the *Sacraments* and on *Church Government*. His *Call to the Unconverted*, and his *Reformed Pastor*, with many other tracts on special doctrines, also belong to the same period. And not only did he write of Christian concord, but he prosecuted zealously various proposals of union among the Presbyterians, Independents, and Episcopalians, and even the Baptists. His views on this subject drew him into controversy with Dr Owen, who, though much less flexible in his notions, both theological and ecclesiastical, yet exceeded our divine in calm judgment and practical temper. These proposals one and all failed, no less than the more famous ones under higher auspices, in which he afterwards engaged.

But Baxter had aspirations also of another kind in those days—aspirations which show how far his Christian zeal ranged above the level of his time, and anti-

---

* His *Unreasonableness of Infidelity*, directed against Clement Writer, of Worcester, who professed to be one of the sect of Seekers, but was either, says Baxter, a "juggling Papist or an infidel."—"An arch-heretic, a fearful apostate, an old wolf, a subtle man, a materialist and moralist," says Edwards, in his *Gangræna*. Baxter, in his later years, wrote two additional treatises in defence of the Christian religion, one of them against Lord Herbert's *De Veritate*.

cipated the triumphs of a later missionary Christianity. He was one of the most active in providing the means for Elliot, the apostle of the Indians, to carry on his great work in America. He maintained a correspondence with this devoted missionary, entered most heartily into his plans, and expressed himself with a mingled wisdom and enthusiasm on his difficulties and aims, well deserving of study even now. "The industry of the Jesuits and friars, and their successes in Congo and Japan, do shame us all save you," he says. Perhaps no career would have better suited Baxter himself than one like Elliot's, in which his fervid and untiring zeal, his evangelical energy, and his impulses to independent movement and government, would have had free and unbounded scope.

The death of Cromwell, and the accession and resignation of his son Richard, found Baxter still at Kidderminster. It is remarkable that, while he looked upon the government of the father with unfavourable and even bitterly hostile feelings, he regarded the government of the son with a friendly interest. The mild respectability of Richard's character, his domestic virtues, his respect for the clergy and "the sober people of the land," as Baxter calls them, attached him, as well as many others, and made them readily submit to his assumption of power. "Many sober men that called his father no better than a traitorous hypocrite, did begin to think that they owed him subjection; which, I confess, was the case with myself." In this expression of opinion we can see already the commencement of the schism between the great body of the nation, who were tired of contention, and who hated the idea of military rule, and the soldiery of the Commonwealth, who had virtually governed

England by their chief during the last ten years.
Richard Cromwell was disposed to represent this
great and peaceful body of his countrymen. He felt
himself more allied in sympathy with them than any
other, and his Parliament was composed mainly of
men of this class. They, in turn, reciprocated his
favourable dispositions ; they not only recognised a
lawful government in his person, but they recognised the House of Lords, as it had been constituted
by his father, and were ready peaceably to co-operate
with it. All this, however, was the very reason why
the soldiery first looked on with displeasure, and then
actively interfered to overturn his Government. The
army had no wish to embroil the country; they had
been satisfied with the late Protectorate; but they had
no intention of letting power slip out of their hands.
Men like Fleetwood, and Lambert, and Harrison, were
not the men to permit themselves to be quietly superseded by the return of the civil forms of the constitution to their old ascendancy. In Oliver Cromwell
they had acknowledged at once the head of the army
and the head of the State; in Richard they only saw
the latter, and that in a very mild and unauthorita-
tive shape. They saw, at the same time, that the
continuance and consolidation of his power and the
power of his Parliament would prove the decay and
extinction of their own—and they resolved to prevent
such a result. An active minority in the Commons,
headed by Sir Harry Vane, abetted their designs.
There were still men like him who believed in a republic; even Owen, with all his practical moderation
and foresight, was of this number.

Before such a combination of parties Richard fell.
The officers of the army united in opposition to him ;

the more violent of the sectaries disowned him ;
"Rogers Feake, and such like firebrands, preached
them into fury, and blew the coals; but Dr Owen and
his assistants did the main work." Richard had not
coveted power, and he retired from it without regret.

During the agitations that followed—the calling
together of the " old Rump," its dismissal once more,
the provisional government in the hands of the officers of the army, and Monk's march upon London—
Baxter still remained in his retirement. But as soon
as the crisis of the Restoration approached, he drew
near to London. He felt the instinct of business, and
that it was well for him to be at headquarters. He
arrived in London in April 1660, and soon after,
along with Dr Manton, held an interview with Monk,
to " congratulate him." L'Estrange, in one of his scurrilous attacks, after the Restoration, accused him of
endeavouring to influence Monk against the King.
Apart from his own express denial, such a charge
refutes itself, as inconsistent with all Baxter's convictions and his prejudices. He confessed, indeed, to
Lauderdale, whom he met on his first reaching London, and "who was just then released from his tedious
confinement in Windsor Castle," that he had scruples
about his "obligations to Richard Cromwell," but
these scruples were removed by the course of events,
and every feeling and sympathy of Baxter induced
him to royalism. He himself explains his interview
with Monk. It was more creditable to his simplicity
and enthusiasm than to his penetration. He went to
request him that "he would take care that debauchery
and contempt of religion might not be let loose upon
any man's pretence of being for the King, as it already
began with some to be." To all such fears there was,

in the mean time, a ready assurance. Charles showered
his proclamations from Breda announcing liberty of
conscience,* and denouncing "debauchery and profaneness in those who called themselves the King's
party." The royal condescension was unbounded at
the moment. The nation reciprocated the confidence
which Charles invited. Men who remembered the
perfidy of the father might urge caution towards the
son; but the current of loyalty had set in too strongly
to be resisted. The most flattering letters as to
Charles's devotion to the Protestant religion were received from Protestant clergymen in France. "Sir
Robert Murray and the Countess of Balcarras" interested themselves in procuring such letters, and they
came in profusion from Daillé and Drelincourt and
Raimond Gaches. From the latter, "a famous pious
preacher at Charenton," Baxter himself received a pom-
pous character of the King, certifying to his regular
attendance on the Protestant worship, even in "places
where it seemed prejudicial to his affairs."

There was everywhere throughout the country an
outbreak of loyal enthusiasm. The nation was wild
with delight; the city bells were rung joyously; bon-
fires blazed in every street; and the health of the
King was drunk amidst uproarious gladness.† Whilst
all this enthusiasm was at its height, the Convention
Parliament met and decreed that the King should be
sent for. The popular joy seems scarcely to have
extended to the Parliament, for "they presently ap-

---

* In his famous declaration, dated Breda, April 4, 1660, Charles pro-
claimed "liberty to tender consciences, and that no man shall be disquieted or called in question for differences of opinion which do not
disturb the peace of the kingdom."

† See Aubrey's description, *Miscell.*, vol. ii.

pointed a day of fasting and prayer;" and on this
occasion Baxter was selected, along with Dr Calamy
and Dr Ganden, to "preach and pray with them at
St Margaret's, Westminster." This is enough to
show the complexion of "the Convention" Parliament.
Loyal, it was yet Puritan and Presbyterian; the cavaliers had been returned in considerable numbers,
but the Presbyterians still formed the clear majority;
and Baxter was now in his element exhorting them.
"In that sermon," he says, "I uttered some passages
which were matter of some discourse. Speaking of
our differences, I told them that whether we should
be loyal to our King was none of our differences. In
that we were all agreed: it being as impossible that
a man should be true to the Protestant principles and
not be loyal, as it was impossible to be true to the
Papist principles and to be loyal. And for the concord now wished in matters of Church Government, I
told them it was easy for moderate men to come to a
fair agreement, and that the late Reverend Primate of
Ireland (Usher), and myself, *had agreed in half an
hour.*"

It was a brief return of Presbyterian power after
long neglect, and Baxter rejoiced in it ; the Independents and Dr Owen had retired out of sight. Milton
was mourning in blindness and solitude the infatuation of his countrymen. Calamy, Manton, Reynolds,
Bowles, and "divers others," along with Baxter, were
the men of the hour. They had it all their own way ;
and, amidst prayer and praises, they hailed the restoration of Charles Stuart. Certain of them went to Breda
to accompany him ; and, as he passed through the city
towards Westminster, "the London ministers in their
places attended him with acclamation, and, by the

hands of old Mr Arthur Jackson, presented him with a richly adorned Bible, which he received, and told them it should be the rule of his actions."

It is impossible to contemplate the conduct of the Presbyterian clergy at this time without very mixed feelings. Pity, and even contempt, mingles with our respect for them. The readiness with which they received Charles's protestations, the facility with which they allowed themselves to be duped by them,* and yet their honest desire to have the nation settled, and the simplicity with which they negotiated with Charles and Clarendon, excite this conflict of sentiment. It must be admitted that they showed themselves but poor interpreters of the national mind, or of the Royal character. In the great crisis in which they and the country stood, it required men of profound policy and far-seeing tactics to uphold the interests which they represented ; they were men merely of sober views and of honest intentions.

When we understand the character of Charles and his advisers on the one side, and of the Presbyterian clergy on the other, it is not difficult to read the meaning of the tangled and unhappy negotiations which followed. Charles himself had no serious feelings on the subject of religion ; he would gladly enough have given way to some modifications of the old Prelatical and Ritual system, if it would have procured him freedom from trouble. He seems even to have had a sort of liking and a feeling of gratitude towards the clergy, who interested themselves in his restoration.

---

* There is something revolting and yet ludicrous in the story of Charles causing the Presbyterian clergy who visited him at Breda to be placed "within" hearing of his (pretended) secret devotions. The baseness of the thing is scarcely more incredible than the simplicity of the clergy.

Baxter's rough honesty and forwardness of speech whetted his careless humour.* But he had no sense of honour; "the word of a Christian King," which he had solemnly pledged at Breda, had no meaning in his mouth; the thought of his engagements never troubled him for a moment; and consequently, when the national feeling, with the assembling of the next Parliament, carried the reaction in favour of arbitrary authority and the old Anglicanism beyond his own hopes, he naturally fell in with it, and abandoned all attempts at holding a fair balance between the Presbyterian and ultra-Episcopalian parties. The Presbyterians, at the same time, had greatly over-estimated their own position and strength in the country; and beyond their own modified schemes of church government and ritual they had no comprehensive policy. They were superior in learning, in earnestness, and moderation, to the bishops who opposed them. Baxter and Calamy, and Manton and Bates, were men of a higher standard, both of intellect and character, than Morley and Sheldon, and Gauden and Sparrow; but their views were scarcely wider, and in principle not less intolerant. They fought for a church theory scarcely less narrow than that of their opponents, while they failed to recognise that their theory no longer represented any national sentiment. The public mind had ceased to interest itself in Presbyterianism. It remained a respectable tradition, but it was no longer a living power. It no longer moved the people. They had gone off into more extreme sects, or, with the dominant impulse of the

---

* In an interview which Baxter had with Charles, October 22, he tells us that he expressed a fear that his plain speeches might be displeasing to the King, who replied that he was "not offended at the plainness, freedom, or earnestness of them, and that for my free speech he took me to be the honester man."

hour, they had returned to swell to its brimming height
the resurging tide of Royalist Anglicanism. It became
very soon apparent that the Presbyterian clergy who
had played so prominent a part in the King's restoration, were destined to have no weight on the national
counsels, and no influence in moulding a new ecclesiastical constitution.

It was necessary, however, for Charles and his advisers to mediate for some time. So long as the Convention Parliament sat, the interests of Presbyterianism
could not be overlooked. The clergy who had surrounded Charles on his return to Westminster, were its
guides and authorities; and an influence which seemed
backed by such a national representation demanded
conciliatory and careful treatment. Several of the
Presbyterian clergy were accordingly selected to be
royal chaplains. Baxter was among the number, and
along with Reynolds, and Calamy, and Spurstow, once
preached before his Majesty. Lord Broghill, afterwards Earl of Orrery, and the Earl of Manchester, were
chiefly active in these proceedings. They were both
men of the early Presbyterian party, and the former as
well as the latter had taken part in the civil wars on
the Parliamentary side ; but the ascendancy of Cromwell and the Independents had driven them into retirement, until they came forward to give their prominent
assistance on the eve of the Restoration.

Through the intervention of these noblemen, a conference was arranged between the King and the Presbyterian clergy. The Lord Chancellor Clarendon was
of course present at the conference ; and, so far as we
can judge from his own account, Baxter was the chief
speaker on behalf of the clergy. The great aim of his
address was, according to a favourite view of his own,

to convince the King of the difference between the
" sober-minded people" (himself and the Presbyterians
generally), " who were contented with an interest in
heaven, and the liberty and advantages of the gospel
to promote it," and the " turbulent fanatic persons in
his dominions." He urged the possibility of a union
between the Presbyterians and Episcopalians—" of
what advantage such a union would be to his Majesty,
to the people, and to the bishops themselves—and how
easily it might be procured, by making only things
' necessary to be' the terms of union—by the true
exercise of Church discipline against sin—and by not
casting out the faithful ministers that must exercise it,
and obtruding unworthy men upon the people." The
audience ended in a " gracious answer," and in such
further assurances of royal interest, and earnest desires
to draw parties together, that an old Puritan minister,
Mr Ash, " burst out into tears of joy, and could not
forbear expressing what gladness the promises of his
Majesty had put into his heart."

It is needless to discuss whether Charles was sincere
now or not. The idea is inapplicable to such a character.
In so far as he cared neither in the abstract for Episcopacy nor Presbytery, he may be pronounced sincere
in wishing that they would be reconciled, and let him
alone ; but in so far as he really used no efforts to
carry out his promises, but gladly abandoned the Presbyterians so soon as the spirit of a new Parliament
permitted him to do so, his want of truth here, as
everywhere, was conspicuous. " Either at this time or
shortly after," the Presbyterian clergy were requested
to draw out a statement of their proposals as to Church
government. The King professed a wish to deal with
a few representatives of either party rather than to

make any general appeal to the body of the clergy. The latter process, which Baxter and others urged, he well said, " would be too tedious and make too much noise." He promised to make the Episcopalians, on their side, draw out a paper of "concessions," so that seeing both together it might be apparent what probability of success awaited the negotiation. The Presbyterian clergy accordingly "appointed to meet from day to day" at Sion College, and in "about three weeks' time" they were ready with a paper of proposals which they agreed to submit to the King, along with Archbishop Usher's form of government, called his Reduction. Mr Calamy and Dr Reynolds were the chief authors of the proposals ; " Dr Worth and Dr Reynolds drew up what was against the ceremonies : the abstract which was laid before the King I," says Baxter, " drew up."

In so far, the leaders of the Presbyterian clergy acted with great wisdom. Their adoption of Archbishop Usher's model as the basis of Church government showed a singular spirit of moderation. Their tolerance of a liturgy, while requiring the amendment of several parts of the Book of Common Prayer and objecting to its rigorous enforcement, was no less commendable. That they should, while making these concessions, have recurred to their old complaints as to the surplice, the sign of the cross in baptism, bowing at the name of Jesus, and kneeling at the altar, was only what might have been expected. The very extent of the concessions they made in the general mode of Church government and worship would only lead them to cling more tenaciously than ever to those accidents which their long struggle had invested with a deeper importance than ever. Had the heads of the Episcopalian party been actuated by the same honest

z

motives as the Presbyterian leaders, it seems as if
the divisions which had so long rent the Church
of England might now have been healed. It seems
so, because in point of fact the wisest men on either
side were not far from one another. Baxter and
Usher had agreed in half an hour, as the former had
told the Convention Parliament in the sermon he
preached before them. Reynolds, who drew up the
paper at Sion College against the ceremonies, afterwards became a bishop. Calamy apparently would
have accepted the offer also made to him if he could
have done so consistently with his former opinions
and the sympathy of his friends. Baxter's scrupulous
temper, more than his principles, prevented him from
accepting a similar offer. Yet here, as everywhere
throughout this varying struggle, it may be doubted
whether there were not fundamental oppositions between the parties as a whole that precluded all idea
of hearty and happy union. It was not any broad
difference of dogmatic principle, but it was a difference
of feeling, of sympathy, of aim—a difference in the
mode of religious thought and the very idea of Christian worship. The literature of the times shows this
in a striking manner. The Puritans, with all their
deep devotional fervency, had become accustomed to
models of worship altogether unlike the old Catholic
forms. Baxter's *Reformed Liturgy*, and the circumstances in which it was written, proves this memorably.
It is difficult to suppose that those who looked upon
the Book of Common Prayer with an affectionate and
admiring zeal, which persecution had only deepened,
could have cordially united with those who regarded
Baxter's *Liturgy* as an appropriate or tasteful expression of devotional feeling. In passing from the one

to the other we enter, beyond doubt, into a changed atmosphere: we leave the calm, tranquil, and hoary sanctities—dim in their antique reserve—of the Catholic past, for the heated, lengthy, and obtrusive utterances of a comparatively modern dogmatism.

But whatever may have been the wish or indifference of the King, or the inclination of the Presbyterians, it must be admitted that the Episcopalian leaders never meant to enter into any compromise. Accordingly, while the former had been debating their concessions at Sion College, the latter had been doing nothing. "When we went with our papers to the King," says Baxter, "and expected there to meet the divines of the other party, according to promise, with their proposals, also containing the lowest terms which they would yield to for peace, we saw not a man of them, nor any papers from them of that nature—*no, not to this day.*" The King, however, received their papers, and expressed himself pleased that they were "for a liturgy, and had yielded to the essence of Episcopacy." It was also announced to them shortly afterwards that the royal intentions as to religion would be made known in the form of a declaration, "to which they would be at liberty to furnish their exceptions." This declaration appeared on the 4th of September 1660. It renewed the King's assurances of liberty of conscience given at Breda, commended the conduct of the Presbyterian ministers who had there waited upon him, and held out the prospect of a meeting to revise the liturgy. Baxter was greatly displeased with this document when he saw it, and wrote a sharp and urgent reply to it, which, however, he modified at the request of Calamy and Reynolds. He had many interviews with the Lord Chancellor on the subject, and also

with some of the bishops ; and after a second reply, or
"paper of alterations," had been substituted for the
first—which, even in its modified form, was "so ungrateful" to the Chancellor that they were never called
upon to present it to the King—a formal interview between his Majesty and the representatives of both parties was held at the "Lord Chancellor's house." The
chief point of discussion at this meeting regarded the
authority of the bishop, whether it should be with the
consent of the presbyters or not—Baxter and his friends,
of course, earnestly contending for this consent. The
wary Chancellor let the Presbyterians understand that
he had received petitions from the Independents and
Anabaptists, and he proposed that they and others should
be allowed to meet for "religious worship, so that they
did it not to the disturbance of the peace." The Presbyterians did not venture to repudiate this proposal,
but they gave it a very cold response. They dreaded
that the toleration would extend to Papists and Soci-
nians ; and "for our parts," said Baxter, "we could
not make their toleration our request." The result of
this meeting was so far good. The "declaration" was
issued in a new and revised form, in which it was
found that the *consent* of the presbyter was recognised.
Baxter was delighted when he first saw this change,
and "presently resolved to do his best to persuade all
to conform, according to the terms of the declaration."

His elation did not last long, and the breath of
suspicion seems to have haunted him even in the
moment of it. For it was only the next day that,
on being asked by the Lord Chancellor if he would
accept a bishopric, he hesitated till he should see
the matter of the declaration passed into a law.
Reynolds, Calamy, and himself, "had some speeches

together " on the subject, and they came to the conclusion that there was nothing inconsistent with their principles in the acceptance of a bishopric; "but all the doubt was whether the declaration would be made law as we then expected, or whether it were but a temporary means to draw us on till we came up to all the Diocesans desired." In the end, as has been already stated, Reynolds was the only one that accepted a bishopric. Baxter's letter to Clarendon, in which he declined the proffered honour, is a touching and noble document, bright in every sentence with his rare disinterestedness. We may regret his scruples, but we must admire his simple-minded indifference to the world and its honours. When, in the close of the letter, he says that, "for the sake of that town of Kidderminster, he would gladly receive the vicarage there, or, if this cannot be managed, that he would willingly resume his old post of curate," his self-sacrifice rises into pathos. A still higher spirit of self-sacrifice, indeed, might have prompted him to lay aside his personal scruples, and have extorted yet more warmly our admiration—but it would not so much have moved and interested our affections.

In the King's declaration it was announced that the Liturgy should be revised and reformed; and Baxter continued to urge the Chancellor to adopt the means for carrying out this part of the royal intentions. The result was the famous Savoy conference in the spring of the following year (1661), which may be said at once to have brought the negotiations to a head, and to have shown the insincerity on the Episcopalian side, which had characterised them all along. Twenty-four commissioners, with certain assistants, were appointed to meet at the Savoy, the Bishop

of London's lodgings, and take into consideration the
subject of the Liturgy. The list comprises all the
well-known names who had hitherto taken the lead
in the negotiations, and the prospect of settlement
might have seemed a fair one. But before the commissioners had met, the election of a new Parliament, and the turn of public affairs, had emboldened
the Episcopalian party to a degree which entirely
destroyed any such prospect. Disinclined in themselves to yield anything, they now perceived that the
nation was prepared to support them in their most
extreme views. Parliament was prepared to outrun
even the zeal of the bishops; and in such circumstances it was not likely that they would be more
ready than they had been to meet the Presbyterians
half way with concession. Accordingly the conference was nearly breaking down at the very commencement on this point. As before—after the deliberations of the Presbyterians at Sion College—the
Prelates had no proposals to make—no concessions to
advance. The Bishop of London, as their spokesman,
opened the conference by saying that it was not they,
but the opposite party, that had been the "seekers of
the conference," and that they had nothing to say or
do till the Presbyterians had brought forward in writing what alterations they desired in the Liturgy. This
was an ingenious Prelatic device, and, to some extent,
served its purpose. Baxter, contrary to the advice of
all his brethren, as he confesses, concurred in the
statement of the Bishop of London; and the issue
was, that he and others agreed to draw out a statement of their exceptions to the Book of Common
Prayer, and of additions or new forms, such as would
meet their approval.

It was the latter part of the task that Baxter undertook, and in the *course of a fortnight* he had completed an entirely new liturgy, to which we have already alluded. This was a fatal attempt. It was impossible that by any plan Baxter and his friends could more effectually have played into the hands of their opponents. The rashness and self-confidence betrayed in the very conception is enough to amaze us. It served to startle even the most moderate among the bishops, while it put the weapon of resistance which they desired into the hands of those who had made up their minds against all change. The result was what might have been expected. It was felt, even before the renewal of discussion, that all hope of settlement was at an end. The paper of exceptions, and a "fair copy of our reformed liturgy," was handed to the bishops, but Baxter expresses his doubts whether they were ever read by the "generality of them." The conference itself degenerated into a series of disputations between some of the more active and zealous of the bench, and our divine as the chief spokesman of the other side. In this rivalry of logic he found a lively interest, and acquitted himself with distinction; but his cause suffered and sank into contempt. Many of the bishops absented themselves, and even some of the Presbyterians, among whom was Lightfoot, followed their example. The attendance dwindled to three or four of either party, besides the chief combatants. Some spectators from "the town" gathered to witness the intellectual combat. Gunning—a clever and well-informed divine of the Laudian school, "noted for a special subtlety of arguing"—took the main share of the debate on the part of the bishops. "The two men," says Burnet,

"were the most unfit to heal matters, and the fittest
to undo them, that could have been found out. . . .
They spent some days in much logical arguing, to the
diversion of the town, who thought here were a couple
of fencers engaged in disputes that could never be
brought to an end, or have any good effect."

The unfortunate issue of the Savoy conference prepared the way for all the harsh and miserable legislation that followed. When men had begun to laugh at
the subject of dispute, the time of renewed intolerance
and persecution was not far distant. The character
of the Presbyterians, besides, had somewhat suffered
from the ill-fated meeting. Their moderation, at first
so commendable that it placed their opponents in a
predicament from which they could hardly escape, save
by yielding their claims, was rendered suspicious by
the idea of a new liturgy, and the general tenor of the
discussion. The effects were immediately apparent.
Baxter, who had lately refused a bishopric, now found
it impossible to obtain his modest settlement at Kidderminster as vicar, or even as curate. He details
at length his dealings in this matter with Clarendon, and Morley, Bishop of Worcester, and Sir Ralph
Clare, "an old courtier," who seems to have been the
man of property and influence at Kidderminster, "the
ruler of the vicar, and all the business." The affair
throughout is painful and discreditable to all engaged
in it saving Baxter himself. It is perfectly obvious
that they had no wish to promote his request. Even
Clarendon, with all his professions, cannot be credited
with any honest wish to befriend him; and he at
length had penetration enough to see this, however
his simplicity may have been at first beguiled. "For
a Lord Chancellor," he says, "that hath the business

of the kingdom in his hand, and lords attending him, to take up his time so much and often about so low a vicarage, or a curateship, when it is not in the power of the King or the Lord Chancellor to procure it, though they so vehemently desire it! But, oh! thought I, how much better do poor men live who speak as they think, and do as they profess, and are never put upon such shifts as these for their present conveniences."

Unable to procure his desired settlement at Kidderminster, he settled in London, and became colleague for some time to Dr Bates, at St Dunstan's-in-the-West, where he preached once a-week. Here began the system of molestation, from which he was scarcely ever afterwards free. Spies waited upon his sermons, and reported their subjects in high quarters,* with insinuations of their seditious tendency. He is said to have frightened and driven them away by his telling exposures in a series subsequently published under the title of "The Formal Hypocrite Detected." The crowds that thronged to his preaching were very great. On one occasion, when preaching at St Lawrence, Jewry, his famous sermon on "Making light of Christ," Lord Broghill and the Earl of Suffolk, "with whom he was to go in the coach," were "fain to go home again," so great was the crowd; while the pastor of the church was glad to get up into the pulpit with him, as the only place where he could find room. On another occasion, at St Dunstan's, an alarm was raised that the edifice was in danger. His calm courage and lofty appeal to the "great noise of the dissolving world" made a deep impression on the

* " I scarce think that ever I preached a sermon without a spy to give them his report of it."

excited and rushing congregation, and succeeded in quieting it.

Baxter continued his preaching till the passing of the Act of Uniformity. While the church of St Dunstan's was preparing, he preached at St Bride's, " at the other end of Fleet Street," and also at Blackfriars, and he held, besides, a week-day lecture in Milk Street, at the request of Mr Ashurst, "with about twenty citizens." He was willing, in however humble a capacity, to serve the Church. His scrupulous disinterestedness would not allow him to receive any remuneration, except for his lectures in Milk Street, for which, he says, "they allowed me forty pounds per annum till we were all silenced."

This issue was fast approaching. The Parliament of 1661 was keen to hurry matters to a crisis. It began its career by requiring every member to take the sacrament after the old manner, and by ordering the Covenant to be burned. The power of the sword was declared to belong inalienably to the sovereign, and all members of corporations were bound to testify that resistance was unlawful. While busy in this work of reactionary legislation, the insurrection of the Fifth-monarchy men, under Venner, took place. Everything seemed designed to carry the tide of reaction to the highest. This insane attempt served as a justification for the proposal of the most extreme measures against all parties disaffected in any degree towards the Church. The Act of Uniformity was passed in May. By this Act every minister was bound, before the feast of St Bartholomew, in the ensuing August, to declare his assent to everything contained in the Prayer-book, under penalty of forfeiting his benefice. Baxter did not even wait for the expiry of the

probationary period, but immediately gave up preaching. "The last sermon I preached," he says, "was on
May 25." His reasons were that he considered himself to be included under a doubtful clause of the Act,
which was supposed to terminate the liberty of lecturers
at that time, and that he wished that his nonconformity might act as an example to others who might
have hesitated.

St Bartholomew's day, the 24th of August 1662,
marks a great epoch in the religious history of England.
Puritanism henceforth merges into Nonconformity. The
ejection of two thousand of the most pious and excellent ministers of the Church carried the struggle which
had been so long waged within it into a different sphere,
and imparted to it a new character. During two years
Baxter had been one of the most prominent men in
the country. In the last efforts of Puritanism to maintain its ground within the ecclesiastical order of the
country, he had been its conspicuous representative.
With the Act of Uniformity he withdrew into private
life, and for ten years is scarcely heard of, save as one
of many victims of the miserable persecutions of the
period, which pursued him to his most retired privacy.

Strangely enough, he commenced this period of his
life by an act which he had hitherto looked upon as
scarcely permissible in the case of a clergyman—he
got married. His wife's name was Margaret Charlton.
She was young and well-born: he was not old,* but
his health had never been good, and his circumstances
were sufficiently gloomy. There is not much wonder,

---

* Her age is stated to have been twenty-two or twenty-three, while
Baxter was in his forty-seventh year. She belonged, according to his
own statement, to "one of the chief families in the county" (Worcester-
shire).

therefore, that the marriage excited great astonishment, according to his own confession. "The king's marriage was scarcely more talked of." It proved, however, in every respect a happy union. Mrs Baxter was not merely a pious and excellent help-mate to her husband, but a noble-hearted and heroic woman, who shared and lightened his imprisonment. She died before him, and he embalmed her memory in what he called a "Breviate of her life."

After his marriage he retired to Acton, where he followed his studies "privately in quietness." He attended the parish church in the forenoon, and in the afternoon preached in his own house to a few friends and "poor neighbours," who assembled with his family. Now and then he spent a day in London. The works on which he was engaged were his chief interest. He completed here his *Christian Directory, or Sum of Practical Divinity,* and also some of his well-known shorter works, his *Life of Faith,* his *Saint or Brute, Now or Never,* and *The Divine Life.* One day as he was preaching "in a private house," a bullet was fired in at the window, passed by him, and narrowly missed the head of his sister-in-law.

During these years that Baxter passed at Acton, the course of public events was marked by a series of startling vicissitudes. In 1663 there was renewed talk of a comprehension, in which he bore his part, but which ended as before in nothing. The King had passed in December of the preceding year an indulgence, including Papists; but Parliament had remonstrated, and followed up their remonstrance by the Conventicle Act (1663), which prohibited attendance on any worship but that of the Church of England, under the severest penalties—three months' imprisonment for

the first offence, five for the second, and seven years'
transportation for the third, on conviction before a
single Justice of Peace. In the close of 1665 the
plague broke out in London, when, Baxter says, "most
of the conformable ministers fled and left their flocks
in the time of their extremity," and the ejected Nonconformists preached in the forsaken churches and ministered to the sick and dying. Yet during this very
time—when the Parliament, in dread of the visitation
which had laid waste London, had taken refuge at
Oxford—Sheldon and Clarendon busied themselves in
riveting the chains of Nonconformity by the infamous Five Mile Act, which prescribed that all who
refused to swear that it was unlawful, on any pretence
whatever, to take up arms against the King, should be
banished five miles from any corporate town or burgh
sending members to Parliament.

The fall of Clarendon in 1667, and the rise of the
Duke of Buckingham, brought some remission from
these bitter exactions; but the strain of intolerance
was only temporarily relaxed. Through various alternations,—renewed proposals for comprehensions by
Lord Keeper Bridgman—a renewed royal indulgence
in 1672—and yet further proposals for accommoda-
tion, in which Tillotson and Stillingfleet took a part,
with Manton, Bates, and Baxter on the side of the
Nonconformists,—the ecclesiastical history of the reign
preserved the same disgraceful character, only equalled
by its court disasters and military dishonour. The
national life and reputation sank gradually to a lower
ebb; while the bishops, with an obstinacy equally
mean and wicked, still stood in the way of any compromise, and delighted to stretch forth the hand of
persecution.

Baxter appears to have lived in studious quietness at Acton till about 1670. The venerable Sir Matthew Hale was his neighbour, and a very pleasant neighbour, with whom he had frequent conferences, "mostly about the immortality of the soul and other philosophical and foundation points, which were so edifying that his very questions and objections did help me to more light than other men's solutions." He greatly commends Hale's piety, moderation, and courtesy. "When the people crowded in and out of my house to hear, he openly showed me great respect before them at the door, and never spoke a word against it. He was a great lamenter of the extremities of the times, and of the violence and foolishness of the predominant clergy; and a great desirer of such abatements as might restore us all to serviceableness and unity." His quiet life of study, and his philosophical discussions with Sir Matthew Hale, were suddenly interrupted by a warrant summoning him before the justices at Brentford. He was accused of holding a conventicle, and of not having taken the Oxford oath. After being subjected to great rudeness, and scarcely permitted to speak in his own defence, he was committed to Clerkenwell Prison. Here, however, his imprisonment was "no great suffering," for "I had," he says, "an honest jailer, who showed me all the kindness he could. I had a large room and the liberty of walking in a fair garden. My wife was never so cheerful a companion to me as in prison." He was liberated at length by a *habeas corpus*, some flaw having been found in his mittimus. This the judge, in dismissing him, took care to point out. The law was against conventicles, he was reminded, and "it was only upon the error of the warrant that he was released."

In order to escape further molestation he returned
to Totteridge, near Barnet. He was afraid " they might
amend their mittimus" and lay him up again, and
this drove him from Middlesex and his pleasant house
at Acton. His present residence was far from comfortable. He had only "a few mean rooms, which
were extremely smoky, and the place withal so cold"
that he spent the winter in great pain, troubled by " a
sore sciatica, and seldom free from much anguish."
Amidst all his discomfort, however, he never inter-
mitted his studies. His great Latin System of Divinity
—his *Methodus Theologiæ*—was now begun. Here
also he wrote his *Apology for the Nonconformists*, and
entered into a long discussion with Owen about the
old ever-recurring subject of the terms of union among
Christians. It was at this time, too, that he had a correspondence with the Earl of Lauderdale, with whom he
had formerly some dealings on the eve of the Restoration. Lauderdale either had a really kindly interest
in Baxter, or he craftily acted at the suggestion of
others, with the view of removing him to scenes where
his influence would be less troublesome. He offered to
take him with him to Scotland, and to make him either
a Bishop there or a Principal of one of the Colleges.
But Baxter pleaded his age and infirmities, and his
engagement in the composition of his *Methodus*,
which, if he lived to finish it, "was almost all the
service he expected to do to God and His Church more
in the world." Hard as was his lot in England, he
was evidently not disposed to commit himself to the
tender mercies of Lauderdale in Scotland.

After the King's "dispensing declaration" in 1672,
he removed to London, and resumed, after an interval of
ten years, public preaching. " The 19th of November

(1672), my baptism day, was the first day," he says,
"after ten years' silence, that I preached in a tolerated
public assembly." From this time on to 1682, or
another space of ten years, he continued to preach
under varying circumstances of difficulty and persecution. It is not necessary to trace his successive
changes during these mournful and unhappy years—
now encouraged by the capricious indulgence of the
royal declaration—and now threatened by the restrain-
ing vigilance of Parliament. Driven from one place of
worship to another—from St James's Market House to
Oxendon Chapel, which the liberality of his friends
built for him—from Oxendon Chapel to one in the
parish of St Martin, then to Swallow Street, and finally
to New Street,—he was hunted by informers, and
worried by persecutors, wherever he went. "I was
so long wearied," he says, "with keeping my doors
shut against them that came to distrain my goods for
preaching, that I was fain to go from my house, and to
sell all my goods, and to hide my library first, and
afterwards to sell it: so that if books had been my
treasure (and I valued little more on earth), I had
now been without a treasure. For about twelve years
I was driven a hundred miles from them; and after I
had paid dear for the carriage, after two or three years
I was forced to sell them." Two warrants for his
apprehension were issued during this period; and on
one occasion constables and beadles, for twenty-four
Sundays, watched his chapel door in Swallow Street
to seize him.

On the 24th of August 1682 he preached in New
Street. "I took that day," he says, "my leave of the
pulpit and public work in a thankful congregation."
He had been in the country to recruit his health, and

returned in great weakness. " When I had ceased preaching," he says, " and was newly risen from extremity of pain, I was suddenly surprised by a poor violent informer, and many constables and officers who rushed in, apprehended me, and served on me one warrant to seize my person for coming within five miles of a corporation, and five more warrants to distrain for a hundred and ninety pounds for five sermons." He was " contentedly" proceeding to jail when a medical friend, Dr Thomas Cox, meeting him, forced him to return to his "couch and bed," giving at the same time his oath before five justices that he could not be removed to prison " without danger of death." The King is represented as having been consulted on the subject, and as having said, " Let him die in his bed." It was determined, however, that his supposed deathbed should be as bitter as possible. "They executed all their warrants on my books and goods, even the bed that I lay sick on, and sold them all." And when he had borrowed some further bedding and necessaries, they threatened to come again and take all, so that he had no remedy but " to forsake his house, and goods, and all, and to take secret lodgings at a distance in a stranger's house." *

Baxter was destined, amidst all his weakness, to survive this harsh and cowardly cruelty, and even worse treatment than this. Again, in 1684, while he lay "in pain and languishing," warrants were sent forth against him. On his refusing to admit them, six officers were set to watch at his " study door, who watched all night, and kept me from my bed and food, so that the next day I yielded to them, who carried me, scarce able to stand, to the sessions, and bound me in four

* *Penitent Confessions.*

2 A

hundred pounds bond to my good behaviour." Repeatedly he was subjected to the same infamous
harshness, and forced, in " all his pain and weakness,
to be carried to the sessions-house, or else forfeit his
bond." It is impossible to conceive oppression at
once more petty and intolerable — cruelty more unnecessary and more tormenting.

In such acts of despotic weakness and cowardly
brutality the last years of the reign of Charles ap-
propriately dragged themselves out. The prisons were
crowded with " aged ministers," the Courts of Justice
were grossly corrupted, thronged by a base and miserable crew of informers—the spawn of an age of lies
and imposture—and presided over by men without
principle or humanity. The Court, the Church, the
Universities were alike without credit or honour.
And while hundreds of the aged Puritan clergy
languished in prison, some of the best blood of England was shed upon the scaffold. The same justice
which was outraged by the sufferings of Baxter turned
with averted eyes from the murder of Russell and
of Sidney.

With the death of Charles and the accession of
James, in February 1685, Baxter's troubles reached their
height. In the beginning of this year he had published a *Paraphrase on the New Testament*, with notes,
in the course of which he was supposed to make
some disparaging reference to the bishops. The charge
was a mere pretence. The real aim was effectually
to silence by imprisonment one who had so long
been a favourite object of resentment to the Church
and the Government. On the 28th of February he
was committed to the King's Bench Prison by warrant of Lord Chief Justice Jeffreys. He applied

for a *habeas corpus*, and by this means was enabled
to secure his liberty till his trial, which was fixed
to take place in May. The indictment, which is
a long Latin document, interspersed with quotations
from his *Paraphrase*, charged him with being a seditious and factious person, of depraved, impious, and
restless disposition, and with exciting others to hostility against the Church and the bishops. On the 18th
of May his counsel moved that, on account of his illness, some further time might be given him before his
trial. Jeffreys exclaimed, " I will not give him a
minute's time more, to save his life. We have had to
do with other sorts of persons, and now we have a saint
to deal with, and I know how to deal with saints as
well as sinners. Yonder," he roared, " stands Oates in
the pillory"—this infamous informer was at the time
expiating his offences in the New Palace Yard—"and
he says he suffers for the truth, and so says Baxter;
but if Baxter did but stand on the other side of the
pillory with him, I would say two of the greatest
rogues and rascals of the kingdom stood there."

The trial occurred on the 30th of May. Baxter came
into court, attended by Sir Henry Ashurst, the son of
his old friend, Alderman Ashurst, who had been so
warm a patron of the Puritan clergy.* Sir Henry had
feed counsel to defend him, and Pollexfen opened the
case on his behalf. As he proceeded, Jeffreys brutally
interrupted him. A question arose as to Baxter's supposed application of the passage about the " long
prayers of the Pharisees," to the Liturgy. " Is he not

* " Among the Nonconformists he acted as a father and a counsellor,
while his purse was ever open to relieve their wants, and his house for
a refuge to them." To Baxter he was a peculiar friend—" my most entire friend," he says.

now an old knave to interpret this as belonging to
liturgies?" "So do others," replied Pollexfen, "of the
Church of England, who would be loth so to wrong
the cause of liturgies as to make them a novel invention, or not to be able to date them as early as the
Scribes and Pharisees." "No, no, Mr Pollexfen," said
the judge; "they were long-winded extempore prayers,
such as they (the Puritans) used to say when they
appropriated God to themselves: 'Lord, we are thy
people, thy peculiar people, thy dear people.'" "And
then, he snorted and squeaked through his nose, and
clenched his hands, and lifted up his eyes, mimicking
their manner, and running on furiously as he said they
used to pray." * "Why, my lord," said Pollexfen, with
grim irony, "some will think it is hard measure to
stop these men's mouths, and not let them speak
through their noses." "Pollexfen," cried Jeffreys, "I
know you well; I will set a mark on you; you are
the patron of the faction. This is an old rogue, who
has poisoned the world with his Kidderminster doctrine, . . . an old schismatical knave; a hypocritical
villain." He accused Baxter of encouraging the late
civil war. Pollexfen appealed to the notorious fact that
his client, along with Mr Love and others, was always
well affected to the King and royal family; and that at
the Restoration his services were rewarded by the offer
of a bishopric. But Jeffreys would listen to no reason.
"What ailed the old blockhead, the unthankful villain,
then," he replied, "that he would not conform? Hang
him, he hath cast more reproach upon the constitution
and discipline of our Church than will be wiped off this
hundred years; but I'll handle him for it; for by G—
he deserves to be whipped through the city."

* *Baxter's Life and Times.* ORME, p. 454.

In the same disgraceful manner the trial proceeded. Jeffreys was drunk with the excitement of hate
and natural ferocity. The intensity of his passion is
at once ludicrous and revolting. When Baxter interposed some remark in his defence, he cried out, " Richard, Richard, dost thou think we'll hear thee poison
the court? Richard, thou art an old fellow; an old
knave; thou hast written books enough to load a cart,
every one as full of sedition—I might say treason—as
an egg is full of meat. Thou pretendest to be a
preacher of the gospel of peace, and thou hast one foot
in the grave; it is time for thee to begin to think what
account thou intendest to give. But leave thee to thyself, and I see thou'lt go on as thou hast begun; but,
by the grace of God, I'll look after thee. . . . Come,
what do you say for yourself, you old knave? come,
speak up. What doth he say? I am not afraid of
you for all the snivelling calves you have got about
you"—alluding to some persons who were in tears
about Baxter. " Your lordship need not," calmly replied the aged divine; " for I'll not hurt you."

There have been many such trials of " cruel mock-
ings;" but few present a more shameful and humiliating spectacle than that of Baxter. Justice has been
in other cases as grossly outraged, but it has seldom
or never been exhibited in an aspect at once more
hideous and contemptible. The trial ended, of course,
in conviction. As the jury retired, Baxter ventured to
say, " Does your lordship think any jury will pretend
to pass a verdict upon me upon such a trial?" " I'll
warrant you, Mr Baxter," said Jeffreys, rejoicing in his
savage coarseness to the last; " don't you trouble yourself about that." He was fined five hundred merks,
and sentenced to lie in prison till he paid it. Jeffreys

is understood to have suggested a severer sentence—
the base indignity of corporal punishment; but to this
his colleagues refused to assent. Baxter was unable to
pay the fine, or probably declined to do it; aware that
his liberty would be soon again threatened by some
equally unjust attack. He lay in prison for nearly two
years. At length, at the instance, it is supposed, of
Lord Powis, he was discharged, and went to live in
Chesterhouse Square, near the meeting-house of Sylvester, a Nonconformist friend and minister.

Here he spent in peace and liberty his remaining
years. Weak and dying as he had seemed to be for
long, he survived the Revolution, and was able even
to take some part in the public measures then devised
for the protection of the dissenting clergy. When all
schemes of comprehension had again failed through
the obstinacy of Parliament, an Act of Toleration was
passed, by which the Nonconformists were brought
under the full protection of the law, on subscribing certain of the Thirty-nine Articles, and taking the oaths
to Government. Baxter availed himself of this act, and
incited his Nonconforming brethren to do so, in a characteristic manner. He drew up a lengthened paper,
setting forth the sense of the articles, as he understood
and was willing to subscribe them. His criticisms
and expositions in many cases show his singularly ex-
ceptive and over-curious logic. It would be difficult
to say that he has made any point more clear by his
distinctions, but he satisfied himself; and no fewer
than eighty dissenting clergy, in London and the neighbourhood, joined with him in his explanations, and
subscribed the required articles. This fact testifies to the
extent of his influence, even at this time, when he had
retired from public life.

Feeble and old as he was getting, his pen rested
not. To this period belongs his elaborate work on *The
True History of Councils Enlarged and Defended*, his
Dying Thoughts, and many other works, controversial and practical. He resumed preaching, so far as
his health permitted. On the Sunday mornings he
took the place of his friend Sylvester, and he held
a meeting also every alternate Thursday morning.
He continued thus to preach for four years and a
half, when he was disabled "from going forth any
more to his ministerial work. So that what he did
all the residue of his life was in his own hired
house, where he opened his doors morning and evening every day."

Thus laboured Baxter unresting to the end. At last
his "growing distemper and infirmities" confined him,
first to his chamber and then to his bed. But even
from his deathbed he may be said to have preached to
the friends who came to see him. "You come hither
to learn to die," he said : "I am not the only person
that must go this way. I can assure you that your
whole life, be it ever so long, is little enough to prepare for death." * He was very humble and resigned.
In the midst of his sharp sufferings, he would say
—"It is not for me to prescribe—when Thou wilt,
what Thou wilt, how Thou wilt." Again—"I have
pain, but I have peace, I have peace." At length, on
the evening before his death, his sufferings became
almost intolerable. He cried out in great agony, till,
somewhat relieved, he was heard softly to murmur
"Death, death.". Early on the morning of Tuesday,
December 8, 1691, he expired.

* Bates.—This old friend, who preached his funeral sermon, has preserved a minute account of his last sickness and death.

Baxter appears before us in such various attitudes, that it would require a very extended criticism to estimate in full his labours, writings, character, and influence.   As a writer alone, his works would furnish matter for long analysis and comment.   What are called his "practical works" fill by themselves four folio volumes, of about a thousand double-columned pages each ; and these, of course, do not comprise his great doctrinal treatises, and many of his controversial, biographical, and historical writings.   His two systematic treatises on divinity, the one in English and the other in Latin, under the respective names of *Catholic Theology*, and *Methodus Theologiæ Christianæ*, extend, the one to 700 and the other to 900 folio pages. His age, it has been said, was "one of voluminous authorship, and Baxter was beyond comparison the most voluminous of all his contemporaries."   Some impression of this voluminousness may perhaps be gathered from a comparative statement of the same writer * who has made this remark :—"The works of Bishop Hall," he says, " amount to ten volumes octavo. Lightfoot's extend to thirteen ; Jeremy Taylor's to fifteen ; Dr Goodwin's would make about twenty ; Dr Owen's extend to twenty-eight ; Richard Baxter's, if printed in a uniform edition, could not be compressed in less than sixty volumes, making more than from thirty to forty thousand closely-printed pages ! "

It would be a weary, and it would not be a profitable task, to enter upon any examination of such a mass of wellnigh forgotten theological literature.   It would, at any rate, be beside our purpose in these pages.   We shall not even attempt any special criticism of Baxter's theological opinions.   They were a

* ORME, *Baxter's Life and Writings*, vol. ii. p. 466.

subject of endless dispute in his own day, and long
after he had sunk to a quiet grave. They touched
distinctions, many of which have lost all vitality of
meaning, and would be scarcely intelligible at present.
To try to revive them would interest none but the
theological reader, and would not, in his case, serve
any good end. It will be more useful, as well as
more consonant with our aim, to endeavour to characterise Baxter's general mode of thought, as representative of that of his time, and of the mass of
theological literature which constituted one of the chief
manifestations of Puritanism. Differing as Baxter
did from Owen and others; involved as he was in
constant controversy with the extreme Calvinists of
his generation; and disposed as some would be to
deny to him the name of a Calvinist altogether,—there
is yet no divine of his age bears, in deeper and broader
impress, the spirit of its religious and theological belief. He rose above a mere formal Calvinism; but
the very processes of reasoning, and peculiarities of
intellectual apprehension, by which he did so, were
Calvinistic. He waged a ceaseless fight with the
Sectarian exaggerations, both of doctrine and ecclesiastical practice, that surrounded him; but the weapons by which he did so were the very same which
had cut out for the sects a more lawless and independent way on the great high-road of Protestantism.
Certainly, of all the men who express and represent
the spiritual thought of the Puritan age, none does so
more completely, and to the very centre of his intelligence, than Richard Baxter.

It was a chief characteristic of this thought, as we
have already seen, to bring within the sphere of clear
and coherent argument—in other words, of a compre-

hensible and didactic scheme, logically related in all
its parts—the various subjects of the Christian revelation, and the various phenomena of the spiritual life.
It systematised religion, both in its intellectual and
practical relations, to a degree scarcely inferior to that
of the old scholastic and mediæval systems. Christian
doctrine was to it a vast body of argued knowledge,
and the Christian life a great "directory of conduct."
Baxter was prominently possessed by both these
ideas. They are to be found in all his writings;
while he has left, in his *Methodus Theologiæ* on the
one hand, and his *Christian Directory* on the other,
his own extended solution of the range of questions,
both doctrinal and practical, which concerns the
Christian.

Of all the divines of his time, none was more bold
and deductive. None carried argument with a more
daring and confident hand into the last recesses of
the Christian mysteries. Others, such as Owen,
were more formally and consistently logical. They
exhibited a more constructive and vigorous power of
thought. But Baxter possessed an inquisitorial and
freely-ranging logic, that out-argued all his contemporaries. His restless acuteness impelled him with an
unshrinking force on all the great problems of Christian theology, while his self-confident subtlety made
him believe that he had explained them by processes
of hypothetical argumentation of the most complicated,
and sometimes of the most imaginary, character. His
principle of trichotomy, laid down in his *Methodus*,
and his views of sufficient grace and of election, are
conspicuous examples of this.

The principle of a "divine trinity or unity" appeared to him to be imprinted on the "whole frame of

nature and morality," and to furnish the only key to a
"true method in theology." What Monadism was to
Leibnitz, as it has been said, Triadism was to Baxter.
It was the "just distribution" into which all natural
and all divine science fell. He saw a threefold unity
everywhere; in the relations of the godhead—in the
spiritual constitution of man—in the method of salvation—in the fruit and grace of it. Father, Word, and
Spirit—life, intellect, and will—nature, grace, and
glory—Governor, Saviour, Sanctifier—faith, hope,
charity,—such are some of the trinal distinctions
which seem to him to underlie all knowledge, and
especially all Christian knowledge. Such divisions
he esteemed a "juster methodising of Christian veri-
ties according to the matter and Scripture than is
yet extant." Nothing can better show the peculiarities of Baxter's mental temperament, as developed and
sharpened in the theological atmosphere of his time.
Such a conception may be considered more an extravagant than a fair representation of the Puritan
mode of thought; but it only brings out, on this
account, more prominently its characteristic tendency.
Its author had exactly that measure of originality
and independence which enabled him to present in
relief the peculiarities of a prevailing system. Owen
would never have yielded to the temptation of such
a speculation; it would have seemed to him a lawless intrusion of human ingenuity into the great province of Christian faith; yet it was the very same
dominance of logical argumentation, the same rage for
systematising within this province, which governed his
own less fanciful and more constructive reasonings on
the mystery of the Atonement. The method of both
was the same—only the one used it with a more sober

consistency and regard to the tenor of the Calvinistic tradition than the other.

The same peculiarity marks all Baxter's distinctive views.   They are modifications of Calvinism; but they are, at the same time, strongly characterised by its hyperlogical scholastic tendency.   It was, for example, one of the chief problems in the Genevan system of doctrine from the beginning, how to reconcile the free invitation of the Gospel to all, with the special gift of grace to some.   The will of God as loving, and desiring the salvation of, all, seemed to come into painful conflict with the same will as only efficacious in the salvation of some.   The spirit of modern theological inquiry, with its comparative disregard of system, is content to acknowledge here a profound mystery, which it does not seek to resolve. It accepts without any qualification, as an express dictate of Scripture, the reality of God's loving will to all men, while it leaves the mystery of opposition to this will to rest simply on the fact of the corresponding reality of a human will, which, in virtue of its very character—because it is a *true will*—may oppose itself to the Divine.   Such a simple appeal to fact, however, was not in the spirit of the old theoretic divinity.   It insisted on compassing the perplexing dilemma by some argumentative solution, and this, too, on the divine side.   The mystery of the divine action must be resolved; and if so, it is clear that it only admitted logically of one solution.   The call of the Gospel is in name, and, according to some hypothetical sense, addressed to all; but in truth it only concerns some.   The principle of logical distinction was fearlessly applied to the last mystery—the relation of the divine and human spirit—in such a manner as to suppose a double or mixed action in the former, whereby it was operative, and yet not effectually or successfully operative, in the bestowal of grace. Baxter here, as everywhere, adopted the principle of the Genevan theology, but developed characteristically his own theory as to the solution of the problem. "As there is a common grace," he says, "actually extended to mankind" (that is, common mercies contrary to their merit), "so there is such a thing as sufficient grace *in suo genere*, which is not effectual." The ordinary Calvinist was content to say that there is common grace and there is special grace, explaining the former in various ways, but with a uniform result — viz., that it is not in a true or saving sense grace at all. Baxter maintained that it is truly grace, and yet not *grace;* or, in his own words, "sufficient" grace, and yet not "effectual" grace— something "without which man's will cannot, and with which it can, perform the commanded act toward which it is moved, when yet it doth not perform it." This is surely to argue, and yet not to explain anything. The spirit of rationalistic inquisition, carried out more boldly and ingeniously, only ends in a more hopeless perplexity — grace sufficient and yet not sufficient! That the case baffles explanation — that this and every relation of the infinite to the finite evades all logical solution — was an admission too plain and direct for the theology of the seventeenth century.

In the same manner he argued regarding the great contrast of *election* and *reprobation.* He supposed, in the genuine spirit of his time, that he explained the inscrutable secrets of the divine mind by the application of modes of human expression which can have no

relation to that mind. He mistook, as such explanations
generally do, a mere verbal inventiveness for a process of thought. He held firmly to election, and, in a
certain sense, to reprobation, yet not, as he said, *pari
passu*, or as both springing equally out of the will of
God. Such a view, which the more consistent Calvinists around him held, was opposed to his deep
and pathetic recognition of the reality of the divine
"call to the unconverted." But, borne away as he
was by the argumentative subtlety of his day in the
treatment of such questions, he tried to fill up the gap
in his logical consistency by hypothetical reasonings
of his own, which, when analysed, have no meaning,
and touch no element of fact.*

When we turn from Baxter's doctrinal writings to
his practical treatment of the Christian life, we meet
with the same spirit of over-zealous and burdensome
argumentativeness. His *Christian Directory, or Sum
of Practical Theology and Cases of Conscience*, fills the
whole of the first volume of the folio edition of his
practical works. It traverses, in four parts, the wide
field of " Christian ethics, or private duties of Christians ; economics, or family duties of Christians ; eccle-
siastics, or church duties ; and of Christian politics, or
duties to our rulers and neighbours." As "Amesius's

* His reasoning, in this particular case, is plainly Arminian. It could
not, in fact, be anything else; as, if such matters are to be reasoned
about at all, the process of reasoning must take one of two fundamental
lines, of which the Calvinistic is, beyond doubt, the only strictly logical
and conclusive. Baxter says, "In election, God is the cause of the
means of salvation by His grace, and of all that truly tendeth to procure
it. But, on the other side, God is no cause of any sin which is the
means and merit of damnation; nor the cause of damnation, but on the
supposition of man's sin. So that *sin is foreseen* in the person decreed to
damnation, but not caused, seeing the decree must be denominated from
the effect and object."

Cases of Conscience were to his *Medulla* the second or practical part of theology," so he designed,
he tells us, his *Directory* as a supplement to his
Methodus Theologiæ. It is impossible, save in the
Romish casuists, to find anything more minute, elaborate, and formal, than Baxter's divisions and subdivisions in this work. The Christian life is not conceived in its related or broader characteristics as
a breathing and full-formed reality, rising in the
" beauty of holiness " from a germ of grace in the
heart, " the planting of the Lord, and honourable ;" but
it is dissected in every fibre and vein of its constitution ; the rounded and spontaneous form stripped off,
and the skeleton framework and unsightly ligaments
everywhere exposed. The outline is not that of an
organic structure, but of an artificial model, end-
lessly divided in its parts,—but without comprehension, or even a just discrimination. The contemplation to which the reader is invited is a deeply
mournful and painful one, over which the heart grows
weary, and the conscience rises affrighted, rather than
gathers strength or quickening. There is no natural
end to the multiplication of questions and cases.
The author seems merely to stop in his catalogues
of sins and duties when his memory is run out for
the time. He admits this. After discussing, for
instance, " thirty tongue sins, and twenty questions
for the conviction of drunkards ; eighteen necessary
qualifications of lawful recreation ; eighteen sorts that
are sinful ; and twelve convincing questions to those
who plead for such pastimes ; thirty-six questions about
contracts ; twenty about buying and selling ; sixteen
respecting theft ; and one hundred and seventy-four

about matters ecclesiastical ;"* he yet regrets that the
want of his library at the time when he composed
the work prevented him from enlarging his enumeration of cases. "The very sight," he says, "of Sayrus,
Fragosa, Roderiques, Tolet, &c., might have helped my
memory to a greater number."

It is perhaps not altogether fair to say that this me-
chanical and unreal treatment of the Christian life, as
an unceasing routine of vices to be avoided and virtues
to be learned, is characteristically Puritan. For the
Romish casuists have carried the same mode of treatment even to a greater and more unhappy excess, and
Baxter's contemporary, Jeremy Taylor, as prominent a
representative of Anglican, as Baxter is of Puritan, theology and piety, has, in his *Ductor Dubitantium*, followed
the same line. It was characteristic of the theological
spirit of the seventeenth century in its varied manifestations. Yet there was that in Puritanism which answered with a peculiar fitness to this casuistical inspection and analysis of life. Its disciplinary system,
as it sprang out of Geneva, was stamped with an inquisitorial authority which sought to touch the individual Christian at every point, and to bring his conduct into conformity with definite rules. The necessity
of this disciplinary training—of the negation not merely
of human passions, but of human folly and amusement,
—by the application of outward restraints, was peculiarly Genevan. In no respect did the Puritans urge their
demands more forcibly while still a minority in the
Church, as in no respect did they carry them out more
intolerantly in the day of their triumph. After looking into Baxter's *Christian Directory*, one can understand how intolerable life would have been made had

* ORME'S *Life and Writings of Baxter*, vol. ii. p. 175.

the stricter form of Puritanism preserved its power, and had it all its own way. It would have set up a court of conscience* in every parish, and drilled human conduct, in its most private activities, into a sombre and harsh routine. As it was, it prescribed, wherever it could, the old country sports, converted Christmas-day into a fast, and punished adultery with death. To such legislative restrictions it would have superadded many yokes for the private conscience, which neither our fathers of the seventeenth century nor their children could bear. And none would have gone further in this way than Baxter, because, with all his perspicacity and sense, he was a man himself of infinite scruples; while his notions both of individual and civil freedom were narrow and unenlightened. In this very work he lays down, in opposition to Hooker, the doctrine of the divine right of government, and consequently the duty of passive obedience, in the most undisguised manner.

But if Baxter represented Puritanism in the over-argumentative and unreal character, which both its religious speculation and its religious discipline were apt to assume, he was also the conspicuous representative of its spiritual energy and fervour; and here every mind will own his greatness. The details of Puritan dogma and ethics may cease to excite interest; but the fire and life of Christian enthusiasm which, especially, made Puritanism what it was, can never cease to stir the heart, and awaken the admiration of all who appreciate the self-sacrifice which is willing to spend and be

---

* Bishop Heber tells us, in his *Life of Jeremy Taylor*, that during Owen's predominance at Oxford, as Vice-Chancellor, a regular court of conscience was held in the university, which the students ludicrously nicknamed the "Scruple Shop."

spent in the service of God. Prophecies shall fail, and
tongues shall cease, and knowledge vanish away ; but
" charity never faileth."   Whatever fate may overtake
dogmatical and ecclesiastical technicalities, spiritual
earnestness still shines with an imperishable lustre.
And there is no form of Christianity which has ever
been more instinct with this spiritual earnestness—
none which has sought more eagerly and intensely to
" win men to Christ," and to count all things but
loss, in comparison with the service and the glory of
God, than Puritanism ; while, of its great preachers,
there is no one who exhibits this feature more than
Richard Baxter. We have already seen what his labours
were as a pastor ; and these labours were only a natural
expression of a divine energy in him, which knew not
how to rest.   There was present, through all his days
and in all his work, such a constant sense of God and
the Unseen—such a practical apprehension of the
awful meaning of salvation in Christ—of men's wretchedness without Christ, and their blessing in Him—that
it coloured and ordered his whole existence. A rare
warmth of Christian sensibility glows in his sermons,
and gives to them and his practical writings the life
they still have. As we read the *Saint's Rest*, or the
Reformed Pastor, or the *Call to the Unconverted*, we
feel everywhere throbbing the pulse of an impassioned
seriousness.   The speech is that of one who, gazing
beyond the mere shadow of earthly things, realises
himself all the " powers of the world to come," and
would have others do the same. Its burden is ever-
more the same message of divine love to perishing
sinners, " beseeching them in Christ's stead to be
reconciled to God."   It is as if his own soul ever
moved responsively to the awful thought which he

says, in his *Reformed Pastor*, should be present to the mind of every preacher. "*O, if these sinners were but convinced and awakened, they might yet be converted and live.*" "What!" he adds, "speak coldly for God and men's salvation? Can we believe that our people must be converted or condemned, and yet can we speak in a drowsy tone? In the name of God, brethren, labour to awaken your hearts before you come; and when you are in the work, that you may be fit to awaken the hearts of sinners." Baxter's own heart, in his more memorable sermons, is on fire with an awakened sympathy. The gleam of spiritual urgency lights up every sentence. The pathos of spiritual tenderness weeps over the sinner, and the awe of a mighty crisis startles and alarms him. He has, as Sylvester said, "a moving πάθος and useful acrimony in his words. When he spake of weighty soul concerns, you might find his very spirit drenched therein." It is the noblest aspect in which we can contemplate Puritanism when we look upon it as summoning men with a terrible zeal from the life of the world and of the flesh to the life of faith in God; and Baxter is the great apostle of its evangelical fervency.

It is in the same point of view that his character rises to its highest lustre. A single-minded earnestness is its pervading feature—in the strength of which every other is absorbed. Intellectually subtle and hyper-logical—of an almost tormenting ingenuity of argument and device—he was, in action, simple and unselfish as a child, with no thought but for the good of others. His rare disinterestedness is conspicuous at every turn of his life. His spiritual devotedness rises to martyrdom. Self was utterly forgotten in the ever-active engrossing thought of doing good, and, above all, of saving men's souls alive. " Love to the souls of men," said one of his friends, " was the peculiar character of Mr Baxter's spirit. All his natural and supernatural endowments were subservient to this blessed end. It was his meat and drink, the life and joy of his life, to do good for souls."

This energy of spiritual enthusiasm, how it lives in all he did and suffered ! His heart is in his work. He carries forward every task with an impulsiveness that glows in its restless zeal—that hurries forward and breaks down obstacles rather than warily meets them. This was not the quality most needed in some of the emergencies of his life, and especially in those miserable negotiations following the Restoration, in which he took so conspicuous a share. His fiery and single-hearted ardour was no match for the cool diplomacy and the wily intrigue of Clarendon. But we love him none the less, but all the more, for this. And when we see this grand and loving energy engaged in its appropriate, its highest, work—of " winning souls to Christ"—"bearing all things, hoping all things, enduring all things, suffering long and yet kind"—we feel how great a hero was this Puritan divine. Few have ever lived more unselfishly, more heroically—for God. Amidst pain and weariness, amidst imprisonment and spoiling of his goods, through disease and in the constant fear of death, he kept a valiant heart, and he gave all its valour to do the will and the work of Christ.

Thus practically great, Baxter's character, like his age, fails in breadth. Catholic in aspiration, and even in principle—for no one has expounded with a more wise and comprehensive moderation the grounds of Christian union—he was yet contracted in sympathy,

and frequently illiberal in feeling. His account of
Cromwell, and his description of the Sects, sufficiently
show this. With all his generosity of impulse, there
was a tinge of harshness in him—a sharpness not of
nature but of temper. His constant suffering affected
his views of life and society, and imparted to them a
sombre tone irrespective of that which sprang out of
the general character of his Puritan faith. Yet in his
harshness there was no malignity, and not the least
trace of cynical indulgence. If sometimes ungenerous
in his appreciation of others, he was intolerant of any
weakness or sin in himself. " I never knew any person," said Dr Bates, "less indulgent to himself. Self-
denial and contempt of the world were shining graces
in him."

Both his self-mortification, and his eager and pleading affection for the spiritual good of others, can be
traced in the worn countenance which his familiar
portraits present. " Abstinence, severities, and labours
exceeding great," are marked in its ascetic lines and
somewhat grim expression ; while the depth of his
ardently affectionate soul speaks in the piercing eye.
Upon the whole, a certain painful severity predomi-
nates. Friends like Bates may have remembered his
countenance amidst its gravity, *somewhat inclining to
a smile ;*" but his portraits show nothing of this. There
is no smile lurks beneath their sad gaze. And so his
character is wanting in hearty vigour—in emotional
healthiness. There is a poverty of the merely natural
life—a lack of genial interest—and of the appreciation
of any mere earthly beauty or art—that takes from
it the richness of a full manhood. He was a Puritan,
and little more. Unlike our two former characters, he
rose but slightly above his time. As its systems con-

fined his intellect, its moral narrowness bound his character. He was strong in its strength ; he was weak in its deficiences. The very intensity of his spiritual earnestness was in some degree born of this one-sidedness. Had he possessed a broader feeling, and sympathies more widely responsive to nature and life, he could not have lived so entirely as he did above the world, and given himself with such an unresting vigilance to the love and ministry of souls. If we look at him as a man, this want of breadth and variety of interest diminishes his greatness ; if we look at him as the Puritan pastor and divine, it was the very singleness of his spiritual energy that made his excellence and crown.

In this view, the life of Richard Baxter must ever touch the Christian mind with the elevation of its self-sacrifice. It was a steady, long-enduring heroism, although the world may little regard him as a hero ; and the more we look beneath the surface we shall find that softer and engaging features were not wanting. Gentleness, if not smiles, lay near to his severity ; and beneath a certain irritability and flashing vehemence, "rather plain than complimentary," there may be also found the mildness of patience, and the beauty of a silent cheerfulness.

IV.

BUNYAN.

BUNYAN.

In our previous sketches we have contemplated Puritanism in its more general and comprehensive aspects. Cromwell and Milton, and even Baxter, are representatives of this phase of our national life in those larger and controversial relations in which it came prominently into public notice, and entered as an element of disturbance or settlement into our national history. In Cromwell we have seen the culmination of its military and political genius—in Milton, the highest expression of its intellect—in Baxter, its ecclesiastical and theological spirit; but in none or all of these have we contemplated, with the distinctness which it deserves, its spiritual and social character. True, there are in these lives many indications of the spirituality which mainly animated and sustained the movement, and made it a national power — which, like a subtle cement, ran through all its parts and compacted them into a great historical whole. It was the strength of this spirituality which, more than anything else, made the bond of connection between Cromwell and his followers, and enabled him to represent them with the effect and triumph that he did. Yet it is mainly as the undercurrent of his life that it appears. The struggles of soul through which the hero

of the Commonwealth passed—and to which many
features of his history and some of his letters testify
in the strongest manner—only rise to the surface here
and there as we survey the restless heroism of his
career. The military and political phases of his character draw away our interest. In Milton, again, the
working of the spiritual life is so strong and consistent
throughout, and so thoroughly interfused with the
growth of his intellectual being, that we can scarcely
distinguish it as a separate element—his whole nature
is so serious, so religious, and formed in its development such a unity of power, that we would try in vain
to disentangle the special influences which entered
into its constitution and gave it such a massive and
controlling harmony; while in Baxter, although we
everywhere come across the pervading spiritual feeling in which lay the whole strength of his life and
the wonderful energy of his work, the prominence of
the theological and ecclesiastical elements distract our
attention, and may be said to form the main characteristics presented to us.

In order to give any adequate picture of Puritanism,
however, it is necessary to survey, as closely and as
much by itself as we can, its distinctive spiritual life.
To the Puritan and the Anglican, religion not merely
presented marked differences in externals—but in its
very spirit—in the mode in which it wrought within
the heart, and coloured and determined the inner
life. The habit of religious thought which came from
Puritanism and that of the old Catholicism of England, were widely distinguished. The Puritan's hatred
of externals, and reaction against the formalities in
which the Anglican piety delighted, drove his devotional feeling to feed more upon itself, and so developed

an intense and passionate spirituality, and a social instinct of a quite peculiar, as it was of a very influential, character. Both in Bunyan and in Baxter we trace the influence of these characteristics, but in the former especially. In the life of the author of the *Pilgrim's Progress* we see them in their most simple and unmixed form. Bunyan is, above all, the spiritualist of Puritanism; while, at the same time, the circumstances of his social position serve to reveal more expressively than we have yet seen, the workings of the system upon the ordinary social existence of those midland counties in which it abounded.

Bunyan's life is a spiritual story, with a very slight setting of external incident and adventure. Its interest is found in the vehement and critical inward struggles which he has himself depicted, and not in any succession of events or any rare development of mental powers. His *Grace Abounding to the Chief of Sinners*—in which he has, with his own very vivid and homely power, set forth the divine dealings with his soul — is nothing else than his autobiography. He had no other life to tell of in comparison; for all his outward activity as a preacher—broken by his long imprisonment—and all his creative fertility as a writer, were the mere expressions of the spiritual passion in which he lived and moved and had his being. In so far, however, as Bunyan's life does take us into the outer world of England in the days of the Protectorate and the Restoration, it serves, as we have said, to bring before us the everyday social aspects of Puritanism, which are apt to escape us in lives of more public prominence.

We have before us a Puritan life comparatively divorced from all excitements of military, or political, or ecclesiastical struggle. With the great events of his time, with which Cromwell and Milton and Baxter come into such close contact, he had nothing to do. He was, in fact, only a youth of twenty-one when the King was beheaded, and when the first great series of events which crowned the Puritan struggle with triumph was completed; and with this series of events we could not connect him at all, were it not for a well known anecdote of his own about the siege of Leicester. Far away, then, from the centre of movement, and in the background, as it were, of that stirring time, runs the career of Bunyan. And yet not the less, but all the more, on that account, he serves to illustrate it in one of its most characteristic features. He is not a prominent actor upon the stage; but his figure in the background is typically expressive of the spirit which animated and governed a host such as him, in everything but his genius. While Puritanism was developing its lofty aims in the high places of the kingdom, it was no less colouring by its influence every village and civic community. While it was legislating for Europe, and writing State-papers in behalf of the persecuted Protestants abroad, it was moving the hearts and ordering the lives of the poor women of Bedford, and of the tinker's son in the neighbourhood; and its working in the one case, no less than in the other, is necessary to enable us to understand its full meaning, and to appreciate its comprehensive and pervading power.

John Bunyan was born at Elstow, a village within a mile of Bedford, in the year 1628, the year in which Charles called his third Parliament—that famous Parliament of the Petition of Right, in which Cromwell

made his first speech. He was, he tells us, " of a low
and inconsiderable generation ; his father's house being
of that rank that is meanest and most despised of all
the families of the land." His father was, in short, a
tinker, and Bunyan himself was bred to the same calling. The father, however, does not seem, any more
than the son, to have pursued his trade in the usual
vagabond-manner we associate with the name. For
Bunyan tells us that he was sent to school " to learn
both to read and to write, the which I also attained according to the rate of other poor men's children, though
to my shame I confess I did soon lose what I had learned, even almost utterly." His boyhood was wild and
thoughtless—very much what we might conceive the
life of a gipsy-tinker boy to be. He revelled in coarse
and profane language, and was careless of the truth,
or of any fear of God. In his own strong simple way he
tells us it was his delight " to be taken captive by the
devil at his will, being filled with all unrighteousness,"
the which " did so strongly work both in my heart and
life, that I had but few equals in both for cursing,
swearing, lying, and blaspheming the name of God."

This, we are to remember, is Bunyan's account of
his boyhood, as he looked back upon it from his later
religious point of view. It would be a mistake—
and yet it is one into which many of his biographers
have fallen—to suppose from the manner in which he
speaks of himself here and elsewhere, that his youth
was peculiarly wicked beyond that of the class to
which he belonged. There is clear evidence to the
contrary in his own statements. A habit of profane
swearing, and a wild and reckless indulgence in Sunday pastimes, are the facts of wickedness with which
his sensitive conscience charges his early years. From

licentiousness his own strong declarations expressly
free him ; and there is no evidence that he was addicted to drunkenness or any form of dishonesty which
we readily associate with his supposed gipsy race and
tinker occupation.   The truth is rather that, from
his boyhood, Bunyan was of a strongly religious turn
of mind.   The great ideas of life and death, heaven and
hell—those spiritual contrasts which afterwards he was
to embody in such rare variety and picturesqueness of
form—had smitten his impressionable imagination
from his youth, and clung to him.   They did not for
many years work themselves into the fibre of his
spiritual being, so as to become its living and effectual springs of action ; but they were there, dormant
and ready to start forth into powerful consciousness.
If practically he now lived without God—and his
habit of profane swearing showed how far religion
was from having any real influence over him—he
was yet so far from being without thoughts of religion, that such thoughts haunted him as living
things, moving in the shadowy background of his
being, and mingling in it every now and then with
a fearful though unpractical effect.   They possessed
him.   They peopled his dreams, and in their constant presence and intimacy made familiar to him
the strangest fancies ; "for often," he says, "after I
had spent this and the other day in sin, I have been
greatly afflicted while asleep with the apprehensions
of devils and wicked spirits, who, as I then thought,
laboured to draw me away with them, of which I could
never be rid.   Also I should, at these years, be greatly
troubled with thoughts of the fearful torments of hell-
fire ; still fearing that it would be my lot to be found
at last among those devils and hellish fiends who are

there bound down with the chain and bonds of darkness unto the judgment of the great day. These things, I say, when I was but a child—but nine or ten years old—did so distress my soul, that then, in the midst of my many sports and childish vanities amidst my vain companions, I was often much cast down and afflicted in my mind therewith; yet could I not let go my sins. Yea, I was also then so overcome with despair of life and heaven, that I should often wish either that there had been no hell, or that I had been a devil, supposing they were only tormentors; that if it must needs be that I went thither, I might rather be a tormentor than be tormented myself."

Although such thoughts did little more than torment him, they never altogether left him. He never appears, amid all his practical recklessness, to have risen above them for any length of time. Every accident served to recall them, and religion rose before his mind as a haunting image, even when he sought to banish it away. There was a tenderness in his heart towards it, while he was yet despising and trampling it under foot. He says, for example, that while taking pleasure in his own wickedness, it was a great grief to him when he saw those who made a religious profession doing wickedly. It made his "spirit tremble." "As once above all the rest, when I was in the height of vanity, yet hearing one to swear that was reckoned for a religious man, it laid so great a stroke upon my spirit that it made my heart ache."

He recalls various incidents in this early period of his life of a providential character. Once "he fell into a creek of the sea, and hardly escaped drowning." Another time he fell out of a boat into the river Ouse, "Bedford River," as he calls it, "but mercy yet pre-

served him." At another time, when in the field with
a companion, he seized, he says, an adder, and "having
stunned her with a stick, he forced open her mouth,
and plucked her sting out with his fingers." He remained unhurt; but had it not been for the divine
mercy, his "desperateness" would have destroyed
him. Most memorable of all, when he was a soldier,
enlisted, it may be supposed temporarily, in defence of
the Commonwealth, he was "drawn out to go to such a
place to besiege it." This was in the summer of 1645
when Charles, having had his army finally broken on
the field of Naseby, sought a few hours' refuge in
Leicester, which he had taken some days before. It
was retaken by the Parliamentary forces a few days
later; and Bunyan believed himself to have providentially escaped death on the occasion. "When drawn
out as one of the besieging party, and just ready to go,"
he says, "one of the company desired to go in my room,
to which when I had consented, he took my place, and
coming to the siege, as he stood sentinel, he was shot
in the head with a musket bullet, and died." *

Following this—a year or two we must suppose,
for even two years would only make him nineteen—
he married; and this event proved of the happiest
character to him. His wife was the daughter of
godly parents, and herself a pious woman. Unpro-

---

* According to this statement, it might seem doubtful whether Bunyan was really engaged at the siege of Leicester. Of Bunyan's military
career, indeed, it cannot be said that we know anything with distinctness or certainty. It remains a matter of dispute, whether he belonged
to the Parliamentary or the Royalist army. His latest biographer, Mr
Offer, who enters on details, inclines to the opinion, that "so loyal a
man joined the Royal army, and not that of the Republicans." If in the
Parliamentary army he was probably engaged at Naseby, as well as present at the siege of Leicester; and, in any case, his military experience
left ineffaceable traces on his memory and imagination, as is abundantly
shown from the conception and composition of the *Holy War.*

vided with worldly goods—"not having so much household stuff as a dish or spoon" betwixt them,—she
had got "for her part," two books—*The Plain Man's
Pathway to Heaven*, and the *Practice of Piety*,—which
turned out of more value to him than a richer marriage-
portion. The study of those books, aided by the religious conversation of his wife, deepened his religious impressions. He was still far, however, from
being a religious man. Outwardly he began "to fall
in very eagerly with the religion of the times;" he
became a regular church-goer, and joined with great
apparent zeal in the service—nay, he was seized with
a fit of superstitious devotion towards all connected
with the church—"both the high place, priest, clerk,
vestment service, and what else belonging to it, count-
ing all things holy that were therein contained, and
especially the priest and clerk most happy, and without doubt, greatly blessed, because they were the servants, as I then thought, of God, and were principal
in the holy temple to do his work therein. This conceit grew so strong upon my spirit, that had I but seen
a priest (though never so sordid and debauched in his
life), I should find my spirit fall under him, reverence
him, and grant unto him; yea, I thought, for the love
I did bear unto them (supposing they were the ministers of God), I could have laid down at their feet, and
have been trampled upon by them; their name, their
garb, and work did so intoxicate and bewitch me."

When Bunyan looked back upon this period of his
life, he could only see its gross superstition. He would
not admit that his conversion had yet begun. "All
this while," he says, "I was not sensible of the danger and evil of sin. I was kept from considering that
sin would damn me what religion soever I followed,

2 c

unless I were found in Christ. Nay, I never thought whether there was such a one or no." But, giving the fullest assent to his own views, we cannot help recognising in the new turn of his thoughts the working of the same religious nature and influences already traced in his earlier dreams and visions.. These influences never forsake him. Now they pursue him as shadowy terrors in his sleep ; and now they make him adore the mere walls of a church, and the ground on which a priest treads. His imagination is steeped one way or another in religious ideas, and paints with its vivid colours his inner life, although his moral energies are as yet unaffected by them.

Practical results were by and by to follow his intense agitation. For a while he struggled against the convictions and imaginations that possessed him, but they were always acquiring a stronger hold of his heart, and making themselves more felt and owned as motives to action. The crises of spiritual impulse through which he passed during this process, almost reached the point of madness. His excited feelings now utter themselves in voices, and now image themselves in features expostulating with him, and looking down upon him. Never, certainly, did any one, by the mere strength of imaginative passion, break down more than Bunyan the boundaries of time and space,—pierce through the objective facts amidst which most men live,—and pass more really into the invisible world. One day he heard a sermon on Sabbath-breaking, and it so filled his mind that, he says, he for the first time felt what guilt was. He went home for the time "greatly loaded" with the sermon, " with a great burden on his spirit." After reaching home, however, and especially after he had "well dined," the effect of the sermon wore off. He shook it out of his mind, and returned with great delight to his old custom of sports and gaming. " But the same day," he tells us, " as I was in the midst of a game of cat, and having struck it one blow from the hole, just as I was about to strike it the second time, a voice did suddenly dart from heaven into my soul, which said, ' Will thou leave thy sins and go to heaven, or have thy sins and go to hell ? ' At this, I was put to an exceeding maze; wherefore, leaving my cat upon the ground, I looked up to heaven, and was as if I had, with the eyes of my understanding, seen the Lord Jesus look down upon me, as being very hotly displeased with me, and as if he did very severely threaten me with some grievous punishment for those and other ungodly practices." As " he stood in the midst of his play," arrested by this voice and vision, the conclusion fastened itself upon his spirit, " that he had sinned beyond pardon, and that it was now too late for him to look after heaven ; and burying all better impulses in this overwhelming thought of despair, he returned desperately to his sport again.

Such extremity of spiritual excitement could not last ; and so we find him soon after this entering upon a new course. Startled out of his evil habit of swearing by the rebuke of a woman at whose shop window he was cursing in his wonted manner, and who, though she was a very loose and ungodly wretch herself, yet protested that he swore and cursed at such a rate as made her tremble to hear, he began a career of outward reformation. He left off entirely the habit which had become a second nature to him; and whereas before he could not speak " without putting an oath before and another behind," he was now able to speak without a single oath, " better and with more pleasant-

ness than ever he had done before." At the same time
he fell into the company of an old man who "made
profession of religion," and whose conversation led him
to the study of the Scriptures, in the historical narratives,
of which, he says, he took great pleasure; "but as for
Paul's Epistles, and such like Scriptures, he could not
away with them."

In this state he continued for about a year, during
which he set the commandments before him "for his
way to heaven." He strove earnestly to keep them,
and when he succeeded in doing so he was comforted; and when at any time he fell away from them he
was greatly afflicted. His neighbours remarked with
amazement his "conversion from prodigious profaneness to something like a moral life;" and when he
heard them commending him, it pleased him "mighty
well." In all this Bunyan found evidence that he was
nothing as yet but "a poor painted hypocrite." On
this period of his life, when he was esteemed "a right
honest man," he looked back with scarcely less complacency than he did upon the preceding period of profaneness. All this while he was "ignorant of Jesus
Christ, and going about to establish his own righteousness." The sharp decision with which he seized the
different features of the religious life, and the realistic
persistency with which he separated and individualised
them, prevented him from seeing the threads of unity
running through the different stages of his career. The
same wonderful imagination that peopled the *Pilgrim's
Progress* with living creatures representative of distinct
qualities and states in religious experience—each with
a separate personality—made him conceive his own
several states vividly apart from one another. During
this period, therefore, he was merely dwelling, accord-

ing to his own figure, in the village of Morality, and
acting the part of Mr Worldly Wiseman. Yet his religious education was advancing more than he afterwards thought. He had not found the true spring
of spiritual life; but he was groping towards it rather than turning out of the way when he felt con-
scientiously concerned about keeping the divine commandments, and found some peace of conscience in
doing so.

The full blessing of grace was about to visit him;
and it came, as God's blessings often come, in what
might seem the most accidental manner. Bunyan
had listened to many sermons, and not without profit,
not without severe excitement of conscience in one
case that we have seen. But "the word fitly spoken,"
and which dropped as good seed into the good and
honest heart, did not come to him from any sermon,
but from the chance talk of "three or four poor women sitting at a door of one of the streets of Bedford.
Their talk was about a new birth, the work of God in
their hearts, as also how they were convinced of their
miserable state by nature; they talked how God had
visited their souls with his love in the Lord Jesus, and
with what words and promises they had been refreshed, comforted, and supported against the temptations
of the devil. And methought," he adds, "they spake
with such pleasantness of scripture language, and with
such appearance of grace in all they said, that they
were to me as if they had found a new world. At
this I felt my own heart begin to shake, for I saw that
in all my thoughts about religion and salvation, the
new birth did never enter into my mind."

The conversation of these poor women in the streets
of Bedford marks the turning-point in Bunyan's life.

Their words about the new birth sank deeply into his heart. When he left them, and went about his employment, his thoughts still "tarried with them," and he returned again and again to their society, till the spark kindled by their words burned into a living and warming flame. For the first time, his spiritual emotions were not merely agitated but soothed. The feeling not merely of his own wickedness, but of God's method of saving him from his wickedness, came home to him, and he was seized with a "very great softness and tenderness of heart," and also with "a continual meditating" on what these poor women had asserted to him from Scripture. He passed, for a time, into a highly ecstatic frame of mind. He was lifted, as it were, out of the earthly and formal life that he had been living, and brought near to the very gates of heaven. He could not get his spiritual aspirations satisfied; and in his intense desires after the things of heaven, this world and all its good seemed to him poor and unprofitable. "Though I speak it with shame," he says, "yet it is a certain truth: it would then have been as difficult for me to have taken my mind from heaven to earth, as I have often found it since to get again from earth to heaven."

He now finally parted from all his old companions; and he gives us a mournfully affecting glimpse of one of them who madly resolved to go on in his evil ways. There is a wild strange pathos in the contrast between the old companions parting on the road of life—the affectionate tenderness of Bunyan, and the dare-devil recklessness of his friend. "There was a young man in our town to whom my heart before was bent more than to any other; but he, being a most wicked creature, I now shook him off and forsook his company;

but about a quarter of a year after I had left him, I
met him in a certain lane, and asked him how he did.
He, after his old swearing and mad way, answered 'he
was well.' 'But, Harry,' said I, 'why do you curse
and swear thus? What will become of you, if you die
in this condition?' He answered me in a great chafe,
'What would the devil do for company, if it were not
for such as I am!'"

But a new trial awaited him in the course upon
which he had entered. The spirit of Antinomianism,
which spread so widely in the wake of the religious
excitement which had long been moving England,
was extending among the religious professors at Bedford. The "Ranters' books" were eagerly read, and
held in high esteem by many. The poor man who
had first by his conversation led Bunyan to the study
of the Holy Scriptures, and with whom he had ever
since maintained a religious intimacy, fell under the
influence of these books. The doctrines of grace were
exaggerated by him into doctrines of license, and he
abandoned himself to his new impulses with all the
vehemency of an enthusiastic nature. "He turned,"
says Bunyan, "a most devilish Ranter, and gave himself up to all manner of filthiness, especially unclean-
ness; he would deny that there was a God, angel, or
spirit, and would laugh at all exhortations to sobriety.
When I laboured to rebuke his wickedness, he would
laugh the more, and pretend that he had gone through
all religions, and could never hit upon the right till
now."

Startling as such contrasts appear, and inconsistent
with all sanity of judgment, they were not uncommon
in this age. Men's minds in such a storm of religious
fervour as prevailed passed rapidly from one extreme

to another.   There was no principle too fixed or sacred
for discussion : all landmarks in religious doctrines
and experience had been torn up, and the spirit of
inquiry, once set in motion, ran in many such cases
as this "poor man," from indifference to earnestness
and the study of the Bible, and from these again,
under some new and irrepressible stimulus, to contempt, and libertinism both of thought and practice.
In this respect Puritanism was merely repeating the
history of every great religious revival.   It seems impossible for multitudes to be moved by the doctrines
of grace and the sweeping and contagious fervour
that comes from a revived interest in these doctrines,
without many yielding, as the wave of religious feeling
begins to ebb, to a certain licence of feeling.   With the
thoughts continually lifted above the practical duties
of morality into that higher region where the Divine
comes into immediate contact with the human,—transported beyond the lower levels of religion to the prime
source whence it issues—in which are all its springs—
it is no wonder if ignorant and unbalanced minds
should try to make the original spiritual element everything, and turn the act of grace into a cover of their
lawlessness.   Certainly there have been those who in
all such times have done so,—whose principle has
been that "God does not and can not see any sin in
any of his justified children."*   The act of grace is
held to be not only primary and absolute, but also
adequate in itself—apart from all moral result ; and
inflamed with this dominant idea, they turn religion
into a frenzy, and piety into a barren ecstasy or a mischievous unreality.

This spirit had been now spreading in England for

* Quoted from the works of Antinomian leaders.—See *Marsden*, p. 224.

some years; and we have already, in our sketch of
Baxter, seen the fruits of it. During the two preceding Stuart reigns there had been hanging on the
verge of Puritanism various sects with a tendency to
doctrinal latitudinarianism, such as the Anabaptists,
Brownists, and Familists. These had risen into new
prominence with the dissolution of the old ecclesiastical bonds; and along with them had sprung up the
other and wilder sects of which we have spoken—
Seekers, Behmenists, and Perfectionists, one and all
seeking the ideal of religion in an arbitrary mysticism transcending the common duties and responsi-
bilities of life. The Ranters were the last and extreme
offshoot of this spirit, many of whom, like Bunyan's
poor friend, seem to have been carried from excess to
excess till they denied the very existence of God;
while others conceived of Him as a bodily shape, and
others as a mere pervading Principle in the universe.
The same spirit readily took the most different shapes
of temporary belief or of no-belief. Ignorance and
vanity, once unbridled, knew no limit to the vagaries
of fantastic spiritualism into which they ran.

Bunyan was in some respects not unlikely to have
fallen under the influence of this spirit. The almost
diseased activity of his spiritual imagination, and his
ignorance of Christian truth, combined with his susceptibility to its broadest and most mysterious representations, might have proved a fitting soil for the reception of this extravagant mysticism. But with all his
religious excitability, he possessed a healthy natural
sense and manliness which saved him from such wild
opinions. He does not deny that they presented
something congenial to him,—that they were "suitable
to his flesh;" but God, who had designed better things

for him, "did not suffer him to accept them." His
increasing love of the Bible, and his growing perception of its cardinal doctrines, enabled him to see how
widely they were opposed to "such cursed principles,"
and preserved him in the right path. The Epistles
of St Paul, which he had formerly despised, now began
to open their meaning to him. "I began," he says,
"to look into the Bible with new eyes; and especially
the Epistles of the Apostle St Paul were sweet and
pleasant to me; and then I was never out of the
Bible, either by reading or meditation, still crying out
to God that I might know the truth and way to
heaven and glory."

But his views of Scripture were withal still dark
and confused. Although he had got into the right
track, his was too intense, and, at the same time, too
ignorant, a nature to go on in an even course of progress. His "Christian" was the type of himself;
and the difficulties and temptations which beset the
"Pilgrim" in his "Progress" from this world to that
which is to come, are not more numerous than those
which beset the author on his own spiritual journey.
In reading the Scriptures, he became greatly perplexed
by the word "faith;" especially this word, "put him
to it." He mused on it, and could not tell what to do.
Without faith he felt he could not be saved; but how to
tell whether he had faith or not baffled all his thought.
At last the idea struck him that the only way in which
he could really learn that he had faith was "by trying to work some miracles;" and one day as he went
between Elstow and Bedford this temptation was "hot
upon him," and took special form in his mind, urging
him "to say to the puddles that were in the horse
pond, Be dry; and to the dry places, Be you puddles."

Just as he was going to make the trial the thought
came to him : " But go under yonder hedge and pray
first that God would make you able. But when I
had concluded to pray, this came hot upon me, that if
I prayed and came again and tried to do it, and yet
did nothing notwithstanding, then to be sure I had
no faith, but was a castaway and lost. Nay, thought
I, if it be so, I will not try yet, but stay a little longer."
But still the thought kept tormenting him, and tossed
" betwixt the devil and his own ignorance," he was so
perplexed that he did not know what to do.

During all this time he seems to have maintained a religious intimacy with the poor women at Bedford whose conversation had been originally so blessed
to him. These women belonged to a small Baptist
congregation which met under the ministry of one
John Gifford, whose history, like Bunyan's own, and
even more than his, presents a strange picture of
the extremes of experience and life through which
many passed in this eventful time. Gifford had been
a major in the Royal army, and, having been engaged
in some Royalist insurrection, was seized, and sentenced to the gallows. By the help of his sister he
contrived to make his escape on the night before his
intended execution ; and after undergoing many hardships, he came to Bedford in disguise, and began the
practice of physic. He had lived in the army, and he
continued in his new profession to live a reckless and
ungodly life, devoted to drinking, gambling, and profaneness. He cherished a peculiar bitterness against
the Puritans, and is said even to have entertained the
design of killing one of their leading men in Bedford,
for no other reason than to gratify his ferocity against
them. Such a man might seem an unlikely subject

ever to become a Puritan and Baptist preacher. But
so it came about. In a fit of desperation, after losing
money in gambling, Gifford happened to look into one
of the books of Robert Bolton, and what he read so
impressed him, that he betook himself to the company
of the persons whom he had so scorned; and, being
"naturally bold," he soon rose to distinction among
them. He formed a number of them, among whom
was the very person he had thought of killing, into a
separate congregation, and became their pastor. To
this small congregation belonged the poor women
whose talk had reached Bunyan's heart; and Bunyan
himself about this time became attached to it. We
can understand the influence that a strong and zealous man like Gifford would exercise over a sensitive and inquiring mind like Bunyan's; and the his-
torian * of the English Baptists has represented him
as the evangelist who pointed out to our perplexed
pilgrim the wicket-gate, by instructing him in the
knowledge of the Gospel. Certainly, the happy spiritual state of "these poor" Baptist people deeply possessed his mind. It imaged itself to him in a kind
of vision," which, both for its own beauty, and the
interesting analogy which it presents to some of the
after-thoughts of the *Pilgrim's Progress*, deserves to
be quoted. "I saw," he says, "as if they were on the
sunny side of some high mountain, there refresh-
ing themselves with the pleasant beams of the sun,
while I was shivering and shrinking in the cold,
afflicted with frost, snow, and dark clouds. Methought,
also, betwixt me and them, I saw a wall that did compass about this mountain; now through this wall my
soul did greatly desire to pass, concluding that if I

* Mr Ivimey.

could, I would even go into the very midst of them, and there also comfort myself with the heat of their sun. About this wall I thought myself to go again and again, still prying as I went to see if I could find some way or passage by which I might enter therein, but none could I find for some time. At the last, I saw, as it were, a narrow gap, like a little door-way in the wall, through which I attempted to pass. Now, the passage being very straight and narrow, I made many offers to get in, but all in vain, even until I was well-nigh quite beat out by striving to get in. At last, with great striving, methought I at first did get in my head; and after that, by a sideling striving, my shoulders and my whole body; then was I exceeding glad, went and sat down in the midst of them, and so was comforted with the light and heat of their sun. Now, the mountain and wall were thus made out to me. The mountain signified the church of the living God: the sun that shone thereon, the comfortable shining of his merciful face on them that were within: the wall, I thought, was the word that did make separation between the Christians and the world: and the gap which was in the wall, I thought, was Jesus Christ, who is the way to God the Father. But forasmuch as the passage was wonderful narrow, even so narrow that I could not but with great difficulty enter in thereat, it showed me that none could enter into life but those that were in downright earnest, and unless also they left that wicked world behind them—for here was only room for body and soul, but not for body and soul and sin."

Bunyan's spiritual perplexities were far from being at an end. In fact, as his mind opened to the deeper mysteries of the Christian faith, and his acquaintance

with Scripture grew in detail, without as yet harmonising into a consistent whole, he became the victim of
anxieties still darker and more tormenting than he had
hitherto experienced. He had been troubled about
faith—he was now troubled about election. In both
cases his temptation was the same—to look away from
Christ to himself—to fix his attention not upon the
fulness of divine grace, but on the limits and conditions
which seemed to accompany the act of grace. As he
had formerly asked, "But how if you want faith indeed? how can you tell you have faith?" so now he
asked, "How can you tell that you are elected; and
what if you should not—how then?" "Why then,"
said Satan, "you had as good leave off, and strive no
further; for if, indeed, you should not be elected and
chosen of God, there is no hope of your being saved.
For it is neither in him that willeth, nor in him that
runneth, but in God that showeth mercy." "By these
things I was driven to my wit's end, not knowing what
to say, or how to answer these temptations." Strangely
enough, he found comfort and strength in this perplexity from a text in the Apocrypha.* It came to
him as a light in the midst of his darkness. As he
was "giving up the ghost" of all his hopes, the sentence fell with weight upon his spirit. It was as if it
talked with him. "Look at the generations of old
and see—did ever any trust in God and were confounded?" He was somewhat daunted to find it only
in the Apocrypha; but he says, very sensibly, that although it was not among those texts that we call holy
and canonical, yet as the sentence was the sum and
substance of many of the promises, it was my duty to
take the comfort of it: and I bless God for that word

* Ecclesiasticus, ii. 16.

—for it was of good to me. That word doth still ofttimes shine before my face."

His next doubt was, "But how, if the day of grace should be past and gone?—how if you have overstood the time of mercy?" As he was walking in the country one day, this doubt came upon him; and with that strange ingenuity with which the spirit learns to torment itself in such a case, the thought suggested itself to him that the small congregation of good people at Bedford was all that God would save in these parts, and that he had come too late, for these had got the blessing before him. At length, however, he thought on the text—"Compel them to come in that my house may be filled—and yet there is room;" and in the light and encouragement of this word he went a pretty while.

About this time he was in the habit of frequenting Mr Gifford's house, "to hear him confer with others about the dealings of God with their souls;" but he derived little or no benefit, he tells us, from these conferences; he only learned the more to see his own wickedness and corruption. "I could not believe that Christ had a love for me. Alas! I could neither hear him, nor see him, nor feel him, nor favour any of his things. I was driven as with a tempest: my heart would be careless; the Canaanites would dwell in the land. Sometimes I would tell my condition to the people of God, when they would pity me, and tell me of the promises; but they had as good have told me that I must reach the sun with my fingers as have bidden me receive or rely upon the promises. All my sense and feeling were against me; and I saw I had a heart that would sin, and that lay under a law that would condemn."

In this state he continued " for some years together."
Like Luther, he could only say, Oh my sins! my sins!
They seemed to cleave unto him, and wholly pollute
him. "I thought now that every one had a better
heart than I had. I thought none but the devil himself could equalise me for inward wickedness and
pollution of mind." And yet all this while he was
" never more tender as to the act of sinning. His
conscience would smart at every touch, and he could
not tell how to speak his words for fear he should mis-
place them." His sensitiveness of conscience was such
that he dreaded even that his very torments should
cease. " For I found that unless guilt of conscience
were taken off the right way—that is, by the blood of
Christ—a man grew rather worse for the loss of his
trouble of mind." And in order that this should not
be his case, he would muse upon the punishment of
sin in hell-fire, that the sense of sin might be kept
alive in his heart. In this condition, a sermon that he
heard on the love of Christ brought for a while peace
to him. The words—"Thou art fair, my love," applied to the poor tempted soul, seized upon him. He
was in great joy for a time. "Thou art my love—
thou art my love." "Twenty times together," this
would sound in his heart, and it grew warmer as the
blessed accents repeated themselves. At length he
felt as if his sins could be forgiven him. "Yea," he
says, "I was now so taken with the love and mercy of
God, that I remember I could not tell how to contain
till I got home. *I thought I could have spoken of his
love, and have told of his mercy to me, even to the very
crows that sat in the ploughed lands before me."*

This time of gladness did not last long. He wished
that he had possessed a pen and ink in the moment of

his elevation, to write down God's goodness to him, for surely he will not forget it forty years hence. "But, alas!" he adds, "within less than forty days, I began to question all again."

The vividness of his spiritual feelings kept him on the rack, and pursued him as a tormenting presence. His imagination gave voice and shape to his inward suggestions; and a text became to him a living being following him, and addressing him. About a week or a fortnight after the last manifestation of grace to his soul, he says, "I was much followed by the scripture—'Simon, Simon, behold Satan hath desired to have you;' and sometimes it would sound so loud within me, that once above all the rest I turned my head over my shoulder, thinking, verily, that some man behind me called me, being at a great distance, methought he called so loud. . . . Methinks I hear still, with what a loud voice these words—'Simon, Simon,' sounded in mine ears; and, although that was not my name, yet it made me suddenly look behind me, believing that he that called so loud meant me." He did not understand the meaning of this at the time, but afterwards it seemed to him as a warning that a "cloud and storm was coming down upon him."

In truth, his temptations assumed now a darker and more fearful form. Hitherto they had concerned his own safety—now they attacked his trust in religion altogether. He was "handled twenty times worse than he had been before;" all comfort was taken from him; darkness seized upon him; after which "whole floods of blasphemies, both against God, Christ, and the Scriptures," were poured upon his spirit, to his great confusion and astonishment. "Whether there were in truth a God or Christ, and whether the holy

Scriptures were not rather a fable and cunning story,
than the holy and pure word of God"—such were the
questions that agitated and darkened him. He could
not rest "from morning to night." He was carried
away with them as "with a mighty whirlwind." His
only consolation was that he felt there was something
in him opposed to such questions. While under this
temptation, he often found his mind suddenly put upon
it, "to curse and swear, or to speak some grievous
things against God, or Christ, his Son, and of the
Scriptures." At times, he thought himself possessed
of the devil. At other times, he seemed as if he should
be bereft of his wits. His agitation certainly verged
on insanity. His will seemed to lose all control. He
compares himself to a child forcibly seized by a gipsy,
and carried away from friend and country. He would
kick, and shriek, and cry, yet he was bound on the
wings of the temptation, and the wind would carry
him away. When he heard others talk of the sin
against the Holy Ghost, the temptation was so strong
upon him to commit this sin, that he says—"I have
often been ready to clap my hands under my chin to
hold my mouth from opening ; at other times, to leap
with my head downwards into some muckhill hole to
keep my mouth from speaking." Like Luther, he
felt the presence of the Tempter disturbing all his
efforts at devotion. " Sometimes I have thought I
have felt him behind me pull my clothes. He would
be also continually at me in time of prayers to have
done—to break off—make haste—you have prayed
enough, and stay no longer—still drawing my mind
away. When I have had wandering thoughts, and I
have laboured to compose my mind, and fix it upon
God, then with great force hath the Tempter laboured

to distract and confound me, and to turn away my
mind by presenting to my heart and fancy the form of
a brute, a bull, a bison, or the like, as if I should pray
to these." In his misery, the animals moved his envy,
and he would gladly have exchanged his condition for
that of a dog or a horse. And yet, while thus bleed-
ing at every pore of his spiritual being, he complains
of his insensibility. His heart was so hard at times,
he says, "that he would have given a thousand pounds
to shed a tear, and could not."

Gradually light began to break upon this period of
his darkness. Various scriptures came to his aid.
One day, as he was sitting in a neighbour's house,
very sad at the consideration of his many blasphemies, this "word" came suddenly to him, "What shall
we say to these things ? 'If God be for us, who can be
against us?' Because I live, ye shall live also." "But
these words were but hints, touches, and short visits,
though very sweet when present." Such "angel visits"
gradually increased ; and Mr Gifford's instructions
proved also wholesome in his distress. He made rapid
progress for a while in faith and in peace of mind.
He was led from truth to truth in a manner that
excited his astonishment, as he recalled it. "Truly,"
he exclaims, "I thus found, upon this account, the
great God was very good unto me; for, to my remembrance, there was not anything that I thus cried unto
God to make known and reveal unto me but he was
pleased to do it for me." He found strength and
comfort even from the contemplation of the errors of
the Quakers, which led him to the study of the
Scriptures, for, as "the Quakers did oppose the truth,
so God did thus the more confirm me in it, by leading
me into the scripture that did wonderfully maintain

it." His elevation and spiritual happiness were remarkable for a time. It would be too long "to stay and tell in particular how God did set me down in all the things of Christ—yea, and also how He did open His words unto me, and make them shine before me, and cause them to dwell with me, talk with me, and comfort me over and over, both of His own being and the being of his Son and Spirit and Word and Gospel." And just as before in his depression, his imagination had conjured up miserable voices and hideous images, which.haunted him as realities—so now, in his elevation, it pictured to him, in visible forms of beauty, the assurance of his salvation. "I had an evidence, as I thought, of my salvation from heaven, with many golden seals thereon, all hanging in my sight;" and the heavenly sight did so ravish him that he wished the last day were come, or that he were "fourscore years old now, that he might die quickly, and that his soul might go to rest."

It is an affecting contemplation this wonderful child-nature of the great Puritan dreamer—now moved to grief—now strung to joy—now plunged in horrors of great darkness—and now raised to heights of celestial blessedness. Reflection scarcely enters into his varying moods; he is not swayed by any calm and coherent succession of ideas. Truth or error, in the abstract, is nothing to him; he cannot hold them before his mind, and contemplate, and weigh the thoughts which they present; but he lives himself in all his thoughts. Transmuted into passions—made living by the ever-burning glow of his imagination—they become all-powerful for the time, and carry him whithersoever they will.

About this time a copy of Martin Luther's *Commen-*

tary on the Galatians fell into his hands, and proved greatly beneficial to him. The copy was so old that it was ready to fall piece from piece if he did but turn it over; but its antiquity only made it the more precious in his eyes; and when he had "but a little way perused," he found his condition "so largely and profoundly handled in it, as if it had been written out of his own heart." This spiritual affinity between Luther and Bunyan is very striking and interesting. In the realistic vividness and fertility of their spiritual imagination they were strongly allied. The divine life imaged itself to them in the same depths and heights, the same representative contrasts, the same agencies of satanic and of angelic and heavenly power. The presence of evil was to Luther the same personal tempter as to Bunyan—reasoning with him, pulling at his clothes, violently and insolently assaulting him; and the idea of deliverance suggested itself to both in the same manner, as an immediate influence from above lifting them out of their sins. The spiritual experience of Luther accordingly was a mirror in which Bunyan might well see his own heart reflected, while the doctrine of the *Commentary on the Galatians* was exactly such as was calculated to minister to his urgent necessities. He never forgot his obligation to this book; he continued to prefer it (excepting the Holy Bible) before all other books, "as most fit for a wounded conscience."

And now, for a brief space, his heart was bound in delightful union with Christ. The day seemed for him to break, and the shadows to flee away. "Oh!" he exclaims, "methought my soul cleaved unto Christ, my affections cleaved unto him. I felt my love to him as hot as fire;" and yet a deeper and more tormenting trial than he had yet experienced was awaiting him. He seemed to have been raised to the heights of love, and to have been gladdened with the sight of the Delectable Mountains, only to be plunged into a deeper "valley of the shadow of death." "Quickly after this my love was tried to the purpose. For, after the Lord had in this manner thus graciously delivered me from this great and sore temptation, and had given me such strong consolation and blessed evidence from heaven, touching my interest in his love through Christ, the tempter came upon me again, and that with a more grievous and dreadful temptation than before."

This temptation was nothing less than "to sell and part with the blessed Christ, to exchange him for the things of this life—for anything." This horrid suggestion haunted him day and night for a whole year. He was not rid of it "one day in a month, no, not sometimes one hour in many days together, unless when asleep." It mixed itself in all he did, so that he could not eat his food, "stoop for a pin, chop a stick, or cast his eye to look on anything," without the thought pursuing him, "Sell Christ for this, or sell Christ for that; sell Him—sell Him." Under the influence of this temptation he was once more reduced to a state bordering on insanity. He was so stirred with the idea of yielding to the horrid suggestion, that his mental agitation showed itself in his bodily movements, and he would thrust forth his hands or elbows in deprecation, still answering, as fast as the destroyer said, "Sell Him,"—"I will not,—I will not: no, not for thousands,—thousands,—thousands of worlds," reckoning in this manner lest he should seem to set too low a value upon Him," until he scarcely knew where he was, or what to do. This lasted for some time; his mind was continually disquieted, and nothing could give him rest; but he still repelled the assaults of the adversary ever as they were renewed; until one morning, as he lay in his bed under unusually fierce temptation, he felt the thought pass through his mind, " Let Him go if He will." The old spirit of resistance relaxed for a moment,—worn out by frequent straining; and he felt his heart, as he fancied, freely consent to the dreadful impulse. " Oh! the diligence of Satan!" he cries, " Oh! the desperateness of man's heart! Now was the battle won, and down fell I, as a bird that is shot from the top of a tree, into great guilt and fearful despair. Thus, getting out of my bed, I went moping into the field, but, God knows, with as heavy a heart as mortal man, I think, could bear, where, for the space of about two hours, I was like a man bereft of life, and as now past all recovery, and bound over to eternal punishment."

There is a strange sad vividness in the picture that he draws of the misery into which he was now plunged —the alternations of fear and horror and partial hope that came upon him. He thought of the passage in Hebrews, xii. 16, 17, about Esau selling his birthright, and afterwards finding no place for repentance, though he sought it carefully with tears; and the words became to his soul " like fetters of brass to his legs, in the continual bondage of which he went for several months together." Yet from the first, too, a casual gleam of hope illuminated the thick darkness of his trial. About ten or eleven o'clock on the same day that he seemed to himself to have committed the fearful sin of selling his Saviour, he says, " As I was walking under a hedge (full of sorrow and guilt, God knows), and bemoaning myself for this hard hap, that such a thought should arise within me, suddenly this sentence rushed in upon me, ' The blood of Christ remits all guilt.'   At this I made a stand in my spirit ; with that this word took hold upon me, ' The blood of Jesus Christ his own Son cleanseth us from all sin,' 1st John, i. 7.   Now I began to conceive peace in my soul ; and methought I saw as if the Tempter did leer and steal away from me, as being ashamed of what he had done." But this pleasant gleam of light and peace by the hedgerows on the first day that he meditated with a darkened heart on his sin, soon left him, and through many suc- ceeding pages he does little but represent the phases of gloomy and despairing thought into which he was plunged.   He imagined he had committed the un- pardonable sin ; and an " ancient Christian," to whom he confided his anxious terror, told him that " he thought so too."   He compared his sin with David's, and Peter's, and Judas' ; and the only relief he had in the retrospect was, that he had not " as to the circum- stances " transgressed so fully as Judas.   Even this bare hope was quickly gone.   It seemed to him as if no sin equalled his own.   " He had sold his Saviour, and there remained to him no more sacrifice for sin." "This one consideration would always kill my heart —my sin was point blank against my Saviour, and that, too, at that height, that I had in my heart said of Him, 'Let Him go if He will.'   Oh! methought this sin was bigger than the sins of a country, of a kingdom, or of the whole world, no one pardonable, not all of them together was able to equal mine ; mine outwent them every one."

A breath of hope sometimes ruffled the current of his misery.   Once as he was walking to and fro " in

a good man's shop," bemoaning his sad and doleful
state, and afflicting himself with self-abhorrence for
his wicked and ungodly thought, " suddenly there was
as if there had rushed in at the window the noise of
wind upon me, but very pleasant, and as if I heard a
voice speaking, 'Didst thou ever refuse to be justified
by the blood of Christ?' To this my heart answered
groaningly, 'No.' Then fell with power that word of
God upon me, 'See that ye refuse not Him that speaketh' (Heb. xii. 25). This made a strange seizure upon
my spirit; it brought light with it, and commanded
a silence in my heart of all those tumultuous thoughts
that did before use—like masterless hellhounds—to
roar and bellow, and make a hideous noise within me.
It showed me, also, that Jesus Christ had yet a word
of grace and mercy for me, that He had not, as I had
feared, quite forsaken and cast off my soul. Verily,
that sudden rushing wind was as if an angel had come
upon me,—it commanded a great calm in my soul ;
it persuaded me there might be hope." Yet again
the Tempter returned. With the resurrection of hope
the spirit of prayer awoke in him, and when about to
humble himself, and beg that God would, of His wonderful mercy, show pity to him, and have compassion
upon his wretched sinful soul, the Tempter suggested
that prayer was not for any use in his case ; that it
could do him no good, because he had rejected the
Mediator, by whom all prayers come with acceptance
to God the Father,—and without whom no prayer can
come into his presence. The most vexatious doubts
sprang from this new root of bitterness. The very
abundance of the grace of Christ seemed to prove an
aggravation of the guilt of his rejection of Him.
The fearful thought of his heart, " Let Him go if He

will" returned upon him in all the darkness of its despairing agony. "Now, therefore, you are severed from Him," the voice kept echoing within him. "You have severed yourself from Him. Behold, then, His goodness,—but yourself to be no partaker of it." "Oh!" thought I, "what have I lost! what have I parted with! what has disinherited my poor soul! Oh, 'tis sad to be destroyed by the grace and mercy of God; to have the Lamb, the Saviour, turn lion and destroyer (Rev. vi.) By such strange and unusual assaults of the Tempter his soul was "like a broken vessel, driven as with the winds." A deep and pathetic gloom settled upon him. What touching tenderness in this picture which he draws of himself! "One day I walked to a neighbouring town, and sat down upon a settle in the street, and fell into a very deep pause about the most fearful state my sin had brought me to; and after long musing, I lifted up my head, but methought I saw as if the sun that shineth in the heavens did grudge to give light; and as if the very stones in the street and tiles upon the houses did bend themselves against me. O how happy now was every creature over I was! for they stood fast and kept their station, but I was gone and lost."

But this was about the crisis of his misery. For as "breaking out into the bitterness of his soul," he heaved a sigh, "How can God comfort such a wretch?" a voice, as if in echo, replied to him, "This sin is not unto death." He was filled with admiration at the fitness and unexpectedness of this sentence; the "power, and sweetness, and light, and glory, that came with it, also, were marvellous." He was lifted for the time out of doubt, and gradually, though still with many struggles and some relapses, he regained composure of mind.

Voices of comfort were heard by him—as formerly voices of woe had rung in his ears. At one time he retired to rest with the quieting assurance, " I have loved thee with an everlasting love." Next morning when he awaked, " it was fresh upon his soul," and he believed it. Again, when renewed doubts assailed him as to whether the blood of Christ was sufficient to save his soul, the words sounded suddenly within his heart, " He is able." " Methought this word *able* was spoke loud unto me—it showed a great word—it seemed to be writ in great letters." Thus he went on for many weeks, " sometimes comforted and sometimes tormented." Upon the whole, he made advance. The darkness cleared away more and more as his mind dwelt upon the promises of Scripture, and he came to understand the harmony of their message in his behalf as a poor sinner. " And now remained only the hinder part of the tempest, for the thunder was gone beyond me, only some drops did still remain that now and then would fall upon me." They were but drops; and then there came " clear shining after the rain." As he was passing into the field one day, still with some dashes in his conscience, fearing lest yet all was not right, suddenly this sentence fell upon his soul, " Thy righteousness is in heaven ;" and therewith he saw, with the eyes of his soul, Jesus Christ at God's right hand, and saw, moreover, that it was not his good frame of mind that made his righteousness better, nor yet his bad frame that made his righteousness worse, for " his righteousness was Jesus Christ himself," the same yesterday, to-day, and for ever. " Now," he adds, in rejoicing language, " did my chains fall off my legs indeed ; I was loosened from my afflictions and irons ; my temptations also fled away. . . . 'Twas glorious to me to

see His exaltation, and the worth and prevalency of all
His benefits ; and that because now I could look from
myself to Him, and would reckon that all those graces
that now were green on me were yet like those cracked
groats and fourpence-halfpennies that rich men carry
in their purses, when their gold is in their trunks at
home ! In Christ my Lord and Saviour. Now Christ
was all ; all my righteousness, all my sanctification,
and all my redemption."

The full and perfect truth of justification by faith
was now owned by Bunyan, and gave him a sure
ground of confidence such as he had not hitherto felt.
He realised the mystery of union with the Son of God
and all the blessings of his representative character ;
and his mind turned from the distractions of his own
spiritual state to rest with assurance on the great work
of Christ for him. He felt himself, through his living
union with Christ, to be truly a sharer in this work,
whose perfection constituted the certainty of his salvation. "For if he and I were one," he says, "then his
righteousness was mine, his merits mine, his victory
also mine. Now, could I see myself in heaven and
earth at once. In heaven by my Christ, by my head,
by my righteousness and life, though on earth by
body or person. Now, I saw Christ Jesus was looked
upon of God ; and should also be looked upon as that
common or public person in whom all the whole body
of his elect are always to be considered and reckoned ;
that we fulfilled the law by him, died by him, rose
from the dead by him, got the victory over sin, death,
the devil, and hell by him ; when he died we died,
and so of his resurrection, 'Thy dead men shall live,
together with my dead body shall they arise.' " *

* Isaiah, xxvi. 19.

These "blessed considerations and scriptures, with many of a like nature," were made henceforth to "spangle" in his eyes; and from this time, although not with a uniform clearness, his soul dwelt in comparative "light and peace." In looking back upon the dark way of his temptations, he ascribed them especially to two causes—a want of vigilance in prayer—and a too material trust in God. He had besought God, on one occasion, to interpose to save his wife from pain, and having received, as he supposed, an answer to his prayer, he was led to "tempt God," by relying upon his interpositions after such a manner. Bitter as had been his experience, he believed that it brought him many advantages. Beyond doubt it did. The wonderful sense that he ever afterwards had of "the blessing and glory of God and his beloved Son"—the "glory of the holiness of God breaking his heart in pieces"—the insight which he acquired into the meaning of the Scriptures, and especially the nature of its promises, and further into the "heights and depths" of grace and love and mercy—"great sins drawing out great grace" —all this sprang as precious fruit from his bitter trial—fruit unto righteousness and life everlasting.

This happy change in Bunyan's condition was followed by his admission to fellowship with "the people of God at Bedford." He joined Gifford's congregation, and was openly baptised by him, probably in the river Ouse, although he himself says nothing of the fact. It is somewhat singular, as Mr Philip, his most copious biographer, points out, that he does not dwell upon the subject of baptism at all in connection with his admission to the society of the Baptists. He speaks of the Lord's Supper, and mentions that the

scripture, " Do this in remembrance of me," was
made a very precious word unto him, " for by it the
Lord did come down upon my conscience with the
discovery of his death for my sins, and as I then felt
did, as if he *plunged* me in the virtue of the same."
He speaks also of the temptations which still pursued
him—how they fastened upon this ordinance, which at
the first had been such a source of comfort ; but he
says nothing of his baptism : it does not seem to have
occupied any important place in his spiritual history ;
the strange drama of his temptations did not find in
it any centre of interest or attraction. Bunyan became a Baptist, in fact, more from accidental association than anything else. He had found the truth
among the poor men and women of the " water-bap-
tism way," as he called it—and therefore he embraced
this way ; but from the very depth and sincerity of
his spiritual nature, he rose far above the mere formalities of the sect, and did not hesitate, with an
unsparing hand, to point out their narrowness and
prejudices when he saw occasion.

About this time he fell into some sickness. The
distress of mind that he had undergone, combined, perhaps, with his wandering and unsettled life, terminated
in this natural result. A nervous system so highly
strung as his could not but suffer from the extremes
of depression and joy which had agitated him. The
very delicacy and sensitiveness of nervous organisation
which made such extremes familiar to him—and out of
which grew the vivid impressions which filled his spiritual imagination—made him, at the same time, liable
to the weakness and disease springing from over-excite-
ment. We are not surprised, therefore, that he was
suddenly and violently seized with what seemed con-

sumption. His life appeared in danger, and he set himself to examine seriously into his state and condition for the future. As he did this, the black troop of his sins came flocking into his mind, and his former state of despair was wellnigh returning upon him; but he was now too fully instructed in the truth to yield to the apprehensions that assailed him. His free justification in Christ came as a reviving thought in the midst of his apprehensions: "Ye are justified freely by this grace through the redemption that is in Christ Jesus."* "Oh, what a turn these words made upon me! Now was I as one awakened out of some troublesome sleep and dream; and listening to this heavenly sentence, I was as if I had heard it thus spoken to me: 'Sinner, thou thinkest that because of thy sins and infirmities I cannot save thy soul; but behold my Son is by me, and upon him I look and not on thee, and shall deal with thee according as I am pleased with him.' At this I was greatly enlightened in my mind, and made to understand that God could justify a sinner at any time; it was but his looking upon Christ, and imparting of his benefits to us, and the word was forthwith done. And as I was thus in a muse, that scripture also came with great power upon my spirit, 'Not by works of righteousness that we have done, but according to his mercy he hath saved us.' Now was I got high. I saw myself within the arms of grace and mercy, and though I was before afraid to think of a dying hour, yet now I said, 'Let me die.' Now death was lovely and beautiful in my sight, for I saw we shall never live indeed till we be gone to the other world. Oh! methought this life is but a slumber in comparison with that above."

* Rom. iii. 24.

This elevation of spirit lasted till another severe fit of illness seized him. His depression returned with this renewed attack. The terrors of death and of judgment again seized his startled imagination, and he felt himself already descending into the pit as one dead before death came. But the words of the angel carrying Lazarus into Abraham's bosom, "So shall it be with thee when thou dost leave this world," sweetly revived him and helped him to hope in God. The text, "O death where is thy sting, O grave where is thy victory?" fell with joyful weight upon his mind. Suddenly he became well. He felt his strength grow as his mind settled into calmness. The evil spirit which had so long troubled him was not entirely gone; but he was rapidly rising above it. Once more a cloud of great darkness hid from him the face of God; but it was only a passing one. After some three or four days, as he was sitting by the fire he suddenly felt the words to sound in his heart, "I must go to Jesus;" and at this his darkness fled away, and the blessed things of heaven once more stood clear in his view. He was for a little uncertain as to the words of encouragement, and in his dilemma appealed to his wife: "Wife," he said, "is there ever such a scripture, 'I must go to Jesus.'" She said she could not tell. But as he stood musing, there came "bolting in" upon him the passage, "And to an innumerable company of angels," * and he felt satisfied and rejoiced. Often afterwards this passage occurred to him, and brought him strength and peace.

After Bunyan had been for some years connected with the Baptist congregation in Bedford, he began to take a part in their proceedings. His earnestness,

* Heb. xii. 22.

mental vivacity, and gifts of expression, soon pointed
him out as fitted for the work of the ministry. "After
I had been about five or six years awakened," he says,
"and helped myself to see both the want and worth
of Jesus Christ our Lord, and also enabled to venture
my soul upon Him, some of the most able among the
saints with us—I say the most able for judgment and
holiness of life—as they conceived—did perceive that
God had counted me worthy to understand something
of His will in His holy and blessed Word, and had
given me utterance, in some measure, to express what
I saw to others for edification : therefore they desired
me—and that with much earnestness—that I would
be willing sometimes to take in hand in one of the
meetings to speak a word of exhortation unto them; the
which, though at the first it did much dash and abash
my spirit, yet being still by them desired and entreat-
ed, I consented to their request, and did twice, at
two several assemblies (but in private), though with
much weakness and infirmity, discover my gift amongst
them, at which they not only seemed to be, but did
frequently protest as in the sight of the great God,
they were both affected and comforted, and gave
thanks to the Father of mercies for the grace bestowed
on me."

Finally, in 1656, "after solemn prayer, with fasting,
he was set apart to the more ordinary and public
preaching of the word." He felt deeply the solemnity
of the work to which he had devoted himself, and was
in no hurry to enter upon it. After his first attempts
he went into the country and addressed small audiences there, privately, for he "durst not make use of
his gift in an open way ;" but gradually the consciousness of his vocation grew upon him, and he felt

a " secret pricking forward thereto." It could not be
otherwise. Gifts such as Bunyan's could not be hid ;
and soon he began to preach openly throughout the
district around Bedford, the Gospel "that God had
showed him in his Holy Word of Truth." Unimportant
as his position had hitherto been, something would
seem to have been known of his history and the wonderful experiences of which he had been the subject, for
he tells that when the country understood that the
profane tinker had become a preacher, "they came in
to hear the word by hundreds, and that from all parts."
God gave him success, for he had not preached long
before " some began to be touched and greatly afflicted
in their minds at the apprehension of the greatness of
their sin, and of their need of Jesus Christ."

The account which Bunyan gives of his preaching
sufficiently explains his success. He tells us that he
" preached what he felt." His own experience made
the substance of his sermons, and we can understand
what life and power this gave to them. The terrors of
the law, and the sense of sin, had lain heavily upon his
conscience. He had felt " smartingly " what it is to
dwell without God and without hope in the world ;
and he " declared that under which his own poor soul
did groan and tremble to astonishment." " I went myself in chains to preach to them in chains ; and carried that fire in my own conscience that I persuaded
them to be aware of." This was the main burden of his
preaching for two years. He cried out against men's
sins, and their fearful state because of them. Then
after this, as he himself advanced in knowledge, and·
peace, and comfort, through Christ, he altered his style ;
" for still," he says, " I preached what I saw and felt.
Now, therefore, I did much labour to hold with Jesus

Christ in all his offices, relations, and benefits unto the
world, and did strive also to discover and remove their
false supports and props on which the world doth both
lean, and by them fall and perish. On these things
also I staid as long as on the other. After this God
let me into something of the mystery of the union of
Christ; wherefore that I discovered, and showed to
them also."

Bunyan's heart, in short, was in his preaching. He
uttered in living phrase his own warm feelings. He
spake as he was moved. He was possessed by the
truths which he addressed to others. It was not
enough for him to say, " I believe and am sure ;" but
he felt " more than sure " of what was life and joy and
peace to his own soul. Everything else to him was
but shadowy and dim in comparison with the realities
of sin and salvation, of wrath and redemption through
the blood of Christ. He lived only in the consciousness of the life of faith, and his preaching was the mere
expression of his constant thoughts and feelings. And
so it touched and awakened the common minds he addressed. The vivid extempore words of such a man,—
coming right from his heart,—were exactly those most
likely to arrest and impress the audiences that gathered
round him. He says, "I never endeavoured to, nor durst,
make use of other men's lines (though I condemn not
all that do), for I verily thought, and found by experience, that what was taught me by the word and Spirit
of Christ, could be spoken, maintained, and stood to by
the soundest and best established conscience. . . . I
have observed that a word cast in by the by hath done
more execution in a sermon than all that was spoken
besides. Sometimes also, when I have thought I did
do good, then I did the most of all ; and at other times,

when I thought I should catch them, I have fished for nothing."

He was not of a disputatious turn. In his preaching he kept clear of such things as were "in dispute among the saints." He had too large a soul to take delight in mere word-splitting, and on different occasions he showed himself above the contentious spirit of his age. But strangely enough it was in a controversial capacity that he was destined to make his first appearance as an author. In 1656 some itinerant preachers of Quakerism had come to Bedford,—and in the parish church, called the "Steeple House," had held a disputation on the subject of their doctrines. They found in Bunyan not only a sturdy but an intelligent and able opponent. Quaker spiritualism—lively and mystic as his own spiritual fancies were—had no charm for him. It seemed to him to destroy altogether the reality of the Gospel salvation, to take away an outward "Christ, born of the Virgin Mary, fulfilling the law, dying without the gate of Jerusalem as a sacrifice for sin, as rising again, as ascending into and interceding in heaven, and as coming from heaven again in his flesh to judge the world." No one was more able than Bunyan to appreciate what was good in Quakerism—its deep inward sense of the Divine—the necessity of *Christ within the heart*, of which it said so much—but he had also a very strong and even vehement feeling of what he deemed its serious errors. A Christ not merely in him but without him ; a Saviour *for him ;* and in whose substantive work on earth, "reconciling the world unto God," he knew himself to be safe — this was to him of the very essence of the truth, for which he was called upon to contend.

With this view he published his first treatise, under
the title, "Some Gospel Truths, opened according to
the Scriptures, on the Divine and Human Nature of
Christ Jesus: His coming into the world: His righteousness, death, resurrection, ascension, intercession,
and second coming to judgment, plainly demonstrated
and proved." The book contains a very sensible and
well-reasoned argument for the divinity of Christ. The
question is argued from prophecy,—from the works of
Christ,—from the whole testimony of Scripture, sometimes not very critically,—yet always reasonably,—
and in a very sound and intelligent spirit throughout.
Nothing could show better Bunyan's strong and sober
judgment under all the enthusiasm of passionate devotion that animated him. It proves also his diligence
as a student of scripture. He misses almost nothing
bearing upon his subject, and if he does not penetrate
below the surface, or bring the old texts into new
combinations, he yet arrays and expounds them in
their accepted meanings, with an impressive and consistent force. In conclusion, he replies to the Quaker
objections with great acuteness and success. Admitting to the full the necessity of a Christ *within*, this
is not, he contends, to be held in opposition to a Christ
without, but in strict and necessary connection therewith; "for where the spirit of Christ is in truth, that
spirit causeth the soul to look to the Christ that was
born of the Virgin for all justification. And, indeed,
here is *my life*—namely, the birth of this man, the
righteousness of this man, the death and resurrection
of this man, the ascension and intercession of this
man for me, and the second coming of this man to
judge .the world in righteousness. I say here is *my
life*—if I see this by faith without me, through the

operation of the Spirit within me, I am safe, I am at peace, I am comforted, I am encouraged ; and I know that my comfort, peace, and encouragement is true, and given me from heaven by the Father of mercies, through the Son of the Virgin Mary, who is the way to the Father of mercies, who is able to save to the uttermost all that come to the Father by Him. This is the rock, sinner, upon which if thou be built, the gates of hell, nor Ranter, Quaker, sin, law, death, no, nor the devil himself, shall ever be able to prevail against thee."

Controversial as the treatise is, its language is, upon the whole, temperate. It is the language of one more anxious to establish truth than to refute error. It would not, however, have been characteristic of the age if it had been altogether free from rudeness and extravagance of epithet, and harshness of feeling. It was a customary device of controversy then to open the attack in the title—to make it as sharp and incisive as possible ; and Bunyan wields this weapon with a hearty goodwill. His secondary title condenses more vituperation than any other part of his book. It runs thus :—" Answers to several Questions, with profitable Directions to stand fast in the Doctrine of Jesus, the Son of Mary, against those blustering Storms of the Devil's Temptations which do at this Day, like so many Scorpions, break loose from the Bottomless Pit to bite and torment those that have not tasted the Virtue of Jesus by the Revelation of the Spirit of God."

The Quakers felt the force of Bunyan's attack ; and one of their leaders, Edward Burroughs, a "son of thunder and consolation," published a reply to it. The reply was entitled, " The True Faith of the Gospel of Peace, contended for in the Spirit of Meekness ; and the mystery of Salvation (Christ within the hope of Glory), vindicated in the Spirit of Love against the Secret Opposition of John Bunyan, a professed Minister in Bedfordshire." Bunyan had put all his fierceness into his title; and after his talk of scorpions, had shown little heat or abuse of language; but Burroughs, all gentleness in the title, breaks out into foaming wrath in his text. His words, "soft as dew, or as the droppings of a summer cloud," portend a storm, such as no doubt won for him his admiring appellation of "Son of Thunder." He thus inveighs—"Your spirit is tried, and your generation is read at large, and your stature and countenance is clearly described to me to be of the stock of Ishmael and of the seed of Cain, whose line reacheth unto the murthering priests, Scribes, and Pharisees. Oh, thou blind priest, whom God hath confounded in thy language, the design of the devil in deceiving souls is thy own, and I turn it back to thee. Thou directest altogether to a thing without disposing the light within and worshipping the name Mary in thy imagination, and knowest not Him who was before the world was, in whom alone is salvation, and in no other. If we should diligently search we should find thee, through feigned words, through covetousness, making merchandise of souls, loving the wages of unrighteousness. The Lord rebuke thee, thou unclean spirit, who hast falsely accused the innocent to clear thyself from guilt. . . . Thy weapons are slanders, and thy refuge is lies; and thy work is confused, and hath hardly gained a name in Babylon's record."

Burroughs was a man of consideration in his party; and in reality, as his letters to his family are said to prove,* a man of tenderness as well as of boldness.

* PHILIP's *Life of Bunyan*, p. 238.

He did not hesitate, as others of his sect, to remonstrate with the great Protector in the day of his power. It is obvious, however, that he showed as little sense as temper in dealing with Bunyan. Humble as the author of *Gospel Truths Opened* was, and with but a modest opinion of himself, he was not to be silenced by mere loudness of tone and stormy language. He replied accordingly with great advantage, quietly exhorting his adversary to preserve a more sober spirit, and some appearance at least of moderation. He tells him that he fights against the saints "with a parcel of scolding expressions." He then returns to his charge against the Quakers. Their "inner light" he argues, is nothing more than conscience. "That light wherewith Christ, as He is God, hath lightened every one that cometh into the world, is the soul of man, which is the life of the body, and yet itself is but a creature. This creature hath one faculty of its own nature, called conscience, which hath its place in the soul, where it is a judge to discern of things good or bad. Now, this conscience, this nature itself, because it can control and chide them for sin, therefore must it be idolised and made a God of. . . . Conscience is not the spirit of Christ, but a poor dunghill creature in comparison with the spirit of Christ." He maintains, in answer to Burroughs' charge of misrepresentation, that the Quakers were in their principles substantially the same as the Ranters, and waxes somewhat bitterly satirical in maintaining this point. To the reproach of covetousness and making merchandise of souls, which Burroughs had recklessly urged against him, he replied, as he well might, in a high, yet patient and well-possessed spirit. "Friend, dost thou speak thus as from thy own knowledge, or did any other body tell thee so? However, that spirit that led thee out of this way is a lying spirit. For though I be poor, and of no repute in the world as to outward things, yet this grace I have learned by the example of the Apostle, to preach the truth; and also to work with my hands both for mine own living and for those that are with me, when I have opportunity. And I trust that the Lord Jesus, who hath helped me to reject the wages of unrighteousness hitherto, will also help me still, so that I shall distribute that which God hath given me freely, and not for filthy lucre's sake."

Bunyan turned from controversy gladly to preaching and the more practical work of the ministry. A truly apostolical zeal animated him to carry the tidings of salvation which had made his own heart joyful to those who were living without any profession of religion. His great desire was "to get into the darkest places of the country, even amongst those people that were farthest off profession." He laboured with unceasing earnestness to see the fruits of his ministry, and if it proved fruitful, nothing else disturbed him —no opposition daunted him. The "doctors and priests vehemently opposed him;" but he quietly pursued his calling, giving no heed to their railing. Sometimes, indeed, in the very midst of his preaching, his old darkness came upon him. The old spirit of fear and evil suggestion still visited him, and at times would so violently assault him with thoughts of blasphemy, that he was prompted to utter them aloud before the congregation. Occasionally, when he had begun to preach with much clearness, evidence, and liberty of speech, before ending he would become "so blinded and estranged from all that he had been saying, that he did not know or remember what he

had been about ; as if my head," he says, "had been
in a bag all the time of my exercise." Then he
would be sometimes lifted up with his apparent success, and some " sharp and piercing sentence," as that
respecting "sounding brass and a tinkling cymbal,"*
would ring in his heart, and bring him to the dust of
humility.

When these spiritual temptations failed to move
him, and his ministry only grew and prospered the
more, because of his constant sense of his spiritual
weakness and his protracted discipline, his adversary
" tried another way," which was perhaps still harder
for Bunyan to bear, although his unflagging spirit and
the testimony of a good conscience no less supported
him here. Malicious and ignorant slanders were put
in circulation against him, as that he was a "witch,
a Jesuit, a highwayman, and the like." Worst of all,
and with the boldest confidence, it was reported that
he had his "misses, whores, and bastards—yea, two
wives at once, and the like." He professed to glory
in these slanders as characteristics of his Christian
profession, even "as an ornament;" but they were not
the less painful to his sensitive spirit, and they roused
him both to unwonted indignation and protest. He
calls them " fools and knaves" who have thus dared
to slander him, and appeals confidently to his established character in refutation of the calumnies. "My
foes," he says, " have missed their mark in this their
shooting at me. I am not the man. I wish that
they themselves be guiltless. If all the fornicators
and adulterers in England were hanged up by the
neck till they be dead, John Bunyan, the object of

* " Shall I be proud because I am a sounding brass ? Is it so much to
be a fiddle?" he says, characteristically.

their envy, would be still alive and well. I know not whether there be such a thing as a woman breathing under the copes of the heavens, but by their apparel, their children, or by common fame, except my wife. And in this I admire the wisdom of God that he made me shy of women from my first conversion until now. These know, and can also bear me witness, with whom I have been most intimately concerned, that it is a rare thing to see me carry it pleasantly towards a woman. The common salutation of women I abhor— it is odious to me in whomsoever I see it. Their company alone I cannot away with; I seldom so much as touch a woman's hand, for I think these things are not so becoming me. When I have seen good men salute those women that they have visited, or that have visited them, I have at times made my objection against it; and when they have answered that it was but a piece of civility, I have told them it is not a comely sight; some indeed have urged the holy kiss, but then I have asked why they made baulks,—why they did salute the most handsome, and let the ill-favoured go. Thus, how laudable soever such things have been in the eyes of others, they have been unseemly in my sight."

There is a charming simplicity in this confession. No one could doubt, after such a statement, the clear-minded honesty and guileless straightness of heart of the tinker preacher. The touch as to "making baulks," on the bestowal of the holy kiss, possesses an irresist-ible *naïveté*, more like the innocent prattle of a child than the maturely recorded experiences of a man. Bunyan was, indeed, and remained, a child in heart. The simplest rules and plainest instincts of duty always guided him, and left his motives and conduct intelligible as the daylight.

He had been preaching about four years, when the Restoration came, and brought serious consequences to him, as to many others. He had been in difficulty before. The book of the Baptist congregation, preserved at Bedford, bears an entry to the effect that, " on the 25th December 1657, the Church resolved to set apart a day for seeking counsel of God what to do with respect to the indictment against brother Bunyan, at the Assizes, for preaching at Eaton." He has not himself said anything of this indictment; and there is every reason to suppose that it was not prosecuted. Probably it was some expression of the dislike of the Presbyterians towards him ; the " doctors and priests, who opened their mouths wide against him" when he began his ministry; but however strongly they might desire to silence him, this was not so easily accomplished, while the firm, but tolerant, hand of Cromwell still held the reins of power.

He was among the first, however, who experienced the persecuting effects of the Restoration. The inoffensiveness of his life, and the comparative obscurity of his ministry, might have been supposed a sufficient shield to Bunyan ; but his plain speaking, and downright sincerity of character, and the popularity of his ministry among the lower orders, made him obnoxious to local vigilance and jealousy. He became a victim to these, rather than to any direct act of vengeance on the part of the Government. As yet, in fact, the Government had taken no steps to control the liberty of preaching. The Act of Uniformity, and the Conventicle Act, were still in the distance. But certain old acts against unordained preachers were sufficient to enable the Justices of Bedford to take steps against him.

He has himself told us the story of his seizure, and the reasons which induced him to risk himself, notwithstanding the dissuasions of his friends. He was engaged to preach at " Samsell, by Harlington, in Bedfordshire." A warrant was out against him, issued by Justice Wingate; and, just as he had met with his friends, and they were ready to begin their exercise,—" Bibles in their hands,"—the constable came in. Bunyan might have made his escape, and was advised to do so ; but he thought that " if he should run and make an escape," it would be " of ill savour in the country ; " his conduct might prove a " discouragement to the whole body." He had no vain ambition to be a martyr, but he honestly looked upon himself as an example to his co-religionists, and, having weighed the whole matter in his mind, he resolved not to fly.

He was brought before the Justice next morning; and the matter would have ended easily, if he would have permitted his sureties to become bound that he would cease from preaching. But to this he would on no account consent. Wingate urged that it was against the law for him to preach, and that he should confine himself to his calling. He replied that he could follow his calling and preach too, and the object of his meetings was only " to instruct and counsel people to forsake their sins and close in with Christ, lest they miserably perish." The Justice withdrew to make out a " mittimus " to send him to jail, and, while he was absent, one Dr Lindale, whom he calls an " old enemy of the truth," came in, and fell to taunting him " with many reviling terms." Lindale appears to have been a beneficed clergyman of Bedford ; and we see in him the natural scorn of the

càvalier churchman for the preaching tinker. They
enter into a railing dispute about the latter's right
to preach ;—Bunyan pleading cleverly the text, " As
every man hath received the gift, even so let him
minister the same ; " and Lindale, throwing in his
teeth the case of " Alexander the coppersmith, who
did much oppose and disturb the Apostles," "aiming
'tis like at me," he adds naïvely, " because I was a
tinker." " You are one of those Scribes and Pharisees who for a pretence make long prayers, to devour
widows' houses," urged Lindale. Bunyan retorted
that "if he had got no more by preaching and praying than he had done, he would not be so rich as
he was."

The interview is painful, but characteristic ; the
impudent dignity of the churchman, the complacency
of the Puritan. In all fairness, we cannot accept Bunyan's idea of Lindale, any more than Lindale's idea
of Bunyan. We know the latter's worth and simplicity, notwithstanding that he seemed to Lindale a
mere fanatical rogue ; and although Lindale was probably no model of an apostolical divine, we have
no reason to think that he was a mere enemy to religion, a mere " Hate-good." Bunyan's most copious
biographer * has not been able to bring any facts
against him beyond those that appear in the narrative, although he has not failed to apply to him op-
probrious language.

As Bunyan was being carried off to prison, some
of his friends appeared, and made another effort to
obtain his release. He was led back before Wingate ;
and another Justice, of the name of Foster, makes
his appearance, of whom we have a very singular,

* Philip.

and not very intelligible, portrait. " When I came to the Justice again," he says, "there was Mr Foster of Bedford, who, coming out of another room, and seeing of me by the light of the candle,—for it was dark night when I came thither,—he said unto me, ' Who is there? John Bunyân?' with such seeming affection, as if he would have leaped on my neck and kissed me, which made me somewhat wonder that such a man as he, with whom I had so little acquaintance, and, besides, that had ever been a close opposer of the ways of God, should carry himself so full of love to me ; but afterwards, when I saw what he did, it caused me to remember those sayings, ' Their tongues are smoother than oil, but their words are drawn swords.' When I had answered him that, blessed be God, I was well, he said, ' What is the occasion of your coming here ?' or to that purpose. To whom I answered that I was at a meeting of people a little way off, intending to speak a word of exhortation to them ; but the Justice hearing thereof, said I, was pleased to send his warrant to fetch me before him."

And then follows a long altercation between them. Foster was evidently no friend of Bunyan, but neither does he seem to have cherished towards him any wilful hostility ; he had rather wished to cajole him, and have the matter hushed up. He was apparently an ordinary specimen of the crafty civic politician, who did not wish the peace disturbed if he could help it ; his conduct is that of the self-important provincial dignitary, who had no dislike to the preacher, save in so far as he interfered with his magisterial responsibility. When he found that he could not move Bunyan's calm sense of duty, he was naturally

angered, and concurred in the sentence to send him
to prison. His friends made still another effort, five
days later, to get him delivered on bail, but this
also was unsuccessful. "Whereat," he says, " I was
not at all daunted, but rather glad." A spirit like
this was not likely to yïeld before the Justices of
Bedford.

After he had lain in prison about seven weeks,
the Quarter Sessions came to be held in Bedford. A
formal indictment was preferred against him, and he
was tried before five Justices, whose names he has preserved. The indictment charges him with " devilishly
and perniciously abstaining from coming to church to
hear divine service," and with being " a common up-
holder of several unlawful meetings and conventicles,
to the great disturbance and distraction of the good
subjects of this kingdom, contrary to the laws of our
Sovereign Lord the King," &c. The only interest of
the trial arises from the glimpses which it gives us
of the popular religious sentiments among Churchmen
and Puritans, at this stage of the controversy. The
discussion turned in the first instance on Bunyan's
opposition to the Church Service, and especially the
Book of Common Prayer. He is very firm and ready,
if not very enlightened or comprehensive, in his arguments. Justice Keeling, his chief disputant, presents
a singular mixture of sense and ignorance. To Bunyan's Scripture texts he can find little or nothing to
say, but he responds with heartiness to the common
sense of some of his remarks ; and although rude and
offensive in his language, he does not appear unjust
or violent beyond the terms of the law. He was a
fair specimen, probably, of a royalist magistrate of the
time—ignorant and somewhat insolent, but good-na-

tured and indifferent,—confounding all religion, except that of the Prayer-Book, with fanaticism and sedition.

Bunyan was pressed to declare his reason for not attending the service of the Church. He pleaded that he "did not find it commanded in the Word of God." Keeling urged that he was commanded to pray. The Puritan admitted this, but said he was not bound to pray by the Common Prayer Book. The prayers in it "were such as were made by men, and not by the motions of the Holy Ghost within our hearts." A man can only pray "through a sense of those things which he wants, which sense is begotten by the Spirit." The Justice owned the truth of this, but maintained that it was possible to pray "with the Spirit, and with the Book of Common Prayer too." He further defended the Prayer-Book as warrantable, "after our Lord's example, who taught his disciples to pray; and that as one man may convince another of sin, so prayers made by men and read over may be good to teach and help men to pray." Bunyan replied with the text, "The Spirit helpeth our infirmities." So far Keeling conducts the argument fairly enough, and not without force. There is a rough sense in many of his statements. By-and-by, however, he falls, along with his brother Justices, into mere railing. Wearied probably with Bunyan's pertinacity, he appears to lose his temper, and to the pious ejaculations of the Puritan, retorts, "This is pedlar's French —leave off your canting."

The result was that Bunyan was sentenced to three months' imprisonment, with a warning that if he did not cease his preaching he would be banished, and if found afterwards within the realm, that he should "stretch by the neck for it." This was all that the Restoration had to say to men like him, and it was

2 F

a somewhat sorry saying. Imprisonment—and then banishment—and then hanging—if you do not conform to the parish church. It met happily a "spirit of power," not to be daunted even by such threats. "If I was out of prison to-day," replied Bunyan, "I would preach the Gospel again to-morrow, by the help of God."

Yet, with all his boldness, he felt deeply the painfulness of his lot. Parting with his wife and children was " like pulling the flesh from his bones ;" and especially the thought of his poor blind child, who "lay nearer to his heart than all beside," made him cry out bitterly—"Oh! the thoughts of the hardship I thought my poor blind one might go under, would break my heart to pieces. Poor child, thought I, what sorrow art thou like to have for thy portion in this world! Thou must be beaten, must beg, suffer hunger, cold, nakedness, and a thousand calamities, though I cannot now endure the wind should blow upon thee. But yet, recalling myself, thought I, I must venture you all with God, though it goeth to the quick to leave you. Oh! I saw in this condition I was as a man who was pulling down his house upon the head of his wife and children ; yet, thought I, I must do it—I must do it."

When Bunyan had been in prison three months another effort was made to induce him to submit to the law, as interpreted by the Justices. They sent to him the Clerk of the Peace, Mr Cobb, to reason with him, and to endeavour to gain his assent to terms which would admit of his being liberated. This seems to have been done on their part in perfect good faith ; there is no evidence of a wish to inflict illegal punishment upon him. Rude and violent as they had been when heated

in altercation with him—prompt and harsh as had been
their vigilance in making his arrest—the magistrates
of Bedford were not yet without some relentings, or at
least desires to be quit of a troublesome business.
They must not be judged unfairly. The Clerk of
the Peace also, who acted as their agent on this occasion, was apparently a reasonable and kindly man—
really anxious to open up a door for his escape
from prison, if he only could be brought to yield a
little. It was conceded to him that he might address
his neighbours in private, provided only that he did
not call together an assembly of the people; but
he would not give up any part of his freedom, and
urged that his sole end in meeting with others was to
do as much good as he could. It was replied by Cobb
that others urged the same in their unlawful meetings,
such as had issued in the late insurrection in London.*
Bunyan declared that he abhorred such practices, and
pleaded his readiness to manifest his loyalty both by
word and deed. Their argument came to nothing.
Bunyan insisted on his right of preaching freely. He
would give the notes of all his sermons, to prevent
occasion of suspicion as to his doctrine; for he seriously desired to "live quietly in his country, and to
submit to the present authority;" but he would not
purchase his freedom by any promise of public silence.
He would lie in jail rather. "The law," he said, "hath
provided two ways of obeying; the one, to do that
which I in my conscience do believe that I am bound
to do actively; and where I cannot obey actively, there
I am willing to lie down and to suffer what they shall
do unto me." At this his interlocutor sat still, and

---

* The insurrection of Venner, which was made the pretext of dealing
severely with the Nonconformists.

said no more, "which, when he had done," he adds, "I thanked him for his civil and meek discussion with me; and so we parted. O that we might meet in heaven! Farewell."

He remained in prison, under sentence of "banishment or hanging," unless he should recant. But just as the time drew near in which he should have "abjured, or done worse," the coronation took place; and, according to a royal proclamation, persons im- prisoned and under sentence were allowed to sue for a pardon within twelve months. This suspended any further proceedings against him; and when the summer assizes came on (1661), he resolved to avail himself of the privilege of petitioning. His friends were either forgetful, or possessed little influence; and it was left to his wife to urge his case before the judges, which she did with a noble and pathetic dignity which has made her memorable, and stamped her as one of the heroines of Puritanism. She was his second wife, whom he had married about a year before his imprisonment. Of his former wife's death we are told nothing. Her early influence for good upon him will be remembered, and everything said of her suggests a favourable impression. His second wife was "worthy of the first"—a gentle, modest, yet intrepid woman, whose meekness and simplicity shine forth under all her hardiness and courage in behalf of her husband.

Sir Matthew Hale was one of the judges, and to him Bunyan's wife first came with her petition. He received her "very mildly," telling her "that he would do her and me the best good he could; but he feared, he said, he could do none." "The next day again," he continues his narrative, "lest they should, through the multitude of business, forget me, we did throw another petition into the coach to Judge Twisdon, who, when he had seen it, snapt her up, and angrily told her that he was a convicted person, and could not be released unless I would promise to preach no more. Well, after this, she again presented another petition to Judge Hale, as he sat upon the bench, who, as it seemed, was willing to give her audience. Only Justice Chester being present, slipt up and said that I was convicted in the court, and that I was a hot-spirited fellow, or words to that purpose, whereat he (Hale) waived it, and did not meddle therewith." The conflict between the willingness of Hale—his wish to do a service to the poor woman before him—and the rude unkindness of his brother judges—the helplessness of the petitioner, "throwing her petition into the coach to Judge Twisdon" as he passed—give us a touching glimpse of the times, and of the unhappy difficulties of honest and good men like Hale who sought to serve the Government of the Restoration.

It might have been supposed that his repulses would have daunted one even so courageous as Bunyan's wife ; but, like the woman before the august Judge, as her husband hints, she resolved "to make another venture." As the Judges sat in the "Swan Chambers, with many justices and gentry of the country in company together," she came before them "with abashed face and trembling heart," yet determined, if possible, to gain a hearing. She directed herself to Hale again, but he told her as before that he could do her no good, because her husband had been held as convicted on his own statements. She continued her pleading, urging that she had been to London, and spoken with one of the House of Lords there, who said that her husband's case was committed to the Judges at the next assizes. Chester and Twisdon would hear nothing on the subject—the one repeating always, "He is convicted," "It is recorded;" and the other urging that her husband was a "breaker of the peace." As she spoke of "four little children,"* the heart of Hale was touched, and he answered very mildly, saying, "I tell thee, woman, seeing it is so, that they have taken what thy husband spoke for a conviction, thou must either apply thyself to the King, or sue out his pardon, or get a writ of error." This was but small comfort to the poor woman: but even so much "chafed" Justice Chester, so that he "put off his hat, and scratched his head for anger." Unable to prevail with them to send for her husband that he might speak for himself, which she often desired them to do, she left in deep distress at her want of success. "I could not but break forth into tears," she says, adding, with a truly Puritanic touch, "not so much because they were so hard-headed against me and my husband, but to think what a sad account such poor creatures will have to give at the coming of the Lord, when they shall then answer for all things."

The result of all was, that Bunyan was left in prison. Fortunately, he found a friend in his jailer, and his imprisonment was mitigated for some time to such an extent as to render it merely nominal. He was permitted to go and come, and even engage in preaching, as he had been accustomed. "I had by my jailer," he says, "some liberty granted me, more than at first, and I followed my wonted course of preaching, taking all occasions that were put into my hand to visit the people of God, exhorting them to be steadfast in the faith of Jesus Christ, and to take heed that they

* The children of his former wife.

touched not the Common Prayer, &c., but to mind the word of God." The harshness which he encountered seems, as in all such cases, to have hardened his polemical hostility to the Church of England. The very consciousness that he was in "bonds" for what he considered the truth, and that his visits and preaching were surreptitious, operated to intensify his zeal, and to call forth a warmer fervour of opposition to those from whom he suffered. His sufferings also served to increase his importance and influence among his own people. Hitherto he had not been in any sense a leader among them. His conflict with the Quaker, Burroughs, may have given him some prominence, heightened by the remarkable circumstances of his conversion ; but it required his imprisonment, and the intrepid defence which he made for his opinions, to bring into full view his claims to respect and influence. It was this rising reputation in his own persuasion which, no doubt, led him to run the risk of going to see " Christians at London," as he tells us he ventured to do, by the indulgence of his jailer. This indulgence, however, cost him severely. His enemies hearing of it threatened the jailer with expulsion from his office, and his liberty was in consequence shortened, so that he " must not look out of the door." It was charged against him that he went to London " to plot and raise " divisions, and make insurrection, which, " God knows," he says, " was a slander."

Bunyan certainly cannot be supposed to have had any hand in political plots against the Government. No man in the country was more honestly loyal. If he had only been allowed to preach, no one was disposed to live a more peaceable life. Southey has indeed said that " the man who distinguished a handful of

Baptists in London as *the Christians* of that great metropolis, and who, when let out by favour from the
prison, exhorted the people of God, as he calls them, to
take heed that they touched not the Common Prayer,
was not employed in promoting unity, nor in making
good subjects, however good his intentions, however
orthodox his creed, however sincere and fervent his
piety." That may or may not be—but it is little to
the point. There is no tyranny that might not urge
such a plea. Neither Bunyan nor his co-religionists
were a whit the worse subjects on account of their
peculiar notions regarding the Prayer-Book and the
number of Christians in London. These notions—right
or wrong—had nothing to do with the civil obedience
of those that held them. Bunyan's confinement, as
Southey goes on to urge, may have proved an advantage to him—it may have given leisure for his " understanding to repose and cool ; " but it was not the less
a gross infringement of civil liberty; and it is but a
miserable defence of a Church and a cause that tries
to find any justification for the hardships inflicted on
the author of the *Pilgrim's Progress.*

He made still some further efforts at the " following assizes " to be released from his imprisonment.
He tried even to have his name "put into the calen-
dar among the felons," and to "make friends of the
Judge and High Sheriff, who promised that he should
be called." His friendly jailer rendered him every
assistance he could, but all his efforts were frustrated.
He blames severely for this his quondam friend Mr
Cobb, the Clerk of the Peace, who had formerly interested himself in his behalf, or appeared to do so. It
would almost seem as if the Justices of Bedford and
their friends felt their position, and the character of

their legal administration, committed in Bunyan's case;
and that some strongly official feeling more than anything else interfered with his liberation. He had been
" lawfully convicted," the Clerk of the Peace argued, as
the Justices had done, and he was, therefore, " not to
be set free except in the ordinary course of the law."
He represents Cobb as running first to the Clerk of
the Assizes, and then to the Justices, and then again to
the jailer, in case his name should get into the calen-
dar through any misrepresentation or informality, and
an opportunity for his release be opened up. So it
was he was "hindered and prevented from appearing
before the Judge and left in prison."

Here he remained during the next seven years—
years of silent but wonderful mental growth to him.
Working with his hands to support his family—making
tag-laces for his wife and children to sell*—his mind at
the same time found work for itself. His imagination
became more intensely and creatively active than it had
ever been. In the solitude of his prison he learned to
dream ; or rather, for he had always been a dreamer,
he learned to depict his dreams. He became the great
artist of that spiritual world in which he lived and
moved and had his being. Shut out from living communication with his fellow-men, and thirsting after
sympathy with the spiritual realities—the diverse forms
of religious passion—with which he had been so con-
versant in his ministerial experience, he called them
into life around him, and peopled his solitude with

---

* Charles Doe, one of his friends, who visited Bunyan in prison, and
afterwards interested himself in the collection of his works, says, " I
have been witness that his own hands ministered to his and his family
necessities, making many hundred gross of long tagged laces, to fill up
the vacancies of his time, which he had learned to do for that purpose
since he had been in prison."—*Memoir,* iv.

their breathing and active presence. From the very darkness and inactivity and solitariness of his outward life was born the faculty which made his inner life bright with the conception of those beautiful and varied characters, and that vivid imagery of incident which compose his allegories. Had Bunyan's spiritual zeal and imaginativeness found scope in outward work,—had he been left practically to direct Christians and Faithfuls and Hopefuls—to exhort the Timorous and Doubting—and to reprove the Pliable, the Formalist, the Hypocrite, and the Talkative,—we might never have had the vivid pictures of these characters that we have from his fertile pen. It was when his living tongue could no longer reach them, when the actual struggle to help the weak and rebuke the erring was no longer possible to him, that his fancy fashioned in a dream the *Pilgrim's Progress*, and all his creative skill was called forth in depicting it. The world of actual religious struggle was removed from him; but, as he dreamed, lo! it was once more around him, and he lived in it, and found his highest interest and pleasure in it. Every form of the reality had stamped itself on his mind, and it came forth to the touch of his fancy true and perfect. He might be hindered from ministering to his flock in Bedford, but none could hinder him from ministering to the flock of his imagination, whose necessities and difficulties—whose hopes and fears—were as real to him as if he had lived in visible contact with them.

Bunyan himself has told how accidentally he hit upon his great plan. He was engaged in the composition of some other book—some have supposed, and not improbably, his *Grace abounding to the Chief of Sinners*, or the autobiographical narrative from which

we have quoted so much in the course of our sketch
—when he "fell suddenly into an allegory." Many
points of similitude between the Christian life and a
journey struck him on the instant, and he noted them
down; the idea once started, it branched off into num-
berless illustrations, and his memory could scarcely
keep pace with the creations of his heated fancy.*

There is reason to think that the *Pilgrim's Progress*
was not the first product of his allegorical faculty,
although it first proved to him its strength. His imaginative dreaming had already found scope in efforts
less happy, but which show no less strongly how naturally his mind turned in this direction. The extended
sermon, entitled *The Holy City, or the New Jerusalem*,
was probably the first of his writings of this kind. It
was published while he was still in prison in 1665,
and he has himself, in his "Prefatory Epistle to four
sorts of Readers," told us the history of its origin. The
statement gives us an interesting glimpse of his prison
life, apart from its own importance. "The occasion of

* " And thus it was: I writing of the way
  And race of saints, in this our Gospel day,
  Fell suddenly into an allegory
  About their journey and the way to glory,
  In more than twenty things, which I set down ;
  This done, I twenty more had in my crown ;
  And they again began to multiply,
  Like sparks that from the coals of fire do fly.
  Nay then, thought I, if that you breed so fast,
  I'll put you by yourselves, lest you at last
  Should prove *ad infinitum*, and eat out
  The book that I already am about.
  Well, so I did ; but yet I did not think
  To show to all the world my pen and ink
  In such a mode ; I only thought to make
  I knew not what ; nor did I undertake
  Thereby to please my neighbour ; no, not I ;
  I did it mine own self to gratify."

my first meddling with these matters," he says, "was as
followeth : Upon a certain fast-day, I being together
with my brethren in our prison-chamber, they expected
that, according to our custom, something should be
spoken out of the Word for our mutual edification ;
but at that time I felt myself, it being my turn to
speak, so empty, speechless, and barren, that I thought
I should not have been able to speak among them so
much as five words of truth with life and evidence ;
but at last it so fell out that providentially I cast mine
eye upon the 11th verse of the one-and-twentieth chapter of this prophecy (Rev. xxi. 11) ; upon which, when
I had considered a while, methought I perceived something of that jasper, in whose light you there find this
Holy City is to come or descend: wherefore, having got
in my eye some dim glimmerings thereof, and finding
also in my heart a desire to see further thereunto, I with
a few groans did carry my meditations to the Lord Jesus
for a blessing, which he did forthwith grant, according
to his grace ; and, helping me to set before my brethren, we did all eat and were well refreshed ; and
behold also, that while I was in the distributing of it, it
so increased in my hand that of the fragments that we
left, after we had well dined, I gathered up this bas-
ketful. Methought the more I cast mine eye upon
the whole discourse the more I saw lie in it. Wherefore setting myself to a more narrow search through
frequent prayer to God, what first with doing and
then with undoing, and after that with doing again, I
then did finish it."

In the process of "doing and undoing, and doing
again," we can imagine Bunyan trying his strength as
a spiritual designer. His own complacency in his
newly-found gift is obvious. He is like a man who,

laboriously striving to learn a task, suddenly finds himself in possession of a more cunning way of doing it. He has started a spring of hidden accomplishment, which works in him henceforth with a joyous and fruitful activity. But the accomplishment is not without its snares. Its very facility to one like Bunyan—all whose thoughts are images—is its danger; and it cannot be said that he has escaped this danger. Certainly he has not done so in his first attempt. In the *Holy City* there is too little concentration—too much of the mere straggling play of fancy—catching at every point, and stretching its capricious tendrils around every clause, and even word. It is tedious in its minute spiritualising, and frequently overdone and mistaken in its applications; but it shows, at the same time, a wonderful consistency and life of treatment. Almost any taste but that of Bunyan's, with its singular instinct of truthfulness, even where it is following out a wrong idea, would have gone lamentably astray in the execution of such a task as he attempted.

Bunyan tried his new powers not merely in prose, but in verse. His poems are supposed to have been chiefly written during his imprisonment. They have feeling and tenderness, and a quaint grace of expression; but more can scarcely be said in their behalf. They have none of the imaginative vigour and life of his allegories. His *Profitable Meditations,** his *One Thing is Needful*, and *Ebal and Gerizzim, or the Blessing and the Curse*, may interest the curious, and even excite the admiration of certain minds; but in them we see Bunyan, not in his strength, but in his weakness. His rhymes at times are deplorable, as any one may judge from looking at the poetical prologues to

* A beautiful edition of these, edited by Mr Offor, has just appeared.

the two parts of the *Pilgrim's Progress*.   Yet there is a
strange, careless felicity here and there—and especially
in his *Divine Emblems*.   In these, more than elsewhere,
he really rises at times into poetry; and the simple
tenderness of his imaginative brooding breaks forth
into touching and expressive pictures.*

During the last three or four years of his imprisonment, its strictness was greatly relaxed.   He was permitted, as before, to visit his friends, and even to
preach.   So little was his action fettered, that he was
really designed to the pastoral office among his old
Bedford congregation before he had formally obtained
his freedom.   He renewed his interest in religious
discussion by making a vigorous attack upon a book
then making some noise, *The Design of Christianity*,
by Dr Fowler, afterwards Bishop of Gloucester.   This
book marked the rising of the new spirit which
was so soon to leaven the theology of the Church of
England.   It was the design of Christianity, according to it, not so much to free man from guilt, and to
grant a free and gracious pardon, as to restore his
nature to its original state of soundness and moral
harmony.   It spoke of a righteousness as a "sound

---

* For example, in the following lines on the "Sun's Reflection upon
the Clouds on a Fair Morning"—

> " Look yonder ! Ah ! methinks mine eyes do see
> Clouds edged with silver as fine garments be ;
> They look as if they saw the golden face
> That makes black clouds most beautiful with grace.
> Unto the Saint's sweet incense of their prayer,
> These smoky curled clouds I do compare ;
> For, as these clouds seem edged or laced with gold,
> Their prayers return with blessings manifold."

If this is scarcely poetry, it is, perhaps, something better ; and there
are others, such as the lines on a "Fruitful Apple-Tree," and those on
the "Child with a Bird at the Bush," that show the same rich simplicity of language, and the same sweet plaintive tone.

complexion of zeal, such as maintains in life and vigour whatsoever is essential to it, by the force and· power whereof a man is enabled to behave himself as a creature indued with a principle of reason, keeps his supreme faculty on its throne, brings into due subjection all his inferior ones, his carnal imagination, his brutish passions and affections." The purity of human nature—the essence of the Divine—was represented as consisting in a "hearty approbation of, and an affectionate compliance with, the eternal laws of righteousness, and a behaviour agreeable to the essential and immutable differences of good and evil."

Such principles were peculiarly obnoxious to Bunyan. They came into conflict with all his own deepest experiences, as well as with his views of Scripture. Christianity, viewed as a mere moral system, was to him no Gospel at all; and he no sooner heard of the book, than he was anxious to see it and reply to it. It was brought to him in prison in February 1672, and in the course of forty-two days he had written his answer to it, under the title of *A Defence of the Doctrine of Justification by Faith in Jesus Christ, proving that Gospel Holiness flows from thence.* His defence is a vigorous and lively argument—not very systematic or coherent, but making up for the want of system by the cleverness and energy of its detailed attacks. He makes short work with the learning and philosophy of the *Design of Christianity ;* and, taking his stand on the simple letter of Scripture, on many points very successfully encounters Fowler. His whole heart was in the work, and he is not sparing in his epithets. He begins as follows:—"Sir,—Having heard of your book entitled *The Design of Christianity,* and that in it was contained such principles as gave

just offence to Christian ears, I was desirous of a
view thereof, that, from my sight of things, I might
be the better able to judge. But I could not obtain,
till the 13th of this 10th month, which was too soon
for you, Sir, a pretended minister of the Word, so
vilely to expose to public view the rottenness of your
heart on principles diametrically opposite to the simplicity of the Gospel of Christ. And, had it not been
for the consideration, that it is not too late to oppose
open blasphemy (such as endangereth the souls of
thousands), I had cast by this answer as a thing out
of season."

Such a mode of attack was too easily retorted; and
Fowler replied in a style that far outdid Bunyan's
abuse. His answer was entitled, *Dirt Wiped Off*, and,
in the course of it, he designated Bunyan by such
epithets as " a wretched scribbler," " a most black-
mouthed calumniator," " so very dirty a creature,
that he disdains to dirt his fingers with him."

Bunyan was pardoned and liberated in September
1772, at the time of the Declaration of Indulgence,
after Charles had formed his secret plans for the re-
establishment of Popery. The story has been, that
Barlow, Bishop of Lincoln, and Dr Owen, were concerned in his liberation; but there seems no good
ground for this story. His old enemies, the Quakers,
appear to have had more to do with it. When Charles
had issued his Indulgence, some of the Quakers sued
for a special act of pardon, which they are said to
have obtained, in consideration of the services which
one of their number had rendered to the King, in
assisting his escape after the battle of Worcester.
Greatly to their honour, the Quakers used their temporary access to the royal favour, not merely for the

good of their own sect; they got included in the "instrument" of pardon the names of many Dissenters, and, among others, that of John Bunyan.[*]

On his release Bunyan devoted himself with renewed and enlarged activity to the duties of his ministry. A private house, which had been licensed as a place of meeting for his congregation, had become "so thronged that many were constrained to stay without, though it was very spacious, every one striving to partake of his instructions." He lived, we are told by one who was a "true friend and a long acquaintance,"[†] in much peace and quiet of mind, contenting himself with that little God had bestowed upon him, and sequestering himself from all secular employments to follow that of his call to the ministry. Besides his labours in Bedford, he visited the neighbouring villages and counties, where he believed he could do good by his preaching or pastoral attentions,—"where he knew or imagined any people might stand in need of his assistance." The regularity of his visitations, and the general respect which began to be paid to him, procured him the appellation of Bishop Bunyan. This may have been said half in "jeer," as his biographer supposes; but even in this sense it testifies to the consideration which he had obtained among his sect, and the wide influence which he exercised.

Notwithstanding his encounter with Dr Fowler, he maintained his character as an uncontroversial and peace-loving man. He spent much of his time in works of peace and charity, "in reconciling differences, by which he hindered many mischiefs, and saved some families from ruin." In such "fallings out" he was

[*] Offor's *Memoir of Bunyan*, Works, i. 61.   Ed. Glas.
[†] Continuation of Mr Bunyan's *Life*.

uneasy till he found the means of reconciliation, and
of establishing again the bonds of affection.

The same peace-loving spirit that marked his private
life distinguished his ecclesiastical views. He was
himself a Baptist, in the strictest sense; he maintained,
that is to say, that adult baptism was the scriptural
rite, and repudiated the baptism of infants; but he
would not, with the great body of his co-religionists,
convert the practice of personal "water baptism," as.
they called it, into a test of communion. In a short
treatise which he published after his liberation, entitled *A Confession of my Faith and a Reason of my
Practice*, he set forth his principles of communion in
a very catholic spirit. He would hold Christian intercourse with all who showed faith and holiness, and
who were willing to subject themselves to the laws
and government of Christ in His Church. His views
met with a storm of opposition from the more extreme
of his own sect. Three of their most able and learned
men—Danvers, Kiffin, and Paul—undertook the defence of sectarianism, and sought to overwhelm him
at once by their learning and abuse. He complained
meekly of the "unhandsome brands that they had laid
upon him," as that he was a "Machiavellian," a man
"devilish, proud, insolent, presumptuous, and the like."
He refused to say in reply, "The Lord rebuke thee—
words fitter to be spoken to the devil than a brother;"
but he appealed to the sense and judgment of his
readers, in a further treatise on the subject, adding
the following noble declaration :—" What Mr Kiffin
hath done in the matter I forgive, and love him never
the worse; but must stand by my principles, because
they are peaceable, godly, profitable, and such as tend
to the edification of my brother, and as, I believe, will

be justified in the day of judgment. That I deny the
ordinance of baptism, or that I have placed one piece
of an argument against it, though they feign it, is quite
without colour of truth. All I say is, that the Church
of Christ hath not warrant to keep out of her communion the Christian that is discovered to be a visible
saint by the Word—the Christian that walketh according to his light with God."

But Bunyan was strong not only in temper, but in
argument. He had a good cause, and felt that he had;
and he was not the man to yield in such a case to any
storm of opposition, however much it might pain him.
He vindicated at length his "peaceable principles and
true,"—met abuse with courageous confession, and sectarian feebleness with a quiet ridicule, which at times
he could employ with great effect. His opponents had
inquired insolently how long he had been a Baptist ;
and remarked that it is "an ill bird that bewrays his
own nest." He replied that he cared little for names
—his only concern was to be a Christian. "As for
these factious titles of Anabaptist, Independent, Presbyterian, and the like, I conclude that they come
neither from Jerusalem nor Antioch, but rather from
hell and Babylon, for they naturally tend to division.
You may know them by their fruits."* One of his
opponents had said, that, "as great men's servants are
known by their livery, so are Gospel believers by the
livery of water baptism ;" to which he satirically replies—"Go you but ten doors from where men know
you, and see how many of the world or Christians will
know *you* by this goodly livery. What! known by
water baptism to be one who hath put on Christ, as
a servant by the gay livery his master gave him?

* Vol. ii. p. 649.

Away, fond man : you do quite forget the text, 'By
this shall all men know that ye are my disciples, if ye
love one another.' " *

After the publication of the *Pilgrim's Progress* in
1678, and some of his more popular tracts, such as
Come and Welcome to Jesus Christ, Bunyan acquired
not only respect but fame. Efforts were made to induce him to leave his congregation at Bedford for a
more public sphere, but he steadily resisted them. As
his friend Charles Doe says, " he refused a more plentiful income to keep his station." He made frequent
visits, however, to London, to preach, and there his
popularity attracted immense crowds to hear him. "I
have seen," says Doe, "to hear him preach, by my com-
putation, about 1200 at a morning lecture, by seven
o'clock on a working day, in the dark winter-time. I
also computed about 3000 came to hear him one Lord's
day at London, at a Town's End meeting-house ; so
that half were fain to go back again for want of room,
and then himself was fain, at a back door, to be pulled
almost over people, to get upstairs to the pulpit."

His popularity, and the attachment of his female
converts, gave rise to a wretched scandal, upon which
one of his biographers † has dwelt with unnecessary
length. We have already quoted his opinion that he
had no power of " carrying it pleasantly with women,"
their company alone he could not away with. One of his
female disciples, however, Agnes Beaumont by name,
courted his company on a particular occasion in such
a manner as to try his firmness and overcome it. He
was on his way from Bedford to preach at a neighbouring village. All his friends were stirred with anxiety
to hear him, and Agnes amongst others. She was to

* Vol. ii. p. 638.   † PHILIP.

have been carried to the "meeting" on horseback, by a "certain Mr Wilson of Hitchin," but he disappointed her. As she stood at her father's door, plunged in grief, Bunyan himself, "quite unexpected," came up on horseback ; and she, trembling with eagerness to go, yet afraid herself to ask to be taken by him, got her brother to do so. He replied, "with some degree of roughness," "No, I will not carry her." But at length he was persuaded to do so. And she, overjoyed, got up behind him on the saddle. The affair, as may be imagined, gave rise to scandal. The *tableau* of Bunyan and a young woman riding together to sermon is amusing to the fancy ; and, with all allowance for the different manners of the time, we can imagine how it would tickle the gossips of Bedford. Save as an illustration of these manners, the story is scarcely deserving of preservation. It has been handed down in the narrative of the woman herself, which is of some length, and full of singularly *naïve* touches here and there.*

Bunyan's reputation and popularity were not for a moment affected by this ridiculous scandal ; it may be questioned, indeed, whether it ever was anything more than a piece of idle talk. He continued his preaching and pastoral labours with unflagging energy. His sermons, when he went to London to preach, drew not only the multitude, but learned and distinguished men to hear him. There is a story told of Dr Owen being greatly taken by his preaching, and on his being asked by the King "how a learned man, such as he, could

---

* As when she says—"I had not rode far before my heart began to be lifted up with pride at the thoughts of riding behind the servant of the Lord, and was pleased if any looked after as we rode along. Indeed, I thought myself very happy that day ; first, that it pleased God to make way for my going ; and then, that I should have had the honour to ride behind Mr Bunyan, who would sometimes be speaking to me of the things of God."

sit and listen to an illiterate tinker," of his answering, "Please your Majesty, could I possess that tinker's abilities for preaching, I would most gladly part with all my learning." The story is at least good evidence of Bunyan's popularity as a preacher. He must have been well known and well admired before he was likely to form the subject of conversation between the King and Dr Owen.

It might be questioned whether Bunyan's sermons, as we read them, bear out his fame as a preacher. They are, like all other sermons of the time, very long, and frequently very tedious in their extension and subdivisions. They are marked strongly by the Puritan characteristic of advancing from point to point through a wide series of didactic and illustrative remarks, without unfolding any new elements of thought —beating out the whole round of scriptural truth, instead of seizing some definite point of doctrine or of duty answering to the text, and summarily expounding and enforcing it. It must be remembered, however, that many of his sermons, like Baxter's, are obviously not so much what he preached, as expanded treatises, composed after being delivered in a shorter form. And amidst all their length and tediousness, we can sufficiently trace in such compositions as the "Jerusalem Sinner Saved," "Come and Welcome to Jesus Christ," the "Pharisee and the Publican," and "The Greatness of the Soul, and Unspeakableness of the Loss thereof," the elements of the lively and remarkable interest that his preaching excited.* The homely pith, simple feeling, and delineative vividness,

* The sermon called "Bunyan's Last Sermon," from John i. 13, may be presumed to be more like the length and general character of his sermons as he preached them.

combined with the spiritual solemnity and unction of these addresses, must have been powerfully attractive in delivery. To all who felt and appreciated the awful realities of which Bunyan spoke, the learned and distinguished, as well as the ignorant and poor, it is easy to imagine what impressiveness there would be in his charming simplicity, plain but pictured earnestness, and his deep and fervid spirit of devotion. The liveliness of his fancy, the very commonplaceness of his argument—never vulgar, only homely—the constant life, sense, and expressive ease of his style, even when the turn of his thought is crude or extravagant, are all among the highest qualities of popular pulpit oratory. An intellectual nature like Bunyan's, the direct growth of the popular religion—apt, imaginative, and eloquent, without any scholastic training—frequently finds its highest expression in preaching. This was not Bunyan's case. His allegories express and embalm his characteristic genius far more completely than his sermons ; but in these also we can see the working of many of his exquisite gifts.

In such labours Bunyan spent the remaining years of his life, which are unmarked by any events of particular importance. He and the Baptist congregation at Bedford had to encounter renewed persecution in 1682, when the Tory and Papal reaction set in against the exclusive and tyrannical spirit with which the Whigs had used their power. His old enemies, the "Justices," were again busy during this period, and the meeting-house for some while was shut up. Bunyan himself, however, does not appear to have been molested. He had sufficiently shown his peaceable and unfactious character, and they could find no excuse for disturbing him.

In the midst of this persecution he published his
Holy War. The popularity of the *Pilgrim's Progress,*
and the success which it had met, not only beyond his
own sect, but beyond the bounds of Puritanism, led
him to the conception and composition of this more
elaborate allegory. As in many other cases, however,
this new effort never attracted the notice nor excited
the interest of the first. As a mere literary composition, there are some points of view in which the
Holy War might claim even a favourable comparison
with the earlier work. The allegorical idea on which
it is based is worked out with a more consistent and
curious art ; there is less rapid and shifting change
of scene, and less confusion of purpose, than in the *Pilgrim's Progress ;* yet, as a whole, it is greatly wanting
in the poetic charm and the nameless interest and
fascination of the latter allegory. It neither seizes
upon the imagination nor touches the heart as the
story of Christian does. Singularly ingenious, elaborate, and coherent in its illustrations and characters, it
is almost as great a marvel, but it is not nearly so
felicitous nor exquisite a product of genius. The
second part of the *Pilgrim's Progress* appeared two years
later (1684). A second part has seldom been handled
with a happier success. The old associations—the familiar scenes—the series of imagery—are all preserved ;
the same simple charm lies on every page ; while in
such characters as Mercy there is a deeper tenderness
—and in others, such as Greatheart and old Honest,
there is a broader and more vivid dramatic outline
than in any of the figures in the first part. The portraits throughout show, if possible, a freer and easier
mastery of hand, although it must yield to the first
in the freshness and life of its scenes and incidents.

These were not—and, in the nature of the case, could not be—rivalled.

On the accession of James, in the following year, Bunyan seems to have apprehended the likelihood of renewed trouble. This is inferred from the fact of his having conveyed at this time any little property or goods he had acquired to his wife. He was destined, however, to finish his days in peace. He continued his pastoral labour till the eve of the Revolution. His last work was that of a peacemaker. It was the character he had always loved, and with no work more appropriate could he have closed his career. A friend of his who lived at Reading had threatened to disinherit his son ; he was approaching his end ; and the idea of his leaving the world unreconciled to his son weighed upon Bunyan's heart. He undertook a journey to Reading on horseback—was successful in renewing the bonds of amity between father and son—and had reached London on his way back. Here, however, he took ill—worn out with the journey—and rapidly sank. He died in the house of his friend Mr Stradwick, a grocer, and was buried in the Campo Santo, as Southey calls it, of the Dissenters—Bunhill-fields Burying-ground. The day of his death is stated in his epitaph, and in the Life appended to his *Grace Abounding*, to have been the 12th of August 1688 ; but other authorities gave a later day of the same month.

Bunyan died as he had lived—a faithful, simple man, intent upon his duty. His character is so simple in its elements, and has been so fully exhibited in the numerous touches of self-portraiture which we have quoted from his autobiography, that little remains to be added on the subject. Naturally a man of deep

and powerful earnestness and firm will—vehement in
his impulses, but moderate in his desires—he would
in any circumstances have proved a remarkable man.
He was, as he believed, before his conversion a notable
sinner ; he became, after conversion, a notable Christian, like his own Greatheart. Had he never been
more than a tinker at Elstow, he must have exercised
over his neighbours a social influence proportioned to
his strength of will and the determination of his convictions. He was not a man to let his life pass idly
by with the current. It is impossible to look at his
portrait, and not recognise the lines of power by which it
is everywhere marked. It has more of a sturdy soldier
aspect than anything else—the aspect of a man who
would face dangers any day rather than shun them ;
and this corresponds exactly to his description by his
oldest biographer and friend, Charles Doe. " He appeared in countenance," he says, " to be of a stern and
rough temper. He had a sharp, quick eye, accomplished, with an excellent discerning of persons. As
for his person, he was tall of stature, strong boned,
though not corpulent ; somewhat of a ruddy face, with
sparkling eyes, wearing his hair on the upper lip
after the old British fashion ; his hair reddish, but in
his later days time had sprinkled it with grey ; his
nose well set, but not declining or bending, and his
mouth moderate large ; his forehead something high,
and his habit always plain and modest."—A more manly
and robust appearance cannot well be conceived, his
eyes only showing in their sparkling depth the fountains of sensibility concealed within the roughened
exterior. Here, as before, we are reminded of his
likeness to Luther. We see in both the same combination of broad, burly humanity with intense spir-

itual passionateness—of simplicity and affectionate-
ness with an obstinate, unflinching, some would say,
a headstrong courage. The Puritan, upon the whole,
is narrower than the Reformer in the range of his
religious sympathies, and in the aspiration of his
genius — in general culture and magnanimity of
mind. There is a freer and larger play of human
feeling, and altogether a grander nature in the German.
There are, however, many special points of intellectual as well as spiritual resemblance between them.
They have together the same intuition of the popular
religious instincts—the same mastery of the popular
dialect—the same love of allegory and story, and the
same picturesque liveliness of delineation—and not
least, the same intense appreciation of the Puritan
doctrine of justification, as the sum and substance of
Christianity—the same susceptibility to states of spiritual darkness and struggle, joined to an unyielding
force of conviction, when once the truth is understood
and seized. We have already seen how much Bunyan
was indebted to Luther. Of all the books that he
found useful in his spiritual perplexities, none, except
the Bible, was so congenial and satisfactory to him as
the *Commentary on the Galatians.* He found his own
spiritual condition so largely and profoundly reflected
in that book, that " it seemed to have been written out
of his own heart."

While rough and soldier-like in exterior, his old
biographer adds that Bunyan was " in his conversation
mild and affable, not given to loquacity or much discourse in company, unless some urgent occasion required it ; observing never to boast of himself or his
parts, but rather seem low in his own eyes, and submit
himself to the judgment of others ; abhorring lying

and swearing; being just in all that lay in his power
to his word ; not seeming to revenge injuries, loving
to reconcile differences, and make friendship with all."
He was, in short, an honest, gentle, and peaceable
man—strong to endure and struggle for the sake of
principle, and in the doing of what he considered duty
—but as little of a fanatic and "pestilent fellow" as
any man could be. As a good soldier of Jesus Christ,
he was ready to endure hardness ; he would submit to
contumely and imprisonment rather than compromise
his conscience regarding the Book of Common Prayer ;
but he was no disturber, he willingly granted to
others the same rights that he claimed for himself.
The longer he lived he cared less for peculiarities, and
set his heart more on the substance of all religion.
He loved to make peace. This genuine spirit of religion showed itself in him, mastering all the earth-
born passions and sectarianism so apt to cling to it.

It was the glory of Puritanism to have produced
many such men—men of a zeal and courage that
soared beyond all worldly considerations, and dared
everything for the truth, as they believed it, and yet
men whose highest instinct it was, if they had been
let alone, to be quiet and faithful in the work to
which God had called them—men who lived in the
fullest radiance of the divine, and yet would have
been content to do good works unnoticed among men.
It was the disgrace of the Restoration that it mistook
and ill-used such men, that it knew not the " sons of
God" save as " rogues " and "knaves," " conceited,
stubborn, fanatical dogs," * to be insulted, imprisoned,
and " stretched by the neck." Puritanism had no
doubt used its own dominance with a high hand ; it

* Jeffreys' language. Baxter's trial.

had been proud and scornful, and sufficiently tyrannical in its day of triumph ; but it never either hated
so blindly, nor punished so indiscriminately and wantonly as Royalism. Narrow as was its spiritual vision
in many ways, and hard its dogmatism, it had a broader
eye and a larger heart than the miserable and degraded fanaticism of licence and cruelty which displaced it,—and which found its natural and appropriate employment in the persecution and maltreatment
of men like Baxter and Bunyan.

The special interest of Bunyan's writings, in our
point of view, consists in the number and variety of
the pictures of popular Puritanism that they contain.
His allegories teem with such pictures. He is the
great artist of the spiritual life of Puritanism. He had
himself lived through almost every phase of its pious
excitement ; his deep, sensitive nature responded to
all its chords of emotion ; and his vividly creative
imagination enabled him to seize and reproduce its
varied experiences in concrete representations, which
have perpetuated them far more lastingly than any
analysis or description could have done. And not
only what he himself had felt and known, but what he
had seen—all the diverse aspects of the religious and
the irreligious life around him—stamped themselves
as pictures on his mind, and reappear in his writings.
The field from which he drew his artistic materials
was strictly limited. It was only its relation to religion—to his own form of it, in fact—that made any
aspect of life interesting to him ; but within his range,
there is no artist has produced so many clearly-marked
individualities of portraiture.

So perfect in many respects is Bunyan's art,—so fer-

tile and easy his creative faculty,—that we are apt to
overlook the extent to which he borrowed directly
from the real life around him. The more, however, we
study the *Pilgrim's Progress* and the *Holy War*, in
connection with his own history and times, the more
will we see reason to believe that their numerous characters directly and broadly reflect both the outer and
inner characteristics of the religious world familiar to
him.

In all his allegories, but especially in the *Pilgrim's
Progress*, there is what may be called a purely ideal
or imaginative element, and a strictly realistic or literal element. The former is their poetic groundwork,
and is, in the main, drawn from Scripture. Bunyan
knew no literature except that of the Bible; his
imagination fed itself upon its grand forms of expression, — its wondrous scenes. It was at once
truth and poetry—all truth, and all poetry—to him.
And, accordingly, his allegories are found constructed
upon such great outlines of imaginative incident and
scenery as he had there learned to admire. All critics have been struck with the simplicity and faithfulness with which he reproduces scriptural circumstance and idea. But, combined with his vivid biblical
imagination, there is also everywhere, in his allegories,
the evidence of a rare power of actual observation,—
of sharp insight into the living characteristics around
him,—and great fulness of artistic skill in drawing
these from the life as he knew and saw them. It is
the religion of the Bible which he portrays; minds
trained in the most opposite schools of Christian
thought have recognised the accuracy of his representations; but it is also religion, such as he saw it
in Bedford and its neighbourhood among his fellow-

Baptists,—among the adherents of the restored Church
—in its Puritan peculiarities,—in its Anglican com-
promises—with the stamp of persecution and exaggeration on the one hand, — and the taint of self-
indulgence and worldliness on the other hand. The
poetical scriptural element seems to give more the
general outline, the varied scenery of the *Pilgrim's
Progress ;* the realistic Puritan element, more the
graphic homely touches that make the characters
start to life before us.

The flight of Christian from the city of Destruction,
the changing difficulties, helps, snares, dangers, delights, and encouragements, through which he passes
on his journey to Mount Zion ; the Slough of Despond, the Village of Morality, the Narrow Gate ;
the Interpreter's house, with all its encouraging and
warning sights ; the place of the Cross, where Christian's burden "loosed from off his shoulders and fell
from off his back ;" the Hill of Difficulty ; the House
Beautiful, with the lions guarding it ; the Valley of
Humiliation, and the fight with Apollyon, "a monster
hideous to behold, clothed with scales like a fish, and
with wings like a dragon, and feet like a bear, and
out of whose belly came fire and smoke;" the terrors
of the Valley of the Shadow of Death ; Vanity Fair,
its persecutions, and the trial and death of Faithful ;
the River of Life, and the meadow " curiously beautified with lilies, and green all the year long;" Doubting
Castle, and the Giant Despair ; the Delectable Mountains, with their gardens and orchards, their vineyards
and fountains of water, and the shepherds feeding
their flocks ; the hill Clear, with the view of the gate
of the Celestial City ; the Enchanted Ground, whose
air naturally tended to drowsiness ; and the country

of Beulah, whose air was very sweet and pleasant,
where "they heard continually the singing of birds,
and saw every day the flowers appear on the earth,
and heard the voice of the turtle in the land;" and,
finally, the River of Death, running very deep between the Pilgrims and the gate of the Celestial City.—
The great and permanent charm of these successive
pictures is the faithfulness with which they reproduce
biblical ideas and imagery. One sees the reflection
of Scripture everywhere. Bright, felicitous, and picturesque as Bunyan's imagination is, he nowhere travels beyond its range. Nature is beheld by him only
in the light of the sacred page, and delineated by him
only in its descriptive language. The Pauline ideas
of sin and of salvation are closely preserved by him
in their great outlines. So far, his representations are
true, not merely to one phase of Christianity, but to
the universal Christian instinct and feeling. All confess, in some measure, to this catholicity in the conception of the *Pilgrim's Progress*—this broad fidelity
and ideal felicity in its treatment.

But, fully admitting this ideal scriptural element—
answering to the almost universal Christian appreciation of the story—it is equally true that, when we
descend from its general imaginative texture to a particular examination of many of its features and characters, we meet with the most literal and direct expressions of his own Puritan observation and experience. In the first instance, his imagination draws
its materials from Scripture—in the second, from life;
and it is, above all, this realistic element that gives
to Bunyan's great allegory its special interest. It is
because he draws so much from outward fact that we
find his pages so living—and linger over them—and

return to them—and find them not only instructive, but entertaining. Spenser, in his great allegory, is richer in poetic feeling, and in the expression of natural beauty—he has represented higher forms of ethical conception, and taken a wider view of humanity—but he has nowhere caught life, and mirrored it, as Bunyan has done. He is a dreamer throughout; his imagination roams wholly in an ideal region ; there is no familiarity, no tangibility, in his portraits ; and hence, even those who most admire the poetry of the *Faery Queen*, feel little interest in its successive stories. It is read for the grandeur, beauty, and luxuriance of its poetical ideas and descriptions ; but whoever read it from any sustained interest in its legends, or the characters—exquisite creations as some of them are—that figure in them? But we read Bunyan for the interest of his story, and especially for the piquancy, variety, and homely expressiveness of the characters that cross his pages. In comparison with all other allegories that ever were written, the *Pilgrim's Progress* is interesting ; and among the main sources of this interest are the diverse portraits of the social and religious life of Puritanism that it presents.

Christian himself, in the deep dejection and misery with which he begins his journey, in his self-conscious absorption concerning his own safety, and his absolute separation from all his old labours and interests, in the dangers that beset his every pause and his every gratification by the way, is a picture of the Puritan Christian. The groundwork—the main features of the character—are broadly biblical and catholic ; but there is also, in such points as now mentioned, the clear practical stamp of Puritanism. The conception

of the world as a city about to be burned up, with no
good and no hope in it—of the Christian life as a swift
and unresting passage from Destruction to Safety in
heaven—is drawn from Scripture, yet drawn with the
tone of exaggeration of the religious ideas in which
Bunyan was nurtured.

Such peculiarities and touches of the practical religious life familiar to him appear strongly in some of
the accessory characters. No character of the time
was more conspicuous than that of the warrior Christian—the religious soldier of the Commonwealth ; and,
accordingly, this idea is one of the author's most frequent inspirations. His best Christians are all fighting
Christians—men who not only hold their own, but slay
giants by the way, and manfully encounter and overcome monsters that impede their progress. Greatheart
is one of his happiest portraits, and he is the portrait
of a warrior Christian, with "sword and shield and
helmet," and who is " good at his weapons ;" who kills
Giant Grim, and Giant Maul, and Giant Slay-good,
and, most of all, takes off the head of Giant Despair,
and demolishes Doubting Castle. He is at once guide,
preacher, and soldier. Old Honest is even a more expressive specimen. His first exclamation, when Greatheart and the others accost him, and ask him what he
would have done if they had come to rob him, as he
for a moment supposed, reveals in full his character.
" Done !" he says ; " why, I would have fought as long
as breath had been in me : and had I so done, I am
sure you would never have given me the worst of it,
for a Christian can never be overcome unless he shall
yield of himself." There is an affecting simplicity in
old Honest ; he has no thoughts but to do his duty
and fight. Then there is Valiant-for-the-Truth, who

fought " till his sword did cleave to his hand." Doubtless Bunyan knew such fighting saints, and the touches
with which he sets them before us may have been
transferred from living specimens of the race. Certainly in such portraits we have before us true and
life-like illustrations of the soldier Christian of the
Commonwealth.

It is remarkable that in the *Holy War*, where the
characters are so entirely military, we have no such
natural and happy portraits as those of Greatheart
and old Honest. Captain Resistance, and Captain Conviction, and Captain Boanerges, &c., are comparative
shadows—mere dim ideals, not half filled up. While
the general intellectual conception of this allegory is,
as we have said, well worked out, with even greater
consistency than that of the *Pilgrim's Progress*, there
is yet throughout it a want of the life and reality of
characterisation that distinguish the earlier allegory.

There was nothing more characteristic of Puritanism
than the conflict and distress of emotion which it associated with religion. All religious life and excellence
sprang out of the darkness of some great crisis of
spiritual feeling. " I live you know where," Cromwell wrote to his cousin, " in Kedar—which signifies
darkness." It is remarkable how prominently Bunyan
has seized and expressed this idea. Considering his
own experience, it would indeed have been strange if
he had not. The Slough of Despond awaits every inquiring pilgrim—the pure-minded Mercy no less than
the sinful Christiana. And even after many pilgrims
have got far on in their journey—after Vanity Fair has
been passed, and the River of Life and the Pleasant Meadow—there is Doubting Castle and Giant Despair. Mr
Feeble-mind, Mr Despondency and his daughter Much-

afraid, Mr Little-faith, and Mr Fearing, who "lay roaring at the Slough of Despond for above a month," are all true but anxious and distressed pilgrims. It is impossible not to see the impress of a prominent feature of popular Puritanism in such characters. The burden of their spiritual weakness oppresses and prostrates them. It is only when Greatheart delivers them from Giant Despair that they have any relief. "Now when Feeble-mind and Ready-to-Halt saw that it was the head of Giant Despair indeed, they were very jocund and merry. Now Christiana, if need was, could play upon the viol, and her daughter Mercy upon the lute ; so, since they were so merry disposed, she played them a lesson, and Ready-to-Halt would dance. So he took Despondency's daughter Much-afraid by the hand, and to dancing they went in the road. True, he could not dance without one crutch in his hand, but I promise you he footed it well ; also the girl was to be commended, for she answered the music handsomely. As for Mr Despondency, the music was not so much to him : he was for feeding rather than dancing, for that he was almost starved." There is queer grim humour in this picture of Puritan mirth. It is but a rare gleam, and a very grotesque one. Mr Despondency had evidently the truer appreciation of his position. The most devoted saint could not live without eating ; but no combination of lute and viol and handsome footing can make the dancing congruous.

While Bunyan has preserved such various types of the Puritan Christian, he has not forgotten their opposites in the Royal Anglicanism, or false religion of the day, as it appeared to him. By-ends is one of his most graphic pictures. He and his friends and companions, Lord Time-server, Lord Fair-speech, Mr

Smoothman, Mr Facing-both-ways, Mr Anything, and the parson of the parish, Mr Two-tongues, all make a group of which Bunyan knew too many specimens. In Puritan times they had been zealous for religion ; while it sat in high places, they had admired and respected it, and seemed to be among its most forward followers ; but they had arrived at such "a pitch of breeding," "that they knew how to carry it to all." From the stricter sort they differed in two small points. "1st, They never strove against wind and tide ;" and, 2d, "They were always most zealous when religion goes in his silver slippers." "They loved much to talk with him in the street when the sun shines and the people applaud him." "They had a luck to jump in their judgment with the present times."

Talkative is a specimen of another phase of pseudo-religious life. It was his great business and delight "to talk of the history or the mystery of things," of "miracles, wonders, and signs sweetly penned in Holy Scripture." He is a capital, if somewhat overdone, picture of the empty religious professor, who learns by rote the "great promises and consolations of the Gospel," who can give a "hundred Scripture texts for confirmation of the truth—that all is of grace and not of works ;" who can talk by the hour, of "things heavenly or things earthly, things moral or things evangelical, things sacred or things profane, things past or things to come, things essential or things circumstantial," but who, notwithstanding all his "fair tongue, is but a sorry fellow." He is the son of one Say-well, and dwells in Prating Row. He can discourse as well on the "ale-bench" as on the way to Zion. "The more drink he hath in his crown," the more of such things he hath in his head. He is "the very stain, and re-

proach, and shame of religion."—"A saint abroad, a
devil at home." "It is better to deal with a Turk than
with him." How many Talkatives must have made
their appearance in the wake of the great Puritan
movement—the spawn of its earnest and grave professions! Bedford and its neighbourhood had, no
doubt, many of them; and Bunyan knew and despised
them in life, as he has fixed them in immemorial disgrace in his pages.

The most complete scene from life probably in the
Pilgrim's Progress is the trial of Faithful at Vanity
Fair. The mob that shouted against Faithful and
Christian, and "beat them, and besmeared them with
dirt," and called them "Bedlams and mad," is the picture of a Restoration mob hooting the persecuted saints.
Lord Hategood, the judge, is the impersonation of the
odious arrogance and ready cruelty of the justices, as
they appeared to Bunyan; the jury and the witnesses
are all more or less portraits; not a feature is filled in
which does not represent some fact or circumstance
well known to him. The indictment is almost his own,
under which his long imprisonment was sealed. "They
were enemies to, and disturbers of their trade; they
had made commotions and divisions in the town, and
had won a party to their own most dangerous opinions,
in contempt of the law of their Prince." Jeffreys himself might be supposed speaking in the words of the
judge. "Thou runagate, heretic, and traitor, hast
thou heard what these honest gentlemen have witnessed
against thee?" Faithful: "May I speak a few words
in my own defence?" Judge: "Sirrah, sirrah, thou
deservest to live no longer, but to be slain immediately
upon the place: yet, that all men may see our goodness toward thee, let us hear what thou hast to say."

The idea and forms of a trial had strongly impressed themselves on Bunyan's mind. It had been one of the most familiar and imposing scenes of his own life, and so had become fixed upon his memory, and a part of his imaginative furniture. It is depicted at great length in the *Holy War*, as well as in the *Pilgrim's Progress*. This shows the homely limits, but at the same time the strength and vivacity, of his fancy. He drew from his own narrow experience—but his art made the dim pictures of his memory all alive with the fitting touches of reality.

This realistic character of Bunyan's allegories is of special interest to us now. We are carried back to Bedford and the Midland Counties in the seventeenth century, and we mingle with the men and women that lived and did their work there. It is in many respects a beautiful and affecting picture that we contemplate. A religion which could produce men like Greatheart, and old Honest, and Christian himself, and Faithful, and Hopeful—and of which the gentle and tender-hearted Mercy was a fair expression, —had certainly features both of magnanimity and of beauty. There is a simple earnestness and a pure-minded loveliness in Bunyan's highest creations that are very touching. Puritanism lives in his pages—spiritually and socially—in forms and in colouring which must ever command the sympathy and enlist the love of all good Christians.

But his pages no less show its narrowness and deficiencies. Life—even spiritual life—is broader than Bunyan saw it and painted it. It is not so easily and sharply defined—it cannot be so superficially sorted and classified. It is more deep, complex, and subtle—more involved, more mixed. There may have been

good in Talkative, with all his emptiness and love for
the ale-bench—and Mrs Timorous, and even By-ends,
might have something said for them.   Nowhere, in
reality, is the good so good, or the bad so bad, as Puritan evangelical piety is apt to conceive and represent
them.   There is work to be done in the city of Destruction as well as in fleeing from it.   The Meadow
with the sparkling river, and the Enchanted Ground,
are not mere snares to lure and hurt us.   There is
room for leisure and literature, and poetry and art
even, as we travel to Mount Zion.   There is a meeting-
point for all these elements of human culture, and the
" one thing needful"—without which all culture is
dead—though Bunyan and Puritanism failed to see it.

Let us reverence with all our heart the spiritual
earnestness of such men as Bunyan, and of the system
they represented ; few things higher or more beautiful
have ever been seen in this world.   But we are also
bound, if we would not empty our earthly existence of
the beautiful and grand—the graceful, fascinating, and
refined in many forms of civilisation and art—to claim
admiration for much that they despised, and a broader,
more tolerant, and more genial interpretation of nature
and life than they would have allowed.

THE END.

ERRATA.

Page 29, line 20, for *on* read *in.*

 ,, 39, ,, 8, for *ten* read *twelve.*

 ,, 93, ,, 21, omit *great* before *key.*

 ,, — ,, 25, for *unexplainable* read *inextricable.*

 ,, 175, ,, 13, for 1624 read 1625.

 ,, 180, ,, 14, for *endueth* read *indueth.*

 ,, 183, ,, 23, for *morn* read *moon.*

 ,, — ,, 8, for *faith* read *youth.*

 ,, 242, ,, 17, omit *it* before *its.*

 ,, 274, ,, 4, for *views* read *vein.*

 ,, 278, ,, 5, for *could* read *would.*

I.

LEADERS OF THE REFORMATION:
LUTHER—CALVIN—LATIMER—KNOX.

By the Rev. JOHN TULLOCH, D.D.,

Principal and Primarius Professor of Theology, St Mary's College, St Andrews.

Second Edition, Crown Octavo, price 6s. 6d.

" We are not acquainted with any work in which so much solid information upon the leading aspects of the great Reformation is presented in so well-packed and pleasing a form."— *Witness*.

" The idea was excellent, and most ably has it been executed. Each Essay is a lesson in sound thinking as well as in good writing. The deliberate perusal of the volume will be an exercise for which all, whether young or old, will be the better. The book is erudite, and throughout marked by great independence of thought. We very highly prize the publication."—*British Standard*.

" We cannot but congratulate both Dr Tulloch and the university of which he is so prominent a member on this evidence of returning life in Presbyterian thought. It seems as though the chains of an outgrown Puritanism were at last falling from the limbs of Scotch theology. There is a width of sympathy and a power of writing in this little volume which fills us with great expectation. We trust that Dr Tulloch will consider it as being merely the basis of a more complete and erudite inquiry." —*Literary Gazette*.

" The style is admirable in force and in pathos, and the book one to be altogether recommended, both for the merits of those of whom it treats, and for that which the writer unconsciously reveals of his own character."—*Globe*.

II.

T H E I S M :
THE WITNESS OF REASON AND NATURE TO AN ALL-WISE AND BENEFICENT CREATOR.—(BURNETT PRIZE TREATISE.)

By the Rev. JOHN TULLOCH, D.D.,

Principal and Primarius Professor of Theology, St Mary's College, St Andrews.

Crown Octavo, 10s. 6d.

" Dr Tulloch's Essay, in its masterly statement of the real nature and difficulties of the subject, its logical exactness in distinguishing the illustrative from the suggestive, its lucid arrangement of the argument, its simplicity of expression, is quite unequalled by any work we have seen on the subject."—*Christian Remembrancer*, January 1857.

W. BLACKWOOD AND SONS, EDINBURGH AND LONDON.

MESSRS BLACKWOOD AND SONS'

PUBLICATIONS.

------◆------

WORKS IN THE PRESS.

In One Volume Octavo,

EGYPT, THE SOUDAN, AND CENTRAL AFRICA.

WITH EXPLORATIONS FROM KHARTOUM ON THE WHITE NILE, TO THE REGIONS
OF THE EQUATOR.

BEING SKETCHES FROM SIXTEEN YEARS' TRAVEL.

By JOHN PETHERICK, F.R.G.S.

Her Britannic Majesty's Consul for the Soudan.

In Two Volumes Octavo,

LIVES OF LORD CASTLEREAGH AND SIR CHARLES STEWART,

SECOND AND THIRD MARQUESSES OF LONDONDERRY.

FROM THE ORIGINAL PAPERS OF THE FAMILY, AND OTHER SOURCES.

By SIR ARCHIBALD ALISON, Bart., D.C.L.

Author of "The History of Europe."

In Two Volumes Octavo,

THE MONKS OF THE WEST.

By the COUNT DE MONTALEMBERT.

An Authorised Translation.

In Two Volumes Octavo,

HISTORY OF THE GREEK REVOLUTION.

By GEORGE FINLAY, LL.D., Athens;

Author of the "History of Greece under Foreign Domination."

Tales from "Blackwood."

Complete in Twelve Volumes. The Volumes are sold separately, price 1s. 6d.; and may be had of most Booksellers, in Six Volumes, handsomely half-bound in red morocco.

CONTENTS.

Vol. I. The Glenmutchkin Railway.—Vanderdecken's Message Home.—The Floating Beacon.—Colonna the Painter.—Napoleon.—A Legend of Gibraltar.—The Iron Shroud.

Vol. II. Lazaro's Legacy.—A Story without a Tail.—Faustus and Queen Elizabeth.—How I became a Yeoman.—Devereux Hall.—The Metempsychosis.—College Theatricals.

Vol. III. A Reading Party in the Long Vacation.—Father Tom and the Pope.—La Petite Madelaine.—Bob Burke's Duel with Ensign Brady.—The Headsman : A Tale of Doom.—The Wearyful Woman.

Vol. IV. How I stood for the Dreepdaily Burghs.—First and Last.—The Duke's Dilemma : A Chronicle of Niesenstein.—The Old Gentleman's Teetotum.—"Woe to us when we lose the Watery Wall."—My College Friends : Charles Russell, the Gentleman Commoner.—The Magic Lay of the One-Horse Chay.

Vol. V. Adventures in Texas.—How we got Possession of the Tuileries.—Captain Paton's Lament.—The Village Doctor.—A Singular Letter from Southern Africa.

Vol. VI. My Friend the Dutchman.—My College Friends—No II. : Horace Leicester.—The Emerald Studs.—My College Friends—No III. : Mr W. Wellington Hurst.—Christine : A Dutch Story.—The Man in the Bell.

Vol. VII. My English Acquaintance.—The Murderer's Last Night.—Narration of Certain Uncommon Things that did formerly happen to Me, Herbert Willis, B.D.—The Wags.—The Wet Wooing : A Narrative of '98.—Ben-na-Groich.

Vol. VIII. The Surveyor's Tale. By Professor Aytoun.—The Forrest-Race Romance. —Di Vasari : A Tale of Florence.—Sigismund Fatello.—The Boxes.

Vol. IX. Rosaura : A Tale of Madrid.—Adventure in the North-West Territory.—Harry Bolton's Curacy.—The Florida Pirate.—The Pandour and his Princess.—The Beauty Draught.

Vol. X. Antonio di Carara.—The Fatal Repast.—The Vision of Cagliostro.—The First and Last Kiss.—The Smuggler's Leap.—The Haunted and the Haunters.—The Duellists.

Vol. XI. The Natolian Story-Teller.—The First and Last Crime.—John Rintoul.—Major Moss.—The Premier and his Wife.

Vol. XII. Tickler among the Thieves !—The Bridegroom of Barna.—The Involuntary Experimentalist.—Lebrun's Lawsuit.—The Snowing-up of Strath Lugas.—A Few Words on Social Philosophy.

Sketches of the Poetical Literature of the Past Half-Century.

By D. M. MOIR.

Third Edition, Foolscap Octavo, price 5s.

The Campaign of Garibaldi in the Two Sicilies.

A PERSONAL NARRATIVE.

By CHARLES STEWART FORBES,
Commander R.N.

Post Octavo. With Plans of the Engagements, and Portraits of Garibaldi and the King of Naples. 12s.

The Poetical Works of Thomas Aird.

Complete Edition. Foolscap Octavo, price 6s.

Cheap Editions of Popular Works.

LIGHTS AND SHADOWS OF SCOTTISH LIFE. Foolscap 8vo, 3s. cloth.

THE TRIALS OF MARGARET LYNDSAY. By the Author of " Lights and Shadows of Scottish Life." Foolscap 8vo, 3s. cloth.

THE FORESTERS. By the Author of "Lights and Shadows of Scottish Life." Foolscap 8vo, 3s. cloth.

TOM CRINGLE'S LOG. Complete in One Volume, Foolscap 8vo, 4s. cloth.

THE CRUISE OF THE MIDGE. By the Author of " Tom Cringle's Log." In One Volume, Foolscap 8vo, 4s. cloth.

THE LIFE OF MANSIE WAUCH, TAILOR IN DALKEITH. Foolscap 8vo, 3s. cloth.

THE SUBALTERN. By the Author of " The Chelsea Pensioners." Foolscap 8vo, 3s. cloth.

PENINSULAR SCENES AND SKETCHES. By the Author of " The Student of Salamanca." Foolscap 8vo, 3s. cloth.

NIGHTS AT MESS, SIR FRIZZLE PUMPKIN, AND OTHER TALES. Foolscap 8vo, 3s. cloth.

THE YOUTH AND MANHOOD OF CYRIL THORNTON. By the Author of " Men and Manners in America." Foolscap 8vo, 4s. cloth.

VALERIUS : A ROMAN STORY. Foolscap 8vo, 3s. cloth.

REGINALD DALTON. By the Author of " Valerius." Foolscap 8vo, 4s. cloth.

SOME PASSAGES IN THE LIFE OF ADAM BLAIR, AND HISTORY OF MATTHEW WALD. By the Author of " Valerius." Foolscap 8vo, 4s. cloth.

ANNALS OF THE PARISH, AND AYRSHIRE LEGATEES. By John Galt. Foolscap 8vo, 4s. cloth.

SIR ANDREW WYLIE. By John Galt. Foolscap 8vo, 4s. cloth.

THE PROVOST, AND OTHER TALES. By John Galt. Foolscap 8vo, 4s. cloth.

THE ENTAIL. By John Galt. Foolscap 8vo, 4s. cloth.

LIFE IN THE FAR WEST. By G. F. Ruxton. A New Edition. Foolscap 8vo, 4s. cloth.

Prayers for Social and Family Worship.

Prepared by a Committee of the General Assembly of the Church of Scotland, and specially designed for the use of Soldiers, Sailors, Colonists, Sojourners in India, and other Persons, at Home or Abroad, who are deprived of the Ordinary Services of a Christian Ministry. Published by Authority of the Committee.

In Crown Octavo, bound in cloth, price 4s.

Prayers for Social and Family Worship.

Being a Cheap Edition of the above.

Price 1s. 6d.

Theism :

THE WITNESS OF REASON AND NATURE TO AN ALL-WISE AND BENEFICENT CREATOR.—(BURNETT PRIZE TREATISE.)

By the Rev. J. TULLOCH, D.D.,

Principal and Primarius Professor of Theology, St Mary's College, St Andrews.

Crown Octavo, price 10s. 6d.

Complete Library Edition of Sir Edward Bulwer Lytton's Novels.

In Volumes of a convenient and handsome form. Printed in a large readable type. Published monthly, price 5s. Sixteen Volumes are published.

"It is of the handiest of sizes; the paper is good; and the type, which seems to be new, is very clear and beautiful. There are no pictures. The whole charm of the presentment of the volume consists in its handiness, and the tempting clearness and beauty of the type, which almost converts into a pleasure the mere act of following the printer's lines, and leaves the author's mind free to exert its unobstructed force upon the reader."—*Examiner.*

The Novels of George Eliot.

In Six Volumes, uniformly printed, price £1, 16s.

SCENES OF CLERICAL LIFE. Third Edition. 2 vols., price 12s.
ADAM BEDE. Eighth Edition. 2 vols., price 12s.
THE MILL ON THE FLOSS. A new Edition. In 2 vols., price 12s.

St Stephen's: A Poem.

OR, ILLUSTRATIONS OF PARLIAMENTARY ORATORY.

Comprising—Pym—Vane—'Strafford—Halifax—Shaftesbury—St John—Sir R. Walpole—Chesterfield—Carteret—Chatham—Pitt — Fox — Burke — Sheridan — Wilberforce — Wyndham — Conway — Castlereagh — William Lamb (Lord Melbourne) — Tierney — Lord Grey—O'Connell—Plunkett—Shiel—Follett—Macaulay—Peel.

Second Edition. Crown Octavo, price 5s.

Lady Lee's Widowhood.

By Lieut.-Colonel E. B. HAMLEY.

With Engravings. Third Edition. Crown Octavo, price 6s.

Works of Samuel Warren, D.C.L.

Uniform Edition, Five Vols., price 24s.

The following are sold separately :—

DIARY OF A LATE PHYSICIAN. 5s. 6d.
TEN THOUSAND A-YEAR. Two vols., 9s.
NOW AND THEN. 2s. 6d.
MISCELLANIES. 5s.

The Poetical Works of D. M. Moir (Δ)

(OF MUSSELBURGH).

A New Edition, with a Memoir by THOMAS AIRD, and Portrait.   In Two Vols., price 12s.

The Sketcher.

By the Rev. JOHN EAGLES, A.M., Oxon.

Originally published in *Blackwood's Magazine.*

In Post Octavo, price 10s. 6d.

"There is an earnest and vigorous thought about them, a genial and healthy tone of feeling, and a flowing and frequently eloquent style of language, that make this book one of the most pleasant companions that you can take with you, if you are bound for the woodland or pastoral scenery of rural England, especially if you go to study the picturesque, whether as an observer or as an artist."

Essays.

By the Rev. JOHN EAGLES, A.M., Oxon. ;

Originally published in *Blackwood's Magazine.*

Post Octavo, price 10s. 6d.

Contents : Church Music, and other Parochials.—Medical Attendance, and other Parochials. —A few Hours at Hampton Court.—Grandfathers and Grandchildren.—Sitting for a Portrait.—Are there not great Boasters among us?—Temperance and Teetotal Societies. —Thackeray's Lectures: Swift.—The Crystal Palace.—Civilisation: the Census.—The Beggar's Legacy.

Sea-side Studies.

By GEORGE HENRY LEWES,
Author of "Physiology of Common Life," &c.

Crown Octavo, price 6s. 6d.

The Moor and the Loch.

CONTAINING MINUTE INSTRUCTIONS IN ALL HIGHLAND SPORTS, WITH WANDERINGS OVER CRAG AND CORREI, FLOOD AND FELL.

By JOHN COLQUHOUN, Esq.

Third Edition, in Octavo, with Illustrations, price 12s. 6d.

Lays of the Scottish Cavaliers, and other Poems.

By W. EDMONDSTOUNE AYTOUN, D.C.L.

Professor of Rhetoric and Belles-Lettres in the University of Edinburgh.

Twelfth Edition, price 7s. 6d.

"Mr Aytoun's *Lays* are truly beautiful, and are perfect poems of their class, pregnant with fire, with patriotic ardour, with loyal zeal, with exquisite pathos, with noble passion. Who can hear the opening lines descriptive of Edinburgh after the great battle of Flodden, and not feel that the minstrel's soul has caught the genuine inspiration?"—*Morning Post.*

Bothwell: A Poem.

By the same Author.

Third Edition, price 7s. 6d.

The Ballads of Scotland.

Edited by Professor AYTOUN.

Second Edition. Two Volumes, price 12s.

"No country can boast of a richer collection of Ballads than Scotland, and no Editor for these Ballads could be found more accomplished than Professor Aytoun. He has sent forth two beautiful volumes which range with *Percy's Reliques*—which for completeness and accuracy, leave little to be desired—which must henceforth be considered as the standard edition of the Scottish Ballads, and which we commend as a model to any among ourselves who may think of doing like service to the English Ballads."—*The Times.*

Firmilian; or, the Student of Badajoz:

A SPASMODIC TRAGEDY.

Price 6s.

"Without doubt, whether we regard it as a satire or as a complete drama, *Firmilian* is one of the most finished poems of the day. Unity is preserved, and the intensity of the 'spasmodic' energy thrown into the narrative carries the reader through every page; while the graces of poetic fancy, and the touches of deep thought scattered throughout, challenge comparison with selections from most modern poems."—*Liverpool Albion.*

The Book of Ballads.

Edited by BON GAULTIER.

Fifth Edition, with numerous Illustrations by DOYLE, LEECH, and CROWQUILL.

Gilt Edges, price 8s. 6d.

Poems and Ballads of Goethe.

Translated by Professor AYTOUN and THEODORE MARTIN.

Second Edition, price 6s.

"There is no doubt that these are the best translations of Goethe's marvellously-cut gems which have yet been published."—*The Times.*

Diversities of Faults in Christian Believers.

By the Very Rev. E. B. RAMSAY, M.A., F.R.S.E.
Dean of the Diocese of Edinburgh.

In Foolscap Octavo, price 4s. 6d.

Diversities of Christian Character.

Illustrated in the Lives of the Four Great Apostles.

By the same Author.

Uniform with the above, price 4s. 6d.

Religion in Common Life:

A Sermon preached in Crathie Church, October 14, 1855, before Her
Majesty the Queen and Prince Albert. Published by Her Majesty's
Command.

By the Rev. JOHN CAIRD, D.D.

Bound in Cloth, 8d. Cheap Edition, 3d.

Sermons.

By the Rev. JOHN CAIRD, D.D.
Minister of West Park Church, Glasgow.

In Post Octavo, price 7s. 6d. Tenth Thousand.

The Course of Time: A Poem.

By ROBERT POLLOK, A.M.
With a MEMOIR of the Author.

In Foolscap Octavo, price 5s.

The Autobiography of the Rev. Dr Alexander Carlyle,

Minister of Inveresk.

CONTAINING MEMORIALS OF THE MEN AND EVENTS OF HIS TIME.

Second Edition. Octavo, with Portrait, price 14s.

" The grandest demigod I ever saw was Dr Carlyle, minister of Musselburgh, commonly
called *Jupiter Carlyle,* from having sat more than once for the king of gods and men to Gavin
Hamilton ; and a shrewd, clever old carle was he."—SIR W. SCOTT.

Lectures on the History of the Church of Scotland,

FROM THE REFORMATION TO THE REVOLUTION SETTLEMENT.

By the late Very Rev. JOHN LEE, D.D., L.L.D.,
Principal of the University of Edinburgh.

With Notes and Appendices from the Author's Papers.

Edited by his Son, the Rev. WILLIAM LEE.

In Two Volumes Octavo, price 21s.

Works of Thomas M'Crie, D.D.

Edited by his SON, Professor M'CRIE.

Uniform Edition, in Four Vols. Crown Octavo, price 24s.

The following are sold separately—viz. :

LIFE OF JOHN KNOX. 6s.
LIFE OF ANDREW MELVILLE. 6s.
HISTORY OF THE REFORMATION IN ITALY. 4s.
HISTORY OF THE REFORMATION IN SPAIN. 3s. 6d.
REVIEW OF "TALES OF MY LANDLORD," AND SERMONS. 6s.

Lives of the Queens of Scotland,

AND ENGLISH PRINCESSES CONNECTED WITH THE REGAL SUCCESSION.

By AGNES STRICKLAND.

Containing the Lives of—

MARGARET TUDOR, Queen of James IV.
MAGDALENE OF FRANCE, First Queen of James V.
MARY OF LORRAINE, Second Queen of James V.
THE LADY MARGARET DOUGLAS, Mother of Darnley.
QUEEN MARY STUART.
ELIZABETH STUART, First Princess-Royal.
SOPHIA, Electress of Hanover.

With Portraits and Historical Vignettes. Complete in Eight Vols., price £4, 4s.

The Eighteen Christian Centuries.

By the Rev. JAMES WHITE.

Third Edition, with Analytical Table of Contents, and a Copious Index.   Post Octavo, price 7s. 6d.

" He goes to work upon the only true principle, and produces a picture that at once satisfies truth, arrests the memory, and fills the imagination.   When they (Index and Analytical Contents) are supplied, it will be difficult to lay hands on any book of the kind more useful and more entertaining."—*Times*, Review of first edition.

" At once the most picturesque and the most informing volume on Modern History to which the general reader could be referred."—*Nonconformist.*

History of France,

FROM THE EARLIEST PERIOD TO THE YEAR 1848.

By the Rev. JAMES WHITE,

Author of the " Eighteen Christian Centuries."

Second Edition, Post Octavo, price 9s.

" Mr White's ' History of France,' in a single volume of some 600 pages, contains every leading incident worth the telling, and abounds in word-painting whereof a paragraph has often as much active life in it as one of those inch-square etchings of the great Callot, in which may be clearly seen whole armies contending in bloody arbitrament, and as many incidents of battle as may be gazed at in the miles of canvass in the military picture-galleries at Versailles."—*Athenæum.*

" An excellent and comprehensive compendium of French History, quite above the standard of a school-book, and particularly well adapted for the libraries of literary institutions."—*National Review.*

Leaders of the Reformation:

LUTHER, CALVIN, LATIMER, AND KNOX.

By the Rev. JOHN TULLOCH, D.D.,

Principal and Primarius Professor of Theology, St Mary's College, St Andrews.

Second Edition, Crown Octavo, price 6s. 6d.

" We are not acquainted with any work in which so much solid information upon the leading aspects of the great Reformation is presented in so well-packed and pleasing a form."—*Witness.*

" The idea was excellent, and most ably has it been executed.   Each Essay is a lesson in sound thinking as well as in good writing.   The deliberate perusal of the volume will be an exercise for which all, whether young or old, will be the better.   The book is erudite, and throughout marked by great independence of thought.   We very highly prize the publication."—*British Standard.*

History of Europe,

FROM THE COMMENCEMENT OF THE FRENCH REVOLUTION TO THE
BATTLE OF WATERLOO.

By Sir ARCHIBALD ALISON, Bart., D.C.L.

A New Library Edition (being the Tenth) including a copious Index, embellished
with authentic Portraits. 14 vols. Octavo, price £10, 10s.

Crown Octavo Edition, 20 vols., price £6.

People's Edition, 12 vols., double cols., £2, 8s. ; and Index Vol., 3s.

Continuation of Alison's History of Europe,

FROM THE FALL OF NAPOLEON TO THE ACCESSION OF LOUIS
NAPOLEON.

By Sir ARCHIBALD ALISON, Bart., D.C.L.

Complete in Nine Vols., price £6, 7s. 6d. Uniform with the Library Edition of
the Author's "History of Europe, from the Commencement of the French
Revolution."

Atlas to Alison's History of Europe.

Containing 109 Maps and Plans of Countries, Battles, Sieges, and Sea-fights.
Constructed by A. KEITH JOHNSTON, F.R.S.E. With Vocabulary of Military and Marine Terms.

Library Edition, £3, 3s. ; People's Edition, £1, 11s. 6d.

Life of John, Duke of Marlborough.

WITH SOME ACCOUNT OF HIS CONTEMPORARIES.

By Sir ARCHIBALD ALISON, Bart., D.C.L.

Third Edition, Two Vols. Octavo, Portrait and Maps, 30s.

History of Greece under Foreign Domination.

By GEORGE FINLAY, LL.D., Athens.

Five Volumes Octavo—viz. :

Greece under the Romans. B.C. 146 to A.D. 717. A Historical View of the
condition of the Greek Nation, from its Conquest by the Romans until the
Extinction of the Roman Power in the East. Second Edition, 16s.

History of the Byzantine Empire. A.D. 716 to 1204 ; and of the Greek Empire
of Nicæa and Constantinople, A.D. 1204 to 1453. Two Volumes, £1, 7s. 6d.

Medieval Greece and Trebizond. The History of Greece, from its Conquest by
the Crusaders to its Conquest by the Turks, A.D. 1204 to 1566 ; and History
of the Empire of Trebizond, A.D. 1104 to 1461. Price 12s.

Greece under Othoman and Venetian Domination. A.D. 1453 to 1821. Price
10s. 6d.

" His book is worthy to take its place among the remarkable works on Greek history,
which form one of the chief glories of English scholarship. The history of Greece is but half
told without it."—*London Guardian.*

" His work is therefore learned and profound. It throws a flood of light upon an important though obscure portion of Grecian history. . . . In the essential requisites of fidelity,
accuracy, and learning, Mr Finlay bears a favourable comparison with any historical writer
of our day."—*North American Review.*

Sir William Hamilton's Lectures on Metaphysics and Logic.

Edited by the Rev. H. L. MANSELL, B.D., LL.D.,
Wynflete Professor of Moral and Metaphysical Philosophy, Oxford;

And JOHN VEITCH, M.A.,
Professor of Logic, Rhetoric, and Metaphysics, St Andrews.

In Four Vols. Octavo, price £2, 8s. Each Course is sold separately—viz. :

LECTURES ON METAPHYSICS. Two Vols., price £1, 4s.
LECTURES ON LOGIC. Two Vols., price £1, 4s.

Thorndale; or, the Conflict of Opinions.

By WILLIAM SMITH,
Author of " A Discourse on Ethics," &c.

A New Edition. Crown Octavo, price 10s. 6d.

Institutes of Metaphysics.

THE THEORY OF KNOWING AND BEING.

By JAMES F. FERRIER, A.B., Oxon.,
Professor of Moral Philosophy and Political Economy, St Andrews.

Second Edition, Crown Octavo, 10s. 6d.

Works of Professor Wilson.

Edited by his SON-IN-LAW, Professor FERRIER.

In Twelve Vols. Crown Octavo, price £3, 12s.

The following are sold separately :—

NOCTES AMBROSIANÆ. Four Vols., 24s.
ESSAYS, CRITICAL AND IMAGINATIVE. Four Vols., 24s.
HOMER AND HIS TRANSLATORS. One Vol., 6s.
RECREATIONS OF CHRISTOPHER NORTH. Two Vols., 12s.
TALES. One Vol., 6s.
POEMS. One Vol., 6s.

NEW GENERAL ATLAS.

To be completed in Ten Parts (Eight Published), price 10s. 6d. each.

The Royal Atlas of Modern Geography:

In a Series of entirely original and authentic Maps, with a special Index to each Map, arranged so as to obviate the former inconvenient method of reference by Degrees and Minutes of Longitude and Latitude.

By ALEX. KEITH JOHNSTON, F.R.S.E., F.R.G.S., &c.,
Geographer in Ordinary to Her Majesty, Author of the "Physical Atlas," &c.

The Concluding Parts will be published early in 1861, *forming a handsome Volume in Royal Folio.*

The Physical Atlas of Natural Phenomena.

By ALEX. KEITH JOHNSTON, F.R.S.E., &c.,
Geographer to the Queen for Scotland.

A New and Enlarged Edition, consisting of 35 Folio Plates, 27 smaller ones, printed in Colours, with 135 pages of Letterpress, and Index.

Imperial Folio, half-bound morocco, £12, 12s.

The Chemistry of Common Life.

By PROFESSOR JOHNSTON.

A New Edition, Edited by G. H. LEWES.

Illustrated with numerous Engravings.   In Two Vols. Foolscap, price 11s. 6d.

The Physiology of Common Life.

By GEORGE H. LEWES.   .·

Illustrated with numerous Engravings.   Two Vols., 12s.

Contents: Hunger and Thirst.—Food and Drink.—Digestion and Indigestion.—The Structure and Uses of the Blood.—The Circulation.—Respiration and Suffocation.—Why we are Warm, and how we keep so.—Feeling and Thinking.—The Mind and the Brain.— Our Senses and Sensations.—Sleep and Dreams.—The Qualities we inherit from our Parents.—Life and Death.

Introductory Text-Book of Geology.

By DAVID PAGE, F.G.S.

Fourth Edition, with Engravings. In Crown Octavo, price 1s. 6d.

"It has not been often our good-fortune to examine a text-book on science of which we could express an opinion so entirely favourable as we are enabled to do of Mr Page's little work."—*Athenæum.*

Advanced Text-Book of Geology,

DESCRIPTIVE AND INDUSTRIAL.

By DAVID PAGE, F.G.S.

Second Edition, Enlarged, with numerous Engravings, 6s.

"An admirable book on Geology. It is from no invidious desire to underrate other works—it is the simple expression of justice—which causes us to assign to Mr Page's *Advanced Text-Book* the very first place among geological works addressed to students, at least among those which have come before us. We have read every word of it, with care and with delight, never hesitating as to its meaning, never detecting the omission of anything needful in a popular and succinct exposition of a rich and varied subject."—*Leader.*

"It is therefore with unfeigned pleasure that we record our appreciation of his *Advanced Text-Book of Geology.* We have carefully read this truly satisfactory book, and do not hesitate to say that it is an excellent compendium of the great facts of Geology, and written in a truthful and philosophic spirit."—*Edinburgh Philosophical Journal.*

"We know of no introduction containing a larger amount of information in the same space, and which we could more cordially recommend to the geological student."—*Athenæum.*

Handbook of Geological Terms and Geology.

By DAVID PAGE, F.G.S.

In Crown Octavo, price 6s.

"'To the student, miner, engineer, architect, agriculturist, and others, who may have occasion to deal with geological facts, and yet who might not be inclined to turn up half a dozen volumes, or go through a course of geological readings for an explanation of the term in question,' Mr Page has carried out the object with the most complete success. His book amply fulfils the promise contained in its title, constituting a handbook not only of geological terms, but of the science of geology. It will not only be absolutely indispensable to the student, but will be invaluable as a complete and handy book of reference even to the advanced geologist."—*Literary Gazette.*

"There is no more earnest living practical worker in geology than Mr David Page. To his excellent *Introductory Text-Book of Geology* and his *Advanced Text-Book of Geology, Descriptive and Industrial,* he has now added an admirable system of geological terms, with ample and clearly written explanatory notices, such as all geological observers, whether they are able professors and distinguished lecturers, or mere inquirers upon the threshold of the science, must find to be of the highest value."—*Practical Mechanics' Journal.*

"But Mr Page's work is very much more than simply a translation of the language of Geology into plain English; it is a Dictionary, in which not only the meaning of the words is given, but also a clear and concise account of all that is most remarkable and worth knowing in the objects which the words are designed to express. In doing this he has chiefly kept in view the requirements of the general reader, but at the same time adding such details as will render the volume an acceptable Handbook to the student and professed geologist."—*The Press.*

The Book of the Farm.

By HENRY STEPHENS, F.R.S.E.

A New Edition. In Two Volumes, large Octavo, with upwards of 600 Engravings, price £3, half-bound.

Book of Farm Implements and Machines.

By JAMES SLIGHT and R. SCOTT BURN.

Edited by HENRY STEPHENS, F.R.S.E.

Illustrated with 876 Engravings. One large Volume, uniform with the "Book of the Farm," price £2, 2s.

The Book of the Garden.

By CHARLES M'INTOSH.

In Two large Volumes, Royal Octavo, published separately.

VOL. I.—On the Formation of Gardens—Construction, Heating, and Ventilation of Fruit and Plant Houses, Pits, Frames, and other Garden Structures, with Practical Details, illustrated by 1073 Engravings, pp. 776. Price £2, 10s.

VOL. II.—PRACTICAL GARDENING—Contains: Directions for the Culture of the Kitchen Garden, the Hardy-Fruit Garden, the Forcing Garden, and Flower Garden, including Fruit and Plant Houses, with select Lists of Vegetables, Fruits, and Plants. Pp. 868, with 279 Engravings. Price £1, 17s. 6d.

ANNUAL PUBLICATION.

The Year-Book of Agricultural Facts for 1860.

Edited by R. SCOTT BURN.

In Foolscap Octavo, price 5s.

Copies of the Volume for 1859 may be had, price 5s.

A Handy Book on Property Law.

By LORD ST LEONARDS.

A New Edition, Enlarged, with Index, Crown Octavo, price 3s. 6d.

The Forester.

A Practical Treatise on the Formation of Plantations, the Planting, Rearing, and Management of Forest Trees.

By JAMES BROWN,

Wood Manager to the Earl of Seafield, and Surveyor of Woods in general.

A Third Edition, Enlarged. In large 8vo, with numerous Engravings on Wood, price £1, 10s.

In Octavo, with Portrait, price 14s.

AUTOBIOGRAPHY

OF

DR ALEXANDER CARLYLE,

MINISTER OF INVERESK.

CONTAINING

MEMORIALS OF THE MEN AND EVENTS OF HIS TIME.

OPINIONS OF THE PRESS.

Edinburgh Review, January 1861.

This book contains by far the most vivid picture of Scottish life and manners that has been given to the public since the days of Sir Walter Scott. In bestowing upon it this high praise, we make no exception, not even in favour of Lord Cockburn's *Memorials*—the book which resembles it most, and which ranks next to it in interest. Indeed, even going beyond the range of our Scottish experience, we doubt whether there is anywhere to be found as trustworthy a record of the domestic, social, and intellectual life of a whole bygone generation, or an appreciation of the individual peculiarities of the persons by whom that generation was led, as shrewd and unprejudiced, as has been bequeathed to us by this active, high-spirited, claret-drinking, playgoing, and yet, withal, worthy and pious minister of the Kirk.

National Review, January 1861.

A more delightful and graphic picture of the everyday life of our ancestors it has never been our good fortune to meet with. . . . It is no slight thing, after such a lapse of time, to have the illustrious men of that age resuscitated by the master hand of their contemporary, and brought again before us in body and soul. With how different a feeling will many a student, when he arises from the perusal of this Autobiography, glance his eye down the shelves of his library, no longer dealing in his mind with empty names of standard authors, but listening to the voices of real men, and entering into their writings in a far more intelligent manner when he has seen them face to face. We do not often pray for autobiographies—for, as a class of literature, they are of very unequal merit—but we shall heartily rejoice to see as many more autobiographies as possible if they are half as well worth reading as *Jupiter* Carlyle's.

Blackwood's Magazine.

Following no master, moulding himself on no model, the charm of these pages is their originality. They are not Boswellian, nor Johnsonian, nor Colley Cibberish, nor traceable to any source. Yet in their liveliness of description, sly touches of satire, and vigorous analysis of character, combined with the naturalness of incident and surprising variety of interest deduced from ordinary adventure, we are constantly reminded of *Gil Blas*.

Daily News.

It will surprise no one that this Autobiography—which, though composed more than fifty years ago, has remained unpublished till now—should prove, as it does, a veritable treasure of information and anecdote relating to Scotch society in the last century. The period over which these reminiscences extend is, indeed, nearly as interesting to English as to Scotch readers. To the great majority of the former we do not hesitate to say that the chief cause of their interest in Scotch history and Scotch manners has been their delighted familiarity with the Waverley novels. But while these have given them more or less interest in every period of Scotch history, they have especially endeared to them one period—the Scotland of "sixty years since" (from the date of the publication of "Waverley")—the Scotland of the "Antiquary" and the "Heart of Midlothian"—the Scotland which Scott himself knew and loved, and was just in time to fix for ever on the canvass in immortal tints before it faded away before the dawn of a new era. Now, this Autobiography is replete with picture and anecdote of Scotch life and character of just this particular period. . . . We might quote from almost every page to the amusement of our readers, though to the questionable benefit of the publisher; but we prefer to recommend them to go themselves to the storehouse of entertainment and instruction provided for them in the Autobiography of this fine old, enlightened, liberal-minded Scotch divine.

Athenæum.

This book overflows with pictures of life, character, and manners belonging to the past century. A more racy volume of memoirs was never given to the world—nor one more difficult to set forth—save by the true assertion, that there is scarcely a page which does not contain matter for extract, or which would not bear annotation. Every reader of the Scott novels (something like every one who can read English) must delight in *Jupiter* Carlyle's Memoirs.

Daily Telegraph.

There are few autobiographies amongst those which have appeared of late to compare with the one now before us. . . . To the public we most cordially recommend this volume as containing a great deal that is entertaining and informing. Carlyle, as a man of enlarged mind, having enjoyed the society and conversation of the most noted men of his time, has brought together in the pages of his Autobiography much that is worth knowing to all persons, especially to young men of the age, who may make a model to themselves advantageously of this long career of a most gifted, agreeable, and amusing observer of the events and personages of the last century.

Critic.

To say that he has written one of the most intensely-interesting books, which we have devoured rather than read, is not to say enough in its favour. . . . If a marvellous acuteness united to a happy though not always merciful power of sarcasm—if an honest outspokenness, and a style pleasantly quaint and always manly and forcible—if these qualities in an author can tend to produce a good book, then Dr Carlyle's book ought to be a good one. He knew well —and we must remind our readers that his knowledge was not of the common vein—Adam Ferguson, John Home, Hume, Adam Smith, and three-fourths of the men who made Scotch society in the last century the most delightful enjoyment on earth. . . . So rich is this volume in pictorial biography, that we scarcely know from what portion of it to choose our extracts.

Literary Gazette.

A shrewd observer of men and manners, living during perhaps the most deeply-interesting period of our history, he was favoured by a happy combination of circumstances such as has seldom fallen to the lot of a single individual. Sufficiently an actor in the eventful scenes of the last century to be accepted as a reliable authority, yet sufficiently secluded from the world to have leisure for a philosophic survey of the events that were passing around him, he has bequeathed to us a picture of the times, which for breadth of colouring and vividness of detail can scarcely be surpassed. . . . We lay down this deeply-interesting volume with a sincere feeling of regret. For marvellous originality and fidelity of description it is unsurpassed in the language.

Edinburgh Witness.

Thus accomplished in mind, attractive in person, essentially social in nature, and free from any taint of the over-religiousness that would have barred his reception into much of the society of his times, Dr Carlyle became in succession the friend and guest of almost all the notability of his day. In spite of his position as minister of the comparatively obscure parish of Inveresk, scarcely a man of the age worth knowing in politics, literature, fashion, law, medicine, or even in philosophy and metaphysics, but came within the wide radius of his acquaintanceship. Few have escaped from the annotations of his diligently recording, quietly humorous, yet not unfrequently sharp and sarcastic pen. The charm of the Autobiography is not the life it professes to record. It lies in its minutely daguerreotyped views of the events and manners of his times, and the faithful, life-like portraits he has hung around himself of his contemporaries. The Autobiography is but the pollard round which a thousand climbing plants have intertwined themselves, and which all but cover with their rich foliage and flower the tree to which they owe their support. We forget the minister of Inveresk as he brings us face to face with the fixed, stern vengeance of the Porteous mob, or leads us through the scenes of the '45; or recalls to us the form, the voice, the living person, of men whose names are identified with the most stirring historical transactions of the last century, and with our literature, philosophy, and science in their young and palmy days, when Robertson, Hume, Hutchison, Home, Adam Smith, Cullen, MacLaurin, and Black, were rising into fame, or reaping the well-earned honours of their genius. By the brief, graphic touches that abound in this volume, life is given back to the history of the last century; and its actors, known to us only through stately biographies, are translated from cold marble figures once more into breathing men.

Scotsman.

The most curious and amusing, if not also, in all respects, the most valuable contribution that has been made for many a day to the political, the ecclesiastical, but especially the social, history of Scotland.

Glasgow Herald.

A book of surpassing interest, and one which excites in us that feeling of gratitude with which we would receive an unexpected gift of great usefulness and princely cost.

Liverpool Albion.

We wish to speak in the very highest terms of this most interesting book, and to recommend its perusal to all of our readers who are interested in the persons who lived, and the great events that happened, in our country one hundred and fifty years ago. Dr Carlyle was only a Presbyterian minister of the Established Church of Scotland, but he lived as an equal among the giants of literature and politics who about that time made Edinburgh the intellectual capital of the country, and his Autobiography is full of pleasant notices of all the best and greatest men of his time.

Scottish Press.

Without question, a more valuable, and at the same time amusing, contribution to the literature of the domestic history of our country has not been made for many years.

Caledonian Mercury.

This is the most readable and enjoyable book of its kind that has been issued from the Edinburgh press for many years. . . . The volume has a distinct historical value, as well as an enchaining and curious interest.

Inverness Courier.

It is one of the most valuable and entertaining works that has appeared respecting the men and manners of Scotland in the eighteenth century, and is written with so lively and graphic a pen that it cannot fail to become very popular in the country.

Dundee Courier.

In the Autobiography of Dr Alexander Carlyle we have one of the most valuable contributions that have ever been made to the social annals of Scotland, inasmuch as it is descriptive of a period of particular interest in the history of our country, and of men of whom in general Scotland has just cause to be proud. . . . The book is a perfect feast. No sooner has the reader entered upon it than he is hurried along with the fascination of a romance. The sketches of society are vivid and racy, and the author's delineations of character appear true to a line, while his descriptions of men and manners are given with a minuteness and fidelity worthy of the pen of Defoe.

Manchester Review.

One of the most valuable contributions to the literary and social history of the eighteenth century that has ever been written; so much so, indeed, as to make us wonder why so charming a book should have been allowed to remain in manuscript so many years.

Ayrshire Express.

Not only *the* publication of the season, but the most notable accession which has been made to this barren yet peculiarly interesting department of our national literature for many years.

Aberdeen Journal.

The book is one of the most remarkable which has appeared for a long time; and while it affords a great deal of matter suggestive of comment, it is pre-eminently a book to be possessed, and read through and through, and over and over again.

Fife Journal.

It is seldom one gets a photograph, as it were, of the days gone by so vivid and true to the life as is afforded by a volume just published. . . . No book for many years has been published so replete with reading for everybody—reading which young and old, learned and unlearned, alike will regard as interesting, and read, and read, and read again.

Glasgow Examiner.

It can scarcely be opened without suggesting the strong common sense—the deep sagacity—the dry humour—the cutting sarcasm—the far-sightedness of the author. It has been truly said that there has been no such delineation of the private life of our great men since Boswell's *Johnson*. . . . There is a strength of thought. a grasp of intellect in his writing beyond any writer we remember. We shall recur to this wondrous volume again.

Dublin Evening Mail.

But we must conclude; and in turning from a book to which we have directed so unusually large a share of our attention, it is scarcely necessary to say that we recommend it heartily to our readers. It is, in truth, one of the most amusing and instructive which has fallen under our notice for many a day.

WILLIAM BLACKWOOD & SONS, EDINBURGH AND LONDON.

www.ingramcontent.com/pod-product-compliance
Lightning Source LLC
Chambersburg PA
CBHW032003110726
47901CB00004B/955